Beginning Django E-Commerce

JIM MCGAW

Beginning Django E-Commerce

Copyright © 2009 by Jim McGaw

ISBN-13 (pbk): 978-1-4302-2535-5

ISBN-13 (electronic): 978-1-4302-2536-2

Printed and bound in the United States of America 9 8 7 6 5 4 3 2 1

Lead Editor: Duncan Parkes
Development Editor: Douglas Pundick
Technical Reviewer: George Vilches
Editorial Board: Clay Andres, Steve Anglin, Mark Beckner, Ewan Buckingham, Tony Campbell, Gary Cornell,
    Jonathan Gennick, Michelle Lowman, Matthew Moodie, Jeffrey Pepper, Frank Pohlmann, Douglas Pundick,
    Ben Renow-Clarke, Dominic Shakeshaft, Matt Wade, Tom Welsh
Coordinating Editor: Jim Markham
Copy Editor: Ralph Moore
Compositor: Mary Sudul
Indexer: Carol Burbo
Artist: April Milne

Distributed to the book trade worldwide by Springer-Verlag New York, Inc., 233 Spring Street, 6th Floor, New York, NY 10013. Phone 1-800-SPRINGER, fax 201-348-4505, e-mail orders-ny@springer-sbm.com, or visit http://www.springeronline.com.

For information on translations, please contact Apress directly at 2855 Telegraph Avenue, Suite 600, Berkeley, CA 94705. Phone 510-549-5930, fax 510-549-5939, e-mail info@apress.com, or visit http://www.apress.com.

Apress and friends of ED books may be purchased in bulk for academic, corporate, or promotional use. eBook versions and licenses are also available for most titles. For more information, reference our Special Bulk Sales–eBook Licensing web page at http://www.apress.com/info/bulksales.

The source code for this book is available to readers at http://www.apress.com. You will need to answer questions pertaining to this book in order to successfully download the code.

This book is dedicated to my parents.

—*Jim McGaw*

Contents at a Glance

Contents

About the Author

Jim McGaw is a web developer with several years experience developing data-driven web applications, particularly search-engine–friendly online catalog and shopping cart sites. He's very thankful that he gets to be a web developer for a living, and is a security, accessibility, and usability advocate. Despite his technical background, he remains in awe of people who are able to design web sites that are visually stunning.

Currently, he lives and works as a software engineer in Santa Barbara, California, where he enjoys hiking, ocean kayaking, and playing the guitar in his spare time. To send him feedback, comments, or questions, drop him a line at: jim@django-ecommerce.com.

About the Technical Reviewer

George Vilches is a software engineer and systems administrator with an unabashed fondness for Python and the web in both disciplines. In the last three years, he has made several contributions to Django, with a focus on the ORM and administrative side of things. He was a principal engineer with Propeller (`http://propeller.com`), and continues to build Django applications with Fortune Cookie Studios, (`http://fcstudios.com`).

George's personal time is split evenly over tinkering with open source projects and enjoying the company of his wife Kate, corgi and two cats, all of whom would prefer he stop tinkering and attend to them more.

Acknowledgments

 A good deal of effort other than my own went into the writing of this book, and I'm grateful to all who helped. Most notably, I'd like to thank the technical reviewer, George Vilches, for his valuable contributions to this book. George strikes me as an extremely knowledgeable person in several different areas as well as a tireless worker, and he really contributed a lot of valuable suggestions. His efforts in reviewing this book are probably near-deserving of co-author credit, and I thank him.

I'd like to thank those on the Apress staff with whom I worked directly, namely James Markham, Duncan Parkes, and Douglas Pundick, whose efforts brought this book together, and to Ralph Moore, who transformed the grammatical sludge of the original writing into a much more readable text. I'd also like to extend my thanks to those people whose names I won't know until I see them on the copyright page of this book in print. That being said, while I had a lot of help, the occasional error might still be lurking in the text. These errors are my fault and not theirs.

I owe a debt of gratitude to my friend Mark Pellerito, who initially got me started doing computer programming, and was always there to answer all the technical questions spewing forth from my knowledge-hungry brain. I'm in this whole mess because of you. Thanks.

Lastly, I'd like to thank Tara, who supported and endured me the whole time I was writing this book. Thanks for making me the luckiest guy on the planet.

Introduction

I read a lot of technical books about software and computer programming. This isn't because I have a great fondness for reading, nor do I actually like owning a massive collection of computer books that's slowly beginning to overtake every room in my home. I do it because at any given time, I'm usually working on a programming project and am faced with a dozen problems that I need to solve. These unsolved problems fester in my head. They scrape away at the surface of my brain like jagged rusty metal hooks. These books provide me sweet relief from these pains.

In my experience, there are two types of computer books: those that act as reference guides and those that act as tutorials. This book falls squarely in the latter category. While you need both tutorial and reference books in order to learn something, I tend to like tutorial books better, simply because they aid you in making better use of the reference books. For this reason, over the course of this book, we will be building one single Django project, to which we will add new features with each chapter and learn new parts of the Django web framework as we go.

There are lots and lots of Django apps floating around on the web. Many of these will contain perfectly good—and in some cases, absolutely spectacular—working code that you can use on your site. In other cases, the code is less than great, but still works. While I've taken a snippet of code from the open source community here and there throughout this book, I've mostly gone the do-it-myself route and implemented things from scratch. The reason for this is simple: when you're learning, rolling your own solutions at a lower level instead of just plugging in an app you found ready-made on Google Code or Django Snippets is much better for making the basic concepts stick to your brain. The drawback of this approach, of course, is that there are parts of the site we're going to develop in this book that are greatly simplified.

However, when you use snippets of code samples that are posted in various corners of the Internet by people all over world, you will still encounter problems. You'll get weird errors when you hook the new code into your site, and you'll end up having to read the Django docs and Django blogs and Django books to determine what's going wrong. My hope is that, after working through the examples in this book, you'll not only be much more adept at developing complex and powerful code with Django from scratch, you'll also have a much better grasp of dealing with these kinds of integration problems with existing third party solutions when they arise. On top of this, you might also find yourself working to extend the functionality of an existing solution to suit your own needs, which is a good ability to have as well.

Who This Book Is For

This book is aimed at developers who are interested in learning more about the process of how to create a Django web site. Over the course of the book, we're going to create a single working e-commerce web site that we'll deploy into production at the very end. In each chapter, we'll tackle a particular feature or group of features that we want to add to the site, outline the requirements and discuss the related concepts, and then write code to implement each feature using Django. This will allow you to see how the different parts of a single Django project all fit together. In the end, you'll have a thorough grasp of how a Django web application is created, secured, optimized for search engines, tested, and finally deployed.

We're going to create a shopping cart site in this book, and while some of the sections cover problems that are specific to e-commerce web sites, most of the content has applications to other types of sites as well. For example, Chapter 8 covers implementation of internal site search so that customers can find things in our product catalog. Search functionality is a requirement of almost any data-driven web site. In Chapter 4, we create a shopping cart for our product catalog, allowing customers to aggregate products before they check out, and here you'll learn more about how you can use Django sessions in order to track information about your customers, whether or not they are logged in. The checkout functionality created in Chapter 5 covers the basics of Python network programming in order to integrate with third-party payment gateways, and the material covered is useful to anyone interested in integrating Django with web services.

This book does assume familiarity with the Python programming language. If you're a complete beginner and have never worked with Python, don't worry... it's a very simple language and you'll be able to catch on very quickly. If you're new to programming and would like an introduction, I'd suggest you take a look at *Beginning Python: Second Edition*, by Magnus Lie Hetland (Apress, 2008). If you're already familiar with at least one other programming language and just need to get caught up on the syntax of Python, I can heartily recommend you read *Dive Into Python*, by Mark Pilgram (Apress, 2004).

The Web Sites In This Book

In this book, I'm going to build a fictional e-commerce site that sells musical instruments and sheet music. The name of the site is "Modern Musician." Developers in the Django community have a penchant for naming their apps and projects after old-time musicians, like John Coltrane, Louis "Satchmo" Armstrong, and Duke Ellington. This tradition was started by the creators of the Django web framework, who chose to name it after guitarist Django Reinhardt, who is regarded by many as one of the greatest jazz guitarists of all time.

It didn't dawn on me until around the time I started writing Chapter 13 that the name "Modern Musician" might be construed as a tongue-in-cheek reference to this tradition in the Django community. In my defense, I originally created the Modern Musician e-commerce site in PHP, as a demo e-commerce site. Later, I implemented roughly the same Modern Musician site using Ruby on Rails, for the sole purpose of learning Rails. So when I got around to spawning this little project in Django, the last thing on my mind when naming the project was any attempt at ridicule. I did so out of tradition.

In the first 15 chapters of this book, we're going to build a single e-commerce web site. For those interested, the site we're going to create is available for public viewing at `http://www.django-ecommerce.com/`. While an administrative interface is part of the site that we're going to create in this book, the public site does not permit altering of data in the product catalog.

In Chapter 16, when we look at putting Django projects up on the Google App Engine, we're going to create a minimal shopping cart site, which is also available for public viewing at `http://django-ecommerce.appspot.com/`.

Source Code and Errata

We're going to write a lot of code in this book. It's not an overbearing amount, as Python is a very concise language and Django syntax tends to reduce the amount of repetitive code that you need to write. In spite of this, you still might find yourself wanting to have a copy of the code on hand so that you don't have to type in every last line. The source code for the site we're going to create in this book is available for download from the Apress web site.[1] (There's also a bunch of awesome books on there.)

If you happen to be reading a digital version of this book on your computer and have the option of selecting text, I'd be careful about copying code from your screen into your editor. Some characters might not transfer from electronic versions of this book into IDEs very well, as they might confuse the Python interpreter. You're much safer just typing it in yourself. You've been warned.

Lastly, while everyone has worked really hard to ensure that this book is grammatically and technically correct, some grammatical and technical "bugs" may have slipped in under our reviewing eyes. ("Bug" is a nice euphemism for "mistake," isn't it?) If you find an error and would like to politely rub it in my face, please feel free to submit it to this book's errata page on the Apress web site.[2]

If you'd like to contact me with any questions or concerns you have about the content of this book, shoot me an e-mail at: *jim@django-ecommerce.com.*

---

[1] http://www.apress.com/book/sourcecode
[2] http://www.apress.com/book/view/1430225351

CHAPTER 1

■ ■ ■

Best Laid Plans

Web development starts in the mind. Sure, it may be done in Python, Ruby, C#, Groovy, or any of the other myriad programming languages out there these days, but all of them are just tools. The code for web sites is created in the mind. Conception occurs in the space (or lack of empty space, hopefully) between your ears, and *implementation* occurs in your programming language of choice.

One of the main goals of this book is to teach you how to architect a site using the Django web framework. But architecting a site, like any piece of software you might be developing, is about a sequence of decisions you need to make for yourself. Some of these decisions are small; others are quite large. A lot of them don't have an easy answer or one that is immediately obvious.

While I can't answer your questions for you, and even though my decisions might end up very different from your own, I'm going to talk you through the process. In this way, I hope to show how to translate your train of thought, and the decisions you make along the way, into workable software. And I hope that it makes you some money in the process.

In this book, we're going to develop an e-commerce application. I chose this kind of web site for a few reasons. First, there is money in selling products online. It's still very possible for would-be entrepreneurs to conceive of business plans that are financially solvent, solely based on selling stuff to people on the web. For this reason, there is likely a demand for this type of application, and an interest in seeing how it's done.

Second, I think e-commerce is interesting. An e-commerce project using any particular framework tends to be fairly complex, with lots of ins and outs. They allow you, as a developer, to start by building a simple product catalog, and then go deeper into hooking into third-party payment processors with web service calls. If you can get your head around the logic behind our Django e-commerce project, then there's probably very little else you won't be able to figure out how to do with Django. Lastly (and don't tell anyone this), I'm pretty bad at visual design. I'm a programmer. Visual design for e-commerce tends to be pretty straightforward. Generally, you don't need to create graphics-heavy grunge designs to wow your audience, like you might need to do for a blog or business-card web site. As far as e-commerce goes: the simpler and cleaner, the better. I can handle that. However, just because we won't be focusing on design in this book doesn't mean that it's not an important part of any e-commerce site. Customers and their purchasing decisions are very much influenced by the look and feel of a web site, so it's well worth your time to learn a bit more about design and make sure that your site doesn't turn customers off visually.

So, let's get right down to it and figure out what our needs are. Maybe you have some idea of what you want to build: I do. Before jumping right in and starting with the coding process, I'm going to take a second to jot down some thoughts about what it is that we're going to create. It's common practice for software developers to write a specification for larger projects before they start coding. There are few different kinds of specifications; the one that we're going to do now is a *functional specification*, which will describe in plain English what our code is supposed to do.

Specifications vary in style and format. They can be extremely stilted and formal, or they can be much less formal. They can be bulleted lists of features, descriptive text, or take the form of user stories that describe the customer experience on the site. How you choose to write your own specification is not terribly important, but it is important that you write *something*, just to make sure that your ducks are in a row and you don't run into unforeseen problems with your plans down the line. If you make any mistakes or run into problems, it's much easier (and cheaper) to change a few lines of text on paper than change lots of written code.

I'm going to start by writing a quick, very informal functional specification for our e-commerce project. Take a moment to do the same, and let's reconvene back here when you're finished. Done? Okay, here's mine: "Modern Musician will be an online e-commerce catalog that sells instruments, sheet music, and music accessories to its customers. We're going to ship orders from the Cleveland, OH location where our retail shop currently does business."

Okay, so that's a little short and doesn't tell us a whole lot. It doesn't refine our goals or help us with our decisions or the overall design process. So, I'm going to have a second and much longer go at it:

"Modern Musician will be an online e-commerce catalog that sells instruments, sheet music, and music accessories to its customers. When the user first comes to the site, the home page will display some featured products, a list of categories, and search box that will let them search the catalog. Navigation will be straight across the top below the banner. Product lists should be thumbnails that include a small image of the product, with the product name. Products can be in as many categories as we want. We need to be able to add products and categories through a form so we don't need to always have computer programmers doing it. These forms need to be protected so only authorized individuals can access them. Products can be added to a cart. Checkout will be a single page where we prompt customers for their information and let them submit the order to us. (How can we inform customers about our privacy policy? Make it always available to them?) We're going to ship orders from the Cleveland, OH location where our retail shop currently does business. Search Engine Optimization (SEO) should always be a priority. Everything should be stored securely. Our site should be accessible to people with disabilities, such as blind people. How should we order products when several are listed on a single page, such as a category page? We need analytics to track conversions and figure out who's buying what. The administrative login also needs a place for us to view orders. Orders can only be placed with a valid credit card on the site, and once the card is approved through a real-time lookup, the order can be submitted with a status of "submitted." Fulfillment will occur on our end, and we'll set the status of the order to "processed" once they've been shipped. We need to handle returns easily. This will require the ability to refund a customer's money, less any handling fees we might charge them. How can we make this information available to the customer? Where should we explain our return policy, during checkout? A hyperlink to a "Return Policy" page."

Okay, so that specification was still pretty short and very informal. That's okay; the point is not to convince venture capitalists to fund us, but to figure out what we're going to do, internally, by getting the mental juices flowing. It can be free-form. Crawl through the site you're envisioning in your mind and jot down any thoughts or questions that come to you. Keep it around and add to it as ideas come to you. The more ideas you have in mind from the start, *before* you start building the thing, the less likely you are to forget something mission-critical and have to go back and redo a bunch of your work.

Selling Stuff Online

I like Shopify. Shopify is an online provider of e-commerce web applications. Sign up with them and you'll have your own store up online very quickly. It's very affordable for small businesses, it's easy to use, and the interface is quite slick. You can even set up a store initially for free, and they'll still accommodate ten sales transactions on your site per month.

But in this book, I'm going to create an e-commerce application. What we're going to create in this book is very similar to Shopify. We're going to create a product catalog, shopping cart, checkout system, and allow users to leave product reviews. Why would you want to roll your own solution from scratch when it's easy, cheap, and takes so little time to use a provider like Shopify?

The reason has to do with a concept in business referred to as a *core competency*. Like most terms in the business world, this refers to a concept that seems drop-dead simple and completely obvious to everyone, but for the sake of writing textbooks to sell to students in General Management courses, a phrase had to be coined. Simply, a core competency is an advantage that your business has over your competitors. Before the patent runs out on those overpriced prescription drugs that pharmaceutical companies produce, before someone else can legally start selling a generic, the drug itself is one of the company's core competencies.

In the prescription drug example, the core competency is the product itself. It's not very often that you'll find a person selling something that you can't buy anywhere else. Prescription drugs are a rare exception because it's possible to create and patent chemical combinations that are not only unique, but for which there is actually a market. Most products are not unique and can't be patented to the point where someone else can't easily rip them off. Generally, the core competencies of a company lie not in their products but in their *process*. It's how they run their business that allows them to gain advantages over their competition.

So what does this have to do with creating your own e-commerce site from scratch? Think about it this way: let's imagine that you have a store that sells oversized stuffed animals. You sell a lot of them in your store, mostly to people who run carnivals, and you want to take this business online, so you can sell to carnival employees all over the world. Now, there's a store right down the street from you, called Huge Stuffed Things, and they have an online store that they've set up with Shopify, and business seems good for them. Huge boxes leave their store each day, presumably filled with huge stuffed animals, to ship to their online consumers.

If you sign up with Shopify to start selling your large stuffed animals too, there will be a drastic limit to what you can do in order to compete with Huge Stuffed Things. Sure, maybe your store has a much better name that doesn't make it sound like a taxidermy shop for game hunters, but really, in this situation, the only way you can compete is through marketing and advertising. You can brand yourself better than they can, and spend lots more money on online marketing campaigns and get lots more traffic to your site. But at its core, the technology you're using (in this case, Shopify's platform) doesn't offer you any advantages over the other guys who are using the same platform, which trickles right down. Your site won't offer your customers any net benefit, either.

Don't get me wrong, I'm not knocking Shopify. Like I said, I like the interface, and there are many very successful sites that are run on its architecture. In addition to this, it can be quite useful for testing the waters. Do people really want to buy gift baskets filled with freeze-dried fruit they can give to their astronaut friends at NASA? Who knows? Set up a store on Shopify and see how many orders you get before you invest too much into the idea. I would encourage that. (And really, I admire Shopify because they're knocking down what are referred to in the business world as *barriers to entry*.)

But for business, *real* business, you need to plan for growth, and a large part of that is starting your online application with a decent architecture that is *your own*, that you can later modify without limit, and that offers you benefits over your competitors. And if you happen to be entering a market where you have no competitors (what business are you in again?), then you either have a terrible idea (why is no one else doing it?), or you will end up with competition very quickly, especially if your venture meets with any success whatsoever. You want to be able to do things better than everyone else, and a key part of this lies in your technology.

I'm not saying that your own system will automatically bring you riches. If you consistently hire poor employees to work for you, or if your base idea is just plain bad, your own e-commerce platform probably won't spin your straw into gold. But the next big, Amazon.com-esque online merchant will not happen on a platform like Shopify.

Throughout the course of this book, you will develop a piece of software that will help your process, and refine the day-to-day operations of your business, to the extent that you can use these savings or quality of service to offer real value to your customers. The purpose of this book is to show you the syntax, illustrate basic concepts, and cover most use cases, so that you can customize things to fit your own business model.

Why Django?

I'm going to use the Django web framework in this book, which was written in the Python programming language. Django is extremely easy to learn and use, and is very lightweight and straightforward, much like the language in which it's written. Choosing a technology to use to construct your site is a tough decision, because you're going to be stuck using it for a while. Even worse, early on, when you're forced to make a decision about what framework you're going to use, you have *hardly any information* about how well it's going to fare against your requirements.

I enjoy Django, but syntactically, it's a little different than most of the other major players out there right now. There are a few things that I think makes Django a very good choice for web development that are not available in other frameworks that I know of. (Let's call them Django's "core competencies.") These include, but aren't limited to:

> *The Django admin interface saves time:* I think this alone is one reason to consider using Django as your web framework. The creators of Django recognized that just about everyone using web pages creates database tables to hold information, and then they must create an administrative interface to manage those records. With only a few small classes, Django creates these administrative forms for you in a slick and easy-to-use interface. It even handles the authentication for you, so only administrators have access to them. This saves you a lot of work and definitely lessens the grade of the learning curve.

> *URL management is easy:* Django allows you to handle how your URLs are formed at the application level and not the server level. This saves you from the headache of putting application logic into your apache conf file where is really doesn't belong. Nice URLs are also very SEO friendly.

> *Python is fast:* As a programming language, developing in Python is quick, and Python, despite being an interpreted language instead of a compiled one, is quick. This means that your development time and running time is also fast.

> *Django is open source:* Django is free to use. You're welcome to take it, extend it, modify it, and do anything that you'd like to your heart's content, and you don't need to pay anybody a dime for it. More specifically, Django is available for free use and modification under the Berkeley Software Distribution (BSD) license,[1] which means that you can safely use it to build a web site and you can rest easy knowing that your use of Django won't ever result in a lawsuit. The main drawback to open source software is, of course, that what you save in software costs you may need to make up for in other opportunity costs, such as developer time. I think Django is easy enough to use, and there isn't a shortage of Python developers, so this probably won't be a problem for you.

You've picked up this book, so you've probably already heard good things about Django, or Python, or both, and are interested in taking it for a test drive. I strongly encourage that, because I'm sure that you'll be happy with both the process and the results. I'm not a salesman; I'm not going to echo the wealth of arguments that are out there on behalf of Django. Besides, the best solution for one application might not be the best solution for your own. It really depends on your own project's requirements.

But I will say this: Django is done in Python, and Python was chosen by Google as the programming language to handle a lot of its dynamic web functionality. Google now employs Python's creator, Guido

---

[1] http://code.djangoproject.com/browser/django/trunk/LICENSE

van Rossum. Even if you don't have the time or desire to benchmark and test Python as one of your options, I'm pretty sure the guys at Google did, pretty thoroughly. You can at least rest easy knowing that your decision is consistent with some of the most successful technical people in the world.

Straying From the Django Philosophy

One big selling point of Django is that it encourages modularity and portability in your web applications. For example, if you create a blog app in your web project, there are ways to set this up in Django so that you can use this blog app in all of your other web projects, without needing to change the code itself. This is very good for code reuse and, if you do things right, can dramatically help you out when you find yourself creating the same basic things over and over again for different web projects.

Oftentimes, the benefits that come from the "Django way" can reduce the amount of code you need to write within a single web project. As one example, in Chapter 3, we're going to create our product catalog, with pages for categories and products. We're going to set it up so that there are two URLs, two view functions, and two template files for these pages, one for category pages and the other for product pages. It would be possible to eliminate one of the view functions, and pass request for categories and products through just one view function, instead of two.

While I think this is pretty neat, I'm going to stray from this approach for the purposes of trying to teach you how to use Django. First off, I don't believe that modularity is always possible for every piece of code you're going to write in a web application, simply because everything ties into everything else. In our e-commerce project, we'll have categories that contain products that can be added to a shopping cart that can be added to an order, and so on. Everything is interrelated, and I think it can get overly difficult trying to abstract away *everything* on the off chance that we might one day want to use all of our code in other places.

And even if it is always theoretically possible, I don't think it's always a good idea. Abstraction has another drawback: readability. If you can't read your code easily, or if everyone that you hire has to squint and stare at your code for long blocks of time, then you've made your application a maintenance nightmare. I mean no offense to the Django community at large, but because I'm trying to teach you how Django works by example, I'm going to err on the side of clarity and simplicity in my examples, instead of always resorting to advanced modularity and abstraction.

However, when the issues regarding modularity come up, I will try and point them out to you where appropriate. I want you to be happy with the work you've done in this book, and if you need to stray from what I do to make your code satisfactory, I would not only encourage that, but insist on it.

A Quick Word on the Software

In this book, I'll be using the following software and versions:

- Django 1.1
- Python 2.5
- MySQL 5.1
- Eclipse 3.4.1 (with the PyDev extensions)
- Apache 2.2
- NginX
- mod_wsgi
- Ubuntu
- Firefox

Django is a web framework based on the Model-View-Controller (MVC) design pattern. Your models are Python classes you use to interact with the database layer, controllers are the layer that handles application logic and sending responses to requests, and views are what the user sees and interacts with. Django doesn't follow this specification exactly, but it's close enough.

We're going to be using MySQL as our relational database. A few of you might be wondering why I'm using MySQL instead of PostgreSQL, especially when the creators of Django say they prefer PostgreSQL. I'm using MySQL because, for better or worse, MySQL is more commonly used. Most people involved in the open source community have done at least one project in which MySQL was involved in some way. PostgreSQL does have a lot of advantages over MySQL, but the point of this book is to teach you how to create an e-commerce site with the Django framework. I decided to use MySQL in the interest of keeping things simple. You might be trying to learn Python and Django while reading this book, and I don't want to make it a whole lot more complicated by forcing you to learn a new database engine at the same time. Most of the code in this book is database-agnostic, and any database guru could easily translate the little MySQL-specific code into PostgreSQL.

As far as integrated development environments (IDEs) go, I'm a big fan of whatever tool helps me get the job done the quickest. If you enjoy using vim, emacs, PythonWin, or Eclipse, choose the one you're most comfortable working in and use that one. I'm going to be using Eclipse with the PyDev extensions involved, which in my opinion is Python's best IDE out there. Feel free to use whatever tool you like the best.

A Note on Version Control

If you're reading this, you're probably a member of the ever-growing open source community, and you've no doubt heard about version control systems like Subversion,[2] Git,[3] or Mercurial.[4] Most of you are probably already using one of these tools for version control on your code, and if that's the case, I'm preaching to the choir, and you can move along to the next section.

If you're not using version control, you should be. I know that hearing one more person like me telling you that you need to start using a version control program is akin to your mother nagging you to eat your beets. I'm okay with that: you *should* be using a version control system. In developing this site, I'm going to be using Git, because it's a favorite among the developer community and is a *distributed* version control system, which has some benefits over Subversion. Bear in mind that over the course of this book, for brevity's sake, I won't subject you to every single checkout, pull, and push that I do...but know that I am using it, even though I'm not bringing it up every time.

There's also the chance that, in order to download some of the third-party items I'm using in this book, you might need Subversion or Git on your system. For example, in Chapter 2, we're going to configure Django to log exceptions in our project, and the code for this is available for checkout from a Subversion repository. So, you'll at *least* need to make sure it's on your system and that you're dimly aware of how to use the most basic commands.

Firefox

You might have a favorite browser with which you prefer to do web development. In case you haven't started doing so, I'd encourage you to use Firefox. There's one very good reason to do this: add-ons. Firefox has loads of useful plug-ins and add-ons that you can use to aid in development. Among

---

[2] http://subversion.tigris.org/

[3] http://www.git-scm.com/

[4] http://mercurial.selenic.com/wiki/

these are Firebug,[5] Tamper Data,[6] and (my personal favorite) the Firefox Accessibility Extension.[7] It's worth checking, *right now,* before you do any more development, to see what's available. If you've never looked into the world of Firefox add-ons, I'm willing to bet you'll find one that proves very useful to you. If nothing else, get Firebug, since it contains very useful tools for inspecting the HTML source of a web page, easily viewing the associated CSS with any markup, and it contains a powerful JavaScript debugger.

Naturally, most of these add-ons, like all open source software, come with no warranty, and force you to check a box accepting a bunch of terms of use that basically ensure that you can never sue the developers of the add-on for anything that ever goes wrong, even if their add-on somehow gets you attacked and mauled by a great white shark. Fair enough. *Caveat emptor.*

Installing the Software

I have some bad news for you that I'll admit up-front: there are a lot of different operating systems out there, and we're using a lot of different pieces of software in this book. If I covered the installation of every software package on every system that my readers might conceivably be using, this book might get so heavy that people would hate carrying it anyplace. If this bothers you, do you know where you *can* find help? The answer is: all over the place. Since we're not using any really obscure software packages, you will likely find documentation on installation on your platform, with the most recent version of the software, on the software's official web site. If this fails, you can generally fall back on guidance from the good citizens of the open source community.

So, I'm going to go over the major ones, and give you some general guidelines on how you can do things on most systems, but this won't be exhaustive. The good news is that all the stuff we're using is open source, so there is a lot of information about how to install Python, Django, and MySQL on all major systems in their respective online documentations.

A quick word on system *shells*: We're going to be doing a lot of stuff from the command line in this book, and I'm assuming that you at least know how to get into the shell on your system and navigate around the directory structure. If not, you can generally get to it by opening up "Terminal" from the application menu or Finder on Linux or Macs. On Windows, choose "Run" from the Start Menu, type cmd, and press Enter.

Whatever shell you might be using, in this book I'm going to preface all commands meant to be issued to your command line by a $ character. So in the next chapter, when you see this:

```
$ python manage.py runserver
```

that means you should type python manage.py runserver into your shell, whatever shell it might be. Your prompt might be different, but for keeping it simple, I'm staying with a $ for all occasions.

Installing Python

First things first, make sure you have Python installed on your system. On any system, you can check by jumping into your shell and typing python. If your system responds to the effect of "cannot be found," you need to download and install Python. If Python is present and installed, you should be dropped into a new prompt that looks like >>>, from which you can start typing in Python code.

---

[5] http://getfirebug.com/

[6] https://addons.mozilla.org/en-US/firefox/addon/966

[7] https://addons.mozilla.org/en-US/firefox/addon/5809

If you're using a Unix-variant or OS X, chances are very good that it's already there. If you're using Windows and need to install it, I highly recommend you download a version of ActivePython, as it takes care of a lot of configuration work for you. The examples in this book are dependent on Python 2.5. If you are running Django on an earlier version (2.3 is the minimum required), you may be forced to change the examples, spelling out the syntactic sugar added in later versions. The most prevalent example in this book is probably the use of Python decorator syntax.

Installing Django

Now that you've got Python installed, you can download and install the Django framework on your system. Download the latest version available from http://www.djangoproject.com/ and untar it to a directory on your system. Inside this directory, you should see a file called setup.py. From within your shell, navigate to this directory and issue the following command:

```
$ python setup.py install
```

You'll probably need to be an administrator, or have sudo-power,[8] in order for this to work. After the install is finished running, you can have a look at the Django base code files. They are on your system in your Python directory under site-packages/django. Most of them probably won't mean a whole lot to you right now, but after working through a few chapters, you'll have a much better handle on how to make sense of the code in the Django source.

There is one item in the bin directory that we're going to take a look at now. It's a file called django-admin.py, and it's going to be an important item during the development process. Make note of where this file is on your system, because when you go to issue any commands that use this file, you may need to specify the full path to this file. For example, if you're on a Unix system, you may need to issue this command:

```
$ /usr/lib/python2.5/site-packages/django/bin/django-admin.py  command_here
```

or on Windows:

```
C:/Python25/Lib/site-packages/django/bin/django-admin.py command_here
```

These may vary depending on your system's exact configuration. If you plan to use the django-admin.py utility a lot, you can save yourself from having to type this every time by adding it to your PATH on Unix, and your Path environment variable on Windows. This isn't terribly difficult to do on Unix: you can create a symbolic link to this file in your PATH.

On Windows, it's a little trickier. Under System Properties, click "Advanced" and click the "Environment Variables" button. In here, in the "System Variables" section, there is a variable called "Path" that should be a semi-colon–delimited list of paths to various utilities you have installed on your system. You can add one at the end. Note that you use backslashes here:

```
C:\Python25\Lib\site-packages\django\bin
```

If you add this entry to your "Path" variable, you will be able to reference django-admin.py without specifying the full path every time.

---

[8] On some Linux systems, it's possible to run a user account that isn't running with full system privileges (for security reasons). However, you can add a user account to the system's sudoers files, which allows the user to run more privileged operations, like installing new programs.

Incidentally, the means of installing Django via the `python setup.py install` is not specific to the Django installation. There are lots of other Python packages you will encounter that you can install in this manner.

Installing MySQL

There's not a whole lot to cover as far as installing MySQL goes. If you install on Windows, be sure you install it as a local service, and during the installation process, configure your MySQL instance to be for use as a developer machine, and select OLTP instead of OLAP. There is also a fantastic GUI program for administering MySQL databases for most operating systems called MySQL-Admin. The program itself was developed and is supported by the MySQL team, so it's well worth your time testing it out. If you're a fan of non-command-line interfaces for getting stuff done quickly and efficiently (as I am), you'll definitely want to install this.

Installing Eclipse and the PyDev Extensions

If you're opting to use Eclipse as your IDE, you're going to have to install a version of the Java Runtime Environment (JRE) first, since the Eclipse IDE is built with and runs on Java. There are a variety of packages you can download that bundle Eclipse and a version of the JRE together that you can use to install Java.

Eclipse is a little strange because, even on Windows, you don't actually run any sort of executable installer to make Eclipse usable. All you need to do is download it, unzip it, and save it somewhere on your system. In the main folder, there is an executable called `eclipse.exe` that you run each time you want to boot up the IDE. If the JRE isn't installed, you won't be able to open Eclipse.

Once you've got Eclipse up and running for yourself, the easiest way to install the PyDev extensions is directly inside of Eclipse. Under the Help menu, select "Software Updates." In this menu, under the tab "Available Software," you can specify a URL where any additions or updates are available, and Eclipse will install them for you. At the right of this window, you should see a button reading "Add Site." Click that one and add the following URL:

```
http://pydev.sourceforge.net/updates/
```

After adding, a new item should appear under "Available Software" that is labeled as the "PyDev Extensions." Check this box and click "Install." After some hard drive spinning, the PyDev extensions should be installed and ready for your use. You may need to restart Eclipse for the new installation to take effect.

Things to Consider Before You Start

You have some work to do before you jump in and start coding. Abraham Lincoln once wrote, "If I had eight hours to chop down a tree, I'd spend the first six sharpening my axe." As great as instant gratification is (and you should achieve that by the end of Chapter 2), your site will always be less work and more successful for you if you take the time to make a few decisions and plan things before you get started building the site.

All of the material that I cover in the next few sections is fairly complex, and each of them could (and do) fill an entire book with material. Obviously, I can't do each of them proper justice, but I will cover the highlights in this book enough to get you off the ground. However, if your site is a substantially large project, you'll probably want to research the material in the following sections more in depth, particularly regarding security.

I'd highly recommend doing this anyway. It'll be less work for you down the line, as most of these things are easier to fix in the planning stage instead of the week prior to launching your site. These are *foundation* issues. You don't build a house and then re-pour the foundation after the fact. I'm sure you can do it, but things will be more stable if you get it right ahead of time.

Security

This is number one. It doesn't really matter how much liability insurance you have to protect your site in the event that any of your confidential user information is compromised; if this is breached in any way, you're not only going to have a mess on your hands, you're going to have a nightmare of a time trying to persuade anyone to shop on your site long after the situation has been rectified. Nothing is ever 100% soup-to-nuts secure, since computer security is kind of an arms race between the "bad guys" finding holes in things and exploiting them, and the "good guys" racing to preemptively find said holes and patch them. You want to make sure that the risk is minimized and, if your site is breached, that there is a limit to the amount of damage that can done once anybody is in.

We'll address some of the major application security concerns as they come up throughout the book. Refer to Chapter 12 for some more in-depth information about security risks, and more specifically, how you can use Django's architecture to reduce the risk. Chapter 12 will not be a definitive reference on how to secure your web application, however. Security is a wide-reaching topic that encompasses several other areas, from the hardening of your web server's operating system to network security concerns. Before launching a site, I would research these issues in depth and check your own configuration for vulnerabilities.

Accessibility

The basic principle of the web was always to make information available to everyone. Or, at least, make it available to everyone with a computer and access to an Internet connection. Web accessibility guidelines are designed to help developers and designers create web sites that are meant to be used by all people, regardless of any disabilities. Your customers may have impaired vision, may not be able to use a mouse, or may be colorblind. There are a few very simple things you can do to make things easier for them to shop on your site.

Regulatory guidelines for web accessibility are defined in Section 508,[9] as part of the amendment to the Rehabilitation Act in 1998. Specifically, Section 508 outlines rules that are designed to make information technology (including web sites) accessible to all users, including those with special needs. If you're not familiar with accessibility guidelines, I strongly recommend you learn at least the very basics about them. They range from making forms and tables easier to browse to more widespread architectural decisions like using CSS for layout instead of HTML tables, as well as making sure your site degrades gracefully when people have CSS turned off.

The basic lesson is that a lot of people might be using your site in a manner with which you might not be familiar. However, on top of supporting a very important cause (accessibility for everyone), it makes good business sense because you're trying to reach as many customers as possible.

There are two major types of approaches that you might take to make your site as accessible as possible to the widest range of users. First, you might determine that you need to create an *entirely separate interface* for your disabled users, so that they have the ability to decide if they want to use the accessible interface in order to shop your site. Amazon.com appears to take this approach. If you visit http://www.amazon.com/access, you'll see a barebones, small site that should be very simple for users with screen readers. (For the record, http://www.amazon.com/mobile redirects to the same interface,

---

[9] http://www.section508.gov/

so setting up a separate accessible page might be coupled with a strategy for creating a mobile interface as well.)

However, a much simpler approach is take the *one* interface that you're creating and just make it accessible to everyone, as best as you can. This makes the most sense, because it forces you to keep the interface *as simple as possible*, which benefits not just disabled users but all of your users. That, and the users with special needs don't feel like they're missing anything by being herded into a separate interface.

I'm going to take the latter approach in this book. I'm not an accessibility expert, but I am going to work the basics into my project where I feel it's necessary. To ease your own development, I highly recommend you download and install the very useful Firefox Accessibility Extension.

PCI Compliance

PCI stands for Payment Card Industry, and a set of recommended practices and guidelines to use when dealing with customer credit card information. If you can avoid it, you should not be storing your customer's credit card information when they place an order, unless you are positive that nobody has easy physical access to your servers, and that you're encrypting the information appropriately. I'll briefly cover how you *could* store credit card data, but we're not going to implement that approach in this book because it's almost always a bad idea unless you really know what you are doing.

There is one alternative to storing the credit card information itself. Some payment gateways, such as Authorize.Net, will store the customer's credit card information for you. In order to charge the credit card a second time (say, in case a customer places a second order), you can reference the transaction ID of the first purchase and use the credit card data stored with Authorize.Net. This does solve the problem of storing the data, but it does have one drawback: it couples our customer accounts to one particular payment gateway. Later, if you want to change payment gateways, you won't be able to take your customer's credit card data with you.

If you decide you don't want to let the payment gateway store credit card information, and you don't store it on your own system, then the customer will have to put in their credit card each time they place an order on your site. This is an inconvenience for them, and that's unfortunate, but we're going to make it abundantly clear to them that while we take security very seriously and have secure servers hosting our site, we're protecting them by not keeping their credit card data where it may be breached.

If you're determined to store credit card data because you simply feel that you must, at least make sure you never store or retain the card verification value (CVV) *anywhere* on your system, in addition to encrypting the data.

Search Engine Optimization

Search Engine Optimization is a weird area of web development because while we have some general guidelines to follow, nobody really knows the exact rules by which we're playing. In *Bang the Drum Slowly*, the characters play a game called "TEGWAR" – The Exciting Game Without Any Rules. The characters always entice some poor sucker to play with them, without mentioning what "TEGWAR" stands for, and the rules of the game always shift so that our poor sucker loses his money to the others.

The odds aren't stacked against us quite as much in the SEO world, but it can feel pretty close. It's a place where the more knowledgeable are always uncertain, and prefer to rely on testing. Take everything anyone tells you with a grain of salt, as the whole area of SEO is fraught with misinformation. My advice, if you're just starting out, is to go straight to the information provided by the biggest search engine: Google. You can read Google's guidelines for SEO at their webmasters page:

```
http://www.google.com/support/webmasters/
```

Besides this, make sure that every page on your site that you would like to have crawled by Google is linked to from somewhere on your site, and make sure each page has a unique title tag and relevant content. I'll cover SEO in more detail in Chapter 11, and in various places throughout the book.

Deployment

Where you are going to end up deploying your application, and how you plan to handle all of the various components, is something you should be aware of up front. If you're deploying to the Google App Engine, some of the code you write for your models may be much different than the code you'd normally write.

During development, all of your project's components are probably going to be on a single development machine, like the desktop you may be sitting in front of right now. That one machine will have your database engine, Django code, style sheets, JavaScript files, images, and any other media on it. When you deploy your site into production, however, these different things are logically split out onto separate machines to maximize the efficiency you get out each one. You'll probably end up having at least one for your database server, one for serving your web pages, and another for static content, such as style sheets and images.

Throughout this book, we're going to construct things so that when production time comes, we'll have a minimum of fuss getting all of the items ported over into their respective areas and still allow them to communicate with one another. I'll cover deployment more in Chapter 15.

Business Requirements

E-commerce is very much rooted in business. To create good software that accommodates the business process, it's helpful to have a little bit of background. Whether you're starting out doing some consulting work for a company looking to go online or trying to take your own sole proprietorship onto the web, knowing some of the basics will help you make some fundamental decisions about how to architect your application.

I know you picked up this book because it's a programming title. You may have very little interest in learning any kind of business background. Most of what I'm going to cover in this section is pretty elementary, and it's not at all comprehensive. My hope is to provide you with enough basic information that you can potentially ask your clients more informed questions, get the creative juices flowing, and provide one or two catalysts for brainstorming sessions. If not that, I hope that this helps you think critically about what you need to develop for yourself.

Of course, if you already know this stuff, or if you're strictly a programmer with a vow never to take any business classes, you can skip to the next chapter and get started creating your Django site.

Accounting & Auditing

It's hard to run any business without maintaining an accurate set of books, both for internal and external reasons. You'll need to keep a set of books so that you have some idea of where your company is, and where it's been, financially, so that you can devise some kind of strategy about where it's going. Furthermore, if you want to scare up capital by going public and issuing stock, you need to release financial statements so that your investors can decide whether or not your company is a safe investment. If you're publicly traded, you may need auditors to come in at least once a year to check for misstatements, either intentional or accidental, in your accounting records.

Accurate financial statements are of paramount importance to everyone, and since a lot of your information will likely be tracked by your application, you should figure out what information you want to collect and how you want to collect it.

One of the main things you'll be tracking is your sales. (You *are* selling something, aren't you?) There are two principles you need to be aware of in deciding how to track your sales that will be of importance to any auditors or other accounting folk reviewing your books. First, there is the *revenue recognition* principle and the *matching* principle. Generally, you should recognize and record your sales after you've performed all necessary business functions you need to order to *earn* them. With e-commerce, this is typically at the point when you've packaged and shipped off the goods to the customer. You also want to *match* the record of your expenses with the corresponding sale.

Typically, this becomes an issue on December 31st, the end of the fiscal year for most companies. Imagine a company that sells Twinkies online, in bulk. On December 31st, at 10PM, some person who's sitting at work on New Year's Eve (for some reason we can't figure out) ordering Twinkies for their business. They order $9,000 worth, and the company that's selling them has an e-commerce system in place that records these sales on December 31st.

On January 2nd, two days later, the packaging and shipping crew arrives energetic and ready to work, punches in, and starts to process the orders. They ship off these $9,000 worth of Twinkies, the original cost of which was half that, $4,500, and then they punch out and go home for the day. (Workdays are short in my imagination.)

The problem here is that the cost of the Twinkies (the $4,500) was recorded in one fiscal period, and the sales ($9,000) were recorded in the prior period. This makes the bottom line of the first year look $4,500 better than it should have, at the expense of making the next year look that much worse. And that's not even factoring in packaging costs, shipping costs, or the wages you had to pay your workers to come in and ship them.

This may sound like a small problem (what's a measly $4,500, really?), but when auditors come in and test these kinds of things, they'll probably check your sales records and make sure that all of them, especially those close to the year-end cutoff, have corresponding shipping records. They find that you missed this $4,500 worth of cost. It doesn't bode well for how good you are at running things, and will cause them to look deeper and charge you more. Also, lots of companies do this intentionally: they record lots of sales toward the end of the fiscal year that should be recorded in the next year, to make the current one look better, a practice called *front-loading*. Be ready for lots of fun if they start suspecting that you did it all on purpose.

For reasons such as this, you want to make sure you have established internal policies about when you record sales. Although we aren't going to do so in this book, you also might like to store the cost of each product along with the selling price, so you can easily figure out your cost of goods sold.

Supply Chain Management

There are two things that fall under this particular umbrella: inventory management and purchasing. As far as purchasing goes, it would be helpful to make sure you can easily determine how much you purchase from each of your suppliers annually. Knowing just how much you spend with them, as well as being familiar with their company and how much their annual sales are, can help you in negotiating lower prices, particularly if what you spend with them is a large chunk of their overall business.

Inventory management is fairly straightforward, but there are a few things you'll probably want to quantify and track to make managing the whole thing a lot easier. You may want to store what is referred to as the *reorder quantity*. The reorder quantity takes into account your lead times from suppliers and determines at what point you should reorder goods to keep a bare minimum of inventory.

Simply put, if you sell two Xbox's on your site each day, and when you order more from your own supplier it takes them four days to ship them to you, you'll want to order more when you have eight left in stock. That way, in theory, the new ones show up just after you've shipped out the last two. Yup, this is the kind of mind-bending mathematics they're teaching to business majors.

You might consider storing your lead time in days with the product, as well as do something to calculate how quickly each product is moving (e.g., how many Xbox's are you selling per day). Then, have a cron job (see the sidebar "Running Daily Tasks") run each night that checks each product and lets you know when you're getting close to the reorder point.

RUNNING DAILY TASKS

In the course of running your Django application, there are a variety of tasks that you might want to run at regular intervals, (e.g., every day or once a week). The operating system on which you're running your application probably has a means for you to set these to run automatically. On Unix systems, these are done by creating a `cron` *job*, which is created by adding an entry to your system's `crontab` file. On Windows machines, you should use the Task Scheduler.

What you *don't* want to do is trigger these kinds of job by hooking them up to an event that is caused by some customer action. For example, at one company where I worked, the product search functionality required copying product data from several database tables into one database table. When a search was performed, it used that one table instead of the other tables that contained the product and sku data.

The problem with this, however, was that the product data was always changing, so in order for the search results to be current, the search table needed to be updated every so often with fresh product data. The "freshness" of the search results table data was checked each time a customer searched on the site. This meant that every few days, one unlucky user who searched the site would have to sit there and wait while the data was all copied over into the search results table. With lots of data, this could make this single search take well over 30 seconds.

There's really no reason to do anything like this to your customers, even if it is just one every few days. Take the burden off of them and use the tools your operating system has provided for you.

Marketing Decisions

When you're doing consulting work, you often get a friendly e-mail or call from the client that goes something like this:

"Hi, one user of our site just called and complained that our site doesn't have *Feature X*. We need to add that as soon as possible."

Before I go any further, I'd like to acknowledge that I'm aware that these kinds of decisions made by marketing teams are the bane of the existence of developers doing consulting work. As a developer, I have a bias in this regard, and I'll admit that up front. This doesn't mean that I don't have a valid point regarding these matters that you should consider when making key decisions about your own projects.

Now, this hypothetical request that came in from a client based on this one user's complaint is ludicrous. You remember the old idiom about the squeaky wheel getting the grease? That's what's going on here. It's possible that implementing Feature X is a terrible idea, and there are a couple of reasons why that might be the case. They have to do with the bias of the feedback you're getting, as well as a cost-benefit of adding the new feature.

First off, people are naturally irritable when they're having a bad day. Never underestimate the trouble a person will go to when they haven't gotten enough sleep to complain to someone about something petty that really doesn't matter one bit. It's possible they used your site once, found that it didn't have one feature that they feel every e-commerce site should have, and felt the self-important need to give you a piece of their mind. For this reason, consider the following when you receive feedback from a user:

- What is the tone of the criticism being voiced? How are they expressing themselves?

- Is this a repeat customer or a one-time user that happened to browse a few products?

Of course, maybe more than one person has voiced their concern about the lack of this particular feature. That's much more helpful, and a good case for considering

But consider this: if your site is getting a few hundred hits a day, a good portion of which are converting just fine, and you get just this one complaint from a person about your missing feature, think about how adding that feature will impact the other few hundred people who *aren't* complaining. If you get an e-mail from someone saying they want to allow customers to ship their orders to multiple addresses, think about how this impacts your site as a whole. You're potentially adding a whole new step to your checkout process, or at least one more box for them to read and check while they're in the flow of trying to purchase your products.

The benefit is that your customers will be able to split a single order to ship to multiple addresses, but what is the cost? *How will this change impact all those people are perfectly happy using your site the way it is?*

Also, you should keep in mind that your site is not impervious to market conditions. This may seem like a low blow, but there will be months when your site underperforms in comparison to your expectation. After launch, you might have five dynamite months of consistent sales and, in the sixth month, they suddenly fall off. It seems like people aren't buying your products anymore. The exact cause or causes of these kinds of changes in consumer behavior can be extremely difficult to track down when you're talking about a website, and for this reason, managers and people in marketing tend to point at the site itself. They come up with one example, like the fact that customers can't set up wish lists for themselves, and decide that the lack of wish lists is the reason customers aren't using their site.

This is just silly. If your site was functionally the same in the first five months as it was in the sixth, there's no reason to suspect that your *site* is somehow causing the downturn. Imagine that you are running a store in a shopping mall that sells designer clothes; it's a little like you walking into this store during a slow sales month and blaming the cash register. It's akin to saying, "Oh, this thing customers are using to swipe their credit cards should be on the right side of the counter, not the left! That's why people aren't buying anything!"

The reason your store, either online or off, is suffering is because of market conditions. There might be another e-commerce site that launched and is selling a lot of the same products you are for cheaper. Maybe those keywords that you bought from AdWords as a part of your search engine marketing campaign have shifted and are not yielding you the same value for your money. Maybe the economy just took a nose dive and people are wary about buying anything that doesn't fit into the lifestyle of a bare minimalist.

I'm not saying that you should never add features to your site; I'm merely saying that you should carefully consider the conclusions you draw when trying to figure out what's wrong with your site. You should add new features and functionality when you think they will add value to your users and their experience using your site, not because you're looking for a quick way to tow your site out of a ditch. In most cases, it's probably not the answer.

In consulting, it's possible you will not always be able to get around this, even if the request is pretty silly. Perhaps, because they're your customer and they're paying you, you'll have to spend copious amounts of developer time implementing Feature X for them, against all better judgment in your mind. This is one of the annoyances of being a developer. The only thing you can do is offer your opinion and hope that, from one professional to another, they at least consider your point of view. Just try to remember that while silly requests like this might be the bane of your existence as a consultant, they are also your livelihood. After all, they are paying you.

Summary

Before you dive into the rest of the book, take a moment to reflect on what you hope to learn about Django by reading this book. Skim the table of contents, and write down any questions that come up about material that you hope to take away from this chapter. Keep this list handy (perhaps next to the "brain dump" plan we created at the beginning of the chapter) while you're reading the rest of the book and jot down the answers as you find them. For the questions that I don't cover, you can always refer to the online documentation later to fill in the gaps.

The point of this assignment is to encourage you to learn with your goals in mind. There's a reason you're reading this, probably because there are things you're hoping to learn. Just make sure you know what they are before you start, and you'll be much more likely to retain the information.

So, let's get started building our application. In the next chapter, we're going to create our Django site and set up our templates so that we have a basic skeleton for our e-commerce application.

CHAPTER 2

■ ■ ■

Creating a Django Site

Now that we have some idea about how our site is supposed to look and function fresh in our minds from the last chapter, we're going to get started by creating the basic skeleton for the site.

First, we're going to create the Django site and have a look at the files that Django creates for you by default, and how you're supposed to use each one to set up the site. As every dynamic web site requires a back-end datastore, we're going to create and configure the MySQL database for our project. Then, we'll learn how Django maps requests to your site to view functions, and how these serve templates back to the users of your site.

We're just going to create something very simple, but don't let this interfere with your own design needs. You're welcome to detract from my setup and use your own custom layout inside of our template files. You should be able to follow along with the technical concepts in the rest of the book using your own HTML and CSS.

A Django-istic Welcome

So, now that we have our development environment up and running, let's create our first Django site! Actually, when compared to getting Django installed and running properly, creating the site and getting to our first default "Welcome!" page is really a breeze. This is probably a good thing: after spending the first chapter plowing through our schemes and configuring all the software we're going to be using, I'm sure you're ready for some instant gratification.

Creating the Project

The first thing to do, whether or not you've opted to use the Eclipse IDE, is to fire up a shell on your system and navigate to the directory where you plan to store your project. On my system, this happens to be in /home/smoochy/eclipse/workspace. Once you're there, run the following command:

```
$ django-admin.py startproject ecomstore
```

Once you've run this, go ahead and run ls to see that a directory called ecomstore was, in fact, created for you. If it's there, change into it and boot up your new site by doing the following:

```
$ cd ecomstore
$ python manage.py runserver
```

You should see a few quick lines about validating Django's models, which I'll discuss in later chapters. More importantly, you should see a URL where you can view your new site in the browser.

Leave the shell open, fire up your favorite browser, and navigate to the URL the shell told you about. It should be `http://localhost:8000/`, or as `http://127.0.0.1/`. The page you get should look something like Figure 2-1.

It worked!
Congratulations on your first Django-powered page.

Of course, you haven't actually done any work yet. Here's what to do next:

- If you plan to use a database, edit the `DATABASE_*` settings in `testsite/settings.py`.
- Start your first app by running `python testsite/manage.py startapp [appname]`.

You're seeing this message because you have `DEBUG = True` in your Django settings file and you haven't conf

Figure 2-1. Hello Django!

Phew! That was easy! Actually, at the risk of being sued by the Staples corporation, I'll gladly amend the latter statement and say: That was Django!

Notice that I named my project "ecomstore" even though we had planned to call our store "Modern Musician." Why didn't I use the store name as the name of our project? The reason is that our project's code will use the project name in our Python code in a few places, and in the interest of keeping things reusable, I've opted to use a more generic name. That way, in a year from now, when you clone your project in an effort to set up "Amazing Athlete" (or whatever), you'll easily be able to migrate over what you've created.

Let's look briefly at the files that are generated with a new Django site.

What Django Creates

Before we start exploring, if you want to open your new project using something other than the command line, open up Eclipse. Go to File New and select "PyDev Project." Type `ecomstore` in as the name of your project, and set the directory as the path to the directory your project is in. (If you've used the default, as I've done, it should already be typed in for you.) Make sure you select the correct version of Python to correspond with what's on your system, then click "Finish." After some quick whirring, the `ecomstore` folder should appear in Eclipse's file navigator.

If you've been following along, there should be at least four items in your `ecomstore` folder: `__init__.py`, `manage.py`, `settings.py`, and `urls.py`. Let's look at each one of these in turn and talk briefly about what it does:

> `__init__.py`: This file should be empty, and exists solely to tell your system that your `ecomstore` directory should be treated like a Python module.[1]

> `manage.py`: A local Python file that enables you to run various commands to administer your Django site. You've already used it to boot up the local development server.

---

[1] Each directory on your system that you want to be recognized by Python should contain this file. One important point about these `__init__.py` files: they can contain Python code, and can be imported by importing the name of the directory. In this case, since our project in on our system's PYTHONPATH, then `import ecomstore` in a Python shell will import the code in the `__init__.py` file.

`urls.py`: The file responsible for mapping incoming requests to their respective responses. It's like the phone operator in the days before cell phones. When you put `http://yoursite.com/product/dwight-schrute-bobblehead/` into your browser and you get back that product page, you can thank the `urls.py` file.

`settings.py`: A configuration file where you'll tell your site what database to use. This is the file where you would put site-wide configuration data, such as cookie expiration lengths, or credentials for a credit card processor. Using this file for such values instead of in your code makes the application easier to maintain, and makes these values easier to change, should you ever need to do so. This file can actually contain Python statements where necessary.

We'll look at each of these in more detail as the need to do so arises. For now, though, let's take a moment to set up our MySQL database.

Creating the MySQL Database

In order to set up the database for our Django project, we need to do the following three things:

1. Create a new database.

2. Create a new MySQL user with a password.

3. Grant the new MySQL user permissions to manipulate the database.

We can't do these from within the Django project. For these, we need to open up MySQL directly and get our hands dirty. Don't worry... this isn't quite as difficult as it might sound. Open up your local MySQL server with root user access however you feel most comfortable. Since I'm using a Unix variant, I'm going to do this from the command line, but feel free to use something more GUI-friendly. Execute the following commands:

```
mysql> CREATE DATABASE ecomstore CHARACTER SET utf8;
Query OK, 1 row affected (0.00 sec)

mysql> CREATE USER 'username'@'localhost' IDENTIFIED BY 'password';
Query OK, 0 rows affected (0.00 sec)

mysql> GRANT ALL ON ecomstore.* TO 'username'@'localhost';
Query OK, 0 rows affected (0.00 sec)
```

Feel free to change the name of the database, the username, or the password (*especially* the password!) to suit your own situation.

MYSQL STORAGE ENGINES

Before pressing on, one important note about MySQL tables. Internally, MySQL offers two different types of storage engines: MyISAM and InnoDB. By default, the tables you create use the MyISAM storage engine, which is missing the ability to handle *transactions*. Transactions basically allow you to execute multiple operations on data in an all-or-nothing fashion; that is, if anything goes wrong during one of the operations, then none of the changes are committed to the database.

The InnoDB storage engine was designed for transaction processing, and can be particularly useful for certain situations in e-commerce web applications. We're not going to use transactions in this book, so we're going to keep to the default MyISAM storage engine for our database tables. However, you should consult the MySQL documentation[2] for more about the differences between the two types to see which one better suits your needs. Also, you can read more about managing transactions in Django documentation.[3]

Back to the database user we just created: why not just run the database as it stands right now? We're doing this for security reasons. When you start up MySQL for the first time, you're probably logging in as "root" with the password you specified when you installed MySQL. This root user has privileges to execute any command on any database that it chooses. If you use the root username and password in your Django project, and someone compromises your Django files, then there's no limit to the damage they can do to all of the databases in your MySQL database server. Taking this extra step limits the damage they can do to *only* the ecomstore database. Consider it a containment strategy.

More than likely, no outsider will ever hack into your application. A much more distinct possibility is as your site and organization grow, you may hire at least one more developer to help you maintain your application. No matter who you choose to hire, there's always a chance your professional relationship will end in a not-so-good manner and you want to make sure there's a limit to what they are able to do. Even if this particular case doesn't apply to you, it's important to be aware of the potential consequences of what you choose to do now.

---

[2] http://dev.mysql.com/doc/refman/5.0/en/storage-engines.html

[3] http://docs.djangoproject.com/en/dev/topics/db/transactions/

mysql utf-8 collation – what gives?

You'll notice that we overrode the default character set when we created our database by explicitly setting it to UTF-8. This may or may not be what you want, and you're welcome to leave this setting off by eliminating the "CHARACTER SET utf8" portion of the CREATE DATABASE command.

The fact that you're setting your database to store Unicode[4] text is important because Unicode allows you to store accented characters, which customer names and addresses might contain. For this reason, you'll want your database to support the storage of Unicode text. Django also has a very adept internationalization framework, so you can display your web site in more than just one language. I'm not going to cover the Django internationalization framework in this book, but if you ever want to start selling your products in, say, Russian, using the Cyrillic alphabet, you'll need your database to support Unicode text. You might want to look into the pros and cons of UTF-8 in your database, as well as how the collation affects your own business requirements. You can read more about the collation settings of your database in the MySQL documentation[5].

The easiest way to configure this is to add this setting when you create the database. This will ensure that all tables created, by default, use UTF-8 to store their data and return query results with the UTF-8 character set.

Now that we have our database set up and our ecomstore user configured, open up your settings.py file in your project. Start scrolling down... close to the top, you should see a list of database settings, starting with DATABASE_, all in caps. The settings should all be empty strings. Based on the database you just created, change the values to read as follows:

```
DATABASE_ENGINE = 'mysql'            # 'postgresql_psycopg2',...
DATABASE_NAME = 'ecomstore'           # Or path to database file...
DATABASE_USER = 'username'           # Not used with sqlite3.
DATABASE_PASSWORD = 'password'        # Not used with sqlite3.
DATABASE_HOST = ''          # Set to empty string for localhost....
DATABASE_PORT = ''          # Set to empty string for default...
```

Provided that you've got your MySQL server installed locally, you can leave the host and port blank (it will assume localhost and the MySQL default port of 3306).

The manage.py file includes a dbshell utility that will enter a MySQL command shell within your project's database, and it provides a means for you to test your database connection. Back in your system's shell, in your project's root, type the following:

```
$ python manage.py dbshell
```

This command should drop you into the MySQL command shell. You're now connected as the user you just created, and, as you had intended, you're only able to access the ecomstore database. You can exit the MySQL prompt by typing quit.

---

[4] http://unicode.org/

[5] http://dev.mysql.com/doc/refman/5.0/en/charset-server.html

If you get an error when trying to enter your MySQL shell, examine the error message that Django displays back at you and try to determine what the problem is. The most common mistake is to try and use the incorrect database information. Check your `settings.py` database values again to make sure they contain the correct database credentials.

Dealing with Django Exceptions

So now that we've done all this work setting up our database, let's put it to good use for ourselves by getting it to log *exceptions* for us. An exception is an unexpected and unusual condition that causes your computer program—whether it's a Python program or a Django web project—to halt normal execution. This could be your site trying to do something it's not allowed to do, or perhaps you've pointed your code to a file that doesn't exist.

For practical reasons, you want to anticipate where potential exceptions might occur in your code and log them so you can review (and hopefully fix) them later. As good a programmer as you might be, as soon as you release your Django project into the wild, there is a slew of things that can potentially go wrong, and you want a means to track these issues. Of course, tracking these exceptions is a very good thing to do during development. And that's what we're going to do with our database right now.

Thanks to the open source community, there's already a solution out there that we can use to log Django exceptions to our database. The package is available at `http://code.google.com/p/django-db-log/`.

Go ahead and download the code (you might need to check it out of the subversion repository as we discussed in Chapter 1) to a directory of your choice, navigate into the directory, and install the package using the standard `distutils` method:

```
$ python setup.py install
```

This will extract the code into your Python's `site-packages` directory. Once this is on your machine, there are a couple of changes you need to make to your `settings.py` file in order for the logging to begin. There are two Python tuples in your `settings.py` file called `MIDDLEWARE_CLASSES`, and `INSTALLED_APPS`.

Add the Django DB Log middleware module to `MIDDLEWARE_CLASSES`:

```
MIDDLEWARE_CLASSES = (
    'django.middleware.common.CommonMiddleware',
    'django.contrib.sessions.middleware.SessionMiddleware',
    'django.contrib.auth.middleware.AuthenticationMiddleware',
    'djangodblog.DBLogMiddleware',
)
```

Be sure you include the trailing comma after that last item in the tuple. Items listed in Python tuples are delimited by commas, which is a simple concept to keep in mind. The problem comes up when there is a Python tuple that contains only a single item. In this case, there must be a comma after the only item in order for Python to recognize it as a valid tuple object. You don't need a comma after this last item, but it's good practice to follow every item in your tuples with a comma to get in the habit. By default, the `INSTALLED_APPS` tuple includes a few apps enabled for your convenience. However, to keep things simple in the meantime, we're going to disable those four and add the Django DB Log. You can comment out lines in your Python files by placing a `#` symbol at the beginning of each line you want to remove. Edit your `INSTALLED_APPS` so that it looks like this:

```
INSTALLED_APPS = (
    #'django.contrib.auth',
    #'django.contrib.contenttypes',
    #'django.contrib.sessions',
    #'django.contrib.sites',
    'djangodblog',
)
```

Once again, don't forget the comma after the last (and in this case, only) element in the tuple. With this in place, hop on back to your shell and run the following command:

```
$ python manage.py syncdb
Creating table djangodblog_errorbatch
Creating table djangodblog_error
Installing index for djangodblog.ErrorBatch model
Installing index for djangodblog.Error model
```

If you've set up your database, you should see a message about the creation of two tables with two indexes added to them. Your Django project will now log all of its exceptions to a database table called djangodblog_error. All we need now is an exception for our application to catch.

Template & View Basics

So now that we have a database in place, let's look at setting up our first custom web page by examining the Django templating system (more on the exception later). First, let's briefly go over how Django handles a request made to our site:

1. The request comes in to the server from the client and this is routed from the web server to our application.

2. The URL resolver examines the request and compares it with a set of regular expressions specified in the project's urls.py files, which are mapped to Django functions called *views*.

3. The request and any additional parameters supplied by the URL are passed to the corresponding view function.

4. After running whatever logic the site needs, the view function returns a response, which typically takes the form of a generated HTML page.

Defining everything as simply as possible, a Django application is little more than a group of Python functions that take HTTP requests and return HTML responses. Your urls.py file just acts as a dispatcher directing what functions the requests are routed to. This may sound a little esoteric in theory, so let's put it into practice.

Here's an example of a Python function that acts as a Django view (you don't have to type this in yet):

```
def catalog(request):
    site_name = "Modern Musician"
    response_html = u"<html><body>Welcome to %s.</body></html>" % site_name
    return HttpResponse(response_html)
```

In this overly simple example, we create two strings, embed one in the other using the string format operator (the %) and Python string interpolation,[6] pass them into a new `HttpResponse` object, and return it to the request. All we'd need to do to make this page usable in the real world is give it a corresponding entry in our `urls.py` file, which might look something like this:

```
urlpatterns = patterns('',
    # other commented code here.
    (r'^catalog/$', 'ecomstore.views.catalog'),
)
```

Given this, if you were to navigate to `http://localhost:8000/catalog/`, you would be presented with the welcome message you created previously. While it's probably not a code sample that will land you your dream job, it does illustrate the basic concept of what a Django view does.

Naturally, in the face of such simplicity with our example, there are some very obvious drawbacks to this approach, which should be immediately apparent to anyone who's spent more than five minutes coding for the web. The first thing you should note is that we've just hard-coded the basic HTML tags for our page in a Python string. Perfect for a "Hello World!" example, but definitely not ideal for a real-world application.

This is where Django templates come in. In almost all practical cases, you'll load a file in your project's directory into a Django Template object that you can use in your response. This file will contain all of the HTML markup that your page has, along with placeholders for variables.

You'll also notice that we passed in the name of the site using the Python string formatter syntax. For larger pages that require a lot of variables to be passed in, this could very quickly become an unmanageable headache. Fortunately, Django templates manage their variables using special objects called *contexts*.

A `Context` object takes one optional parameter, which is a Python dictionary of name-value pairs. These values are the variables you can use in your templates, and reference by name, when you return them to the response.

So, if we refactored what we did previously to follow Django standards, we might create a file called `sample.html` within our project's template directory (which we haven't made yet) containing the following HTML:

```
<html><body>Welcome to {{ site_name }}.</body></html>
```

and we would change our Python view function to look like this:

```
def catalog(request):
    my_context = Context({ 'site_name': 'Modern Musician' })
    response_html = return_to_string('sample.html', my_context)
    return HttpResponse(response_html)
```

This makes things much simpler and more flexible. You create a `Context` object and pass it a Python dictionary with one entry: the name of your site. You then call the `return_to_string()` function, passing it the name of your template and the `Context` object you created. Then, like before, you return the response.

Don't worry if you're completely lost about how things are supposed to really come together in Django at this point. You might be wondering how Django knows where to look when it's loading your template file, or why we'd do anything as inane as specifying our site's name in a local variable in a

---

[6] http://www.python.org/dev/peps/pep-0292/

single view function. I've only provided these examples so that you get some idea of how you create a template and the means by which you pass in any variables.

In particular, take note of the double curly-braces in the template: `{{ site_name }}`. That is Django's syntax for a variable. When the Django templating engine parses this code, it will stick the name of your site—in this case, "Modern Musician—in the `{{ site_name }}` placeholder.

Advanced Templates with Inheritance

As a Django programmer, you'll be loading templates and creating `Context` objects very often during the development of your site. For this reason, you want to take the easiest approach possible. We're now going to leave the realm of theoretical examples and implement a real page with the tactics that will carry us through the rest of the book.

Templates are made easier in Django with functionality referred to as *template inheritance*. If you're familiar with object-oriented programming, template inheritance is much like class inheritance: child templates take the content of their parent template, and custom content can be added to the child to override and extend that of the parent.

Let's put this thought into action. First, create a new folder in the root of your project and called it `templates`. Then open up your `settings.py` file and find the variable `TEMPLATE_DIRS`, which should be an empty tuple by default. You'll need to put the absolute path on your system to the directory or directories where you plan to keep your template files. On the Ubuntu box I'm using, this looks like this:

```
"/home/smoochy/eclipse/workspace/ecomstore/templates",
```

On a Windows machine, your path will likely start with `C:/`, and should take only forward slashes. Make sure not to copy the backslashes from your Explorer window because they won't work.

A quick word about what we just did: we opted to put the template files into a directory inside our project. Depending on your particular requirements, this may not be what you want. The Django community, as well as the Python community at large, prides itself on maximum flexibility, and being able to reuse work that you've already done in other Django projects is a large component of that flexibility. It's not a requirement that your template directory is within your project... it could be just about anywhere on your system that your user account has the proper permissions to access.

I've chosen to contain them within our project for simplicity and convenience, and because I'm pretty sure any future sites I'll be coding will have drastically different layout needs, I want to set things up so that later, when I need to edit one site, I don't have to edit them all. I prefer the templating for each project be decoupled from all of the others, and any base similarities can merely be copied from the other projects at the start of development. Despite this philosophy, if you think you'll be doing lots of other projects and want to put them elsewhere, outside of your directory, I would be the first person to insist on it.

Typically, to allow yourself some "wiggle room" as far as the templates go, Django templates should be three levels deep. The template in the first level contains all of the elements that are common to all HTML pages on your site, like the opening and closing `html`, `head`, and `body` tags, and any `meta`, `link`, or `script` tags inside of the `head` tags. The template directly below this will contain the HTML for your site's overall layout structure, marked up with `id` and `class` attributes for CSS styling. The third and last level should contain content specific to individual pages. To start creating our templates, let's look at the needs that will be fundamental to most every HTML page on your site. You can safely assume you'll have a Document Type Declaration, and opening and closing `html`, `head`, `body`, `title`, and `meta` tags. Create a file in the templates directory you just created and call it `base.html`. Put the following code into the file:

```
<!DOCTYPE html PUBLIC "-//W3C//DTD XHTML 1.0 Strict//EN" "XHTML1-s.dtd" ><html
xmlns="http://www.w3.org/1999/xhtml" xml:lang="en" lang="en">
```

```
<head>
    <meta http-equiv="Content-Type" content="text/html; charset=utf-8" />
    <title>{% block title %}{% if page_title %}{{ page_title }} - {% endif %} ↵
        {{ site_name }}{% endblock %}</title>
    <meta name="keywords" content="{{ meta_keywords }}" />
    <meta name="description" content="{{ meta_description }}" />
</head>
<body>
    {% block site_wrapper %}{% endblock %}
</body></html>
```

Okay, I see some hands starting to pop up in the back of the room. I realize that I covered the placeholders for template variables with the double curly braces, but you haven't yet seen the Django template blocks. Django blocks in a parent template are spaces reserved for content in the child templates. So, if you create a template that inherits from base.html, you'll be able to specify a block in the child template called site_wrapper and put whatever content you would like into it. Whenever one of these children is rendered, the content of site_wrapper will be nested in your base.html template. Neat, huh?

The first Django template block we've defined, called title, contains some logic and variables for the corresponding tags in the head element of our site. We'll come back to the {% if %} Django template blocks later, but basically, they allow you to put logic in your templates the same way you would your code. Of course, the amount of actual logic you put in your template should be small. Even though Django templates come equipped to handle programming flow, they are intended to act as a thin presentation layer for your application. You should keep its use to a minimum to keep your templates simple and maintainable.

In this case, our template is checking for the presence of a variable called page_title and if it's present, the template renders it before the name of the site, with a dash separating them. Make sure that the title block is only on one line, since line breaks will be included in the content of the tag.

There are also two variables for meta keywords and meta description inside of the standard meta tags, which we'll set later when we write our view functions.

The next level down should contain the layout that will be used by most of the pages on the site, like the homepage, category and product pages, and any static content pages, such as an "About Us" or "Privacy Policy" page. This layout will include a side bar with extra content. When we get around to making the checkout pages, we will probably create a different second-level template. We want to allow ourselves the options to do this, so we can change pages based on our needs. For example, we might remove the side bar from the checkout pages so that users are less likely to get distracted during the checkout process and click somewhere else.

Create a new file in your templates directory called catalog.html and put in the following content:

```
{% extends "base.html" %}

{% block site_wrapper %}
<div id="main">
    <a href="#content" class="skip_link">Skip to main content</a>
    <div id="banner">
        <div class="bannerIEPadder">
            <div class="cart_box">
            [link to cart here]
            </div>
```

```
                Modern Musician
        </div>
    </div>
    <div id="navigation">
        <div class="navIEPadder">
            [navigation here]
        </div>
    </div>
    <div id="middle">
        <div id="sidebar">
            <div class="sidebarIEPadder">
            [search box here]
            <br />
            [category listing here]
            </div>
        </div>
        <div id="content">
            <a name="content"></a>
            <div class="contentIEPadder">
                {% block content %}{% endblock %}
            </div>
        </div>
    </div>
    <div id="footer">
        <div class="footerIEPadder">
            [footer here]
         </div>
    </div>
</div>
{% endblock %}
```

The key thing is to make sure that {% extends "base.html" %} is the first line in the file. This is the directive that tells catalog.html to inherit from base.html.

In the rest of the file, you see that we've overridden the content of the site_wrapper block with a bunch of markup for the site layout. We've also created a new content block called, aptly enough, content, which we'll use for the content of individual pages. We'll see the CSS that accompanies this markup in a moment.

Finally, create a third template in your templates directory that we'll use for the homepage, and name it the traditional index.html. Within that template, put the following:

```
{% extends "catalog.html" %}

{% block content %}
    <h2>Welcome!</h2>
{% endblock %}
```

Our content block has a cordial welcome message in it. Look over these three templates and make sure you understand how things are flowing from top to bottom. In a moment, we'll see what they look like all put together.

Before we go further, it's worth retracing our steps and examining the blocks in our templates that open and close with curly braces and percentage signs. We used them to create blocks in our templates, but these tags are much more versatile in Django templates. They are used for if statements, for loops, including blocks of template code, and other directives much like the {% extends... %} we saw before. We'll come back to those other uses at various points in the book.

Greater Ease with render_to_response()

Now that we've done all of this work setting up the templates, we just *have* to test them to see if everything's been done correctly. We still have more work to do, but let's gratify ourselves with a quick peek at our layout so far.

Code inside of a Django project resides inside of individual subdirectories called apps, which we'll learn more about in the next chapter. For now, we're going to create an app to store code for this simple preview. Inside your project's root directory, execute the following to create an app called preview:

```
$ python manage.py startapp preview
```

Inside this new app directory, you should find a file named views.py. Open up that file and add the following code to create a single view function:

```
from django.shortcuts import render_to_response

def home(request):
    return render_to_response("index.html")
```

That's interesting. Using render_to_response() sure *seems* to make everything quite a bit quicker than the sample views we looked at before. As it turns out, the Django developers created the render_to_response() function to do the heavy lifting for us whenever we are writing Django view functions , which allows us to handle a very common case using only a single line of code. In our case, we just passed it the name of the template to render, but it takes an optional second argument: a Python dictionary of variables. The render_to_response() function takes the template, populates it with variables, and then returns the generated content to us in form of an HttpResponse.

In most web frameworks, such as ASP.NET, PHP, and Ruby on Rails, the URL is mapped to a *file* on the file system that contains application code, such as Default.aspx or index.php. In Django, your URL ends up being mapped to a *function* in Python code, which in turn renders a template file on the file system. It's a different way of doing things, but you'll get used to it quickly, so don't sweat it.

So, we have a simple view for testing our homepage. Unfortunately, we still don't have a way of navigating to it, so open up your urls.py file and add the following line:

```
urlpatterns += patterns('',
    #other commented code here
    (r'^catalog/$', 'preview.views.home'),
)
```

With this in place, jump back to the shell and boot up the server (if it's not running already):

```
$ python manage.py runserver
```

Once that's up, fire up a browser and navigate to `http://localhost:8000/catalog/`. You should see some black on white text that lacks any formatting whatsoever:

```
Skip to main content
[link to cart here]
Modern Musician
[navigation here]
[search box here]
[category listing here]
Welcome!
[footer here]
```

The reason we're not seeing anything particularly pretty is because we haven't yet attached our CSS file. That's all right… I deliberately left out that step so we could check what our site looks like without any CSS markup. Remember, there are people out there with special browsers that don't render CSS, and you don't want to preclude them from being able to use your site conveniently. Sure, the preceding markup on a product page might be awkward, but the flow is still there in good order, and we're not preventing anyone from checking out.

Make it a point to check your site during the various stages of development to ensure that the layout looks okay, and that elements are logically ordered, without the aid of any CSS styles. You actually don't have to remove the CSS link from your template code each time you want to do this. If you're using Firefox, with the Firefox Accessibility Extension toolbar installed, you can easily disable CSS from the "Style" menu by toggling off the "Author CSS" setting.

Adding in the CSS

There's one piece of the puzzle still missing, and it's the CSS for our layout in `catalog.html`. To add the CSS, create a directory called `static` in the root of your Django project and create a file called `css.css` within your new `static` folder. Enter the following CSS:

```
*{
    margin:0;
    padding:0;
}
html{
    font-size:medium;
}
html,body{
    background-color:Silver;
}
.cb{
    clear:both;
}
.fr{
    float:right;
}
.fl{
```

```
        float:left;
}
.bn{
    border:none;
}#main{
      margin: 0 auto;
      width:900px;
      background-color:White;
}
.bannerIEPadder, .sidebarIEPadder, .contentIEPadder{
      padding:10px;
}
.navIEPadder, .footerIEPadder{
      padding:5px;
}
#banner{
      width:900px;
      height:75px;
      background-color:DarkOrange;
      color:White;
      font-size:36px;
      font-weight:bold;
      position:relative;
}
div.cart_box{
      position:absolute;
      top:10px;
      right:10px;
      font-size:medium;
}
div.cart_box a{
      color:white;
}
#sidebar{
      width:200px;
      float:left;;
}
#content{
      width:700px;
      float:left;
}
#footer{
      clear:both;
      background-color:#98AC5E;
      color:White;
      text-align:center;
}
```

```
a.skip_link{
    position:absolute;
    left:-1000px;
    top:-1000px;
}
```

Some browsers come equipped with some default settings, such as margin and padding for elements. These default styles can create differences in appearance between browsers, so the solution is to use a CSS reset to set all padding and margin to zero. The preceding code contains a CSS reset (which is the style attached to the asterisk * character), some basic classes I will be using, and the more specific classes and attributes contained in our HTML markup. One thing that may jump out at you is the "Skip to main content" link we set at the top of our page. You'll notice that we're using CSS to hide this link. Why the invisible link?

This is for accessibility reasons. Users that have impaired vision may be listening to the markup of the page being read aloud to them, and with each new page they navigate to, they will have to start listening at the very top. That means that with each new page, they might potentially need to hear the banner, navigation, and side column markup before they get to the content. Putting in a skip link at the very top of the pages enables them to jump right to the start of the page content, thus making your site much more usable to people using screen readers. You can see that this link is not visible to all users when CSS is on, so it won't distract or interfere with people who don't need it. If the CSS is not available or rendered, as is the case with screen readers, then it appears right at the top of the page above the logo.

WHY THE "PADDER" CLASSES?

You might have noticed that I've got some divs nested in our layout divs, with classes that start with "padder". I'm doing this to accommodate IE 6's box model issue. This has to do with any div element that has a fixed width and a specified border or padding.

As an example, if you have a div that is 500px wide, with 10px of padding, standards-compliant browsers will expand the box to be 520px wide in total. However, IE 6 will make your div 500px wide, with 10px of padding inside of this, and your content will be compressed into an area that is 480px. The simple solution is not to add padding, borders, or margins to any elements that have a fixed width.

I'm not a designer or a CSS professional, but this is one issue that I've seen drive CSS newcomers absolutely batty when trying to maintain consistency in their layouts across major browsers. While this may or may not affect you (officially, IE 6 doesn't have this problem, although I've encountered it under "normal" conditions), I think it's helpful to be aware of it. You can read more about the issue at: http://en.wikipedia.org/wiki/Internet_Explorer_box_model_bug.

Now we need to attach the CSS file to our template files. This is simple enough, but there is one issue we need to address before we do so. When you're developing your site on a single machine, you have everything running on that one computer: the database, images, style sheets, JavaScript files, and so forth. However, in real-world sites deployed into production, these items are usually split out onto different machines. The creators of Django believe (and rightly so) that for scalability reasons, the server that is serving your site's pages shouldn't be the server that is hosting and serving up your static media, such as style sheets or images.

During the development phase, configuring a full web server such as Apache to serve your site's static media can be kind of a hassle, so there is a workaround for this while you're developing locally. Go into your urls.py file and add the following entry to refer to the static directory with your CSS file in it:

```
urlpatterns = patterns('',
    # other commented code here
    (r'^catalog/?', 'views.home'),
    (r'^static/(?P<path>.*)$', 'django.views.static.serve',
        { 'document_root' : '/home/smoochy/eclipse/workspace/ecomstore/static' }),
)
```

This will point any request to your site made to http://localhost:8000/static/ into the static directory you created. Next, go into your base.html file and add the following line to your site's head:

```
<head>
    <link rel="Stylesheet" type="text/css" href="/static/css.css" />
    <meta http-equiv="Content-Type" content="text/html; charset=utf-8" />
```

Make sure you include the slash before static in the href attribute.

This approach is a hack, albeit a useful one, that should *never* be used in production. We've got things set up for ourselves in the meantime, but definitely make a substantial mental note to change this later. We'll cover the change you should make, and how to do things correctly, in the chapter on deployment much later in the book.

Optionally, you could add logic to your urls.py file to only include the static media path as a URL entry if your site is not currently in production. Before deploying your site, one thing you should do is set the DEBUG property in your settings.py file to False. You could conditionalize this by importing your settings module into urls.py and adding it if DEBUG is set to True:

```
from ecomstore import settings

urlpatterns = patterns('',
# other urlpatterns defined here

if settings.DEBUG:
    urlpatterns += patterns('',
(r'^static/(?P<path>.*)$', 'django.views.static.serve',
        { 'document_root' : '/home/smoochy/eclipse/workspace/ecomstore/static' }),
)
```

Notice that this code block is separate from the first urlpatterns block, and we're using the += operator, which adds the static URL pattern to the existing urlpatterns block.

You can read more advice about this hack at http://docs.djangoproject.com/en/dev/howto/static-files/.

SERVING STATIC CONTENT ON WINDOWS

The static content you just set up will look a little different for windows users. Instead of the '/home/…' path, you'll probably need to use something that starts with your drive letter and maps to the directory in much the same way:

```
{ 'document_root': 'C:/Documents and
Settings/Smoochy/Eclipse/Workspace/ecomstore/static' }),
```

As mentioned earlier, note that forward slashes are used and not back slashes.

With our CSS now attached, go back to your browser and refresh the site. You should see a colorful layout that resembles Figure 2-2.

Figure 2-2. Ta-da! Our homepage, viewable at http://localhost:8000/catalog/.

I'd like to reiterate one point that I made in Chapter 1: I'm not a visual designer, I'm a programmer. Yes, programming code is a form of design, but I know nothing about color theory and couldn't tell you what psychological effect this orange and green color combination might have on our potential customers. Maybe it will make them laugh, and maybe that's a bad thing. Remember that the design in this book is just a placeholder. When you have the resources and the wherewithal, you can hire a designer to overhaul your catalog.html file and make it look the way you want.

A quick note on CSS: for very large sites, you might want to break out your CSS into multiple files and import them into the one that you include in the link element in your site's head. You could conceivably put this into your css.css file (must be the first thing in the file):

```
@import 'layout.css';
@import 'styles.css';
@import 'links.css';
```

The content of these three other files will be downloaded with your one style sheet. This can be extremely useful for partitioning areas of your CSS, especially for large projects, but be aware that each of your @import directives makes the loading of your site require an additional HTTP request. For performance optimization, you don't want to go "import crazy" and have 20 imports for relatively small files. If your project will be fairly tiny, like mine, it's probably better for you to do as I will, and just use a single CSS file.

Location, Location, Location

We are repeating ourselves in the `settings.py` file with regard to one particular configuration: the path to our project on the system on which it's running. For example, there are two places in `settings.py` and one place in `urls.py` where the following path is located:

```
/home/smoochy/eclipse/workspace/ecomstore… (etc)
```

Clearly, this is suboptimal and we want to not only have this information declared in one place, but it should also be determined for us automatically, at runtime, based on the project environment.

As it turns out, Python comes with a very simple function that returns the path to the current directory as a string. The following code will do this and return the path as a Unicode string:

```
import os
os.path.abspath(os.path.dirname(__file__).decode('utf-8'))
```

Simple as that. One problem with this approach is that it will not work on Windows. If you run this function on a Windows box, the directory delimiters will be two backslashes: one that's really supposed to be a backslash and one that's escaping the backslash character. So, we can perform a simple find and replace on our string in order to get this working correctly on Windows boxes by replacing double backslashes with single forward slashes.

Let's set a constant in our `settings.py` file that encapsulates this information. In your `settings.py` file, enter the following two lines of code somewhere near the top of the file:

```
import os
# hack to accommodate Windows
CURRENT_PATH = ⏎
    os.path.abspath(os.path.dirname(__file__).decode('utf-8')).replace('\\', '/')
```

Now, wherever you reference the path to your project in your configuration files, just replace the text with the `CURRENT_PATH` variable. Here is my `TEMPLATE_DIRS` tuple reconfigured:

```
TEMPLATE_DIRS = (
    os.path.join(CURRENT_PATH, 'templates'),
)
```

Here we are using another method that ships with the `os.path` module. The `join()` function takes the `CURRENT_PATH` variable and appends the `templates` subdirectory to it. Now, if your project moves around between multiple machines during development (as mine tends to do), and regardless of where it ends up on the system when you deploy the site, you don't need to alter these directory paths after each move.

A Site Navigation Include

Things are set up for us to start developing the site pages, but I'm going to show you one last template item briefly before we continue. The placeholder reading [navigation here] will be replaced by a set of anchor elements leading to the pages on our site. This is simple enough for HTML gurus that we can do this now.

Create a directory within your templates folder called tags, and create a new file inside of your tags directory called navigation.html. Put the following HTML into that file:

```
<ul>
    <li><a href="/catalog/">Home</a></li>
    <li><a href="/catalog/">About</a></li>
    <li><a href="/catalog/">Privacy</a></li>
    <li><a href="/catalog/">Products</a></li>
    <li><a href="/catalog/">Contact</a></li>
</ul>
<div class="cb"></div>
```

Next, open up your project's CSS file and add in the following styles for our navigation list of hyperlinks:

```
#navigation{
    width:900px;
    height:auto;
    background-color:#98AC5E;
    text-align:middle;
}
#navigation ul{
    list-style:none;
}
#navigation ul li{
    float:left;
    margin-right:15px;
}
#navigation ul li a{
    color:White;
    font-weight:bold;
    text-decoration:underline;
}
#navigation ul li a:hover{
    color:#616161;
    background-color:White;
    text-decoration:none;
}
```

You should now have this file set up in your project at: /templates/tags/navigation.html. We're going to use a Django templating option that allows us to separate out the template code, by using an include directive. Open up your `catalog.html` file and find the placeholder for the navigation. Replace it with the following line:

```
{% include 'navigation.html' %}
```

The `include` directive looks in your template directories for the file you specified, and if it finds it, inserts the HTML it finds in the template file into that spot in your template. If you come from a PHP background, this should look very familiar to you. This template has nothing to do with our inheritance model we structured earlier. Instead, it's merely an easy means of breaking out chunks of HTML in your site (in this case, the navigation) into a separate file that you can inject in your template where you want. This helps keep your templates more manageable, as it allows you take large blocks of HTML content and keep them out of your base templates, which should only contain markup related to the overall site structure.

So, with this code in place, load up the `catalog` page. If you get an error, and a message on the error page that says something like `TemplateSyntaxError` and a message about an exception that was caught while rendering the exception, then bravo.

You haven't done anything wrong. Remember earlier in the chapter when I promised you a Django template exception to test our error handling code? Our `include` tag is incorrect because we didn't specify the correct directory. Remember, we put the `navigation.html` file into `/templates/tags/navigation.html`, and not just in our `/templates` directory. Our Django project is looking in the `templates` directory for the file, and not inside any subdirectories.

So, to fix your `include` tag, alter it so that it looks like this:

```
{% include "tags/navigation.html" %}
```

Try reloading your page again. You should be greeted with the same page as before, except now you should have five navigation links at the top, styled according to your CSS (and that, when clicked, don't take you anywhere).

So let's check for that exception you just caused. Drop down into your database, either using the `manage.py dbshell` or otherwise, and run the following:

```
SELECT * FROM djangodblog_error;
```

You should get back at least one row, and the last one should contain the same details about the `TemplateSyntaxError` that were on the page when you encountered the exception. So why did we take the trouble to log the details about Django exceptions when we can plainly see the details about exceptions on the pages that throw them?

As mentioned in the last section, in a production setting, there will be one crucial difference: your site will not be running in debug mode. In the `settings.py` file, near the top, is a variable called `DEBUG`. You'll notice that right now, it's set to `True`.

This is one thing you need to change before deploying, and when you do, Django will, among lots of other things, display a custom generic "Sorry, we encountered an unexpected error!" page to display to the users of your site. The two most common errors are the 404 Page Not Found error, which is returned when a customer makes a request for a URL that doesn't exist, and the 500 Internal Server error, which occurs if Django raises an exception. The default files that are shown in this case lie in the root templates folder of the Django source, and are aptly named `404.html` and `500.html`.

Ensuring that `DEBUG` is set to `True` is good for security, as these generic template files prevent your users from easily finding out that you're using Django, or reading the traceback of your site's code that potentially gets displayed on an error page in debug mode. However, you need to have this information accessible to you somewhere, if for no other reason than to let you know where an exception occurred and any details you might need to fix it. This is the reason we've taken the trouble to log these errors to our database.

One last thing: now that you know how to make a page, you might be tempted to jump in and start creating your "Privacy Policy" or "Contact" pages. Hold off on that. There's a much easier way, using a Django app called flatpages, which will help you do this without needing to create a bunch of static template files. We'll come back to that later in the book.

A Word (or Two) About URLs

Before we jump into coding our models and adding lots of templates to inherit from our catalog.html template, let's talk about URLs. The creators of Django didn't like messy URLs in their pages. If you've ever tried to type in a URL in by hand that looks something like:

```
http://www.somesite.com/products/product.php?product_id=5674&category=bananas&lang=
en-us
```

then you know just how terrible and unreadable these can be. Django handles the mapping of cleaner URLs to its pages in a very simple way. If you've ever used Apache's mod_rewrite[7] to make your URLs look better, Django has a very similar functionality built in. The only difference is that in Django, the mapping is handled at the level of your web application and not by the web server. This is particularly useful when you're dealing with a shared hosting environment, and you're not allowed to tweak the Apache conf files directly.

Let's take a quick look at URLs. You added the one line for the /catalog/ page earlier:

```
urlpatterns = patterns('',
    #other commented code here
    (r'^catalog/$', 'views.home'),
)
```

Each entry in the patterns tuple takes a regular expression and the name of the view function to call as its arguments. I sense that some of you might be a little taken aback by the first part. Regular expressions? Aren't those things really hard? And isn't Django supposed to make things easier on us?

In response to all three of those questions: yes. Regular expressions are pretty tricky to get the hang of. My advice to you is not to worry about it, since most of what you'll be doing will only involve a small handful of regular expression tips and tricks. And for the most part, when a problem arises that isn't covered in this book, a little Googling around for the answer will probably get you what you're looking for.

---

[7] http://httpd.apache.org/docs/2.2/mod/mod_rewrite.html

Summary

We set a lot of important groundwork in this chapter. We created our Django application, configured exception logging to our database, and set up a hierarchy of templates for most of our site's pages. We now have a basic site layout and appearance that will act as a simple interface while we set up all of the back-end architecture in the next chapter, where we'll create the product catalog with a category structure and even some stuff customers can browse.

In the next chapter, we're going to put our database to good use, and create categories and products. Then we'll really sink our teeth into creating content for our site by creating their corresponding pages.

CHAPTER 3

■ ■ ■

Models for Sale

Imagine walking into your favorite traditional brick and mortar store. It may be a book store, a retail clothing outlet, or perhaps even a music shop that sells CDs. You know what to expect when you walk in the door; you probably plan to turn and go right to one particular section that has the goods you want to peruse. But, imagine that when you first enter the store, you notice something very askew: all of the shelves are empty. There are no products anywhere in sight.

Since you really like this store, you're very curious about what's going on, so you walk over to the purveyor and ask them: what gives? Where'd all of their stuff go?

To which the owner of the store replies: "It's in the back room. Due to technical difficulties, I can't let you look at it right now." And, after a long hearty laugh at this absurd response, most of us would probably let our feet do the talking and leave pretty quickly.

Regardless of what kind of e-commerce store you're creating, and what type of product you want to sell online, there is one fundamental truth you need to get your brain wrapped around: the importance of your data. You might have a massive warehouse filled with products that are ready to move and make you a hefty profit margin, but when it comes to selling, you need to give your customers access to your products. In the offline retail world, that's obviously the purpose of a storefront; to allow your customers to browse (and purchase) your products.

In an e-commerce store, your web application is acting like the physical store, but without your data, it would be an empty shell. It's like the imaginary store you just entered in daydream-land with all those empty shelves. Your data is the interface that lets your customers find and buy what they want. And, like a real store, you have to protect your data just as you would your products because they can be mangled, destroyed, or even stolen. (We'll look at safeguards against the latter threat in this chapter, and the others throughout the book.)

In this chapter, we're going to set up your database with your product data. This isn't actually as difficult as it may sound. Creating the tables in your database is as easy as writing some basic Python classes with the fields you want each table to have and then running a command to create the tables. That is one of the beautiful things about Django: the database layer is abstracted away behind Django's object-relational mapper (ORM). This allows you to access data with some very simple Python code that will not take you long to write.

After that, we'll create our first Django app. A Django app is a block of Django code that performs some function, which may be coupled with your project or used across multiple projects. For example, one Django app may be created within your project to control the site's news articles. Your app would contain your models for the articles and article categories, as well as the views that control how the content is displayed to your users. Once that's in place, we'll take a closer look at how the Django admin interface greatly reduces the amount of work you need to do in order to start administering your product catalog via a web interface. Then, we'll cover how the data gets from your database to the pages of your web site, writing view functions that pull the data from the database and return them to the user. Finally, we'll look at the basic syntax of Django templates and how to wrap the data into the site skeleton we created in the last chapter.

Over the next few chapters, our focus is going to be on getting something basic up and running quickly. The site will not scale for larger sites that have thousands of products; we're going to cover those techniques in Chapter 13, where we'll introduce caching and other techniques to aid your site in terms of performance.

We're going to cover quite a bit of material in this chapter. My advice is to take it slow, particularly if you're extremely new to the subject matter. While I always encourage that readers code along with their technical books, I strongly urge you to read this chapter once through in its entirety, before you start working through the examples. Once you understand the big picture, the details will make a lot more sense.

Lastly, go grab yourself a glass of water and keep the gray matter between your ears hydrated.

Databases 101

As I mentioned in Chapter 1, we're going to use MySQL as our relational database backend. If you've never worked with a database before, don't worry. I'll cover the basics quickly to get you up to speed on the few concepts you should be familiar with in order to make things work. Chances are good you'll work through the rest of your Django project without needing to write any SQL whatsoever, but knowing the concepts of how SQL manipulates your data can be invaluable to your understanding as a programmer.

If you've never worked with relational databases and would like to learn more about them in-depth, I highly recommend you pick up *The Definitive Guide to MySQL, Third Edition* by Michael Kofler (Apress, 2005) to get up to speed on the theory and practice.

An Introduction To SQL

In this section, we'll go over the basics of SQL syntax, as well as some very basic theory about how to properly set up a relational database. While you won't necessarily use SQL a whole lot while we're developing our Django project, and instead rely on Django's powerful ORM layer, it still helps to have a grasp of what's going on behind the scenes, so you know how to use Django to its full potential, even if the syntax between SQL and Django is much different. If you already know SQL and the other DBA stuff, feel free to skip to "What Django Gives You – The ORM".

First off, SQL stands for Structured Query Language, and it's the language that we use to communicate with a database engine, such as MySQL. In other words, make sure you understand the distinction between SQL and MySQL: SQL is the language we use to communicate with the actual database program that stores our data. One way to think of it: SQL is to MySQL what English is to England.

A database stores its data in tables. These tables are best described as grids that contain data, very similar to an Excel spreadsheet. The header contains the name of each column, and each row represents a particular record. For example, you might have a spreadsheet with product data in it (which you need to put into your database), with column headings called "Name," "Description," "Price," and "Category." Each row contains the data for one product.

If you've worked with a spreadsheet, you've almost certainly seen this arrangement before, and have likely worked with large amounts of data in this fashion. It's intuitive enough, although using Microsoft Excel as a database is a fairly big headache when you are trying to maintain this data, or develop a program that needs to access it on a regular basis. (As any programmer will tell you, there's no shortage of business people trying to pass around data in CSVs.[1]) A closer approximation of this can be found elsewhere in Microsoft Office, in a database program called Access.

For practical purposes, we want to create database tables that have ways of enforcing uniqueness across each row. You might think that this is easy and that you can just use the category name as the unique field, because you're unlikely to create two categories that are both called "Ukuleles" on your

---

[1] "Comma-separated values." Excel spreadsheets are often exported in CSV format for portability.

site. However, one day, when your site is huge and you have a team of developers running things for you, this kind of collision is much more likely. And if it's even remotely *possible* that this uniqueness requirement can be violated, then it's a problem. If you try to select the category from the database by name using the Django ORM get() method, which expects only a single result, and you get multiple results returned to you, this will raise an exception. Of course, having two categories with the same name also creates some ambiguity for customers about where to find things, so it's also a usability issue.

The model layer is responsible for storing data in Django applications, but it's also responsible for enforcing the business rules of your database. In this context, the term "business" has nothing to do with the business side of things, and merely refers to the constraints you need to set on your database. For example, when storing numbers for shopping cart quantities, you may want to enforce that the number stored is a positive value, and *not* zero or negative. This type of constraint can be defined on the field in the model class definition.

Django makes it very easy for you to enforce uniqueness on a field in a database table by setting a property called unique equal to True when you define the model. So, if you want to ensure that no two categories ever have the exact same name, set unique to True for the fields that you want to constrain. Then, if anyone ever tries to create a category with the name of an existing one, the Django ORM will halt the creation of the new category by raising an exception.

Most relational databases, including MySQL, allow you to specify a *primary key*, which is one field that is *absolutely* guaranteed to be unique. If you try to add two records to your data table that both have the same value in their primary key field, then the second insert will fail at the database level because of the primary key constraint. And instead of forcing you to ensure that your product names are always unique, every Django model by default is created with an integer field called id. This field starts with 1, and increments automatically by one with each record you add. This auto-counter field is used by Django to help manage relationships between your models. (See the next section for more on relationships.)

In a database table, much like in Excel, there are four basic operations you can perform to maintain your product information: Create, Read, Update, and Delete. These have earned a term of endearment in the computer industry, affectionately being referred to as the CRUD commands. They're pretty self-explanatory: you can create, read, update, or delete one or more of the rows in your product database.

The "CRUD" acronym doesn't translate directly to SQL syntax. A more appropriate mnemonic would be "ISUD", where Create and Read are replaced by INSERT and SELECT, respectively (although that's not a whole lot better… a less popular one is DAVE, for Delete, Add, View, and Edit). So, in keeping with our product data example, running these commands on your data might look like this:

```
SELECT name, description, price, category FROM product_table;
INSERT INTO product_table (name, description, price, category) ↵
    VALUES ('Ruby Axe Guitar', 'Great guitar!', 299.99, 'Electric Guitars');
UPDATE product_table SET price=249.99 WHERE name = 'Ruby Axe Guitar';
DELETE FROM product_table WHERE name = 'Ruby Axe Guitar';
```

The latter two commands are generally performed with the WHERE clause. If you have 10,000 products in your product table, and run the DELETE command without a WHERE, you will delete all 10,000 products! Similarly, if you run UPDATE without a proper WHERE clause, every single product will be updated with the change you intended to make to just one. These are pretty easy mistakes for a developer to make, particularly at the end of a long workday. My advice is that when you're working directly with SQL at the command line or within the shell, you should type your WHERE clause first. SELECT can also take a WHERE clause, so you could try running a SELECT with your WHERE clause to test that it really does only retrieve the rows you want to UPDATE or DELETE.[2]

---

[2] If nothing else, this mistake is one of the many reasons that you should be performing regular backups on your application's database!

Lastly, regarding raw SQL queries, we should discuss the inclusion of an ORDER BY clause in your SELECT queries. If you retrieve more than one record, you have the option of specifying an ORDER BY clause, which lets you explicitly determine how your results will be sorted. As a simple example, the following query will return the product records the same as before, but they will be ordered, alphabetically, by the name field:

```
SELECT name, description, price, category ⤶
FROM product_table ORDER BY name
```

ORDERING AND CASE SENSITIVITY IN DATABASE ENGINES

When you sort results by an integer column, the sorting behavior will make sense. When sorting by a field containing character data, the exact ordering of query results when you use an ORDER BY clause depends on the way that your database engine orders different strings lexically. By default, MySQL sorting is case-insensitive, while PostgreSQL is very case-sensitive. How the results are sorted is affected by the collation setting of your database engine. If the field is able to contain NULL values—that is, the absence of any value at all—then you may not get the exact ordering you were hoping for.

For more on the nuances of ORDER BY clauses, consult the documentation for your own database server.

What Makes a Relational Database

Of course, any real site out in the wild is going to have more than one table in which it will store its data. Your e-commerce site is going to be storing customer information, orders, and shopping carts as well as product data. As it happens, these tables almost never stand alone; they are linked to one another in a logical way through relationships between their records.

While you might get away with coding an entire Django project without writing a single line of SQL, you'll be hard-pressed to architect anything without understanding these relationships between models. They aren't terribly complicated: there are three types of these relationships: one-to-many, many-to-many, and one-to-one. These describe relationships between the specific records in your tables. Let's look at these individually in turn.

> *One-to-many:* Occurs when a single record in one table can be linked to one or more records in another table. As one example, take products and their corresponding product reviews. Products can potentially have one or more reviews, but reviews typically belong to only one single product. This a very common relationship that you'll be using extensively throughout this book, so it's key that you take a moment to understand how it works and let the concept sink in.

> *Many-to-many:* This relationship can be found when a single record in one table can be linked to one or more records in another table, and a single record in the other table can be linked to one or more records in the first table. We'll see a perfect example of this coming up shortly in this chapter, between categories and their products. A category can, of course, have more than one product. There will be more than one guitar that we're listing under "Electric Guitars." However, the converse can also be true: a product may fall into more than one category. You may create a category called "Hammers of the Gods" for

those top-of-the-line Gibsons and Flying Vs, and any one guitar may fall under this category, as well as "Electric Guitars."

Relational databases like MySQL do not support many-to-many relationships between two tables. The solution is to create a third table that acts as a join between the two tables, and holds records that represent relationships between them. We'll come back to that when we set up our tables.

One-to-one: This is when one record in a table can be linked to exactly one record in another table. In all likelihood, you'll rarely ever use this type of relationship in practice, simply because if you have a one-to-one relationship between tables, it will usually make more sense to combine the data from the two tables into a single table.

So why all the linking? The most important reason to spread data out across multiple tables is to eliminate redundancy. This makes things terribly convenient for you. Ideally, whenever you add, edit, or remove data, you'd like to do it in just one place.

Let's look at how this could help you. Here is a listing of some dummy product data that we were talking about doing in Excel earlier:

Name	Description	Price	Category
Ruby Axe Guitar	This is a great guitar!	249.99	Electric Guitars
Erlang Metronome	Good metronome!	39.99	Accessories
Haskell Drum Set	Bang on these!	599.99	Drumsets

Notice that we've got the category name stored in this data. That's okay for now, because we only have one product in each category. But what if we start adding electric guitars? We're going to be putting in the text "Electric Guitars" quite often, once for each product. Also, if we ever decide to change the name of the category from "Electric Guitars" to "Killer Axes," we're going to have to update the category name for every single product in this category. Furthermore, there is not a way to map a product to more than one category, unless you start storing duplicate records of the product data. Clearly, this will quickly turn into a maintenance nightmare where database angels fear to tread, and not a viable solution for us.

The best thing for us to do is create two tables, one for category data, and one for product data, and link them together. In the case of a simple one-to-many join between the tables, we would place an integer field called `category_id` in the product table that references the `id` field in the category table. When the primary key of a table appears as a reference to that table in another table, that field is referred to as a *foreign key*.

This process of spreading data out across multiple, linked tables in order to reduce duplicate data is called normalizing your database. The most common methods of normalizing data in tables are numbered, starting with the non-first normal form (NF^2), first normal form (1NF), and so forth, up to sixth normal form (6NF). Despite the range of choices, there are data redundancy issues with 2NF and below, and complexities that arise with 4NF and above, which make them poor choices given the requirements of our project.

The third normal form (3NF) is the level of data normalization that database administrators tend to shoot for when designing their databases. At this level, any attributes on the model that don't describe something about the model itself are normalized into a different table. In the list of products in the preceding table, where the category is listed with each product, the data does not represent 3NF. While the category *does* describe the product, it's not really an attribute of the product. Logically, it makes sense to give categories their own table with their own primary key, and link them to products.

The correct pattern of normalization is highly subjective to your project's business requirements, and for some systems, can get complicated very quickly. It's one of the reasons that DBAs make the big bucks, and spend lots of time revising links between little boxes on company whiteboards. However, for our project, 3NF will solve most of the potential problems that might arise from poor database design. If you're interested in learning more about designing databases, I found *Beginning Database Design,* by Clare Churcher (Apress, 2007) to be a valuable resource.

Even if you're still a little uncertain about exactly what we're going to do, don't fret. It always helps to put theory into practice, and that's what we're going to do when we create our models.

What Django Gives You – The ORM

As mentioned briefly in the first chapter, the Django framework is based loosely on the model-view-controller (MVC) architectural style. This chapter is all about the "M" component of that acronym: model. In Django, models represent your data. You create a product model that has all the data you want to keep about your products, and then you start creating models, which are stored in your database.

For those of you who've worked with other web frameworks, such as ASP.NET or PHP, you might be familiar with n-tier architecture. This generally involves dividing your application into layers (usually three of them, referred to as three-tier) that all have a specific role to play. At the top, you have the Presentation Tier, which is your UI part of the web application that your user interacts with. At the bottom, you have the Data Tier that stores your information, typically in a relational database. Between both of these, you have the Business Tier (or Business Logic Layer), which facilitates communication between your Presentation and Data Tiers. Under n-tier architecture, when a customer requests a product page, the request is passed by the Presentation Tier down to the Business Tier, which turns around and makes its own request to the Data Tier. The response from the Data Tier is passed back up the chain to the Presentation Tier, which is then presented to the customer.

This architecture is quite good, but if you've ever set up a site this way, you know how much work it can be to set up initially. In your Data Tier, you need to create the database tables and any SQL stored procedures for manipulating your data, and in the Business Tier, you create classes in your server code (C# or PHP) that you populate with data and hand off to the Presentation Tier. After a while, you'll find yourself doing the same basic work for different objects, whether they're orders, products, or news articles.

In Django, a lot of this work is done for you, based on a few simple assumptions that tend to hold true:

- One business tier class is mapped to one table in the database.

- One business tier object instance is mapped to one record in the database table.

- There are a limited number of things you can do to manipulate your data, based on the CRUD commands we covered earlier.

First, one product object in your code tends to represent one record in the products table in your database. This isn't necessarily always true; for example, your product object could contain its category name, which might come from a different table. However, for our purposes in examining Django, it's safe to assume that one product object and its data can be mapped to one database record. From this, it makes sense to remove some of the repetition and do the work only in one place, and that's exactly what Django models do for you.

Django models provide an object-relational mapping from your Python code to your database. That means that with only a few small exceptions, you'll only ever need to interact with your database via Python code. You can make a request for a Python object, and the Django ORM hands off the request to the relational database, gets the returned data, and then passes it on to you in the form of a Python object (hence the term "object-relational mapper"). You don't need to write SQL to get at your data or call your database explicitly. As long as you have your database settings correctly configured in `settings.py`, you don't need to set this up from scratch.

In a lot of ways, the Django model layer is acting as both your Data Tier and your Business Tier. Of course, that isn't entirely accurate. You still have a MySQL database storing your information, and this has nothing to do with the Django model layer. However, the model layer does abstract away a lot of the work you would otherwise have to do with a web framework that didn't offer an ORM.

Creating the Catalog App

Before we jump into creating the models for our e-commerce project, a very quick note on Django apps. Typically, you'll divide your Django project up into different "apps." Each app contains view functions and a set of models that are all related to one particular type of functionality you need in your Django project.

For example, it makes sense to create a Django app within your project to handle checkout functionality. This checkout app would contain models for order information and views for your site's checkout process, as well as any functionality that your checkout process requires in integrating with a payment processor (we'll get to that in Chapter 5 when we cover checkout).

We're going to put our code and models for categories and their associated products into a Django app called `catalog`. To create the `catalog` app, open up your command line shell and, from the document root of your `ecomstore` project, enter the following:

```
$ python manage.py startapp catalog
```

This will create a directory within your project called `catalog`, which should contain four items: `__init__.py`, `models.py`, `tests.py`, and `views.py`. Let's quickly have a look at each one:

- `__init__.py`: much like the one in the root of your project, this should be empty, and it's just there to let your system know that your catalog app contains Python code.

- `models.py`: contains the classes mapped to your database tables, as well as any other information about your application data.

- `tests.py`: if you run automated tests for your code, the test runner will check this file for any test functions you have defined. We'll cover tests more in Chapter 14.

- `views.py`: contains the view functions for your Django app.

Another quick word about Django apps: the ability to partition different parts of your project into separate units is to facilitate the ease of code reuse. Much like your template directory, a Django app directory does not have to reside within the confines of your project directory. The `djangodblog` app that we added to our project in Chapter 2 is a perfect example of this. So, if you create a Django app that may be useful to you in more than one project, you are free to include it in any project you please. In our case, I find it more convenient to keep the `catalog` app, as well as the other apps I'll create in this book, inside the project directory, but as always, you are free to refactor anything I do to meet your own needs.

With the `catalog` app in place, let's move along and do what you've been itching to do since the beginning of the chapter: set up your product data.

Creating the Django Models

So now that your head is swimming around in all of this theory of system architecture, let's do something a little more fun. We are going to create the product and category models and the database in this section, but first, you need to do something else.

You need to determine what information you need to store about your products.

I could jump right in and start droning on about how you can store strings, numbers, dates, and boolean fields (I'll get to that in a minute, I promise), but before you start thinking about your data in terms of data types, the way engineers and DBAs like to do, I want you to put this book down and reflect on what you need.

As mentioned as the start of this chapter, the value of your site to customers hinges on the data. That is the logical start for things. Unfortunately, the data hinges on your ability to figure out what data you need to track. In terms of your products, you want to think long and hard about the information you need your system to have on each product. If you have 200 products that you want to sell on your site at launch time, you really don't want to put in 200 products only to figure out that you've forgotten one key field, like meta keywords for SEO for each product. You'd then have to go back and add these for each of your 200 products. Oops.

You might have realized that your products require more than just the two tables for categories and products that we're going to create in this book. Forget about how you're going to normalize your data for right now. Forget about relationships. Forget about what the maximum length of your product names will be.

Sure, it's tough to develop the user interface without your data, and it can be tough to think about what your site data needs to be to get the user interface you want. The simplest solution to this chicken-and-the-egg nightmare is to forget about your database for right now and focus on the product page itself.

So put down this book and pull up your favorite tool for creating a visual representation of your product page. It may be Photoshop, Dreamweaver, or GIMP. Personally, I find that using a piece of paper and a pencil is the most efficient way of getting something down quickly, as it allows you to quickly make edits. It's the least intrusive way of letting the creative side of your brain express itself because you're sketching on paper, and you're not interacting with a computer while you do it. Sketching also lets you get the ideas from your head to paper as quickly as possible. It's important not to underestimate just how quickly ideas come to your brain and, on the flip side of the same coin, realize how quickly you can lose them. You might be interrupted in the process of creating another Photoshop layer, and if you didn't get that one fabulous idea down, it might be gone forever.

What we're doing here is a process that's sometimes referred to as *paper prototyping*. While paper prototyping generally involves the informal creation of an interface that can be shown to prospective users in order to gain feedback on its usability, it has other uses as well. The best thing about designing things in this fashion is that it's quick and easily amenable, in case you don't get everything right the first time.

I'm going to create a quick sketch of my product page, and I suggest you do the same. Think of a product you plan to sell and draw the basic layout, complete with a photo and any other information. My only guidance about what you draw is this: think about an e-commerce store where you really liked the experience, and try to base it on that. You don't need to copy it exactly, but try and capture the same essence. Just be sure you create something you like, and that you think your customers will like too.

The results of my sketching can be seen in Figure 3-1.

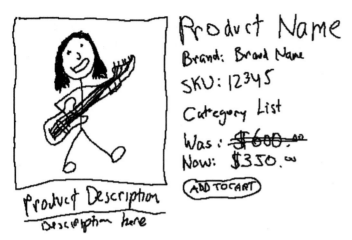

Figure 3-1. A rough sketch of the content of our site's product page.

The point of this exercise is simple: to determine what your database needs to store about its products by looking at the front-end first. Database creation is fairly cut and dry, and there's not a whole lot of room for creativity. Taking this approach at least engages you for a little while.

After you've created the sketch, look it over and see what kinds of information it contains. One thing you'll note about mine is that it has a "was" price and a "now" price. This is one important detail that we might have missed if we hadn't drawn the sketch; we might have just stored one single price and only realized much later, after lots of other work had already been done, that we need to store two prices. (Of course, that wouldn't be a terribly difficult fix...but you'll want to be thorough.)

Start to jot down a list of the things you see on the page, and make any additional notes about the information you might need. It doesn't have to be a formal spec... just some free-form, stream-of-consciousness scribbling will do just fine. It should also include anything you don't see on your sketch that you might need to store, such as meta tag content.

My list looks something like this:

- Name of product
- Brand name
- Product SKU
- Which categories is the product in?
- Price
- Sale price, plus old price
- Product image
- Meta description
- Meta keywords
- Quantity in stock
- Date product was created
- Date product was last updated
- Product status (active or inactive)

This list is simple enough, and thankfully, it's also very easy to translate this into the Python code that will set up our database. Before we get to that, let's make a quick list going over the required fields for our category pages. You're welcome to a sketch for these pages as well, but I'm just going to create a list of items, like our product:

- Name of category

- Category description

- Meta keywords

- Meta description

- Date category was created

- Date category was last updated

- Category status (active or inactive)

Set aside your two lists of data that you want to store, and let's talk about what your databases can store for you. It won't be that tedious…I promise.

Model Field Data Types

Databases can store different types of data in different fields, which fall into four basic categories. The first type, and the most important, are strings, or character data. This is the most important data your web application will store because search engines like content, and content typically takes the form of text. The users shopping on your site will be using text to make buying decisions, and will submit text to your site in the form of product reviews that will help other users make decisions as well. Because strings are so important, there are a few different kinds of fields you can use to store this data in your relational database. The following is a list of field types that store string data, and a brief description of when you should use each:

- `CharField`: used to store text that is less than or equal to some determinate length. For example, you might determine that your longest product name is 147 characters long. In that case, you should use a `CharField` for your product name and set its length to be 175 characters or so.

- `TextField`: used to store large amounts of text that you don't want restricted by length. Product descriptions are a perfect example; they may contain any amount of descriptive content or HTML for formatting, and you want this. You want to provide enough information to your customers so they can make an informed decision… as well as give search engines lots of content to index.

- `SlugField`: a specialized text field that is designed to be used in URLs. When a user requests a product page, they'll access a URL reading `/products/product-name-here/` in order to request your product. Suffice it to say, this value should be unique to each product.

This list of string types is not exhaustive, and before we get to coding our models, it might behoove you to read the online documentation.[3] You may get some more ideas about the kind of data you want to store.

---

[3] `http://docs.djangoproject.com/en/dev/ref/models/fields/`

WHY USE A SLUG FIELD TO LOOK UP RECORDS?

The mere presence of the `SlugField` field type for Django models belies the origins of the framework. Django was created for Lawrence Journal-World, a newspaper publication in Kansas. The term "slug" is a journalism term. Slugs are the names given to articles in production by editors to identify and describe each article. Like so many other computer terms,[4] the word "slug" started out as something not at all computer-related, but has found its way into the world of computer programming by its application. In the context of a Django project, slugs are used in URLs to identify pages.

So why are we going to use a `SlugField` in our category and product models to look up the data instead of an integer field? After all, isn't that terribly slow and inefficient by comparison? Yes, in a way, it is. When you pass a string field in your URL and use that to perform the lookup in your database, it must do a character-by-character comparison of the string from your URL and the slugs stored in your data table. This is slower than just using a category or product id and performing a lookup in your table based on this integer value.

The reason we're doing it this way to is thwart content theft. If we used our product id, which is an auto-incrementing integer field, then our product page URLs would look like this to our users:

```
/product/1
/product/2
/product/3
```

And so on. It's pretty easy to figure out the pattern here, and makes it all the easier for someone to automatically steal all of your content with a simple awk script that does a series of `wget` requests.

Of course, it's also a good idea because it lets you define the link and describe its content to your human visitors. If someone copies your URL and links to your page from a forum on another site, having the product name in the URL will help other users determine the content of the link and enable them to determine if they should follow the link, and `product-name'` is quite a bit more helpful than `/16545sdfkb/`.

Lastly, let's not forget the SEO value of keywords in your URL to your robot visitors as well.

Remember when you are defining your string fields that you want to use a `CharField` in most cases. You might be tempted to simply use a `TextField` for everything since it doesn't constrain you in terms of length. For performance reasons, this is a horrible idea. When your application starts searching and sorting your data, `TextFields` will slow down your application because most database engines cannot optimize nearly as well for fields designed to hold larger amounts of text. This will degrade the speed and performance of your web site as the number of records in your table grows.

The next crucial data type is the one used to store currency values, which for an e-commerce application, is pretty important. Real numbers (in the mathematical sense) are stored in integer fields, but currency values require a higher degree of precision, as they require storage of decimal places, which integers cannot accommodate. There are a couple of other options for dealing with this precision in Django: floats and decimals, which are represented in Python by the float and Decimal types, respectively. When dealing with currency values, decimals are much more appropriate than floats, so we're going to store our monetary values using `DecimalFields`.

---

[4] One of the first computer "bugs" was literally a bug. (`http://en.wikipedia.org/wiki/Software_bug`)

The other three data types you're apt to use are integers, Booleans, and dates. These are also important, although there's much less to them than strings and don't require much initial discussion. When you need to store a number, a true/false value, or a date/datetime value, you use one of these fields. The cases when you need one of these are pretty easy to spot.

Now that you have some idea of the types of data that you can store with your models, let's get back to creating the models for our product catalog.

Creating the Category Model

So, going back to the very basics, we're going to group all of our products into categories. This will help organize our content so that a customer browsing the site has some direction, and is more likely to be able to find what they need. As we discussed, we're going to set up our site so that there is a many-to-many relationship between categories and products, which simply means a category can have lots of products, and a product is allowed to reside in more than one category.

■ **Note** If you're planning to deploy your project onto the Google App Engine, the models you code might have to be different than these in order to be compatible with Google's database layer. See Chapter 16 for more information.

The category model looks very simple compared to the product one, so let's start by coding that one. In your `catalog` app directory that you just created, open up the `models.py` and add the following code to the file:

```python
from django.db import models

class Category(models.Model):
    name = models.CharField(max_length=50)
    slug = models.SlugField(max_length=50, unique=True, ⤸
        help_text='Unique value for product page URL, created from name.')
    description = models.TextField()
    is_active = models.BooleanField(default=True)
    meta_keywords = models.CharField("Meta Keywords",max_length=255, ⤸
        help_text='Comma-delimited set of SEO keywords for meta tag')
    meta_description = models.CharField("Meta Description", max_length=255, ⤸
        help_text='Content for description meta tag')
    created_at = models.DateTimeField(auto_now_add=True)
    updated_at = models.DateTimeField(auto_now=True)

    class Meta:
        db_table = 'categories'
        ordering = ['-created_at']
        verbose_name_plural = 'Categories'

    def __unicode__(self):
        return self.name
```

```
@models.permalink
def get_absolute_url(self):
    return ('catalog_category', (), { 'category_slug': self.slug })
```

This code sample contains a definition for a Django model called `Category`. You first define a class which, in Python form, inherits from a special Django class called `models.Model`. Then, we list the fields that we want to become columns in our categories database table. Take particular note of how you're declaring these fields: you declare the name for each, and then assign it a particular type of field with some optional parameters. And don't worry, just because you've typed in this code doesn't mean it's in the database; we still have to run that `syncdb` command we ran in Chapter 2 (*don't* run this yet).

Let's look at each of these fields one at a time and discuss what we're doing here in a little more detail.

```
name = models.CharField(max_length=50, unique=True)
```

This is pretty easy to understand. You've declared a name field that will be a string containing a maximum of 50 characters. By setting `unique=True`, your database will enforce a rule that each category must have a name that is distinct.

```
slug = models.SlugField(max_length=50, unique=True, ↩
    help_text='Unique value for product page URL, created from name.')
```

This is our `slug` field. It shares the same length as the category name, and we're also constraining it so that our application will require that each one is unique for every category we have. If we try to add a second category with the same slug as another, it will not add the category. The `slug` field has to be unique, since the category slug is a component of the URI that will point to our category page. If there was one slug that pointed at two different categories, you can see how our application would get confused.

One more thing to note is the `help_text` property we're specifying. Later, we'll set up an administrative interface, complete with a form where you can enter new categories. The help text will be displayed on that page. It's a good way of noting the use of each field to your user if it isn't immediately obvious. And remember, while you might understand what a slug is right now, six months from now you might be up to your eyeballs in shipping online orders, and when you go to add a new category, it will help tremendously if you have notes that explain what each field is for.

You'll also notice that I'm saying the slug field will be filled out automatically from the category name... stay tuned and I'll get to that shortly.

```
description = models.TextField()
```

This is our category `description` field, which will appear at the top of the category page. It's a text field, meaning that it can be huge, without any character limit.

```
is_active = models.BooleanField(default=True)
```

This is a True/False field that lets us turn the category on or off. You might think that if you ever want to remove a category from your site, you'll simply delete it, but bear in mind that deleting is forever. When using the Django ORM, it's very easy to inadvertently wipe out information because of the way deletions are cascaded to child objects. For example, if you have a product with several product reviews, the reviews will be deleted if you delete the product. While the loss of a few product reviews is unlikely to be detrimental, it wouldn't help matters if you accidentally deleted important financial information, such as order items associated with products. The best solution is to structure your application to just ignore a little True/False field, like this one, you'll have a much easier time turning things on and off.

```
meta_keywords = models.CharField(max_length=255, ⤶
    help_text='Comma-delimited set of SEO keywords for meta tag')
meta_description = models.CharField(max_length=255, ⤶
    help_text='Content for description meta tag')
```

These are two fields that I'm requiring each category page to have, and they'll be used right where you're thinking: for the meta tag content. It is important that you explicitly set these for each page for SEO purposes. Keywords are important, and if you're outlining an SEO strategy, coming up with them is important, even if you just plan to use them in your page's content. And while you might think that you can use the ordinary "description" text field that we created previously for our description meta tag, remember that field can be of any length. Your meta description tag should be shorter, and more to the point. It also cannot contain HTML tags, which your ordinary description field might.

```
created_at = models.DateTimeField(auto_now_add=True)
updated_at = models.DateTimeField(auto_now=True)
```

These are two DateTime fields that will track when you added each product, and when each product was last updated by an administrative user. The two fields are created by declaring a DateTimeField and passing it auto_now_add=True, which fetches and stores the current date and time once when your category is created, and auto_now=True, which stores the current date and time every time your category is updated.

After we're done declaring all of the information that we want to store, we then declared a class called Meta inside our Category model class. This class contains any additional information, or *metadata*, about the information your model will contain.

Our Meta class looks like this:

```
class Meta:
    db_table = 'categories'
    ordering = ['name']
    verbose_name_plural = 'Categories'
```

The first item is a variable named db_table, which, when defined in our internal Meta class, allows us to explicitly set the name of the database table. By default, your tables will be named by the following formula:

```
[app_name]_[model_name]
```

Left to its own devices, our database table for categories would end up with the name catalog_category. While there's nothing overtly wrong with this, I prefer to keep the names simple. categories is not too ambiguous for an e-commerce database, and so it's not going to confuse any database administrator when they start playing around with the tables.

Next, we set a variable called ordering, which takes one or more items in a Python list object that specify the ordering of more than one object when they are retrieved from your database. In this case, I've set them to be sorted by name, in ascending order. If you wanted to sort them by name, but in *reverse* order, you would simply put a minus sign (-) in front of the name of the field within the quotes.

Imagine that you wanted to have the categories show up with the newest ones appearing first, and the oldest ones last. You could use your created_at DateTimeField for this, and specify a reverse sort order:

```
ordering = ['-created_at']
```

The last item is rectifying a small problem with pluralizing the name of your model. Django tries to create the word for the plural by tacking an "s" onto the end of the name of your model. In most cases, this works just fine. However, some plural cases require "es", or in the case of the word "category," one letter needs to be changed and "es" needs to be added. Instead of having your model displayed as "Categorys" wherever the plural version is rendered, I've chosen to explicitly override this setting by defining my own. This will matter later on, when we set up the admin interface where we can administer our catalog data.

Below the inner `Meta` class, we've defined two methods on our class, the first of which looks like this:

```
def __unicode__(self):
    return self.name
```

This method is returning a string representation of our `Category` model. Don't worry about this one for the moment, we'll come back to it when it starts to matter. Just keep in mind that it will be called whenever you refer to a particular `Category` object in a context where a string is needed; Django will fall back on this method.

The next one is far more important to you as a web developer:

```
@models.permalink
def get_absolute_url(self):
    return ('catalog_category', (), { 'category_slug': self.slug })
```

The first line, which starts with the `@` character that prefaces the actual definition of the method, is referred to as a *decorator*. This will let your Django project know that this method will be used to generate links. Whenever you call the `get_absolute_url()` method in your templates, the link will be generated from your `urls.py` file, which is in turn being used to map requests to your Django views. In this way, this method and your `urls.py` file are both used to *generate* links as well as *route* them.

CAVEAT: PYTHON DECORATORS

If you're using a version of Python prior to 2.4, or if you plan to distribute your code to anyone who might be using an earlier version of Python, you won't be able to use the decorator syntax with the @ symbol right before your method definition. Instead, you'll have to use the earlier syntax and rewrite your code like this:

```
def get_absolute_url(self):
    return ('catalog_category', (), { 'category_slug': self.slug })

get_absolute_url = models.permalink(get_absolute_url)
```

However, in this book, I'm assuming that you're using Python 2.5 or higher, and that the code is going to remain on development and production machines of your choosing, so we'll be using the @ decorator syntax instead.

Why is this so useful? Headaches in maintaining web applications usually don't hit you all at once. Instead, they creep up on you slowly over long periods of time. Imagine creating a web site with category pages, and you start linking to them from your homepage to allow users to click through and start shopping. You define the link to the category page like this:

```
<a href="/category/{{ category_name}}/">Category Name</a>
```

Of course, this link might work fine. It works so well that a week later, when you need to link to the category page from another page, such as in your product templates, you use it there, too. Little needs for links to category pages within your application start cropping up and you use this solution, and pretty soon the /category/{{ category_name}}/ form is everywhere on your site.

Then one day, you need to change the way these links are all formed. Suddenly, it needs to be something like /shop/category/{{ category_name }}/ instead, and you find yourself having to iterate through every last page on your site, looking for these old links and updating them to the new form.

Django's philosophy is that the models should have as much information about themselves as possible. In this case, we're encapsulating the structure of the internal links to our category pages within the Category models themselves. When we need to link to a category, we define the method and use it in our application, instead of hard-coding it in a bunch of different templates.

Defining the link to models in one place, and one place only, is following the DRY principle. This stands for "Don't Repeat Yourself," which is a programming virtue you should make every effort to adhere to. If you find yourself repeating the same work twice, do yourself a favor and *stop right there.* Anything you do in two separate locations might end up being done in three, or four, and so on. Stop, and rethink your approach.

Take a moment and let that information sink in. As a matter of fact, you may feel your brain starting to melt after all that code. Get out of your seat, stretch, and grab some coffee. Hang in there and you'll see shortly what's so great about what we're doing.

Creating the Product Model

The Product model is a little more complex than the category one, but fortunately, there are a lot of parallels between the two, and these should help you get your head around the code. In your models.py file, *below* the declaration of the Category class, enter the following lines of code:

```
class Product(models.Model):
    name = models.CharField(max_length=255, unique=True)
    slug = models.SlugField(max_length=255, unique=True,
        help_text='Unique value for product page URL, created from name.')
    brand = models.CharField(max_length=50)
    sku = models.CharField(max_length=50)
    price = models.DecimalField(max_digits=9,decimal_places=2)
    old_price = models.DecimalField(max_digits=9,decimal_places=2,
        blank=True,default=0.00)
    image = models.CharField(max_length=50)
    is_active = models.BooleanField(default=True)
    is_bestseller = models.BooleanField(default=False)
    is_featured = models.BooleanField(default=False)
    quantity = models.IntegerField()
    description = models.TextField()
    meta_keywords = models.CharField(max_length=255,
        help_text='Comma-delimited set of SEO keywords for meta tag')
    meta_description = models.CharField(max_length=255,
        help_text='Content for description meta tag')
    created_at = models.DateTimeField(auto_now_add=True)
    updated_at = models.DateTimeField(auto_now=True)
    categories = models.ManyToManyField(Category)

    class Meta:
        db_table = 'products'
        ordering = ['-created_at']
```

```
def __unicode__(self):
    return self.name

@models.permalink
def get_absolute_url(self):
    return ('catalog_product', (), { 'product_slug': self.slug })

def sale_price(self):
    if self.old_price > self.price:
        return self.price
    else:
        return None
```

This code should make a little bit more sense to you, now that we've already walked through the Category model. There are a few things you should notice that are new, such as the use of a DecimalField to store the product prices. Both of these take two arguments in their declaration: max_digits and decimal_places. With a max_digits value of 9, and decimal_places value of 2, we store values with 2 decimal places, and up to 7 digits to the left of the decimal point. That means our products can be up to $9,999,999.99, which should suit most e-commerce sites, save for the ones that are selling commercial airliners. Of course, if you're selling Boeing 747s, you're probably not selling a lot of them to your customers via a shopping cart web interface.

You'll also notice that there's an additional argument being passed to our old_price field reading blank=True. By default, blank is set to False, meaning that all of your model fields require a value of some sort, unless you specify otherwise. old_price is the first field where allowing a blank field makes sense, because we don't necessarily want *every* product to appear as though it's on sale. We also set a default value for this field so that if the user doesn't enter anything, a value of 0.00 is automatically entered into the field.

Along the same lines, we've also created a new method in our Product model:

```
def sale_price(self):
    if self.old_price > self.price:
        return self.price
    else:
        return None
```

This will be used to create a different display in our catalog templates for products that are on sale, and those that aren't. Since we can define a portion of this logic in the model as opposed to in our template code (Django templates have their own {% if %} statement tags, as you saw in the last chapter), it makes sense to do so to keep the templates as simple as possible.

Next, we specify a mere string field to store the product image. We'll come back to this in a later chapter, when we cover how to deal with product images. Django actually provides a couple of special fields you can add to your models, designed specifically for handling the uploading of files. These are ImageField and FileField, which handle images and files. For now, we'll just use that to store the name of the file and use our templates to point to the correct directory where the image resides on our file system.

Boolean fields are extremely handy, and I've created two others, on top of the is_active we created for our Category model: is_featured and is_bestseller. The only difference with these latter two is that they are set to False by default, which makes sense because we expect the bestseller and featured labels to apply to only a small handful of products, while we expect almost every product in our system to be active.

True/False fields are an excellent way to manage your products. When you get around to creating the home page, you'll have a box containing some "featured products." By editing a few of your products and checking the featured field, you can control which products show up to the user. This easily gives you control over which products you are going to present to your user as soon as they arrive at your site, much like you might create a display filled with products in the front window of a retail shop.

But what about bestsellers? Shouldn't you just use your order history and actually show people what products are actually bestsellers? Sure, you could do this, but there are a couple of problems with that approach. First, as your site grows and you start storing more and more order history, querying the order tables to determine which products have historically moved the most units will slow things down. A lot.

That, and if you're displaying your bestselling products somewhere prominent, like in a side column on every page, more users are likely to click on them and purchase them than the non-bestsellers. This creates a sort of feedback loop that makes your site's "bestseller" list very resistant to change, and believe me, you're going to want to change it at some point in the future. Accept that you need to tell this small fib to your customers and allow yourself to have more control. Don't over think it because your customers won't really care, so long as you are offering a list of bestsellers that adds value to their experience using your site.

The last, and by far the most important, piece of code in your Product model is the last field we declare before creating the inner Meta class. Have a long, hard look:

```
categories = models.ManyToManyField(Category)
```

This is the field that defines the relationship between your Product and Category models. Remember the discussion earlier about many-to-many relationships, about associating each product with many categories, and vice versa? This one line of code is the workhorse that makes all of that happen. When you run the script to create your two tables for products and categories, a third table will be created to manage and hold the relationships between the two models. This enables you to assign a product to as many different categories as you'd like.

We've created the relationship by creating a field that we're calling categories in our Product model, and although this happens to match the name of the categories table we created, bear in mind that you can call it whatever you'd like. The name "categories" was just logical, so I used it. Also, there will never be a categories field in the product table in your database. It's just something you declare in the model to set up the relationship.

One caveat worth pointing out is that the Category model class declaration needs to come before the Product model class. You're passing in "Category", the name of your Category model, as an argument to the ManyToManyField, and if the Category class comes after this line of code, Django won't understand where this model is coming from, and you'll get an error when you try to sync up your database.

The Django Admin Interface

Now that you have a couple of models to put data in, let's set up the Django admin interface so that you can start adding categories and products! This requires that we do a couple of things. First, we need to install the apps that Django requires for us to use the admin interface. Second, we need to create some code that informs the admin interface about our models.

The first item just requires a few small configuration changes to our settings.py file. Remember those four lines of code that I had you comment out in the last chapter, under the INSTALLED_APPS section? We're going to uncomment those same lines out, as we're going to need them now. Open the file and edit that section, removing the '#' characters, and add the extra two lines:

```
INSTALLED_APPS = (
    'django.contrib.auth',
```

```
    'django.contrib.contenttypes',
    'django.contrib.sessions',
    'django.contrib.sites',
    'ecomstore.catalog',
    'django.contrib.admin',
    'djangodblog',
)
```

Notice that you've added a line specifying your Django `catalog` app in your project, and another line right below that to install the admin interface. The other four that you've uncommented out are also very necessary to making the admin site work. Since the admin interface is behind a login, we need to enable sessions so that you can create a user, and then track their login using a cookie. (We'll cover sessions more in the next chapter.)

You'll need to be able to navigate to your admin interface once it's up and running, and for that, you'll need to make a quick edit to your project's `urls.py` file. Open it, locate the lines near the top related to the admin interface, and uncomment them:

```
# Uncomment the next two lines to enable the admin:
from django.contrib import admin
admin.autodiscover()
```

Make sure that you also remove the extra space between the hash (#) character and the start of the line. Remember, Python is quite moody about indentations! Next, scroll down and uncomment the line within your `urlpatterns` tuple:

```
# Uncomment the next line to enable the admin:
(r'^admin/', include(admin.site.urls)),
```

With these changes made, you just need to tell your Django project about the models you want available through the admin interface, which we're going to do in the next section.

Product and Category Admins

Registering your models with the admin site requires us to create a new file, in your `catalog` app directory, called `admin.py`. Create this file now, and add the following code to it. We'll go through this code shortly:

```
from django.contrib import admin
from ecomstore.catalog.models import Product, Category
from ecomstore.catalog.forms import ProductAdminForm

class ProductAdmin(admin.ModelAdmin):
    form = ProductAdminForm

    # sets values for how the admin site lists your products
    list_display = ('name', 'price', 'old_price', 'created_at', 'updated_at',)
    list_display_links = ('name',)
    list_per_page = 50
    ordering = ['-created_at']
```

```
    search_fields = ['name', 'description', 'meta_keywords', 'meta_description']
    exclude = ('created_at', 'updated_at',)

    # sets up slug to be generated from product name
    prepopulated_fields = {'slug' : ('name',)}

# registers your product model with the admin site
admin.site.register(Product, ProductAdmin)

class CategoryAdmin(admin.ModelAdmin):
    #sets up values for how admin site lists categories
    list_display = ('name', 'created_at', 'updated_at',)
    list_display_links = ('name',)
    list_per_page = 20
    ordering = ['name']
    search_fields = ['name', 'description', 'meta_keywords', 'meta_description']
    exclude = ('created_at', 'updated_at',)

    # sets up slug to be generated from category name
    prepopulated_fields - {'slug' : ('name',)}

admin.site.register(Category, CategoryAdmin)
```

The code in our `admin.py` file contains two class declarations, one for each model. Each one subclasses `admin.ModelAdmin`, and there is a handful of fields we've set on each one. These fields relate to customizing the appearance and functionality of the admin interface. We'll look at each of them briefly.

`list_display`, `list_display_links`, `list_per_page`, `ordering`, and `search_fields` all control the functionality of the admin interface. The admin interface will create a list of your categories and products for you to browse, and here, we're customizing how they appear in that list. `list_display` is a Python tuple that takes the list of fields you would like to appear on the listing page for each item. `list_display_links` is a tuple that takes a list of fields that you want to be hyperlinks that will take to you an "Edit Item" page. `list_per_page` defines how many will be displayed per page, and if there are more than that, "Next" and "Previous" links will be displayed to let you navigate through the pages. `ordering` simply defines the order in which the items are displayed, and is set up the same way the ordering variable was in our model classes.

Your products and categories listings will be searchable in the backend. `search_fields` is a Python list of fields against which you want to match text. If we search our products for "acoustic," any product with the word "acoustic" in its name, description, or meta tags will be listed for us. Also, each item will be given its own "Edit" page, where you'll be presented with a form where you can change the item's values. It makes little sense for us to display `created_at` and `updated_at`, since the user was never meant to edit those fields. Because of this, we list the two fields in a tuple that is assigned to a variable called `exclude`. With this in place, these date fields will not appear on the "Edit" form.

There is also a `prepopulated_fields` variable for each admin model. We'll see how this works in just a moment when we get to our interface.

Lastly, we register the model, and its corresponding admin model, with the admin interface by calling `admin.site.register(Model, ModelAdmin)` twice, once for each model.

That's it! Setting up these classes and registering their associated models with the admin is very simple.

So, there is one last bit of code in the `ProductAdmin` model that you might still be curious about, and that's the line reading `form = ProductAdminForm`. We've put this in place because we need some *validation* on our models, which we're going to examine in the next section.

WHAT ABOUT AN INTERNAL "ADMIN" CLASS?

You may have seen some code out in the wild that doesn't create a separate `admin.py` file to get your models hooked up to the admin interface. Instead, an internal class called `Admin` is created inside the model class, very similar to the internal `Meta` class, and it contains all of the information to customize your admin interface.

This method was used in versions of Django prior to the 1.0 release. If you're working with an earlier version, you'll have to consult the online docs in order to determine how to hook up your models. Most of the syntax is the same… you just need to do that one thing differently.

A Note on Model Validation

One key part of setting up your data, and maintaining its integrity, is setting up validation on your models. For example, you don't want a category or product name to be blank, their slug fields must be different for every record, and you enforced a maximum length on many of your fields. If you try to add any category or product that violates these constraints, the add operation will fail.

A lot of this was done implicitly, without us having to do anything out of the ordinary. This is more based on luck. Django's default settings on model fields just happened to suit our needs, and we overwrote them when there was an exception to the default rules. For the most part, this is acceptable; the default rules are good ones. Just make sure you're familiar with them, so you know what you need to change. If nothing else, at least remember that all fields cannot be empty unless you set `blank=False`.

Sometimes, however, the default validation is not enough. Your admin interface will enforce a few rules, but your models might have some custom rules that you need enforced. One perfect example of this is your product price. It should never be zero or a negative number, but right now, users can enter whatever number they want.

Django's models don't support validating number ranges just by specifying an argument in the field declaration in the class. So, we need to do a little extra work. Django allows you to hook up your own custom validation to its admin interface forms by declaring your own, and then associating the form with your admin model. Have a look at the `admin.py` code, and reread the three import statements. Notice the third one:

```
from ecomstore.catalog.forms import ProductAdminForm
```

If this is confusing to you, don't worry; it doesn't exist because we haven't created it yet. Go ahead and create another file in your `catalog` directory called `forms.py`, and add the following code to it:

```
from django import forms
from ecomstore.catalog.models import Product

class ProductAdminForm(forms.ModelForm):
    class Meta:
        model = Product
```

```
def clean_price(self):
    if self.cleaned_data['price'] <= 0:
        raise forms.ValidationError('Price must be greater than zero.')
    return self.cleaned_data['price']
```

This code bears a closer look on our part. We declare a new class called `ProductAdminForm`, which inherits from `forms.ModelForm`. You can call this class anything you like, but `ProductAdminForm` is a good name that makes its purpose clear to anyone reading the code. Inside, we declare an internal class called `Meta`, just like within our model classes, inside of which we tell our class which model it should be associated with.

Then, we declare one method that actually performs the validation. These methods take the form of `clean_[field name]`. Because our field is called `price`, we create a method named `clean_price`. The methods prefaced by `clean_` are run before the data is allowed to be saved into the database. We can access the value of `price` from a Python dictionary named `cleaned_data`, by looking it up by name. We check the value and, if it's less than or equal to zero, we raise a forms `ValidationError` with a message informing the user of the error. Of course, if no error is encountered, the error is not raised and the data is returned to Django for saving the model instance (in this case, one of our products).

The admin form for the product is already set up for us, but we just needed to inject a little bit of extra code that enforces our one rule regarding the price.

Syncing Up the Models

Now, after all of that hard work, we're finally going to run our `manage.py syncdb` script again and create our product, category, and join tables. Before we do this, there are a couple other scripts available from `manage.py` that you might find quite useful.

The first one is `validate`. Go ahead and run the following in your shell from the root of your project:

```
$ python manage.py validate
```

This will scan your models to make sure that the syntax you've used in entering them is correct. If there is anything you missed, it will let you know something is wrong before you commit these models to your database. Think of it as spell check for your model code. If you've entered everything correctly, you should get the following output:

```
0 errors found
```

It won't catch everything, but it's a nice safety net. If you do get any errors, read the information it gives you and use that to fix any problems.

The next one allows you to get a look at the Data Definition Language (DDL) output that Django will run on your database in order to create the tables. This is how Django talks to your database… it translates all of the Python code for your model classes into a language that the database will understand. This is much easier on you, since you would otherwise be creating this DDL by hand.

In MySQL, this DDL takes the form of `CREATE TABLE 'products'`, followed by a comma-delimited list in parentheses of all your fields and their data types. To view the DDL, run the following command:

```
$ python manage.py sqlall catalog
```

The word `catalog` you've supplied is the name of the app containing the models you want the DDL for. You can request the DDL for more than one app, if you would like. When you run this, you should see three tables being created, along with some `ALTER TABLE` commands settings up foreign key constraints.

If you've made it this far without any problems that made your `manage.py validate` spew up large quantities of error text, congratulations! You're ready to commit everything. Run the `syncdb` script:

```
$ python manage.py syncdb
```

Running this with your admin apps uncommented for the first time, you're likely to be prompted about creating a superuser account for your Django project. This is setting up the login account so you can access the admin interface. Go ahead and enter the information it asks for, which should be as simple as a username, e-mail, and password. The password will be encrypted before stored, so don't worry about it being stored in plaintext.

If on the off chance your setup happens to skirt the whole "create superuser" prompt, you can do so manually by using one of `manage.py` utilities:

```
$ python manage.py createsuperuser
```

Again, you might run into a couple of errors when running your `syncdb` script. If you do, just make a note of the details that the error message gives you and try to remedy the error. Then run the sync script again.

That's it! Once the sync goes smoothly, you're ready to login. Boot up the server in a shell using the `runserver` command, as you did in Chapter 2.

```
$ python manage.py runserver
```

With this shell still open (remember that if you close the shell, your development server will stop running), fire up a browser and navigate to the URL that your shell mentioned. To get to the admin interface, this should be `http://localhost:8000/admin/`, although it might be slightly different.

At this URL, you should be prompted with a login screen, which should look like Figure 3-2. Enter the username and password of the superuser account you just created a moment ago. From here, you should be taken to the Django Administration Home Page, as displayed in Figure 3-3.

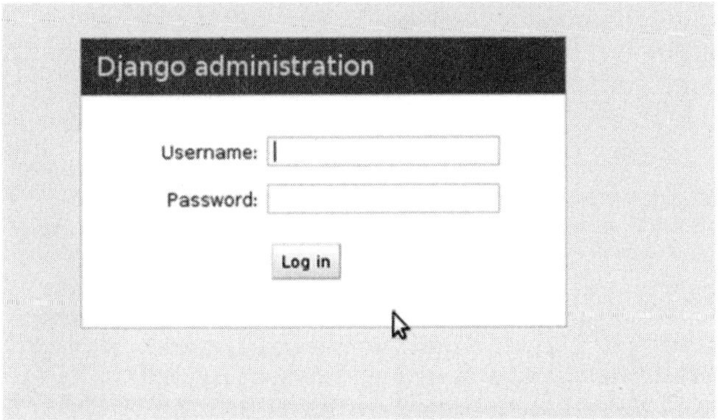

Figure 3-2. The Django admin interface login screen.

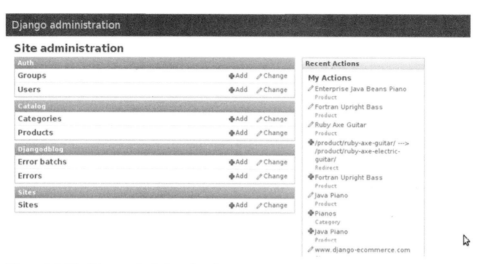

Figure 3-3. The Django admin interface homepage.

You should be presented with a few boxes, one for each installed Django app. One of these boxes should have "Catalog" in the title bar, and two entries below it for "Categories" and "Products." Click on the "Categories" link. Here, you'll find a listing of the current categories you have on your site. Go ahead and click the "Add category" link in the top right corner of the page.

You should be taken to a form that lets you input information for a new category, such as name, description, and so forth. Feel free to enter one category to see how this works.

Notice that when you start typing the name, the slug field starts populating itself automatically! Go back and have a look at the code you entered for your admin models, and look at the `prepopulated_fields` variable you set up in your admin class for each model. With this setting in place, your admin interface will convert anything you enter in the title and convert it to all lowercase letters, as well as translate any spaces or URL-illegal characters to dashes. You're welcome to edit the slug field manually, to add a keyword or two that you don't want in the category name itself, but there's no reason you need to.

You should have no trouble using the admin form to add a few categories. Go ahead and add one or two right now. If you're feeling testy, leave one of the required fields, such as Name, blank, and try to save it. You'll see the Django form validation at work; it will come back with an error message shrouded in red telling you that Name is required.

After you've added a couple of a categories, find your way back to the admin interface homepage and click on "Products," and then "Add product." You should see a form that looks very much like the screenshot in Figure 3-4. On the Add product form, you'll see that, toward the bottom, there is one box that lists your site's categories, and when you add a new product, you're able to select multiple categories in order to assign that product to them. This is how you maintain the relationships between the two models.

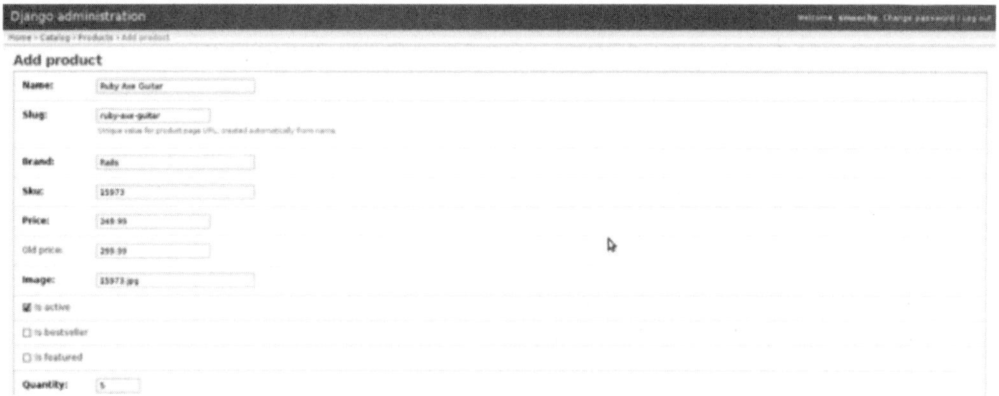

Figure 3-4. The Add product form in the Django admin interface.

One thing to point out as far as setting up model relationships go: order matters. We specified the `ManyToManyField` in the product model, and not the category one. In truth, we could have put the `ManyToManyField` in the category model, and then the setup would be just the opposite: when you add a category, you'd be able to select multiple products to be in that category.

Logically, our way is much simpler. It's easier to think about the few categories that each product should be in as opposed to the multitudes of products that each category might have. Also, there is a certain order of operations of that you should consider. If we added products first, then added categories and chose from a list of products which should be in that category, it's much more likely we'd end up with orphaned products that aren't mapped to any category. Making sure each and every product is in a category, and thus can be found on our site by browsing categories, is much easier at the product level than at the category one.

Create a few products, save them, and make sure that you see them in the product listing page after you've saved them. Notice that, on both the product and the category listing pages, you can see the fields you set up before, when you specified `list_display`, `list_display_links`, and so forth. Note that the ordering of the categories and products should be by name, since that's what we specified in our `ordering` variable. Also, try performing a search on your models. You should get back results matching the fields you listed in `search_fields`.

One thing to note about product images: just put in the name of the image that you will be using. If you have more than one, such as a thumbnail and a larger one for the product page, just use the name of the larger one and we'll come back to them later in the chapter. Just make sure you only use the name of the file and don't store any directory information, for example, forward slashes, in this field.

Now that you understand how the admin interface works (and how useful it will be in helping you manage your online catalog), feel free to go back and change any aspect of your model admin classes to customize what data you see, as well as how your data is being shown.

From the admin interface homepage, you'll also see our Django DB Log app, which you can click into and browse the exceptions you've logged so far. Next time you're stuck trying to figure out what is going wrong in your project, remember that this can be a useful tool.

One last note about the Django admin interface: while I think it's a pretty nice-looking interface for a piece of open source code, some people don't like its appearance. For this reason, it is possible to customize the look and feel of the admin interface by changing its colors and layout. You can learn more about customizing the admin interface in the Django online documentation.[5] We'll come back to the admin interface in the chapter when we cover adding and managing user accounts.

---

[5] http://docs.djangoproject.com/en/dev/obsolete/admin-css/

Playing with Model Structure and Data

Now, before we get to the really interesting part and start coding our views, there are a few things we need to do first. Let's have a quick look at how we can play with our model data. From your command line, enter the following to drop into a shell within your Django project:

```
$ python manage.py shell
```

Inside this Python shell, enter the following lines of code to import your models, load a single product, and then type the name of the product variable and hit Enter:

```
>>> from ecomstore.catalog.models import Product, Category
>>> p = Product.objects.get(slug="ruby-axe-guitar")
>>> p
<Product: Ruby Axe Guitar>
```

You'll need to use a slug value that belongs to one of your actual products. Now, we have access to one of our product models in memory, but what can we *do* with it? If we merely echo back the variable p, we get the string representation of the product, as supplied by our __unicode__() method we wrote earlier, but this doesn't do us much good.

The most useful function I've found in playing around with models is called dir(). dir() takes an object, function, property, or exception and returns a list of the object's attributes, which include any methods you can call on the object. For example, go back to your Python shell and keep going with your single product:

```
>>> dir(p)
```

As you can see, entering this gets you back a whole lot of junk. The results are a Python list, which includes properties and methods you can call on the object, as well as any potential exceptions that might be raised in attempting to load your product object. Let's try and get a list of all the categories in which this product resides, shall we? Have a look at your list of results... there's one item called categories. Let's enter that:

```
>>> p.categories
<django.db.models.fields.related.ManyRelatedManager object at 0x9f71eac>
```

Okay, so that isn't useful to us. Let's pass this into our dir() method too, and see what we get:

```
>>> dir(p.categories)
```

The results from this look a little more helpful. Another Python list with calls we can make on p.categories. One of the returned items is called all. Let's try calling that:

```
>>> p.categories.all()
[<Category: Acoustic Guitars>, <Category: Electric Guitars>]
```

There are also cases where you'll want to be able to evaluate your models at runtime to see what attributes they contain. Objects in Python have an attribute named __dict__ (there are two underscores on either side of dict), which returns a Python dictionary containing entries for the attributes. You can call this attribute either on a model class or on an instance of that class.

Following the preceding example, you can do the following to obtain a dictionary representation of the attributes of the model instance:

```
>>> p.__dict__
```

Or, you can use it on the `Product` model class itself, in order to get more detail about the available functions, methods, exceptions, and other attributes available to the class:

```
>>> Product.__dict__.copy()
```

The `dir()` function and the `__dict__` attribute are extremely useful, and I've found that when I'm trying to figure out how to do something, this can be much quicker than browsing through books or online documentation. Even if you take nothing else away from this chapter, you'll save yourself a lot of time by keeping `dir()` and `__dict__` by your side.

Templates, URLs, and Views

So now that we have our product and category data set up, and now that we have a few dummy items that our site is ready to sell, we can set up our category and product pages. Don't worry, I know you've just spent a ton of time typing in your model classes. The good news is that you've already done most of the heavy lifting in this chapter and the last, so setting up the pages will be relatively easy.

First of all, we're going to equip your app with its own set of URLs. Create a new file inside your `catalog` app directory called `urls.py`, and inside this file, put the following code:

```
from django.conf.urls.defaults import *

urlpatterns = patterns('ecomstore.catalog.views',
  (r'^$', 'index', { 'template_name':'catalog/index.html'}, 'catalog_home'),
  (r'^category/(?P<category_slug>[-\w]+)/$', ⏎
       'show_category', {
'template_name':'catalog/category.html'},'catalog_category'),
  (r'^product/(?P<product_slug>[-\w]+)/$', ⏎
       'show_product', {
'template_name':'catalog/product.html'},'catalog_product'),
)
```

Wow... confusing. Let's come back to this in a moment after we've configured everything else. We're building the start of a pipeline that will take users who request the homepage or a category or product page, and then forward them to our templates. We won't cover each individual piece of this pipeline until we create the entire thing, so we can go over the whole picture.

Next, open up the `urls.py` file that's in the root of your project. In the last chapter, you may have added a line for the `catalog/` page. Feel free to remove this line now, and update your `urlpatterns` tuple so it looks like this:

```
urlpatterns = patterns('',
  # other commented code here.
  (r'^admin/(.*)', admin.site.root),
  (r'^', include('catalog.urls')),
  (r'^static/(?P<path>.*)$', 'django.views.static.serve',
       { 'document_root': '/home/smoochy/eclipse/workspace/ecomstore/static' }),
)
```

Of course, the last line might be different, depending on where on your system your static files are located. The new line you should have added here is the one with the `include('catalog.urls')`, which refers to the `urls.py` file you just created in your `catalog` app directory.

Configuring Page Titles and Meta Tags

Next, we need to set things up for our little e-commerce project so that we can easily configure our page titles, as well as our meta tags. Search engines don't look favorably on what they regard as *duplicate content*. According to one source, it's even possible for crawlers to conclude that two pages with the exact same page title are duplicate content and penalize you for it.[6] For search engine optimization purposes, you should be working to make sure that each page has at least a distinct page title. (See Chapter 11 for more on search engine optimization (SEO).)

Page title text is displayed in the top bar of your browser application. It should be set to six or seven words that describe your page's content. In the case of our category and product views, it makes logical sense to use the category and product names as unique page title text.

A lot of sites use their site or company name in every single page title on their site. This isn't strictly necessary unless you're really trying to brand yourself on the internet; in a lot of cases, you may be better off using the space you would use for a company name for other content. However, if you are, your company name probably shouldn't be the first thing in your title tag. Instead, the unique text should come before the site name, separated by something like a dash. This is what we're going to do for Modern Musician. Our page titles will have some brief text, following by a hyphen, and then the site name on every page.

Even though we're only going to be writing three views in this chapter, we're going to create a module in our project that will let us automatically set the page title and meta tags. We'll configure defaults in our `settings.py` file so that, even if we fail to specify our own title or meta information, there will be content to fall back on so the tags will not appear empty on any page.

Let's set up these defaults now. Open up your `settings.py` file in the root of your project and add the following lines in at the bottom:

```
SITE_NAME = 'Modern Musician'
META_KEYWORDS = 'Music, instruments, music accessories, musician supplies'
META_DESCRIPTION = 'Modern Musician is an online supplier of instruments, ⤷
    sheet music, and other accessories for musicians'
```

Next, scroll up in the file and find the value named `MEDIA_URL`, which should be set to an empty string. Update the value to reflect the location of your static media:

```
MEDIA_URL = '/static/'
```

Now, anywhere in your code that you'd like to use these values, you can simply import your settings file and call them by name.

Because our page title and meta tag functions need to be available to our entire project, we're going to create an app that all of our views can use. Create an app in your project called `utils`. Before we continue, make sure that you add this new `utils` app to your `settings.py` file, under the `INSTALLED_APPS` section:

```
'ecomstore.utils',
```

In our views, we're going to set up a list of links to our category pages on the sidebar. This information is going to be made available to every page, and there's no reason we need to call it in every

---

[6] http://www.seobook.com/archives/001796.shtml

last one of view functions. There is other information you might want access to as well, such as a default page title, or the name of our site. Django handles this dilemma of making some information available to all pages with something called *context processors*.

Your project already has some context processors installed by default, but you won't find them in your settings.py file. To have a look under the hood and see what's going on here, you need to open your global_settings.py file. This file should be in the Django installation directory wherever on your system Python is installed, which might vary based on your OS. Under your Python installation, you can find it under site-packages/django/conf.

Don't feel like looking it up right now? That's okay. I've copied the comments and code out of that section and put them here:

```
# List of processors used by RequestContext to populate the context.
# Each one should be a callable that takes the request object as its
# only parameter and returns a dictionary to add to the context.
TEMPLATE_CONTEXT_PROCESSORS = (
    'django.core.context_processors.auth',
    'django.core.context_processors.debug',
    'django.core.context_processors.i18n',
    'django.core.context_processors.media',
)
```

In order to create a valid context processor, you merely need to create a function that, just like a view, takes an HttpRequest object, and return a Python dictionary with all the information you need available to your templates. When you return a template at the end of any view function, you have the option of passing in a RequestContext, which is a glorified set of default variables that you can use in your templates.

Create a new file called context_processors.py inside your utils app directory, and add the following code to it:

```
from ecomstore.catalog.models import Category
from ecomstore import settings

def ecomstore(request):
    return {
        'active_categories': Category.objects.filter(is_active=True),
        'site_name': settings.SITE_NAME,
        'meta_keywords': settings.META_KEYWORDS,
        'meta_description': settings.META_DESCRIPTION,
        'request': request
    }
```

Now, you just need to make this particular context processor available to your project. To keep things simple, copy the TEMPLATE_CONTEXT_PROCESSORS section out of your global_settings.py file and paste it somewhere inside your project's settings.py file, along with the new line for our new context processor function:

```
TEMPLATE_CONTEXT_PROCESSORS = (
    'django.core.context_processors.auth',
    'django.core.context_processors.debug',
    'django.core.context_processors.i18n',
```

```
        'django.core.context_processors.media',
        'ecomstore.utils.context_processors.ecomstore',
)
```

With this in place, you can create views that pass in the `RequestContext` object, and they will have access to all of the variables you specify in your `ecomstore()` context processor function. We've set up five default variables here, which will be available to any template to which we pass the default `RequestContext` object, which we'll see in a moment when we code our views.

Have a look back at the template we created in Chapter 2 called `base.html`. Look at the three tags in the header section. As you can see, the template checks for three variables called `page_title`, `meta_keywords`, and `meta_description`. If these are not supplied by our view functions (which we're getting to, I swear), then the template falls back on these variables we just set in our `context_processor.py` function.

Now, I'm going to confess one thing here: if you look back at the code that sets the variables, the list of active categories really doesn't *belong* there. The list itself is going to end up in the side column on every page of the site. Ideally, any database calls we make should be encapsulated in that one part of the site, and not *everywhere*, like our site name needs to be. Don't worry… in the next chapter, when we learn how to create custom template tags, we're going to get rid of this kludge. For now, you have a list of categories to aid in browsing the site.

Coding Up the Catalog Views

So, let's code our view functions! You may be thinking back to the alphabet soup we talked about earlier: MVC. Naturally, since this stands for "model-view-controller," it would make sense for you to assume that your Django views are the "view" part of that acronym. This isn't really the case. In the MVC design pattern, the controller is responsible for handling the logic in your application. It talks to your models, fetches instances of them, and returns to the views. Your view functions will do this, more than act as real "views" in the MVC sense of the word.

In fact, as ludicrous as it sounds, your templates are really your view layer, while your view functions are more your controller layer. Confused yet? Yes? Well, the good news is, it doesn't really matter. You understanding where in the theoretical MVC pattern each part of your project falls isn't crucial to you getting it built.

Let's get down to it. Open the `views.py` file inside your `catalog` app directory and enter the following import statements and three view functions:

```python
from django.shortcuts import get_object_or_404, render_to_response
from ecomstore.catalog.models import Category, Product
from django.template import RequestContext

def index(request, template_name="catalog/index.html"):
    page_title = 'Musical Instruments and Sheet Music for Musicians'
    return render_to_response(template_name, locals(),↵
        context_instance=RequestContext(request))

def show_category(request, category_slug, template_name="catalog/category.html"):
    c = get_object_or_404(Category, slug=category_slug)
    products = c.product_set.all()
    page_title = c.name
    meta_keywords = c.meta_keywords
    meta_description = c.meta_description
```

```
    return render_to_response(template_name, locals(),↵
        context_instance=RequestContext(request))

def show_product(request, product_slug, template_name="catalog/product.html"):
    p = get_object_or_404(Product, slug=product_slug)
    categories = p.categories.filter(is_active=True)
    page_title = p.name
    meta_keywords = p.meta_keywords
    meta_description = p.meta_description
    return render_to_response(template_name, locals(),↵
        context_instance=RequestContext(request))
```

These are the views for the home page, category, and product pages. You'll see that these functions are making good use of the page title and meta tag functions we created in the last section. As you know, if any of our products have blank title or meta data, our project will fall back on the defaults. Other than that, what you're seeing should make sense.

We are using another Django shortcut here: get_object_or_404. Typically, if a user enters a URL for a product or category slug that doesn't exist, it will raise a DoesNotExist exception in your Django project. We'd much rather pass along an informative and courteous message to the user letting them know they've tried to access a page that doesn't exist, by returning a 404 Page Not Found. This is exactly what get_object_or_404 does. Pass in the name of one of your model classes, as well as any arguments used to look up the particular record you want. If it looks up the given category or product by its slug and does not find a match, it will raise a 404 exception that our Django project can use to present a slick "Page Not Found" error to the end user.

We're also making heavier use of our render_to_response() function in this chapter. We're passing in three arguments instead of just the one. The first is the name of each template, through the template_name variable, which we haven't created yet, but will be coding in the next section. Because we're using a variable name as a keyword argument to our view function, the actual view code itself isn't cluttered up with the name of the template.(save for its inclusion in the view's list of arguments).

The second is a function called locals(), which is a useful shortcut when returning a response to the user. As the second argument, you could create a dictionary listing all of the variables that your view function is passing into the template, such as page_title, c, and so forth. However, this is a lot of typing that can get old quickly. The locals() function sucks up all the variables you've declared in your function, creates a Python dictionary out of them, and makes them available to your template, without you needing to explicitly list all of them.

The last argument passed in is called context_instance. This takes a RequestContext object that can contain any variables you might want to pass to multiple pages. As you can see, we're just passing in the RequestContext object created by the ecomstore() function we created in the last section. Any view that passes in this RequestContext will have a list of active categories, a site name, default meta keywords and description, and the request object variables made available to it.

Creating the Template Files

So, now all we need to do to see some pages is create the templates. Let's make a quick change to our base.html file so that we're using our context variable to set the location of the CSS file. Open it and change the link tag in your site's head to look like this:

```
<link rel="Stylesheet" type="text/css" href="{{ MEDIA_URL }}css.css" />
```

Here, you're updating your page to make use of the MEDIA_URL you entered into your settings.py file. Now, where is *that* coming from? We didn't add it to our context processor function, so how is our template able to use it? As it turns out, the MEDIA_URL value is already passed to your template, via the following context processor:

```
'django.core.context_processors.media',
```

So, you can easily change the location of your static content when you deploy, and you won't lose the link to your CSS.

Now we're going to create three new ones, to correspond with our three views. We're interested in keeping our application manageable, especially as it gets much larger. Right now, you should only have two or three template files in your templates directory, but as you start adding new apps and new models, the number of them may start to grow by leaps and bounds. To keep things organized, we're going to adopt a practice of organizing our templates by the app to which they belong. So, create a new directory in your templates folder called catalog, and create three new HTML files in it: index.html, category.html, and product.html.

index.html will be the simplest one for us to do, so open that file first and add the following code to it:

```
{% extends "catalog.html" %}


{%block content %}
<h1>Welcome to Modern Musician!</h1>
{% endblock %}
```

As you can see, we're merely extending our catalog.html template from the last chapter, and adding a very brief welcome header to greet the user. The home page is the most important page on your site, since it will give the user an overview of everything your site has to offer, and will help them determine whether or not they should stick around.

For this reason, it's usually prudent to save the planning of your home page for last, after you've decided what content your site will include. You might end up adding news articles, a blog, a shopping cart, wish lists, user accounts, and so forth. We'll be adding some of those items, and later come back to presenting all of this to the user at the end, when we've finished most of our site. For now, since we're not yet live, we can stand to leave a simple welcome message as a placeholder for things to come.

Next, let's move on to the category page. Open up category.html and enter the following code:

```
{% extends "catalog.html" %}

{% block content %}
    <h1>{{ c.name }}</h1>
    {{ c.description }}
    <br /><br />
    {% for p in products %}
        <div class="product_thumbnail">
            <a href="{{ p.get_absolute_url }}">
                <img src="{{ MEDIA_URL }}images/products/thumbnails/{{ p.image
}}" ⏎
    alt="{{ p.name }}" class="bn" />
                <br />
                {{ p.name }}
            </a>
        </div>
    {% endfor %}
{% endblock %}
```

As you can see, things are starting to get a little juicier in our templates. This one is pretty clear: we have a couple of variables that are displaying information about our categories, and a Django template `{% for %}` loop that runs through our products and displays a thumbnail, with the image, for each one. We haven't set up the image folders quite yet.

Now, let's do the category page last. Open your `product.html` file and enter this code:

```
{% extends "catalog.html" %}

{% block content %}
    <div class="product_image" >
        <img src="{{ MEDIA_URL }}images/products/main/{{ p.image }}" alt="{{ p.name }}" />
    </div>
    <h1>{{ p.name }}</h1>
    Brand: <em>{{ p.brand }}</em>
    <br /><br />
    SKU: {{ p.sku }}
    <br />
    In categor{{ categories.count|pluralize:"y,ies" }}:
        {% for c in categories %}
    <a href="{{ c.get_absolute_url }}">{{ c.name }}</a>
    {% if not forloop.last %}, {% endif %}
        {% endfor %}
        <br /><br />
     {% if p.sale_price %}
        Was: <del>$ {{ p.old_price }}</del>
        <br />
        Now: $ {{ p.price }}
    {% else %}
        Price: $ {{ p.price }}
    {% endif %}
    <br /><br />
     [add to cart button]
    <br /><br />
    <div class="cb"><br /><br /></div>
    <h3>Product Description</h3>
        {{ p.description }}
{% endblock %}
```

There's a little bit more going on here. We're using a few template variables, some `if` blocks, and a couple other things you might not have seen before. Below the product name, we're listing as links the categories that the product is in. We're basing the appearance of our "In categories" text by using a Django *template filter*. Filters let you format the output of variables at the point you display them in the page.

For example, let's say you have a variable supplied by a site user that could potentially contain malicious JavaScript that could make your site vulnerable to Cross-Site Scripting attacks. You can use a template filter to strip out HTML tags, or HTML encode the content of the variable, from the output in your templates.

In our simple example, we're basing the display of the word "categories" on how many categories the product is in. If the category count is only one, the word "category" will be displayed. If the count is more than one, however, than the word "categories" will be used instead, through the use of the `pluralize` filter: In `categor{{ categories.count|pluralize:"y,ies" }}`.

Next, notice that as we loop through our categories and output the links, there is a nested `if` loop that looks like this:

```
{% if not forloop.last %}, {% endif %}
```

The syntax is simple enough… this almost looks like pseudo-code. This delimits your category link list with commas, but the comma will not be appended to the last category because it is the last item in the loop.

Next, we're using the custom `sale_price()` method that we specified in our product model. If you refer back to the code, this method will only return a value if an old price is set that is higher than the price field. So, our `{% if %}` block will only evaluate to true if the product is on sale. In this case, a "before" and "after" price will be displayed, with a strike through the "before" price. If the product is not on sale, the price field is simply displayed.

There are a few simple things we need to add before we get a sneak preview of our site. First, there are some new CSS classes, so open up your `css.css` file and add the following styles:

```
a{
     color:#98AC5E;
     font-weight:bold;
     text-decoration:none;
}
a:hover{
     text-decoration:underline;
}

/* category page styles */
div.product_thumbnail{
     text-align:center;
     float:left;
     width:150px;
     height:200px;
}

/* product page styles */
div.product_image{
     float:left;
     padding:0 10px 10px 0;
}
```

Product images need a place to live on our site, and we've already set aside a small corner inside our `static` directory. Create an `images` folder inside your `static` folder. Inside this, create a `products` folder. Inside *here* (provided you're not lost yet), create two directories for your products called `main` and `thumbnails`. If you have some product images already created for any of the products you've added through the admin interface, go ahead and put them in here now. Be sure that they're sized correctly, since our templates don't resize our images in our template markup.

A Category Link List

Now, we're going to use the list of active categories that all of our templates have as a variable, but currently are not configured to use in any way. Go into your `catalog.html` template file and find the line of text in your site's sidebar acting as a placeholder for your category list. Get rid of the [category listing here] and replace it with the following line of code:

```
{% include "tags/category_list.html" %}
```

Create the `category_list.html` file inside the `tags` subdirectory, and add this simple loop code to it:

```
<h3>Categories</h3>
{% for c in active_categories %}
    <a href="{{ c.get_absolute_url }}">{{ c.name }}</a><br />
{% endfor %}
```

This will list the active categories in your product catalog in the side navigation bar of your site.

Our Code in Review

At this point, take a moment to review the directory structure and files in your project. If you've been following along, your project should be structure like this:

```
ecomstore/
    catalog/
        __init__.py
        admin.py
        forms.py
        models.py
        tests.py
        urls.py
        views.py
    static/
        images/
            products/
                main/
                    image1.jpg
                thumbnails/
                    image1.jpg
        css.css
    templates/
        catalog/
            category.html
            index.html
            product.html
        tags/
            category_list.html
            navigation.html
```

```
        base.html
        catalog.html
        index.html
        utils/
                __init__.py
                models.py
                views.py
                tests.py
                context_processors.py
    __init__.py
    manage.py
    settings.py
    views.py
    urls.py
```

Now that this is all set up properly, go ahead and fire up your development server from your shell using `manage.py runserver`, and navigate to the homepage. You should see your site load up with the "Welcome!" header that you created in your `catalog/index.html` template.

■ **Note** Your site directory structure might also contain files with the extension `.pyc`. When you run your code, the Python interpreter will attempt to create compiled versions of your Python files. Compilation isn't necessary, as Python is an interpreted language; it's just a means of optimizing the speed of your code.

You can see that our side navigation now has a list of categories displayed. Click on one that you know has products in it, and you should be taken to that category's page, complete with a listing of products. Click on one of the products, and see if that page loads correctly. My product page looks like Figure 3-5. Click around on the site for a while, make sure everything is working the way you expect it to. Make note of the URLs, and make sure you understand how they are structured.

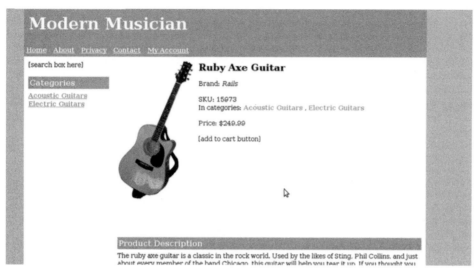

Figure 3-5. My product page.

You'll notice that the page contains a placeholder for the "Add to Cart" button, which doesn't do anything yet. We'll be adding this functionality in the next chapter.

So How Does It All Work?

Let's walk through a request step by step, and review the way our code is handling all of this. A request to the site is first routed through the urls.py file in our root directory, and the requests to the homepage, category, and product views are now being routed through the one line with our include() function in it:

```
(r'^', include('catalog.urls')),
```

This in turn maps to the urls.py file we added to our catalog app. The urlpatterns variable in this file looks like this, in its entirety:

```
urlpatterns = patterns('ecomstore.catalog.views',
  (r'^$', 'index', { 'template_name':'catalog/index.html'}, 'catalog_home'),
  (r'^category/(?P<category_slug>[-\w]+)/$', ⏎
      'show_category', {
'template_name':'catalog/category.html'},'catalog_category'),
  (r'^product/(?P<product_slug>[-\w]+)/$', ⏎
      'show_product', {
'template_name':'catalog/product.html'},'catalog_product'),
)
```

Any incoming request to your site is going to go through the one in the root of your project first, and, when it gets to the line with the include() function, every last request will match it. Regular expressions use the ^ and $ characters for two very particular tasks in matching string patterns: the beginning and the end of the string pattern, respectively. A regular expression on your site that looks like `(r'^contact/$', 'contact_view_function')` will match that inner string tacked on to the end of your site's domain. So this request would match that particular regular expression exactly: `http://www.yoursite.com/contact/`.

This first pattern just uses the `^` without a corresponding `$` character that will match everything, even an empty request to `http://www.yoursite.com/`. So, every request will continue on the `urls.py` file in your site's `catalog` app folder. When you get to the regular expression (`r'^$'`), this is the URL entry that matches your home page URL. Because you now have the `$` character determining where the end of the string is, it will only match a URL that is empty after the `http://www.yoursite.com/`.

After this home page match, we then pass it the name of the home page view function: `'index'`. There's a little bit of a mystery here. How does our site know where the `index()` function resides?

The answer lies in the first line in our catalog `urls.py` file. While this is an empty string in our root file, here we've specified `'ecomstore.catalog.views'`. In effect, this translates to "preface every URL view function we specify with this location in our application." This means that these three views all reside in this file, and instead of having to type out the full location each time, we can just type it once, at the beginning of the `patterns()` function.

The `category` regular expression bears a little bit more examination. Sure, there's still `^` and `$` characters, but there's a whole lot of stuff between them:

```
(r'^category/(?P<category_slug>[-\w]+)/$', ⤸
     'show_category', {
'template_name':'catalog/category.html'},'catalog_category'),
```

The syntax of using parentheses that start out with "?P" is the syntax for using a named argument in your view function. This tells your application that in this part of the URL, you expect to receive some text that should be a category slug. You denote the name of the argument in angled brackets (`< >`), followed by a regular expression that should tell your pattern what kind of content your named argument might contain. In this case, `[-\w]+` matches any number of letters, numbers, or hyphens... exactly the characters your slug field might contain.

So, navigating to the URL:

```
/category/my-category-name/
```

is the same as calling your view function, by hand, like this:

```
show_category(request, category_slug="my-category-name", ⤸
     template_name="catalog/category.html")
```

After passing in the name of the view function (`show_category`) in your URL entry, there are two more arguments here, the likes of which we haven't seen before. The first one is a dictionary we're passing in, which can contain any view function arguments you want to make available to that particular view. We are passing in the name of the template we're planning to return to the view function, instead of hard-coding it in the `render_to_response()` function.

The last one is a little strange: `'catalog_category'`. What gives? Go back to your category model class definition and find the `get_absolute_url()` function:

```
@models.permalink
def get_absolute_url(self):
     return ('catalog_category', (), { 'category_slug': self.slug })
```

As you can see, the first argument here matches the last mysterious argument back in our URL definition. This is mapping the `get_absolute_url()` function to your `urls.py` file, so that whenever you call it, it looks up the location of the category in your `urls.py` file. Therefore, if you want to change the format of the URL where your categories are located, you would just need to update your `urls.py` file and your project will automatically take care of updating all of the hyperlinks on your site (provided, of course, that you're using the `get_absolute_url()` method).

The product URL entry is pretty much the same as the category one. Just make you understand how the internal plumbing is working, and how `get_absolute_url()` is determining how to construct its links.

File Not Found and Custom 404s

In the last chapter, we briefly covered the template files that are used when your project encounters an error. You've equipped your project to return 404s when it doesn't find a category, and while the Django default `404.html` template would work just fine, let's set up a custom template so that our "Not Found" page is consistent in appearance with the rest of the site. Create a file called `views.py` in the root of your project and enter the following 404 function definition into it:

```
from django.shortcuts import render_to_response
from django.template import RequestContext

def file_not_found_404(request):
    page_title = 'Page Not Found'
    return render_to_response('404.html', locals(),↵
            context_instance=RequestContext(request))
```

Now, create a file called `404.html` in your `templates` directory and put the following code into it:

```
{% extends "catalog.html" %}

{% block content %}
    The page or resource you requested was not found.
    We apologize for the inconvenience.
    Please go back and check to make sure you typed in the URL correctly.
{% endblock %}
```

Next, open up the `urls.py` file in the root of your project and, *below* the `urlpatterns` variable, put the following line of code:

```
handler404 = 'ecomstore.views.file_not_found_404'
```

Now, when your site encounters a 404, it will return this template you just created. Note that this won't be visible to you, or your site users, until you change the `DEBUG` variable in your `settings.py` file from `True` to `False`. Your project assumes that while in development, your project will be in debug mode, and that during development you'll want to read those spiffy and verbose error messages that a 404 would give you.

While it may seem unnatural to you at first, you'll get into a quick flow, in which you'll create your URL, create your view, and then create your templates. Once you've gotten into the habit, creating pages with Django will go quickly.

Summary

So, after all of that delightful coding work, we now have a small e-commerce catalog. We went over the basics of model creation, setting up relationships between you models, and learned the very basics about database design. We created product and category models, set up the admin interface for each one, added a few of each, and got the views, templates, and URLs set up so that users can browse our products. In the process, we learned more about how to set up URLs, pass arguments into view functions, and the great amount of flexibility that Django templates give you in creating your user interface.

In the next chapter, we're going to set up our own custom shopping cart so that users can start aggregating our products for eventual checkout.

CHAPTER 4

■ ■ ■

The Shopping Cart

Anyone who's ever done any shopping, either on the Internet or off, understands the concept of a shopping cart. It allows customers browsing your products to aggregate some products from your catalog and then, once they've gotten everything they want to buy, go through the checkout process with all the items in their shopping cart.

In this chapter, we're going to create a shopping cart on our site, to which users can add the products in our catalog. We're going to create the shopping cart page, where they can review their selections, adjust any purchase quantities, or remove any items before beginning the checkout process. In doing so, we'll take a much closer look at the Django templating system and what you can do to extend Django's templating system with your own custom template filters and template tags.

Shopping Cart Requirements

Before we get to coding up our shopping cart models and creating our templates, let's write a quick spec outlining the basics of our cart requirements, and talk a little bit about the purpose of sessions.

I'm going to do a quick write-up to serve as an overview of the functionality that our shopping cart requires. Feel free to do your own and remember, yours might end up looking a whole lot different than mine for lots of different reasons. The only piece of advice I'm going to give you is to call your shopping cart just that… a "shopping cart." While you might think it's a good idea to come up with a different metaphor that fits into the particular theme of your site, I would strongly advise against this.

I remember shopping on an e-commerce site for a hardware store that sold tools and garden equipment, and they called their shopping cart a "wheelbarrow." Sure, that's cute and all, but most web shoppers are familiar with the shopping cart metaphor. When they are finished shopping and are ready to check out, they will scan your site looking for the cart so they can complete their purchase, but if all they see is "wheelbarrow," there's always the chance that a few of them will get confused about what they are looking for. Hardware stores don't give you a wheelbarrow to shop with, so why should we get creative with an online storefront anyway?

If you want to detract from the usual name and go with something a little more quaint, I believe that "basket" is a close second choice to "shopping cart."

In any case, here is my quick outline of our needs for the shopping cart. Just as before, in Chapter 1, my functional spec is not bound by the formalities or procedural bureaucracies of any organization, so it may sound like unorganized gibberish. However, in my defense, I'd like to point out that my spec is very *human-readable* gibberish:

"A link to the shopping cart must be present on every page. This link should include a quick summary about how many items are in the cart, maybe a small icon of the shopping cart? This needs to be on every page so that whenever the user gets the itch to check out, no matter what page they are on, they should be able to figure out how to do it quickly and without any confusion. Once they click on the

<section>79</section>

shopping cart link, they should be taken to the cart page where they can review their items and edit quantities or remove single items as they need. A checkout link should be present only if the cart is not empty. IMPORTANT: Users, even anonymous ones that haven't registered or logged in, should be able to add items to their cart."

Very simple and direct. If your own spec gets much more complicated than this, you might consider breaking it into sections.

As I mentioned in the last chapter, it's usually in your best interest to start with your data, set up the structure and relationships of your models, and then develop the rest of the site from this foundation. Before we jump into the models, a quick bit of theory about how web sites track anonymous visitors is in order.

An Introduction to Sessions

Do you know what sessions are and why web developers use them? You do? All right, you're off the hook, feel free to skip ahead to the next section and you shouldn't have any problems understanding what's going on. The rest of you will have to read the following story.

I live in California, which is home to about 98% of the remaining functional 1970s flower-covered Volkswagen Vans left in the entire world. Let's imagine that one day, a driver of one of them cuts me off on the highway and I take it very personally. I decide to write a letter to my governor and let him know that I think he ought to ban VW Vans from the roads and highways of California, if for no other reason than I'm bored and would like to complain.

So, I write up a letter to Governor Arnold Schwarzenegger (yes, I had to look up how to spell that) and tell him how much those pesky VW vans are annoying me and give him a piece of my mind. I write his address on an envelope and drop the letter into a mailbox, then sit on my hands and wait patiently for his reply.

A week later, a return letter from Mr. Schwarzenegger's shows up in my mailbox, and I open it eagerly. No, he has written back, he will not ban VW Vans from the 1970s, and that's the silliest thing he's ever heard. He also pleads with me to get a job so I stop worrying about what kinds of cars are on the road.

Now, I might be a little put off by his reply, and want to tell him how I feel about it. But notice that the only way for me to do this is to write him another letter. At this point, the line of communication has ended. The correspondence is complete. I've sent him a request, and he's sent back a response, and now this entire plan of mine to eliminate VW Vans is all but *kaput*. The only way for me to try and spark up this whole process is to initiate the whole thing from scratch, by writing another letter.

However, let's imagine that Arnold S. receives a whole ton of letters each day, to which he always sends a personal reply. After replying to each and every letter, he immediately tosses the original letter and forgets the name of the person who sent it to him. He just doesn't bother retaining any information

This is how the Internet works. The entire thing is based on a request-response system between clients and servers, kind of like me writing to Arnold in the VW story. When you type in http://www.google.com/ in the address bar of your browser and hit Enter, you are transmitting a request (as a client) to Google (who is the server), which will take your request and then return a response to you. Think of it like tossing a rubber bouncy ball at the wall: the ball is not at rest until it's back in your hand.

This shouldn't be too big of a shock, since this is what your view functions were doing in the last chapter. They accept an argument aptly named "request" and then render a "response" in return. After the response, there is no longer any open line of communication. This is in the interest of conserving server connections. Web servers tend to have a limit on the number of concurrent connections they can have open. If every site visitor was given their own dedicated connection from the web server, the server's performance would not scale as well. Also, keeping connections open only long enough to transmit information and closing them as soon as possible conserves bandwidth, which is an expensive and very finite resource on the Internet.

Contrast this to a regular desktop program that you might install and use on Windows, such as Excel. When you're using something that's installed on your local machine, and not running it in a browser, there is a direct line of communication between you and the program. You enter data into a few cells and the program accepts it right there. This is akin to me giving Arnold a call on the telephone and talking directly to him (assuming that he didn't just hang up on me right away).

The World Wide Web doesn't have these direct lines open, and instead has to rely on the request-response means of communicating. If you want to sound like a very technical and well-read person, you refer to this principle on the Internet as the *statelessness of HTTP*. A bunch of faceless requests come in, and the servers reply to them, but the servers don't have a means of aggregating all of the requests that originated from one particular machine.

Back to Arnold on his state of California throne. In the interest of getting re-elected, he decides to start keeping a filing system. He files away the letters that he gets by the name and address of the person who sent them, instead of carelessly throwing them away. That way, with each letter, he can check and see if the writer has ever sent him a letter in the past. This enables him to tailor his response to that person in particular.

So when I write him next month and tell him how much I hate palm trees and how I think we should get rid of all the palm trees in California, he can reply back to me and say, "Hello Jim, no, we won't be doing that either. That's an even stupider idea than getting rid of all the VW Vans you mentioned last month. Please reconsider my advice for seeking gainful employment. Sincerely, Arnold." You see? With that reply, he addressed not only the letter I had sent but the one before it as well. The response feels more personal, like he's really listening to me, and I really get the impression that he *cares*.

You want your customers to think, and know, that you care. Web developers have been using a technique to identify and track all of those anonymous requests that come in from web surfers for a long time now, using *cookies*. A cookie is a small text file that you write to each user's computer, via their browser, with some information that you can use to uniquely identify that user on that computer. We can use this for all sorts of things that will let us tailor the experience that the user has on our site specifically for them.

The beauty of this approach is that it allows customers who aren't registered or logged in to still shop on our site, adding items to their cart for eventual checkout. This is the best approach, because you want to make everything as easy as possible for your users, particularly the new ones. If you concern new users with registering before they can even start shopping on your site, you're going to annoy some of them and they're going to leave. Just because the register-first-then-shop approach works for Costco certainly doesn't mean it's a good idea for your site.

We're going to use this cookie information to help track the shopping cart data. When a user first adds an item to their cart, we're going to create a long and crazy string of random characters that will uniquely identify their cart and the items in it, and write this to a cookie in their browser. Then we'll store this long string with the associated cart items in the model. Whenever they interact with their cart, or add other items to it, we'll reference this identifier to pull the corresponding cart items from the database.

There is an important distinction to point out here, about how we're using session information. There are lots of examples floating around out on the Internet that demonstrate how to use sessions in Django, and while the examples are programmatically correct, they are architectural nightmares that, if implemented, wouldn't scale *at all*.

Let's say you want to restrict product reviews to one per product per customer on the site, and you decide to use the Django session framework in order to track which products a user has reviewed to prevent them from posting more than one for any given product. Now, what you *don't* want to do is write a cookie for each product that the user reviews and track them that way. There is a limit to how many cookies you should be writing to each user's browser, and in practice, it's somewhere between 30 and 50 cookies. (As a matter of fact, the number of cookies you actually use will likely be much smaller than that.) Since a user might write hundreds of product reviews (in theory), filling up a user's machine with hundreds of corresponding cookies is bad architecture.

Admittedly, this is a poor example, because you would more than likely track a user's reviews with an e-mail or a user account. My only point is that sessions are one tool in the Django arsenal, they can be used for tracking anonymous users, and you certainly don't want to start storing large quantities of detailed information in them. That's what your database is for.

The Shopping Cart Model

Let's continue this chapter with a very quick review of setting up models, just like we did in the last chapter. Before we get started, I'd like to remind you that source code for this chapter can be downloaded from the Apress web site, if you want to spare your wrists some mileage at the keyboard.

First, we're going to create a new app within our project to house all of the shopping cart information. I'm going to call my app cart.

From the root of your project, run the following:

```
$ python manage.py startapp cart
```

This will create the directory with the default Django app files, and that's just *so* Chapter 3 that I'm not going to repeat the list again for you here.

First, let's talk about what we need for our shopping cart models. What data do you need to store? Turns out this requires a little more thought than the product data, and once again, I welcome you to sketch up a mock of what you envision your cart should look like and go from there. Here's one hint: don't store any information that's associated directly with the product (like the price) or anything that's *calculated* (like the extended price) in the cart models.

For my simple little cart model, I came up with four things that I need to store with each item in a user's shopping cart:

1. Our unique Cart ID value

2. Product ID

3. Date product was added to the cart

4. Quantity in the cart

This is simple. Exceedingly simple. It's so straightforward that we really only need one model for storing this information. Open up your models.py file in your new cart app and add in the following code for your cart item class:

```python
from django.db import models
from ecomstore.catalog.models import Product

class CartItem(models.Model):
    cart_id = models.CharField(max_length=50)
    date_added = models.DateTimeField(auto_now_add=True)
    quantity = models.IntegerField(default=1)
    product = models.ForeignKey('catalog.Product', unique=False)

    class Meta:
        db_table = 'cart_items'
        ordering = ['date_added']

    def total(self):
        return self.quantity * self.product.price

    def name(self):
        return self.product.name

    def price(self):
        return self.product.price
```

```
def get_absolute_url(self):
    return self.product.get_absolute_url()

def augment_quantity(self, quantity):
    self.quantity = self.quantity + int(quantity)
      self.save()
```

As you can see, the CartItem class and its associated methods borrow a lot from the related Product model. When we call the name, price, and the link to the cart item, we're actually going to be calling for those items on the related product that we've set up in our model as a foreign key. Items on the cart page will be linkable, but the items will link to the product page, since they don't have their own dedicated templates. There's also one method, called total(), that returns the extended price, which is calculated from the product's price and the quantity of the cart item.

Now that we've added a new model, we need to make sure that we add the new app to our settings.py file and run manage.py syncdb to create the database table. Open up your settings.py file and add the following line to your INSTALLED_APPS section:

```
'ecomstore.cart',
```

Then, inside your system's shell, run the following command in your project:

```
$ python manage.py syncdb
```

The database table for the CartItem model class should now be created and ready to start storing shopping cart items.

Let's back up one step: why are we only using one model instead of two? In a cart with more than one item, we're going to be storing the Cart ID for that user in more than one place. In a properly normalized database, you're trying to reduce the amount of redundancy as much as possible, because you want to ensure that when the time comes to change the data, you'll only have to remember to change it in one place. Given this thought, it makes more sense to give the Cart ID its own table and link it, in a one-to-many relationship, with the items it contains.

I've chosen to merge the cart data into one table, and potentially store redundant Cart IDs across multiple records, for a couple of reasons. First, the Cart IDs are going to be a big blob of character data from the session cookie that is not going to change. The only thing that can happen is the customer clears their cookies, or switches computers or browsers, in which case we'll just assign them a new Cart ID.

But second, and much more importantly, when you pull your model information in your views to show the user, two separate tables with the cart information would do one of two things. It would either require you to do a query for the Cart ID, and then do a second query for the associated items in the cart, in which case you've performed an extra query, or you would have to perform a *join* on the two tables in order to get the information you need in one shot. Queries are expensive, and joins on tables to query data from more than one table are also quite expensive.[1] And after all, in our case, there isn't any additional information that a second table would contain, other than the Cart ID.

The last method, augment_quantity(), will be used by our site just in case someone adds an item to their cart and, by some weird coincidence, finds their way back to that product page and adds the exact same item to their cart a second time. Instead of adding it again, we'll just adjust the quantity.

---

[1] With the proper use of indexes in your database tables, however, joins might be less expensive than tables with several columns. See Chapter 13 for more about indexes.

Django Sessions Overview

So how long do Django cookies last? Once you identify a user and they start adding items to their cart, how long does that cart persist in their browser? The best answer I can give you to these questions is to point you directly to where the answer lies: in the Django global configuration file. We saw this file in the last chapter. It's called global_settings.py, and it resides in your Django installation folder on your development machine.

Open this file and navigate down to the section labeled SESSIONS surrounded by lots of pound (#) signs. You should see about 10 configuration settings related to cookies, which have self-describing names and comments that should help you understand the purpose of each one. In case you don't feel like opening the file yourself, here are the most important ones:

```
# Cookie name. This can be whatever you want.
SESSION_COOKIE_NAME = 'sessionid'
# The module to store sessions data.
SESSION_ENGINE = 'django.contrib.sessions.backends.db'
# Age of cookie, in seconds (default: 2 weeks).
SESSION_COOKIE_AGE - 60 * 60 * 24 * 7 * 2
# Whether a user's session cookie expires when the Web browser is closed
SESSION_EXPIRE_AT_BROWSER_CLOSE = False
# Whether the session cookie should be secure (https:// only).
SESSION_COOKIE_SECURE = False
```

As you can see, cookies last two weeks before they expire in the user's browser. At these two weeks of idle activity, if the user returns to your site, their shopping cart will appear to be empty, even if they had previously filled it up with 10 different kinds of jaw harps and banjo strings.

That last value is the most important one to examine, because it makes a very important point: *cookies are not secure.* Cookies are only as secure as the transmission protocol they're sent over, and plain ol' HTTP is not secure. We discussed not storing large amounts of complex information in cookies, but you certainly don't want to start storing any sensitive information in them. As a way-too-obvious example, don't store customer credit card information in cookies.

■ **Note** Setting your SESSION_COOKIE_SECURE value to True does *not* in any way secure your cookies. That just means they won't work in your web project unless the user is browsing your site over SSL. (I'll discuss SSL in more detail in Chapter 5.)

Lastly, notice that, while the database is used to store session information by default, you can change this configuration to use one of the other options. Your project can use a file in your project's directory to track user session information. Because performance is superior with the database approach, we're not going to use the file approach in this book, but you do have the option, in case your project isn't using a database.

If you feel the need to change any of these default settings, my advice to you is not to edit this global settings configuration file. As a matter of fact, as far as changes go, leave the Django source code alone. Like any computer code, a change in one area of the source code might inadvertently break things in other places. This shouldn't be a problem for you, since you can override any of the settings in the global settings file by adding the same configuration setting to your project's settings.py file.

For example, if you want to set cookies so that they last 90 days instead of 2 weeks, you can add this line of code to your `settings.py` file:

```
SESSION_COOKIE_AGE = 60 * 60 * 24 * 90
```

Or, if you want to make it unreadable to anyone that doesn't have a calculator at hand:

```
SESSION_COOKIE_AGE = 7776000    # the number of seconds in 90 days
```

The two are functionally equivalent. However long you would like your carts to last is entirely up to you and your own needs. I'm going to set my cookie to last for 90 days, to give my users enough time to think about their buying decisions. If you want to test this setting, set it to some ridiculously low, like three seconds, add an item to your cart, and watch how quickly it disappears after you start refreshing the cart page.

Enabling and Using Sessions

The good news is that you already have sessions enabled. Back in Chapter 3, when you uncommented out this line of code in your `settings.py` file under the `INSTALLED_APPS` section:

```
'django.contrib.sessions',
```

the tables that your database needed to track sessions were created as soon as you ran the `syncdb` command in your shell. In addition, your project came equipped with another batch of code in the `MIDDLEWARE_CLASSES` section.

The `request.session` object is an instance of a special `SessionStore` class, which is similar in concept to a Python dictionary object that you can use in your Django code to store and retrieve session information with each request. So, when a user adds an item to their cart on the product page, and you want to set the value of their Cart ID, you can use the following code:

```
request.session['cart_id'] = 'cart_id_value_here'
```

Later, when you want to retrieve it, you can just as easily get at it with this:

```
request.session['cart_id']
```

The syntax is simple, but things get a little sticky when you try to access a user's Cart ID before you've set it, and you can't set the value each time it's accessed, because you'd just be overwriting the value that was already there. To solve this problem, we're going to check for the existence of the Cart ID, set it if it doesn't exist, and then return that value.

Here is the function for the Cart ID for our cart module (we haven't created the cart module yet):

```
def _cart_id(request):
    if 'cart_id' in request.session:
        request.session['cart_id'] = _generate_cart_id()
    return request.session['cart_id']
```

As you can see, we use the Python dictionary's get() method to check for the Cart ID, and if the key `cart_id` is not found, an empty string is returned and our `_generate_cart_id()` method is called to create one for us.

So what is our Cart ID going to look like? In our project, we're going to generate a random string of fifty letters, numbers, and other non-alphanumeric characters. Here is the implementation of our function to generate random Cart IDs:

```
import random

def _generate_cart_id():
    cart_id = ''
    characters = 'ABCDEFGHIJKLMNOPQRSTUVWXYZabcdefghij ↵
        klmnopqrstuvwxyz1234567890!@#$%^&*()'
    cart_id_length = 50
    for y in range(cart_id_length):
        cart_id += characters[random.randint(0, len(characters)-1)]
    return cart_id
```

I should point out that the random module is not actually "random" enough for serious security purposes, but it's random enough for our purposes in trying to make sure two poor shoppers out there don't end up with the exact same Cart ID. Each of our generated Cart IDs is 50 characters in length, and with 72 possible characters for each of the 50, there are 50^{72} possible Cart IDs… which is really a lot of Cart IDs. This makes the likelihood of a collision *extremely* improbable.

Of course, we cannot say with absolute certainty that no two customers will ever end up with same Cart ID, but the chances are so remote that for practical purposes, we don't need to worry about it. You can rest easy knowing that the guy trying to buy a death metal distortion pedal doesn't end up with a harmonica in his cart, and vice versa.

Using Django Forms

When you get right down to it, web developers probably enjoy creating, designing, and testing forms for usability about as much as users enjoy clicking around them. They're clunky, awkward, and there's not a lot of room for creativity. They're a functional requirement. You're users have to be able to add items to a cart and give you their order information, or else you're not going to be able to make any money.

Django has an interesting approach for dealing with forms: create a Python class, much like you did with your models, that represents a form, instantiate one in your view code, and pass it to your template just like you would any other variable.

If that sounds a little odd, don't worry. It is a rather unique approach to creating forms, but once you get used to it, you'll be amazed at the amount of flexibility you have in using them to create forms for your user interface. The first form we're going to create will be the "Add to Cart" form on the product page. It's just a baby, with only a small handful of inputs.

The Add To Cart Form

I mentioned the use of cookies earlier in the chapter. One caveat is that cookies are not always enabled in the user's browser by default. It's very easy for a user to turn them off so a site cannot write cookie values to their machine.

Our site requires that customer's surfing our site must have their browsers configured in order to accept cookies. Since our site requires that cookies be enabled before anyone can add anything to the cart, we need to check to see if cookies are enabled and, if they are disabled, display a message to the customer letting them know that they need to enable cookies in their browser before they can use our site.

This may sound kind of Draconian, like "Turn on your cookies or get lost," and I understand your concern. You don't want to annoy anyone, but if I were you, I wouldn't worry too much. These days, almost *everyone* has their cookies enabled, and almost *every site* requires them. If you don't believe me, go ahead and turn your own cookies off, and try browsing the web for a while. You'll get an error message from just about every reputable site that has a login or a shopping cart.

For the most part, this shouldn't be an issue for you, but you do want to make sure that if any super-paranoid, hacker-fearing customer tries to add something to their cart, they get some feedback about why their attempt to add to the cart didn't work.

As it turns out, Django has the plumbing built right in to test whether cookies are available. You can write a test cookie to the user's browser, which you can then check for to make sure it exists, and delete it when you're done using it.

To write this dummy test cookie, we use the following line of code:

```
request.session.set_test_cookie()
```

Then, when you need to check for that cookie's existence in your code, you use the following function, which will check for the cookie and return `True` if it finds it:

```
request.session.test_cookie_worked()
```

Lastly, you can destroy this dummy cookie with:

```
request.session.delete_test_cookie()
```

We're going to use these three methods in our form code to check if cookies are enabled and, if they aren't, let the user know they can't buy anything from our site until they are enabled.

Go back into your `catalog` app directory and find the file called `forms.py`. Open it up and add the following class definition for our "Add To Cart" form, below the `ProductAdminForm` class:

```python
from django import forms  #this import should already be at the top

class ProductAddToCartForm(forms.Form):
    quantity = forms.IntegerField(widget=forms.TextInput(attrs={'size':'2', ⏎
        'value':'1', 'class':'quantity', 'maxlength':'5'}), ⏎
        error_messages={'invalid':'Please enter a valid quantity.'},
        min_value=1)
    product_slug = forms.CharField(widget=forms.HiddenInput())

    # override the default __init__ so we can set the request
    def __init__(self, request=None, *args, **kwargs):
        self.request = request
        super(ProductAddToCartForm, self).__init__(*args, **kwargs)

    # custom validation to check for cookies
    def clean(self):
        if self.request:
            if not self.request.session.test_cookie_worked():
                raise forms.ValidationError("Cookies must be enabled.")
        return self.cleaned_data
```

Each field definition in the form class is assigned a given field type, based on the type of data you are asking the user for. These fields take a "widget" argument that allows you to control exactly how the input is rendered on the page. As you can see, this is a very simple form that only takes a quantity that the user can input, and a hidden input field that represents our product slug to identify just which product is being added to the cart.

The quantity field will be rendered as a textbox input to the user, with some extra attributes like size, value, and class. We've also specified a custom error message that will be displayed to the user if they try and submit the form with an invalid value.

The hidden input will never be displayed, so we don't have to waste valuable CPU cycles in our brain determining how it should look on the page. We're just going to assign it a value in our view code, just before we pass it to our templates.

Following the field definitions are two function definitions. The first one overrides our form's default *constructor* with its own __init__() function definition, which enables us to pass the current request object into our form instance, so we can check to see if cookies are enabled.

The second function definition, clean(), is called on our form to actually perform the validation. If cookies are disabled in the user's browser and test_cookie_worked() returns False, then we raise a ValidationError with a quick message letting the user know they need to enable cookies to shop our site.

Processing the Form

The HTTP protocol, the one sending web pages from servers to client machines all over the world, uses different verbs in order to process requests. There are two verbs that are in widespread use: GET and POST. These are really not so much like verbs as they are *adverbs*, in that they are defining how we are requesting instead of changing the action itself. The majority of the time, the GET verb is the one being used. When you click a hyperlink and load up a web page with some local news on it, you're doing just that: you're GETting something.

Now, the POST verb is used when you want to do something. It's telling the server to create or modify some resource on the server instead of just passively asking for a web page. Usually, in order to make a POST request to a page, you have to click something with your mouse, like a button that submits a web form to the server.

So what does that have to do with our "Add To Cart" form? Think about how you're going to implement the form for adding items to the cart. You might be thinking it will end up looking something like this:

```
<form action="/add/to/cart/product_slug/" method="post">…etc
```

The problem with this approach is that you've got this funky URL to which you're posting your form, which means that you'll need to set up that URL and map it to a view function, which isn't even really a view function because no one will ever see it. It's just going to process adding to cart and redirect to the cart page when it's done.

We're going to keep out this clutter by having the "Add To Cart" form on the product page post back right onto the product page itself. Just like the scarecrow in *The Wizard of Oz*, we're going to give our view function a *brain*, so that it can differentiate what it does based on whether the request coming in is a GET or a POST. Here's the general idea:

```
def show_product(reqest, product_slug):
    # … more code here …
    if request.method == 'POST':
        # someone's adding to cart…do something here.
    else:
        # just a normal GET request
    # … etc …
```

So if a POST request comes in, we assume that someone just tried to add our product to the cart, then, um… add it, and send them off to the cart page. If it's just a boring old GET, then we do just what the view does now, and display the product page. The flow of this can be tricky to get your head around because you're skipping a whole block of it the first time around, so the whole process just doesn't seem linear.

Don't worry about adding this code to your view right now. We'll get to it in a moment.

Putting It All Together

Okay, now, in order to get our "Add To Cart" form working so that you can start testing your code, we've got to jump around a lot and implement a lot of little things all at once. If you've been skimming the rest of this chapter so far, sit up in your chair and pay attention. This won't take long.

Let's take a quick moment to set up the URLs for our cart app, as well as a dummy "Cart" template that will show up after we've added something to the cart. Open up the urls.py file in the root and add the following line to your patterns tuple:

```
(r'^cart/', include('cart.urls')),
```

Then create a urls.py file within your cart app and add this code to it:

```
from django.conf.urls.defaults import *

urlpatterns = patterns('ecomstore.cart.views',
    (r'^$', 'show_cart', { 'template_name': 'cart/cart.html' }, 'show_cart'),
)
```

Now, we need to create a template for this URL so that it doesn't spit up a TemplateNotFound exception like we got at the end of Chapter 2. We're passing in a variable named template_name, just like in the last chapter, to specify the template our cart page will use.

In your project's templates directory, create a cart subdirectory and a cart.html file that contains the following simple code:

```
{% extends "catalog.html" %}

{% block content %}
    <h1>Cart Page Here</h1>
    Cart item count: {{ cart_item_count }}
{% endblock %}
```

And then, finally, create the view function in views.py:

```
from django.shortcuts import render_to_response
from django.template import RequestContext
from ecomstore.cart import cart

def show_cart(request, template_name="cart/cart.html"):
    cart_item_count = cart.cart_item_count(request)
    page_title = 'Shopping Cart'
    return render_to_response(template_name, locals(),
context_instance=RequestContext(request))
```

It's far from complete, but now, when we add in the "Add To Cart" functionality, it will at least have someplace to go. Now, we're going to create all of those fun cart functions we were talking about earlier. With your project's cart app directory, create a new file, and call it cart.py. Add the following code to this file:

```
from ecomstore.cart.models import CartItem
from ecomstore.catalog.models import Product
from django.shortcuts import get_object_or_404
from django.http import HttpResponseRedirect
```

```python
import decimal    # not needed yet but we will later
import random

CART_ID_SESSION_KEY = 'cart_id'

# get the current user's cart id, sets new one if blank
def _cart_id(request):
    if request.session.get(CART_ID_SESSION_KEY,'') == '':
        request.session[CART_ID_SESSION_KEY] = _generate_cart_id()
    return request.session[CART_ID_SESSION_KEY]

def _generate_cart_id():
    cart_id = ''
    characters = 'ABCDEFGHIJKLMNOPQRSTUVWXYZabcdefghij ⤸
        klmnopqrstuvwxyz1234567890!@#$%^&*()'
    cart_id_length = 50
    for y in range(cart_id_length):
        cart_id += characters[random.randint(0, len(characters)-1)]
    return cart_id

# return all items from the current user's cart
def get_cart_items(request):
    return CartItem.objects.filter(cart_id=_cart_id(request))

# add an item to the cart
def add_to_cart(request):
    postdata = request.POST.copy()
    # get product slug from post data, return blank if empty
    product_slug = postdata.get('product_slug','')
    # get quantity added, return 1 if empty
    quantity = postdata.get('quantity',1)
    # fetch the product or return a missing page error
    p = get_object_or_404(Product, slug=product_slug)
    #get products in cart
    cart_products = get_cart_items(request)
    product_in_cart = False
    # check to see if item is already in cart
    for cart_item in cart_products:
        if cart_item.product.id = p.id:
            # update the quantity if found
            cart_item.augment_quantity(quantity)
            product_in_cart = True
    if not product_in_cart:
        # create and save a new cart item
        ci = CartItem()
        ci.product = p
        ci.quantity = quantity
        ci.cart_id = _cart_id(request)
        ci.save()

# returns the total number of items in the user's cart
def cart_distinct_item_count(request):
    return get_cart_items(request).count()
```

This code is almost twice as long as it really needs to be, because I've commented the *heck* out of it. I'm generally very liberal with my commenting, because a week later, when I have to come back to it and change something, I don't have to decode it all. Also, it helps my co-workers when they're using my code. (At least I think it does.)

The art of commenting your code isn't terribly difficult to get the hang of. My first inclination is to say you should comment liberally, but you can go overboard. The point of commenting your code is not to document it thoroughly, but to explain to those reading your code things about your code that may not be immediately obvious from the code itself. When in doubt, comment your code when you need to explain *why* you're doing something, and avoid too many cases when you're merely explaining *what* your code is doing.

In the last chapter, I didn't use many comments in my code because there wasn't a whole lot of logic in what was happening. There were some Django models and views, and not a whole lot more. But look at the add_to_cart() function. It makes perfect sense to me because I just wrote it, but for the rest of you reading this, it's just a big hairy *mess* without any comments. You're welcome.

First of all, you'll notice that the name of two of our functions start with an underscore (_). If you're coming from the Java or C# camps, you might be familiar with *access modifiers*. These are the keywords you put before function definitions, such as public, private, protected, and so forth, which determine what code can call your functions. The private keyword, for example, ensures that the function can *only* be called by code within the same class.

In Python, there are no such access modifiers, but in practice, if you preface a function name with an underscore, you're telling other developers that the function is only intended to be used within the same module. So, these two functions, while they *can* be called from other files, are only intended to be accessed from other code in your cart.py file.

Now, back to the add_to_cart() method. You see that we create a copy of the data that came in our request object via the POST. We request the product (returning a 404 if the requested one can't be found) and request all of the products in the user's cart. We loop through the cart contents to see if the product is already in the cart. If it is, we just add the quantity to the existing quantity. If not, we create a new cart item, and save it. Next, we need to tweak the views.py file in your catalog app directory so that it can handle this sudden barrage of POST requests we're hoping that it receives from shoppers eagerly filling up their carts. Open that file, and add the following import statements and extra lines to your product page view function. Comment as liberally as you see fit.

```
# this stuff goes at the top of the file, below other imports
from django.core import urlresolvers
from ecomstore.cart import cart
from django.http import HttpResponseRedirect
from ecomstore.cart.forms import ProductAddToCartForm

# new product view, with POST vs GET detection
def show_product(request, product_slug, template_name="catalog/product.html"):
    p = get_object_or_404(Product, slug=product_slug)
    categories = p.categories.all()
    page_title = p.name
    meta_keywords = p.meta_keywords
    meta_description = p.meta_description
    # need to evaluate the HTTP method
    if request.method == 'POST':
        # add to cart…create the bound form
        postdata = request.POST.copy()
        form = ProductAddToCartForm(request, postdata)
        #check if posted data is valid
        if form.is_valid():
            #add to cart and redirect to cart page
```

```
            cart.add_to_cart(request)
            # if test cookie worked, get rid of it
            if request.session.test_cookie_worked():
                request.session.delete_test_cookie()
            url = urlresolvers.reverse('show_cart')
            return HttpResponseRedirect(url)
    else:
        # it's a GET, create the unbound form. Note request as a kwarg
        form = ProductAddToCartForm(request=request, label_suffix=':')
    # assign the hidden input the product slug
    form.fields['product_slug'].widget.attrs['value'] = product_slug
    # set the test cookie on our first GET request
    request.session.set_test_cookie()
    return render_to_response("catalog/product.html", locals(), ⏎
        context_instance=RequestContext(request))
```

Here, we put the new product page form we coded earlier into action. You'll notice that we create a new variable, simply called form. If this request is coming from a POST request, we pass the accompanying post data into the creation of the form variable, which binds the values the user submitted to the form. An unbound form will have a value of "1" (we specified that when we wrote the code for the form class earlier in the chapter), but a bound form will display the value that the user submitted. So, if they enter "5" and submit the form, the value of "5" will be retained instead of being reset to "1." In this particular case, this will only matter when there's a validation error and the page is redisplayed to the user.

Then, we ask Django to validate the form via the form.is_valid() method call. If the user entered any value that isn't a number, or if the user has cookies disabled, then our form class will raise an "invalid" error and display our custom error message.

However, if the form *is* valid, we delete the test cookie, add the item to the cart, and then redirect the user to the cart page. We do this using a built-in Django function:

```
url = urlresolvers.reverse('show_cart')
```

This reverse() method looks through your project's list of URLs and returns the matching one. The show_cart value corresponds to the fourth parameter in your URL, the one that comes *after* the dictionary. In this case, the name of our view function is also show_cart... but the reverse() method is looking at the fourth parameter in your urls.py module.

And finally, whether or not the HTTP request verb is GET or POST, we set the hidden input in our form to match the product slug.

```
form.fields['product_slug'].widget.attrs['value'] = product_slug
```

So now you can rest easy knowing that you can access, and manipulate, the values of your forms programmatically.

Okay, we're almost done here. The last step is to add the form variable to your product template. Open the product.html file inside of your templates/catalog directory and find the line reading [add to cart button]. Replace that code with the following:

```
<form method="post" action="." class="cart">
    {{ form.as_p }}
    <br />
    <input type="submit" value="Add To Cart" name="submit" alt="Add To Cart" />
</form>
<div class="cb"></div>
```

And that's all you need. Notice that the *entire* form isn't built for us… we still need to create the opening and closing form elements, and the input still needs to be added by hand. But as for the other inputs, you just call the as_p() method on your form variable (notice that the parentheses are omitted when you call methods on variables in templates) and it renders the inputs in your form class in the way that you specified your "widget" arguments.

Have a closer look here. Go ahead and fire up a product page in a browser. Not much has changed, but you should see something that looks like Figure 4-1.

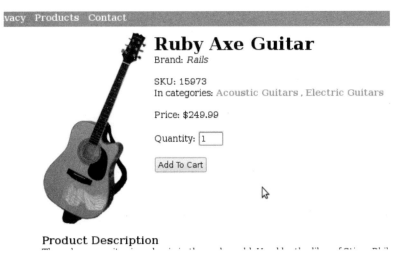

Figure 4-1. *Our product page with the new "Add To Cart" form.*

Okay, now, I think this is really cool: have a look at the source of the "Add to Cart" form, and look at the two inputs that were generated by the as_p() method. You'll notice that these were created and wrapped in a set of <p></p> elements. If you want more control over how these inputs are displayed, you can also call the as_table() or as_ul() methods if you want them to be rendered differently.

The neat thing here is that, as far accessibility goes, Django has done *exactly* the right thing. People who use screen readers and other assistive technologies may have trouble with the following HTML input on a form:

```
<p>Quantity: <input type="text" value="1" /></p>
```

The problem with this HTML is that a screen reader has absolutely *no* way of figuring out that the input textbox next to the text "Quantity:" is the input for the quantity. Sure, users can guess at it, but they really have no way of being certain. And this doesn't even take into account situations where there are dozens of input fields on a single page, all mashed into some messy HTML table, and the screen reader is reading all of this garbage to the poor user, who has to really work to figure out which input is which.

The solution is to use the following syntax:

```
<label for="quantity">Quantity</label><input type="text" id="quantity" value="1" />
```

In this example, the for attribute of the label and the id attribute of the input are matched up so that screen readers can clearly communicate to the user exactly which input they're using. And, as you can see in your product page's source, Django has constructed the quantity form input using just this syntax. Yay!

So, go ahead and add one of your products to the cart. You should be taken to the cart page and see that you have one item in the cart. You can go back and test adding as many as you like. Just remember that if you keep adding the same product, this count won't augment, as it's counting product types in the cart, and individual items.

Make sure you also try and enter an invalid number, or disable cookies in your browser, and then click the "Add To Cart" button. You should see the product page redisplayed, with the error message telling you to enter a valid quantity. The problem here is that the message doesn't really reveal itself, since it's just black text on white. It looks like the rest of the product page.

If you look at the source of this error message, you should see:

```
<ul class="errorlist">
    <li>Please enter a valid quantity.</li>
</ul>
```

Well, we can solve that problem by styling it. Open up your project's CSS file and add the following line of CSS code:

```
/* style for Django error messages */
ul.errorlist{
    background-color:Red;color:White;
}
```

Now, your error message should really jump at the user, as it appears in Figure 4-2. The new styles will make them realize that there's an error that they need to fix.

Figure 4-2. *The new styled error message on display.*

Cart Form Code in Review

Okay, so we just jumped all around and added code to a bunch of different places. I wouldn't be at all surprised if you were completely lost about what's happening. Sure, maybe your code is working, but maybe you're not entirely sure *how*. Or maybe it isn't working, and you don't have the slightest clue how to start debugging it.

Let's quickly walk through the steps of the user experience:

1. The user navigates to a product page from somewhere else, via a GET request. An unbound form is created and passed to the template, and shown to the user with a default value of 1. At this point, we also write the dummy test cookie to the browser.

2. The user, because they were dropped on their head several times as a child, enters "B" into the quantity box and tries adding to the cart. Our product view detects the POST, but the form is invalid, because "B" is not a valid value for an IntegerField in the form. The error message is displayed.

3. The user fixes their mistakes and adds a quantity of "2" quantity and resubmits. The product view detects the POST, validates the form, and then calls the add_to_cart() function in our cart.py module, passing in our product slug.

4. "Add To Cart" requests the current user's Cart ID. Because it doesn't exist, a new one is generated and set in the session. It returns this to the adding-to-cart operation in progress.

5. After the item is added to the cart, the user is redirected to the cart page. Right now, they only see the number of products in their cart.

If you're getting any kind of error, try and trace through the flow of the code and find where the error is occurring. Try commenting out a block around the area where you think the error is happening and see if you can get it to throw a *different* error, which might provide an additional clue about what's wrong.

Otherwise, let's move right along and code up the view for the shopping cart page.

Creating the Shopping Cart Page

For the most part, our shopping cart will be little more than just a single HTML table that we're going to use to display the list of items in our cart. While HTML tables were long ago phased out for site layout in the interest of simplicity, maintainability, and (most importantly) accessibility, HTML tables are still the best option when you need to display a grid of information on a single web page.

Even though a single HTML table is still pretty straightforward, we are going to add a few things to the markup of our table that you might have never seen before, in the interest of making the cart page as *accessible* as possible to everyone. The HTML of our shopping cart table will have six columns, and look something like this:

```
<table summary="Your Shopping Cart" id="shopping_cart">
    <caption>Your Shopping Cart</caption>
    <thead>
        <!-- header info here -->
        <th scope="col">Product</th>
        <!-- …etc… -->
    </thead>
    <tfoot>
        <!-- footer info here -->
    </tfoot>
    <tbody>
    <! - - loop through cart items here -->
    </tbody>
</table>
```

We're making use of three things here. First, we're creating a caption element within our table so that it's officially labeled. This is akin to the <label for=""></label> markup for each form input. It helps people using assistive technologies identify the contents of the table as their shopping cart.

Also, each th element in the table will have its scope attribute set to col. This way, when screen readers are reading out the contents of the table, they will preface the contents of each cell with the header information. So, as it reads through the cart items, it will sound like: "Product. Ruby Axe Guitar. Price. $249.99." It's one very tiny addition to our table that helps make our cart page much more usable.

Lastly, we're using the thead, tfoot, and tbody elements so that the header, footer, and content information of the table are explicitly identified in the markup.

Django Template 'if' and 'for' Tags

In the last chapter, we already got a look at both of these template tags in action, and as a programmer, you're probably already intuitively familiar with how these work. It's very possible that the designer touching your template files will have no programming background. If this is the case, the bare minimum is that the graphic designer/CSS guru who's designing the markup code for your site at least needs to understand the Django template syntax, and what the {% if %} and {% for %} tags do.

Django {% if %} tags allow your templates to handle conditional logic. This is most commonly used when you want to check for the existence of a variable and, if it exists, display it on the page. On our shopping cart page, we're going to use the {% if %} statement tags in a couple of places. First, we're going to check and see if there are any items in the user's shopping cart. If there are, we're going to list them. If not, we'll instead display a friendly "Hi, your cart is empty" message letting them know they haven't added anything yet.

Also, if you refer back to the functional spec that I coughed up at the beginning of this chapter, you'll notice that we want to display a link to the checkout page *only* if there are items in the cart. Again, the {% if %} tag will come to the rescue here as well. There is also a corresponding {% else %} tag that you can use inside of a block of {% if %} tags.

The Django {% for %} tag is used to iterate through sets of items. Our list of shopping cart items is just such a group of items that we want to run through, one at a time, and roll them out as rows inside of our table.

There's not much more to it than that. In a moment, we'll see both of these in action inside the Django template/HTML code for our cart page.

Custom Template Filters

Django *template filters* are a powerful way for us to control the appearance of our output directly inside our template code. There are a ton of template filters that come with Django by default, and it's well worth your trouble to have a look at the Django documentation so that you know which ones are available for your use. Among the more important ones are those for encoding or stripping HTML (to prevent cross-site scripting attacks), converting text to all upper- or lowercase, taking operations on sets or groups, or formatting strings. We already used one of these in the last chapter, the pluralize filter that customizes the display of a word based on a numeric value (for example, "category" versus "categories" on the product page).

If any of the default filters don't do what you want, you are free to create your own. Since we're creating an e-commerce site, I already feel myself putting dollar signs ($) all over the site, which might be fine for the moment, but will pose a problem for us when we want to start selling stuff in other countries. To make sure that our site propagates as needed, we're going to create a custom "currency" filter for displaying price information.

In order to create a custom template filter, we just need to create a Python function definition that takes a value as an argument, and returns a string to display in our template. This function just needs to be in a directory called templatetags inside one of our project's installed apps. Go ahead and create this folder inside your project's catalog app, and add two files to it: __init__.py, and catalog_filters.py. The first, of course, is the obligatory empty file that merely identifies your directory as a Python package. The second will contain our code. Add the following to catalog_filters.py:

```
from django import template
import locale

register = template.Library()

@register.filter(name='currency')
def currency(value):
    try:
        locale.setlocale(locale.LC_ALL,'en_US.UTF-8')
    except:
        locale.setlocale(locale.LC_ALL,'')
    loc = locale.localeconv()
    return locale.currency(value, loc['currency_symbol'], grouping=True)
```

I'm using a very useful part of the standard Python distribution, called locale, which is used for formatting and displaying currency values based on the locale that is set by our code. The preceding function definition will use a comma to separate dollar values by the thousands, and use a dollar sign for the currency symbol. We use decorators to register our filter with the template system using the Python decorator syntax and name it currency.

I have to admit that before I found the locale module in Python, I spent about a half-hour trying to design my own custom solution to this problem. Never underestimate the resourcefulness of the Python community. Keep in mind that if you dig deep enough, you can probably find a solution to your problem somewhere on the Internet.

■ **Note** The locale module is dependent upon the locales that have been configured with your operating system. If you run into problems with the preceding code, you may need to take explicit steps to set these up on your system. On Unix systems, you may trying running the following as root locale-gen en_US.UTF-8 to configure the locale.

In order to use the filter in our template, we just need to load it inside our template file, with the following line of code at the top of the file (but make sure it's *below* the extends directive. That must always come first!):

```
{% load catalog_filters %}
```

The load directive is the Django template equivalent of the Python import statements at the top of your Python files. It scans through all of the templatetags subdirectories that it finds in your project's list of installed apps, and loads in any custom template tags or filters that it finds.

After you're finished with the cart page, go back into your product page template file and add your new currency filter. You just need to add the {% load %} directive and add the filter to any price you're displaying on the page.

Creating the Cart Page

Open up your CSS file and add the following style definitions for your shopping cart table:

```
/* styles for shopping cart page */
table#shopping_cart{
```

```
        width:100%;
        border-collapse:collapse;
        color:#616161;
}
h1,caption{
        text-align:left;
        font-size:x-large;
        margin-bottom:15px;
        color:Black;
}
th,td{
        text-align:left;
        padding:3px;
}
thead th{
        color:White;
        background-color:#616161;
}
tfoot th{
        height:40px;
}

table#shopping_cart th.right, td.right{
        text-align:right;
}
a.cart{
        color:DarkOrange;
}
```

Then, open up your cart template that you create earlier and replace what's in there with the following markup:

```
{% extends "catalog.html" %}

{% load catalog_filters %}

{% block content %}
<table summary="Your Shopping Cart" id="shopping_cart">
    <caption>Your Shopping Cart</caption>
    <thead>
    <tr>
        <th scope="col">Product</th>
        <th scope="col">Price</th>
        <th></th>
        <th></th>
        <th></th>
        <th scope="col" class="right">Total</th>
    </tr>
    </thead>
    <tfoot>
    <tr>
        <th class="right" colspan="5">
        Cart Subtotal:
```

```
            </th>
        <th class="right">
            {{ cart_subtotal|currency }}
        </th>
    </tr>
    {% if cart_items %}
    <tr>
        <th class="right" colspan="6">
            <a href="/url/to/checkout/">Checkout Now</a>
        </th>
    </tr>
    {% endif %}
    </tfoot>
    <tbody>
    {% if cart_items %}
        {% for item in cart_items %}
        <tr>
        <td>
            <a href="{{ item.get_absolute_url }}" class="cart">
            {{ item.name }}
            </a>
        </td>
        <td>{{ item.price|currency }}</td>
        <td class="right">
        <form method="post" action="." class="cart">
        <label for="quantity">Quantity:</label>
        <input type="text" name="quantity" value="{{ item.quantity }}" id="quantity" ⤵
            size="2" class="quantity" maxlength="5" />
        <input type="hidden" name="item_id" value="{{ item.id }}" />
        </td>
        <td>
        <input type="submit" name="submit" value="Update" />
        </form>
        </td>
        <td>
        <form method="post" action="." class="cart">
        <input type="hidden" name="item_id" value="{{ item.id }}" />
        <input type="submit" name="submit" value="Remove"/>
        </form>
        </td>
        <td class="right">{{ item.total|currency }}</td>
    </tr>
    {% endfor %}
    {% else %}
    <tr>
        <td colspan="6" style="height:30px;">
        Your cart is empty.
        </td>
    </tr>
    {% endif %}
    </tbody>
</table>
{% endblock %}
```

The indentation in this code is somewhat mashed, for the sake of preserving space. You can see that we're using our new currency filter function definition for all of our prices. Before you start trying to type that in, have a look at Figure 4-3, so you have so idea of what it's supposed to look like.

Notice that we've got two forms for each line item that have a POST method that post back to the cart page. That means that we're going to handle these processing requests in our view function, right? Exactly.

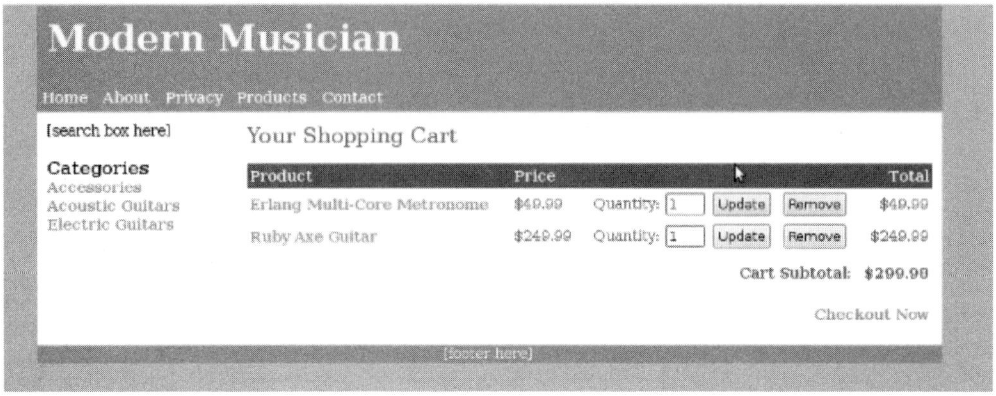

Figure 4-3. *Our cart page, with items ready for purchase.*

With the template and corresponding styles in place, we can now turn our attention on the last bit of code we need to write, which is our view code and the corresponding functions in our cart.py module. Open up your views.py file and change the show_cart() view function so that it looks like this:

```
def show_cart(request, template_name="cart/cart.html"):
    if request.method == 'POST':
        postdata = request.POST.copy()
        if postdata['submit'] == 'Remove':
            cart.remove_from_cart(request)
        if postdata['submit'] == 'Update':
            cart.update_cart(request)
    cart_items = cart.get_cart_items(request)
    page_title = 'Shopping Cart'     cart_subtotal = cart.cart_subtotal(request)
    return render_to_response(template_name, locals(), ↵
        context_instance=RequestContext(request))
```

And lastly, add the following four function definitions to the cart.py module, so that our view code actually has some corresponding code to call:

```
def get_single_item(request, item_id):
    return get_object_or_404(CartItem, id=item_id, cart_id=_cart_id(request))

# update quantity for single item
def update_cart(request):
    postdata = request.POST.copy()
    item_id = postdata['item_id']
    quantity = postdata['quantity']
    cart_item = get_single_item(request, item_id)
    if cart_item:
```

```
        if int(quantity) > 0:
            cart_item.quantity = int(quantity)
            cart_item.save()
        else:
            remove_from_cart(request)

# remove a single item from cart
def remove_from_cart(request):
    postdata = request.POST.copy()
    item_id = postdata['item_id']
    cart_item = get_single_item(request, item_id)
    if cart_item:
        cart_item.delete()

# gets the total cost for the current cart
def cart_subtotal(request):
    cart_total = decimal.Decimal('0.00')
    cart_products = get_cart_items(request)
    for cart_item in cart_products:
        cart_total += cart_item.product.price * cart_item.quantity
    return cart_total
```

You should be starting to get the hang of the flow at work here, and hopefully, the preceding code is making some sense to you. Most of the code in our `cart.py` module is stuff that would have been put in the would-be "cart" model, if we had chosen to create two separate models. For example, one of the preceding methods, `cart_subtotal()`, is returning the subtotal of the user's cart for display on the page. Logically, this would have gone in the cart model if we had created one, and we would call this method on the instance of our user's cart.

Have a look at the forms that are on the cart page. Here, I've opted to build them from scratch instead of coding up Django form classes to create them for us. One of them takes one quantity input, very similar to our product page, and updates the quantity in the cart. If the quantity is zero on an update submission, than we simply delete the item from the cart. The other form contains a `Remove` input that removes the item from the cart.

Adding Custom Template Tags

One last thing that we need to add is a link somewhere at the top of the page that links to the cart, so our browsing users are free to check out whenever they would like. We're going to create a custom Django template tag to contain our "Link to Cart" box. We'll have this information display at the top right in the banner, inside an absolutely positioned div element. Create a new include template file called `cart_box.html` inside your project's `template/tags` directory. Add the following markup to it:

```
{% with cart_item_count as cart_count %}
    <a href="{% url show_cart %}">
        Shopping Cart
        <br />
        {{ cart_count }} Item{{ cart_count|pluralize }}
    </a>
{% endwith %}
```

Remember when we used the built-in `urlresolvers.reverse()` method to fetch the URL location of the cart page? Turns out, you can use a Django template {% url %} tag to achieve the same thing in your templates. We pass it the string `show_cart` and it finds the corresponding URL definition in our `urls.py` modules. Pretty slick, eh?

We're also using a new Django tag: {% with %}. The Django {% with %} tag allows you to give a variable an alias and cache it in the template, so that your database isn't hit with the query to get the number of items in the cart each time a new page is loaded. Here, we're assigning the value of `cart_item_count` to a variable called `cart_count`, and using that variable in our actual template code.

Lastly on the template side of things, we need to load our new templates and insert the tag in the appropriate spot. Add the following line of code near the top of your template:

```
{% load catalog_tags %}
```

And then add this to your `catalog.html`, inside the `cart_box` div:

```
<div class="cart_box">
    {% cart_box request %}
</div>
```

Here, we're calling on our new `cart_box` template tag and passing in the current `request` object as a variable. Now we get to the *real* Django magic. Inside your catalog app's `templatetags` directory, right alongside your `catalog_filters.py` module, create a new module called `catalog_tags.py`. This file will contain the functions for our template tags. Open up `catalog_tags.py` and add in the following lines of Django code:

```
from django import template
from ecomstore.cart import cart

register = template.Library()

@register.inclusion_tag("tags/cart_box.html")
def cart_box(request):
    cart_item_count = cart.cart_distinct_item_count(request)
    return {'cart_item_count': cart_item_count }
```

In the `inclusion_tag()` function call, you pass in the name of the template file you want to use, which in our case is the `cart_box.html` file we just created. Our template function tags the `request` object as a parameter (which we passed in our use of the tag in the template) and then returns a Python dictionary of variables that our template will be able to use. You can see that this is how our template is getting the `cart_item_count` variable we aliased and used in our actual template file.

With these simple changes, we now have a link to our Shopping Cart page on every page of our site, which also tells the user how many distinct products are in their cart. We're also making good use of the Django `pluralize` template filter and the excellent {% with %} tag.

	Price				Total
re Metronome	$49.99	Quantity: 1	Update	Remove	$49.99
	$249.99	Quantity: 1	Update	Remove	$249.99

Figure 4-4. Site banner, now with cart page link.

Re-creating the Category List Tag

Keep that new catalog_tags.py file open, because we're not done with it quite yet. We can apply this same template tag logic to the list of categories that we're using in the sidebar of each page, and, at the same time, make a couple of improvements. First, we can use this new {% with %} tag to cache our list of categories and save a hit to the database on each one. On top of that, we'll set up some logic so that if the user is currently on a category page, we'll deactivate the link to give the user a small visual cue about where they are.

As long you've got it open, add the following code to your catalog_tags.py file:

```python
from ecomstore.catalog.models import Category

@register.inclusion_tag("tags/category_list.html")
def category_list(request_path):
    active_categories = Category.objects.filter(is_active=True)
    return {
        'active_categories': active_categories,
        'request_path': request_path
    }
```

Now, open up the category_list.html file you created back in Chapter 3 and change its contents to the following:

```html
<h3>Categories</h3>
<ul id="categories">
{% with active_categories as cats %}
    {% for c in cats %}
    <li>
    {% ifequal c.get_absolute_url request_path %}
        {{ c.name }}<br />
    {% else %}
        <a href="{{ c.get_absolute_url }}" class="category">{{ c.name }}</a><br />
    {% endifequal %}
    </li>
```

```
    {% endfor %}
{% endwith %}
</ul>
```

Here, on top of the {% with %} tag again, we're also using a new template tag, the {% ifequal %} tag, which takes two parameters, compares them, and returns True if they have the same value. As you can see, the function takes the current request.path (in a variable called request_path) and compares it with the get_absolute_url() returned by our category. If the two are equal, that means the user is on that particular category page, and we deactivate the link to just be plain text.

There are some CSS styles that go along with this. Add these to your CSS file:

```
h3{
      background-color:#98AC5E;
      color:White;
      padding:3px;
      margin-bottom:6px;
}

ul#categories{
      list-style:none;
}
ul#categories li{
      font-weight:bold;
      color:#616161;
}
ul#categories li a{
      text-decoration:underline;
}

div#footer a{
      color:White;
      font-size:small;
      text-decoration:underline;
      font-weight:normal;
      margin-right:10px;
}
```

And finally, we just need to tweak the catalog.html file so that our site uses our new template tag instead of the include tag we created before. Find this line:

```
{% include 'tags/category_list.html' %}
```

and change it to this:

```
{% category_list request.path %}
```

You're all set. Your category link list at the side of the site now has its data call and functionality neatly wrapped up in one template file and one template function. At this point, you can go back to your context_processors.py file in your catalog app and remove the variable active_categories from your return dictionary, as you don't need this to be called here anymore.

Static Content with Flatpages

In the next chapter, we're going to create the site checkout and order processing system, and before we do that, we need to set up a bunch of pages with static HTML content on them. Customers who shop online, particularly at small sites, will be interested in your organization's *privacy policy*. People want to be reassured that you're not going to hand out their e-mail and phone number to every spammer on the planet, who will then try to contact them at every possible opportunity to buy a renewal on the warranty on their vehicle which is about to expire, and what have you.

There are lots of other pages you might want to create, such as a "Contact" or "About" page, for which we set up placeholders in Chapter 2 in our `navigation.html` file. You might also need to create a "Return Policy" page so that your customers can be reassured that they'll be taken care of in the event that their product ends up being broken on arrival, or any of the other things that can go wrong during shipping.

The need for these static pages, that will only contain a header and some basic text as content, is a very wide one. Since it's such a common requirement for most sites, Django comes equipped with an app called `flatpages` that is designed to help you create simple static pages.

Hooking up the `flatpages` app is just as simple as adding the app to your project. Open your `settings.py` file and add the following line to your `INSTALLED_APPS` tuple:

```
'django.contrib.flatpages',
```

Then, add this line to your `MIDDLEWARE_CLASSES` section:

```
'django.contrib.flatpages.middleware.FlatpageFallbackMiddleware',
```

Finally, run the `manage.py syncdb` utility in order to set up your database tables for the models:

```
$ python manage.py syncdb
```

If that runs successfully, you can now add static pages to your admin interface. Go ahead and fire up `http://localhost:8000/admin/` in a browser window, log in, and notice that there's now a section of your admin interface named "Flat pages."

Before we jump into that, notice that there's also another section called "Sites" that we've ignored so far. Go ahead and click on this, and you should see one site listed as `example.com`. Let's go ahead and change that information to match our own site. Click that domain name and you'll be taken to an edit screen where you can change the domain name and the display name of your site. Go ahead and put in your information, as I have in Figure 4-5.

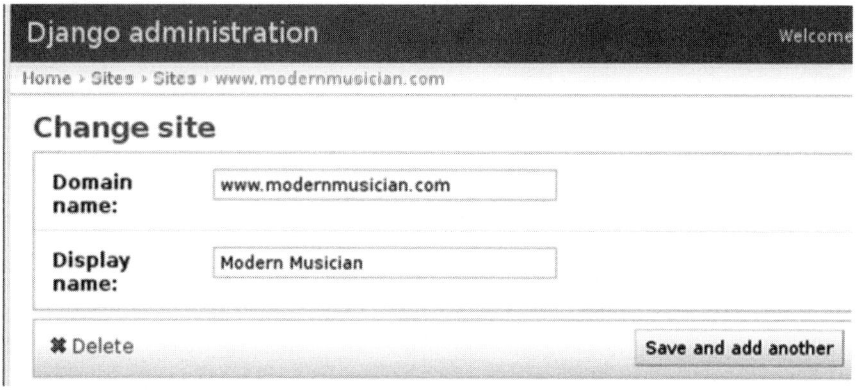

Figure 4-5. *Editing the site domain and display name.*

Now, click back to the admin interface homepage and go into the "Flatpages" section. Click the "Add Flat Page" button at the top right and you'll be taken to a form that asks you for four things: a url where the site should reside, a title, content, and the choice of a site in a select box, which should now contain your own domain information.

Enter in some values for a test page. I'm going to put in my site's contact page information, as shown in Figure 4-6.

Figure 4-6. *Add a Contact static flatpage.*

When you're choosing URLs for your flatpages, you'll want to be careful to avoid entering URLs that are used by other pages. Also, make sure you select the site in the select box or else you'll get an error when you try to click "Save." Under the "Advanced Options" tab, you can specify the exact name of the template that will be used to render the page, but in our case, we're just going to fall back on the default template.

Save this page, and you should be taken back to a page that lists your flatpages, of which there is just one. Feel free to create a bunch more pages for your project.

After you're done adding pages, go back to your project files. In your project's `templates` directory, create a subdirectory called `flatpages` and create a single file called `default.html`. This is the file that the flatpage module will use in rendering each page. Put the following code into the `flatpages/default.html` file:

```
{% extends "catalog.html" %}

{% block title %}
    {{ flatpage.title }} - {{ site_name }}
{% endblock %}

{% block content %}
    <h1>{{ flatpage.title }}</h1>
    {{ flatpage.content }}
{% endblock %}
```

As you can see, we're overriding the site title block with our own content, where we inject the page title manually. The content is little more than just a header with the title, and contains the content for this page below it.

Navigation Tags

While we're at all of this, let's create an inclusion tag for our footer, which will be a list of links that includes all of our new flatpages. Inside your project's `templates/tags` directory, create a file called `footer.html` and enter the following template code:

```
<a href="{% url catalog_home %}">Home</a>
{% with flatpage_list as pages %}
    {% for page in pages %}
        <a href="{{ page.url }}">{{ page.title }}</a>
    {% endfor %}
{% endwith %}
<a href="{% url show_cart %}">Shopping Cart</a>
```

This contains a link to the homepage, the shopping cart page, and between them, lists all of your flatpages. Then, inside your `catalog_tags.py`, enter the following code:

```
from django.contrib.flatpages.models import FlatPage

@register.inclusion_tag("tags/footer.html")
def footer_links():
    flatpage_list = FlatPage.objects.all()
    return {'flatpage_list': flatpage_list }
```

Lastly, inside your `catalog.html` template, change the placeholder line of text:

```
[footer here]
```

to this custom tag:

```
{% footer_links %}
```

Now we have a footer with actual navigable content that includes any flatpage we might end up adding in the future.

For the navigation at the top, I'm not going to go crazy and create another Django inclusion tag. Truth be told, we're probably going to want to be able to control the list and ordering of the navigation at the top manually. Since we'll want this level of control, let's merely edit the existing `navigation.html` file in the tags directory, and edit our list of links:

```
<ul>
    <li><a href="{% url catalog_home %}">Home</a></li>
    <li><a href="/about/">About</a></li>
    <li><a href="/privacy-policy/">Privacy</a></li>
    <li><a href="/contact/">Contact</a></li>
</ul>
<div class="cb"></div>
```

You may have to change this list a little bit to match your own flatpages. With this in place, fire up a browser and see how the site looks now. My contact page looks like Figure 4-7, which, with the exception of the search box placeholder text, is looking just about complete.

Figure 4-7. Our completed Contact page, courtesy of the Flatpages app.

Summary

The site is coming together very nicely. We now have a functional catalog with a working shopping cart! The rest of the site certainly looks like it's ready to be deployed pretty soon (save for, perhaps, my choice of the orange and green color scheme).

If you've been following along at home, and making your own customizations to the code as you go, now would be the perfect time for the first round of usability testing. Go grab someone you know, in your home or at work, sit them down, and ask them to shop your site. Tell them to find some products they like, add them to the cart, and then update or remove them on the cart page. Go on, do it. You might find something terribly wrong with the design of my UI. I don't care if you're out alone reading and working on this at Starbucks on your laptop… go ask that barista you think is really cute, that you just *haven't* had the *guts* to ask out, if they can take five minutes out of their busy drink-making day to help you out with this little project you've been working on. See if there's anything about our site so far that they're unable to figure out how to make work. Then consider fixing it. For larger sites, such informal usability testing this early on in the process might not be sufficient…but getting some feedback at this point couldn't hurt matters.

In the next chapter, we're going to go the extra mile and create an order creation system for our site, so customers can check out with their shopping carts. Then, we'll integrate our little site with payment processing gateways so customers can actually start paying for the items that they order.

CHAPTER 5

■ ■ ■

Site Checkout & Orders

We're almost at the tipping point for our online catalog site. Customers can shop, they can put stuff into a cart, but the final piece of the puzzle is still lacking: checkout. Without a way to collect orders and payments from customers, our site is never going to be able to send merchandise to customers and won't ever turn a single cent of profit.

This is the problem we're going to correct in this chapter. First, we're going to implement a quick integration with Google Checkout, where customers shop on your site and then are forwarded to the Google Checkout service to provide their billing information. This lets your customers use their Google accounts securely, and is the quickest solution if you're looking to deploy your site in a hurry. Google Checkout provides merchants with an interface that allows you to manage orders easily.

Next, we'll look at integrating our site with Authorize.Net, customizing the checkout process so that customers can complete the checkout process right on our own site, and use the admin interface we saw in Chapter 3 in order to manage order processing. We'll also look at how to hook in a Secure Sockets Layer (SSL) to our checkout pages to secure the information we're transmitting using some custom middleware created by the Python and Django community.

Google Checkout API

To start with, we're going to go the express route and hook in to the Google Checkout API. The customers on our site will browse the products in our catalog, add them to a shopping cart, and review their purchases on our shopping cart page. Then, when they're ready to checkout, we forward them to Google Checkout, where they can use their own Google account to log in and pay, or they can checkout anonymously.

So is this really a good idea? I've overheard lots of people talk about how *unprofessional* it seems when you're shopping on a site, filling up a cart, and when you go to checkout, you're redirected to some third-party web site to handle the checkout. I agree that this *can* be a bad idea. It can be a terrible idea, depending on how you implement it, and the company that you choose to use.

I think that one of the main advantages of relying on a third-party site to handle your checkout process is because people are really unsure of themselves when it comes to computers and security in general. Next time you turn on the television, notice how many credit card commercials there are trying to scare the living daylights out of people. One of them uses imagery of thousands of Vikings attacking as a metaphor for identity theft, which means… um, I don't know.

But the point is that identity theft is not unknown to the general public. Most Internet users are acutely aware that giving their credit card information is not a trivial thing to do, so they tend to be very careful about to whom they provide this information.

So, there is an advantage here, but it's an advantage that we gain *only* if the third-party processor that you choose has more credibility than us. People might not trust Modern Musician enough for them to give us their credit card information, but if we decide to forward them to some dippy, obscure checkout system of which they've likely never heard, like the Two Guys in their Mom's Basement Checkout, Inc., then it's not very likely that they're going to trust *them* with their personal information, and in this case, we've gained absolutely *nothing*.

My guess is that people trust Google. They've got corporate brand recognition, tons of street cred in the Internet community, and I'm convinced their employees are out helping old ladies cross streets or selling cookies door-to-door for some really good cause. People get that warm fuzzy feeling with Google. It's very unlikely any of your customers are going to be put off when they go to checkout and *Google* pops up. This has the added benefit of letting your customers use already existing accounts that they've created with Google, and use credit cards that they've stored with Google, which is undoubtedly a healthy portion of overall Internet users.

After the customer completes the checkout and the credit card is processed, Google will store the information for each order, and provide an interface that will let you manage and fulfill the orders. It's nothing fancy, but it's perfect for a small operation shipping items from a backroom or very small warehouse.

Of course, it's also worth mentioning that the use of this service isn't free. Google does take a small chunk of each sale for their trouble. As your site and your sales grow, then outsourcing your checkout process to a third-party probably will, and should, be a placeholder for your own checkout solution later on. For much smaller sites that need to get up and running right now, though, it's the simplest solution to the checkout problem.

Let's get started.

Signing up with Google Checkout

The first thing we need to do is sign up for a merchant account with the Google Checkout API. To do this, you just need to sign up for a Google Checkout Merchant Account. If you have a business entity or business contact information, keep it handy. You're going to need to provide one of three things: either an Employer Identification Number, a credit card number and a Social Security number, or just a credit card number. Don't worry, they won't charge you until you have a full account and they have a valid reason for doing so.

You'll want to make sure that initially, for development purposes, you opt to create a sandbox account. A sandbox account allows you to test your code by putting in test credit card numbers that Google will process and log like regular orders in their Merchant interface, so you can test that your Python code is working correctly. Later, when you're ready to actually take real orders, you can switch the account from a sandbox account to a live one that will actually process payments.

Let's take a moment to set up a sandbox account with Google Checkout.[1] Click the "Sign up now" button and you'll be taken to a screen where you can start creating your account. Make sure when you're signing up that slanted red text appears in the background reading "Sandbox. This is a system for merchants to test Google Checkout."

On this sign up form, follow the instructions. You'll need to create a Google Account or, if you already have one you're using for AdWords or Gmail and would like to use that account for the Merchant API, then enter that information. If not, create a Google Account with them now.

From here, you'll be taken to a page where you'll be asked to provide your company information, contact information, and the nature and name of your site. They'll also ask you for your financial information at this point. Again, don't sweat it. They won't be charging you for anything without a good

---

[1] https://sandbox.google.com/checkout/sell/

reason, and as long as you have a sandbox account, such a reason shouldn't come up. Remember to read, and comply with, the Google Checkout Terms of service before completing the sign-up process.

After finishing the sign-up, you should be taken to your Merchant Account home, which should also have that red "Sandbox…" message tiling the background, in order to reassure you that the development we're doing right now is all just pretend, and nobody is going to charge you money yet. It should look like Figure 5-1.

Figure 5-1. *The Google Checkout home, politely demanding my bank information.*

Before we get started coding, you might want to have a look at the developer documentation for the Google Checkout XML API,[2] which is the API that we'll be taking advantage of when building our site.

Submitting Orders to Google

In order to have Google process our orders for us, we need to supply Google with the cart contents of each of our customers when they go to checkout. There are two ways of doing this. First, you can embed an XML version of the cart and our Google Checkout Merchant Key as encoded hidden inputs in a form that posts to the Google API, or you can use your server to create the request in Python code and post it to Google that way.

There are a couple of large drawbacks with the first approach. First, anyone who views the source of your cart page will be able to see your Merchant Key right in the clear. Second, the encoded version of the cart is right in the page and is submitted as part of the form, which means that it's very easy for people to tamper with values when the form is submitted. While this is unlikely to invite too much trouble, we're going to play it safe and take the second approach here. After the user clicks the "Checkout" button on our shopping cart page, our server code is going to start whirring and perform a few simple steps:

1. Create an XML version of the contents of the user's shopping cart.

2. Create an HTTP request object to *post* to Google's XML API.

---

[2] http://code.google.com/apis/checkout/developer/

3. Add headers to the request, one of which is an authorization value we'll create from our Google Checkout Merchant info so that Google can validate that we made the request.

4. Post the request to Google's API and get back the XML response.

5. Parse the URL out of the XML response and redirect the user to this URL, where the user will find a Google Checkout page, with their cart's contents, waiting for them.

6. The customer completes the checkout and we get money for our order. This is the point at which, as a celebratory gesture, everyone would throw their hats into the air.

In step #5, it's important to note that once we dump the user into the Google Checkout process, they can see the contents of their cart, but they cannot alter the cart at that point. We have to make sure that the user does not click the checkout button until after they've reviewed their cart.

The most difficult part is building the XML request to post to Google's API, which is kind of tedious when you do it all in Python code. Tedious, but not difficult. If you've ever built an XML document in code, you probably know exactly what I'm talking about. Let's take a gander at that whole process now.

Building XML Documents in Python

XML is a means of formatting text in a self-describing, easy-to-read manner that has the bonus of being transferrable across different platforms. Google Checkout accepts a user shopping cart built as an XML document, which means that almost any site, no matter what technology is behind it, can construct this simple text document and submit the data to it. Most major programming languages offer a means to construct and parse XML documents.

In case you're unfamiliar with XML documents, let's have a quick look at one of them. This is an example of the shopping cart XML we're going to construct from the contents of our user's cart:

```xml
<?xml version="1.0" encoding="UTF-8"?>
<checkout-shopping-cart xmlns="http://checkout.google.com/schema/2">
  <shopping-cart>
    <items>
      <item>
        <item-name>Ruby Axe Guitar</item-name>
        <item-description>Ruby Axe Guitar</item-description>
        <unit-price currency="USD">249.99</unit-price>
        <quantity>1</quantity>
      </item>
    </items>
  </shopping-cart>
  <checkout-flow-support>
    <merchant-checkout-flow-support>
      <shipping-methods>
        <flat-rate-shipping name="FedEx Ground">
          <price currency="USD">9.99</price>
        </flat-rate-shipping>
      </shipping-methods>
    </merchant-checkout-flow-support>
  </checkout-flow-support>
</checkout-shopping-cart>
```

This is an XML representation of a shopping cart that contains one item, and will offer the user one shipping option when they checkout on the Google Checkout interface. Even if you've never seen any XML before, as a programmer, the document listed here should make perfect sense to you. Here are some basic rules that well-formed XML documents must adhere to:

1. There must be a document type declaration. (aka DTD, e.g., the line reading `<?xml...>`)

2. There must be exactly one "root" element, which opens right after the DTD and closes at the end of the document. In this case, it's the `checkout-shopping-cart` element.

3. All opening elements must have a corresponding closing element, or must close themselves if they don't contain any child nodes or content. (Our sample XML doesn't have any self-closing tags.)

4. Elements must close in the reverse order in which they opened. Read from beginning to end, elements should open and close like a LIFO stack. Open Element 1, Open Element 2, Close Element 2, Close Element 1.

If you'd like to know more about XML and how to create well-formed XML, I'd recommend consulting http://www.w3.org/XML/ for more detailed information about the specification.

Building XML in Python is fairly straightforward. Take the following bit of Python code:

```
from xml.dom.minidom import Document

def build_me_some_xml():
    doc = Document()
    # generate the root node.
    root = doc.createElement('checkout-shopping-cart')
    # add an attribute to the root node
    root.setAttribute('xmlns', 'http://checkout.google.com/schema/2')
    # add this root node to document
    doc.appendChild(root)
    # create another node, append to root node
    shopping_cart = doc.createElement('shopping-cart')
    root.appendChild(shopping_cart)
    # return the xml doc to whatever function called it
    return doc.toxml()
```

And you can continue in this fashion, creating new element nodes and appending them as child nodes to existing ones, as many levels deep as you desire. This code produces and returns the following XML as output:

```
<?xml version="1.0"?>
<checkout-shopping-cart xmlns="http://checkout.google.com/schema/2">
  <shopping-cart />
</checkout-shopping-cart>
```

In this case, the `shopping-cart` element is a self-closing tag because it doesn't contain any child nodes or text. However, this document is nothing more than semantic markup without any content, making it about as useful as mammary glands on a bull. However, as a working example, it's quite useful. With this code, all of the methods we need to create our full XML document are there. We can create a document, add nodes, and add attributes.

113

There are other libraries out there for building XML. I've had good experiences with the ElementTree[3] library, but the standard XML libraries in Python will do for our purposes. If you've got another library that you want to use to build the document, feel free to use that instead.

Making HTTP Requests in Python

The next piece of the puzzle lies in generating an HTTP request, and posting it to a given URL, in Python code. Python comes equipped with a library for making these HTTP requests called urllib2, which we're going to use here in order to post our order data to Google's Checkout API.

Take this bit of Python code, which illustrates the basics of constructing a POST request (don't type this in, as the code itself will not work):

```python
import urllib2
from urllib2 import Request, urlopen

def make_dummy_request():
    my_url = 'http://checkout.google.com/whatever/url/to/checkout/'
    # calls another local function for XML Cart
    cart_xml = get_cart_xml()
    # build request with
    req = Request(url=my_url, data=cart_xml)
    # set one header, containing content-type
    req.add_header('Content-Type', 'application/xml; charset=UTF-8')
    # read the response into a local variable for processing
    response_data = urlopen(req).read()
```

The real heavyweight here is the urlopen() function, which is actually posting the request and its corresponding data to the URL we specified, and then reading the response. Coming from the Google Checkout API, the response data will be an XML document that contains the URL to which we should redirect the user.

Python comes equipped with a means of detecting exceptions where they might occur, through the use of the try keyword. If you expect that some code might raise a particular exception, you can use the following syntax in order to anticipate errors:

```python
try:
    # code that might raise a HTTPError
    # exception goes here.
except HTTPError, err:
    raise err
else:
    # if there was no exception encountered,
    # run some more code here.
```

When we try to open up our request to Google Checkout, we are expecting a couple of possible exceptions: HTTPError and URLError. We need to check our code block that is responsible for connecting to Google Checkout for these two types of exceptions, in that order, and raise them if they occur.

Lastly, in our actual request to Google, one of the headers we're going to attach to our request will need to be a base64-encoded string. While this shouldn't be particularly intimidating, here is the code that will encode a string:

---

[3] http://docs.python.org/library/xml.etree.elementtree.html

```
import base64

encoded_string = base64.encodestring(my_string)
```

Let's jump back to our user-friendly Google Checkout Merchant home page and start putting these pieces together.

Your Google Merchant ID and Key

Before we can start coding things up, we need to put a couple of things into our project. When we signed up for our sandbox account with Google Checkout, we were issued two things: a Merchant ID and a Merchant Key. You can find both of these if you click on the "Settings" tab at the top of the page and then click on the "Integration" link at the left side of the page, as shown in Figure 5-2.

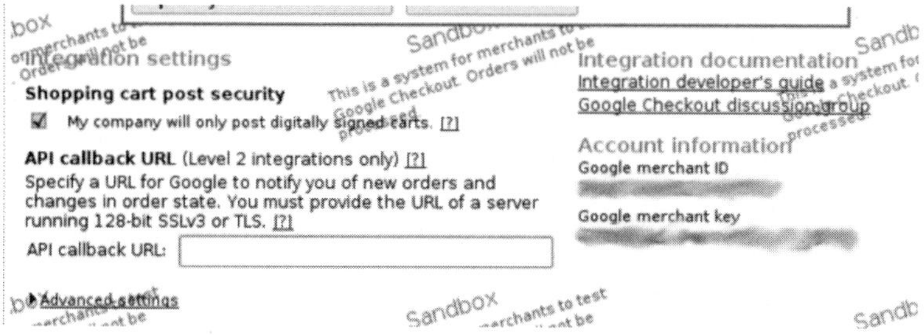

Figure 5-2. *Your Google Merchant ID and Key. Keep the Key a secret!*

With this page open, bring up your `settings.py` module and add the following lines to it:

```
GOOGLE_CHECKOUT_MERCHANT_ID = 'your id here'
GOOGLE_CHECKOUT_MERCHANT_KEY = 'your key here'
GOOGLE_CHECKOUT_URL = 'https://sandbox.google.com/checkout/ ↵
    api/v2/merchantCheckout/Merchant/' + GOOGLE_CHECKOUT_MERCHANT_ID
```

With these entries in your `settings.py` file, you can now write the code that is necessary for integrating with Google Checkout. If you do have values that may change, like the Merchant Key or ID, or that are not directly related to the logical code flow or processing that your code is doing, you don't want to stick these values directly in your Python functions. It's much better to have these values stored as constants in a configuration file. That way, later on, if any of these values changes, you won't need to update any of the Python code in your checkout package. You simply need to update the constants in your `settings.py` file.

The Python Property Decorator

There's one last thing I'm going to point out before we implement our checkout. Have a look at the following code, which accesses properties on an instance of our `CartItem` model:

```
item = CartItem()
quantity = item.quantity
product = item.product
price = item.price()
```

The last item looks a little out of place. We have to do it this way because a call to price is actually a call to a method named price(), which we defined in the model:

```
def price(self):
    return self.product.price
```

This is simply a means of getting the price of the CartItem's related product. This is a little strange, because while price() is a method, intuitively it makes much more sense as a property, like the rest of the fields in the model.

We can explicitly use the @property decorator on our price() method definition so that we can call it like a property instead of a method. So altering the method to this:

```
@property
def price(self):
    return self.product.price
```

actually makes the following call on a model instance valid:

```
price = item.price
```

While this isn't necessary, it's a nice little trick to keep your code a little more consistent and logical. Bear in mind that property is read only, and acts only as a "getter" property. Also, this will break any existing calls that use the method syntax of item.price(). This won't affect us if we change it now, since the only place we're calling this method is in our templates, where we omit the parenthesis on method calls anyway.

So, go ahead and add the @property decorator on your total(), name(), and price() methods on your CartItem model, and on the sale_price() method on your Product model.

Creating the Checkout App

Inside your project's shell, create a new app called checkout:

```
$ python manage.py startapp checkout
```

Of course, you need to add this new app to your INSTALLED_APPS in your settings.py file:

```
'ecomstore.checkout',
```

Inside this new app, we're going to create a new file that will contain the code to build the XML cart and submit the carts to Google Checkout. Create a file called google_checkout.py and add the following code to it:

```
from xml.dom.minidom import Document
from xml.dom import minidom
from django.http import HttpRequest, HttpResponseRedirect
from urllib2 import Request, urlopen, HTTPError, URLError
import base64

from ecomstore.cart.models import CartItem
from ecomstore.cart import cart
from ecomstore import settings

def get_checkout_url(request):
```

```
        redirect_url = ''
        req = _create_google_checkout_request(request)
        try:
            response_xml = urlopen(req).read()
        except HTTPError, err:
            raise err
        except URLError, err:
            raise err
        else:
            redirect_url = _parse_google_checkout_response(response_xml)
        return redirect_url

def _create_google_checkout_request(request):
    url = settings.GOOGLE_CHECKOUT_URL
    cart = _build_xml_shopping_cart(request)
    req = Request(url=url,data=cart)
    merchant_id = settings.GOOGLE_CHECKOUT_MERCHANT_ID
    merchant_key = settings.GOOGLE_CHECKOUT_MERCHANT_KEY
    key_id = merchant_id + ':' + merchant_key
    authorization_value = base64.encodestring(key_id)[:-1]
    req.add_header('Authorization', 'Basic %s' % authorization_value)
    req.add_header('Content-Type','application/xml; charset=UTF-8')
    req.add_header('Accept','application/xml; charset=UTF-8')
    return req

def _parse_google_checkout_response(response_xml):
    redirect_url = ''
    xml_doc = minidom.parseString(response_xml)
    root = xml_doc.documentElement
    node = root.childNodes[1]
    if node.tagName == 'redirect-url':
        redirect_url = node.firstChild.data
    if node.tagName == 'error-message':
        raise RuntimeError(node.firstChild.data)
    return redirect_url

def _build_xml_shopping_cart(request):
    doc = Document()

    root = doc.createElement('checkout-shopping-cart')
    root.setAttribute('xmlns', 'http://checkout.google.com/schema/2')
    doc.appendChild(root)

    shopping_cart = doc.createElement('shopping-cart')
    root.appendChild(shopping_cart)

    items = doc.createElement('items')
    shopping_cart.appendChild(items)

    cart_items = cart.get_cart_items(request)
    for cart_item in cart_items:
        item = doc.createElement('item')
        items.appendChild(item)
```

117

```python
        item_name = doc.createElement('item-name')
        item_name_text = doc.createTextNode(str(cart_item.name))
        item_name.appendChild(item_name_text)
        item.appendChild(item_name)

        item_description = doc.createElement('item-description')
        item_description_text = doc.createTextNode(str(cart_item.name))
        item_description.appendChild(item_description_text)
        item.appendChild(item_description)

        unit_price = doc.createElement('unit-price')
        unit_price.setAttribute('currency','USD')
        unit_price_text = doc.createTextNode(str(cart_item.price))
        unit_price.appendChild(unit_price_text)
        item.appendChild(unit_price)

        quantity = doc.createElement('quantity')
        quantity_text = doc.createTextNode(str(cart_item.quantity))
        quantity.appendChild(quantity_text)
        item.appendChild(quantity)

    checkout_flow = doc.createElement('checkout-flow-support')
    root.appendChild(checkout_flow)
    merchant_flow = doc.createElement('merchant-checkout-flow-support')
    checkout_flow.appendChild(merchant_flow)

    shipping_methods = doc.createElement('shipping-methods')
    merchant_flow.appendChild(shipping_methods)

    flat_rate_shipping = doc.createElement('flat-rate-shipping')
    flat_rate_shipping.setAttribute('name','FedEx Ground')
    shipping_methods.appendChild(flat_rate_shipping)

    shipping_price = doc.createElement('price')
    shipping_price.setAttribute('currency','USD')
    flat_rate_shipping.appendChild(shipping_price)

    shipping_price_text = doc.createTextNode('9.99')
    shipping_price.appendChild(shipping_price_text)

    return doc.toxml(encoding='utf-8')
```

The code that we've written should make sense to you. It may be a mile and a half long, but really, the longest part of it is the _build_xml_shopping_cart() function, which is the block of Python we've created to build our shopping cart in XML. The items in the cart are added to the items element one at a time in a Python for loop, which iterates through all of the cart items and builds a child item element for each one.

Notice that we have added one shipping option in our XML cart: FedEx Ground for $9.99 per order. The user will be able to select from the options that you specify in the shipping-methods element. In our case, we've only created a single option, so every user will be forced to choose this one shipping method. This probably isn't what you want, but it would be very easy to create a ShippingOptions model with the different types of shipping you'd like to offer customers, and add it to the XML with a second for loop.

The other functions are the ones responsible for submitting the request to Google Checkout and parsing the URL where we need to forward the customer out of the response the API sends back to us. We create a Request object, which takes the URL of the Google Checkout API and the cart XML as keyword arguments. Then, before submitting to the API, we add three headers to the request detailing the authorization of our request, the type of content in our request, and the type of content we will accept in response.

We then submit the request, using a Python try block. Provided that we don't encounter any exceptions in making our request, we read the contents of the response into a variable called response_xml. We then parse through this request to get at the URL that Google Checkout sends back to us. For your reference, here is an example of the XML that Google will return back to us with the URL:

```
<?xml version="1.0" encoding="UTF-8"?>
<checkout-redirect xmlns="http://checkout.google.com/schema/2"
    serial-number="981283ea-c324-44bb-a10c-fc3b2eba5707">
    <redirect-url>
    https://checkout.google.com/view/buy?o=shoppingcart&amp;shoppingcart=8572098456
    </redirect-url>
</checkout-redirect>
```

As you can see, our code merely parses out the text contained in the redirect-url node. This is a string we assign to a variable we call redirect_url, which is then returned to the calling function. We will use this in our view function to redirect the user to the correct Google Checkout page.

If we get an error back from Google, we will detect the error-message node instead of the redirect-url, and we'll raise a RuntimeError with the details of the error, which are inside the error-message node.

Next, create a file called checkout.py inside your project's checkout app, and add the following lines of code:

```
from ecomstore.checkout import google_checkout

def get_checkout_url(request):
    return google_checkout.get_checkout_url(request)
```

This simple bit of code called the get_checkout_url() function we created in our other google_checkout.py file, and this is what we're going to call from our view. In this way, if we later decide to change the third-party order processor, or when we want to have our customers checkout on our own site, we can change this function without touching any of our views.

Now, we need to jump back to the cart page, where we'll have to add the "Checkout" button to our template and add logic to the cart view to handle the process of someone clicking it. In your templates/cart directory, open up your cart.html file and find the following block of code for the checkout link:

```
<a href="/url/to/checkout/">Checkout Now</a>
```

This link only shows up if there are items in the customer's shopping cart. Alter this block of template code so that it reads the following:

```
<form method="post" action=".">
    <input type="hidden" name="submit" value="Checkout" />
    <input type="image" name="Google Checkout" alt="Fast checkout through Google"

src="http://sandbox.google.com/checkout/buttons/checkout.gif?merchant_id={{ merchant_id }}
        &w=180&h=46&style=white&variant=text&loc=en_US" height="46" width="180" />
</form>
```

One of the terms of the Google Checkout API's terms of use is that you must display one of the many Google Checkout buttons (which all basically look the same, but are different sizes) as the "Checkout" button on your site. Personally, I don't think this is a bad thing. (Am I starting to sound like a manager yet?) Whenever you're about to send the user off your site for any reason, it's important to give them a MASSIVE visual cue so that they know they'll be leaving your site. The Google Checkout button is perfect for this, and I've gone with the largest one so that it's readable and clear exactly where pushing that button is going to take them.

The request for the image of the "Checkout" button requires your Merchant ID to be passed to the cart template as a variable, so we'll have to make sure we add that to our view.

In your cart app, open up the views.py file and change the show_cart() function so that it looks like this (the code I've added to the file is in bold):

```
# other imports omitted here.

from django.http import HttpResponseRedirect
from ecomstore.checkout import checkout
from ecomstore import settings

def show_cart(request, template_name):
    if request.method == 'POST':
        postdata = request.POST.copy()
        if postdata['submit'] == 'Remove':
            cart.remove_from_cart(request)
        if postdata['submit'] == 'Update':
            cart.update_cart(request):
        if postdata['submit'] == 'Checkout':
            checkout_url = checkout.get_checkout_url(request)
            return HttpResponseRedirect(checkout_url)
    cart_items = cart.get_cart_items(request)
    page_title = 'Shopping Cart'
    cart_subtotal = cart.cart_subtotal(request)
    # for Google Checkout button
    merchant_id = settings.GOOGLE_CHECKOUT_MERCHANT_ID
    return render_to_response(template_name, locals(), ⏎
        context_instance=RequestContext(request))
```

As you can see, this code simply handles our view in the event that someone just clicked the "Checkout" button in our template. If it detects the submit as part of the form, with the value of Checkout, then it calls our checkout.py module for the URL to which it should redirect the user. checkout.py is actually calling the google_checkout.py module for the URL, passing the current request object down the chain for processing. google_checkout.py returns the URL and sends it back up the chain to our view, which uses the Django HttpResponseRedirect utility to send the user to Google Checkout.

Go ahead and pull up your site in a browser, add one product to the cart, and have a look at the cart page as it stands now. You should see the Google Checkout button on your cart page, like mine in Figure 5-3.

Figure 5-3. *Our Shopping Cart page with the Google Checkout button.*

As long as we have this set up now, let's take it for a test drive. All you need is another Google Account, different than the one you used to sign up as a Google Checkout Merchant. In order to test checkout using the sandbox account, Google provides four test credit cards that you can use to place orders without anybody actually getting charged for anything. They are strictly for making sure that you coded everything correctly. At the time I wrote this, these are the four dummy credit cards you can use, which are listed in Table 5-1.

Table 5-1. *Test credit cards for use with your sandbox Google Checkout account*

Card Type	Card Number	CVC	Expiration Date
American Express	3782 8224 6310 005	any four digits	any future date
Discover	6011 1111 1111 1117	any three digits	any future date
MasterCard	5555 5555 5555 4444	any three digits	any future date
VISA	4111 1111 1111 1111	any three digits	any future date

Let's go through it right now, so you have some sense of what your customers are going to see. Click the big bright and shiny "Google Checkout" button that's now adorning your cart page and you should be redirected to the first step of the Google Checkout process, which should have a summary of your cart contents. On my computer, I'm already logged in to my personal Google Account for testing this, and I'm prompted for credit card and billing information.

If, by chance, you're still logged in under your Google Account you used to become a Merchant, you won't see anything in your cart. You need to click back to the cart page on your site, log out of that Google account in another browser tab, and then click the "Google Checkout" button again. Also, if you're having some unexplained problem when you're being redirected to the Checkout API, try adding `/diagnose` to the end of your `GOOGLE_CHECKOUT_URL`. This is the setting you can use to debug problems, and after the redirect, the Google Checkout interface will show you a brief message explaining the nature of the error.

The first step, with the cart summary and billing information, should appear like Figure 5-4.

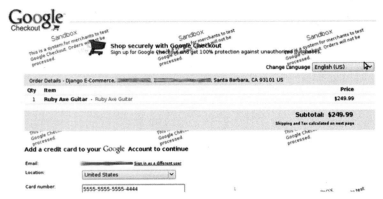

Figure 5-4. Shot of Step 1 with Google Checkout. I'm logged in.

Put in the information for one of the test credit cards from Table 5-1. The cardholder name, expiration date, and CVV don't really matter since you're just testing. Submit this information and you'll be taken to a confirmation page where you can select shipping and opt in to special offers. Notice that they can select to receive promotional offers from your site in Figure 5-5.

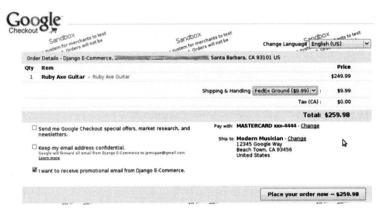

Figure 5-5. Notice the "promotional email" box is checked.

The details in Figure 5-5 might confuse you, because the "Ship to" information I'm using as a fake customer happens to be the same as the vendor, and the vendor information is "Django E-Commerce" instead of "Modern Musician." In the real world, the "Ship to" information would be your customer's information, and your own address would appear at the top.

Go ahead and click the "Place your order now" button. You'll be taken to a "Thanks!" page that shows the customer a link back to your site and information on how they can track their order. Google Checkout will even send them an e-mail with details about the order they placed on your site.

Figure 5-6. The Thanks! page after finishing up with Google Checkout.

Now that the customer has placed the order, it's up to you as the vendor to fulfill it. The Google Checkout Merchant system makes this whole process fairly easy. Log out of your personal Google Account with which you just placed your test order, and log back in to the Google Account you used to sign up as a Merchant.

If you check the corresponding Gmail account, you'll find that you've received an e-mail letting you know that a customer has placed an order on your site and requires your attention. You can use this Gmail account to get notifications of your orders as they come through. E-mails can be forwarded from this account to another primary e-mail that you're using to manage your store. I've also found the Gmail Notifier to be extremely useful, which will display a small Gmail icon in your system's taskbar that will pop up a little alert each time you receive an e-mail.

Go back to your Google Checkout Merchant homepage. In your Inbox, you should see the single test order that you've placed. Go ahead and click the Order Number link and you'll be taken to a page with the details of that order, akin to what you see in Figure 5-7.

Figure 5-7. The details of your first order. Too bad it's not real.

So far, Google Checkout has authorized the charging of these funds, but it hasn't actually captured them. As the Merchant, this is something you'll need to do through the Google Checkout interface. Go ahead and click the "Charge order" button in order to capture the (fake) money from this customer's (fake) order.

This will actually charge the credit card (which, if you'll please remember, was fake) and put the money into your bank account. This might not happen immediately, but you've initiated the actual process of getting payment for the merchandise you're about to ship.

After this step, the next step will be to actually ship the product. If you click the "Send shipping notice" button that appears on the order details page, a small inlay will pop up allowing you to put in details about the shipping carrier and a tracking number. This information is for the customer's convenience, so they can track where their order is while it's in transit. It will also send them a friendly e-mail letting them know that their order has actually been shipped. The interface also lets you handle refunds without much effort.

Before you start selling stuff, you should probably establish company policies about when customers are charged in relation to when you will actually ship the merchandise, in a way that makes sense for your order processing workflow and that complies with local laws and regulations relating to e-commerce. My general advice (not legally binding, of course) is that you charge customers the same day as you ship the merchandise. You don't want the gap between when you charge customers and when you ship the merchandise to get too large or else you run the risk of forgetting to ship something, which is fraud, and you don't want *that* on your conscience, I'm sure.

In order to put the work that we've done here into production, you'll need to upgrade your account from a sandbox one to a full Google Checkout Merchant account, so that you stop seeing that annoying red "Sandbox" message tiling the background of all the Merchant pages and actually receive some money. You'll also need to change the URL to which you're submitting your orders to the following:

```
GOOGLE_CHECKOUT_URL = 'https://checkout.google.com/api/checkout/ ↵
    v2/merchantCheckout/Merchant/' + GOOGLE_CHECKOUT_MERCHANT_ID
```

That's about it. Google gives you most of the tools you need to make this whole process of selling stuff online, and charging and shipping orders, fairly painless.

Order Checkout Requirements

Using Google Checkout actually sets the bar pretty high. It handles the collection of data, secure transmission over HTTPS, shipping methods and tax information, and order processing tasks. Truth be told, we won't be implementing 100% of these. One of our main constraints is our heavy use of the admin interface, which doesn't allow for the read only access to things. That means that you or whoever else is accessing the order data can accidentally change the shipping address, save the record by mistake, and all of the sudden, you'll have to contact the customer asking them for their address in order to get the order out properly.

Besides this, we have everything we need to start replicating what just happened on Google Checkout right on our own site. Since we're doing e-commerce and security is the first priority, we're going to start by looking at setting up SSL for our checkout pages.

SSL Middleware

Obviously, when you need to send people's sensitive data over a public network like the Internet, you absolutely should make sure that you secure the data so that if the Bad Guys intercept it, they won't be able to use it to do malicious things. Since we're capturing our customer's credit card data, we have to make sure we encrypt the data while it's in transit.

The standard way of doing this is with the Secure Sockets Layer, or SSL. With this configured on your site, any information is transmitted with the HTTPS protocol, which is different from HTTP and gets its own dedicated port (it's 443, whereas standard HTTP is done over port 80). Behind the scenes, this uses public-key cryptography in order to ensure that data is securely encrypted in transmission, and that the data can be decrypted and understood by the client and server on each end of communication.

You can see this in action on any major site that asks you for your credit card information. The URL should be prefaced with https:// instead of http://, and there should be an indicator in your browser that the site is secured with SSL, which is generally a padlock symbol.

■ **Caution** It's important to point out that even though a site is secured with SSL, this does *not* mean that the *entire site* is secure. It means that any data sent between the client and server will be *transmitted* securely, but doesn't ensure that the site itself will store it securely. It's possible for a site to use SSL to obtain data in a secure fashion and then carelessly store it in a database in plaintext, where anyone with access to the database can read it.

While this is terrific, the problem is that we don't want SSL enabled on every single page of our site. There is overhead associated with processing pages served over HTTPS, so you only want to use it where you know that it's needed to protect sensitive information, such as authentication pages or checkout pages. So, we need a systematic and simple way to apply SSL to some pages on our site.

As you've seen, view functions are the Django tool that handles individual request/response operations. Django provides an interesting capability out of the box to interact with each and every request that comes into the site or response that goes out, without the need to put this code into every view function on your site. It provides this ability via *middleware*.

Middleware classes provide a nice alternative to writing a particular block of code into every single view. Django uses them to manage user sessions, authentication, and even the flatpages app that we hooked up in the last chapter. Middleware is also the perfect candidate for enabling SSL on our site, since this is something we need to systematically evaluate in each view, but we'd rather not have some "To SSL or not to SSL?" code block cluttering up each of our views.

The Python and Django community have actually already created a solution for us. The following snippet is a piece of SSL Middleware created by Stephen Zabel and Jay Parlar. We can hook this into our Django project in order to handle enabling SSL in some, but not all, of our views:

```python
from django.conf import settings
from django.http import HttpResponseRedirect, ⏎
    HttpResponsePermanentRedirect, get_host

SSL = 'SSL'

class SSLRedirect:
    def process_view(self, request, view_func, view_args, view_kwargs):
        if SSL in view_kwargs:
            secure = view_kwargs[SSL]
            del view_kwargs[SSL]
        else:
            secure - False
        if not secure == self._is_secure(request):
            return self._redirect(request, secure)

    def _is_secure(self, request):
        if request.is_secure():
            return True
        if 'HTTP_X_FORWARDED_SSL' in request.META:
            return request.META['HTTP_X_FORWARDED_SSL'] == 'on'
        return False

    def _redirect(self, request, secure):
        protocol = secure and "https" or "http"
        newurl = "%s://%s%s" % (protocol,get_host(request),request.get_full_path())
```

```
    if settings.DEBUG and request.method == 'POST':
        raise RuntimeError, \
    """Django can't perform a SSL redirect while maintaining POST data.
        Please structure your views so that redirects only occur during GETs."""
    return HttpResponsePermanentRedirect(newurl)
```

If we hook this in to our project, we can pass an additional variable called SSL and set it to True in each of the views we want secured. Here are some sample URLs:

```
# this view will be served securely
(r'^secure_data/$', 'secure_view', { 'SSL':True }, 'secure_view'),
# and this view will not be secure
(r'^not_so_secure/$', 'insecure_view', { 'SSL':False }, 'insecure_view'),
```

If the SSL variable is not passed to a given URL, then it's not served securely. So, we don't even need make sure we add 'SSL':False to all the views that don't require SSL. As long as we have it present, and set to True, for all views that require secure transmission, we're all set.

At least, we're all set as far as our little web project goes. Unfortunately, the test server we've been playing around with so far in the book is *not* equipped to handle serving pages over SSL. That's a bigger job that needs to be handled by an actual HTTP web server, such as Apache. We'll look more at the settings for our project in Chapter 15 when we cover deployment.

For right now, let's hook the SSL Middleware[4] into our project. Once you have your hands on this code, save a copy of it in a file called SSLMiddleware.py and put it in the root directory of your project. Then, in the MIDDLEWARE_CLASSES section of your settings.py file, add the following line:

```
'ecomstore.SSLMiddleware.SSLRedirect',
```

Now you can start using SSL in your views. While we're in settings.py, go to the top of the file and add the following lines of code to define a constant:

```
# Change to true before deploying into production
ENABLE_SSL = False
```

Now, we can just use this ENABLE_SSL Boolean variable in our URLs. That way, when we deploy into production and are ready to start serving pages over HTTPS, we can simply change this one value to True and it will be applied where we've specified.

DRY Models and Forms

So far, we've created models for our data, and we've created one form in the last chapter for adding products to the shopping cart. This has been simple, and most of the form-to-model interaction has been handled by our Django admin interface. When you get down to doing more significant work, such as creating a checkout form for capturing order data that will eventually go into an order model, you'll find that you're repeating yourself quite a bit.

For example, both the form and the model for order data will contain shipping and billing address information. That means on the model, you might create fields for this data, and then in the form, you'll create fields that will probably have the exact same names. When you take this data from the user in a form instance, you'll end up copying these values from each form field into the fields on the model.

---

[4] http://www.djangosnippets.org/snippets/85/

Clearly, this is more work than we should be doing. The creators of Django realized this and worked in a very handy solution through the use of a ModelForm. Once you define a model, you can create a form with fields that are based directly on the fields listed in your model. You can exclude the fields from your model that you *don't* want to show up on the form or be subject to validation, add fields to your form that aren't in the model, and easily save an instance of your model based on the form your user sends back to you.

Let's walk through a very quick example of how this works. Look back over the code in the last chapter. Our CartItem model and our ProductAddToCartForm are two classes that have overlap. Both of them define a field called quantity, and these refer to the same piece of data. The form is supposed to take it from the user, and through some Python code, we put it into an instance of the model.

Now, *don't* actually sit there and start changing the code we wrote in the last chapter, because the code we wrote in the last chapter is *fine*. But, let's walk through what we could have done as a way of getting a quick handle on the use of ModelForm.

Here is a summary of our CartItem model class, omitting import statements, methods, properties and Meta class:

```
class CartItem(models.Model):
    cart_id = models.CharField(max_length=50)
    date_added = models.DateTimeField(auto_now_add=True)
    quantity = models.IntegerField(default=1)
    product = models.ForeignKey(Product, unique=False)
```

Now, let's say we wanted to make full use of our ModelForm option. We would create a form class that inherits from ModelForm and specifies its associated model in an inner Meta class:

```
class ProductAddToCartForm(forms.ModelForm):
    class Meta:
        model = CartItem
        fields = ('quantity',)
```

Now, because we've subclassed ModelForm and attached it to the CartItem model, the form will contain the fields from the model. We can create an instance of this form on the product page, and in this case, it would include *only* the quantity field since we've explicitly stated that in our Meta class. When you've got a model with a dozen or more fields that needs a form for the UI that mostly mirrors the fields in the model, this approach can save you a lot of typing.

The tricky part comes when we want to take the populated form instance from our POST request and save it into an instance of the model. The form subclass instance of ModelForm has a method called save() that returns and stores an instance of the model in your database.

You should make sure the form is valid before trying to call save on it:

```
if my_form.is_valid():
    cart_item = my_form.save()
```

Now, the call to the is_valid() method on the form instance won't work and will raise a ValueError exception. Even though the *form* is valid, the *model* requires the cart_id and product fields to have values before you save it to the database. Therefore, you need to manipulate the fields on the model before you save it.

The save() method takes an optional keyword argument called commit. By default, this is True, but if you explicitly set its value to False, then save() will wait until you call save() a second time before actually storing it in the database. Between these two calls to the save() method, you can change the values of the fields on the model to whatever you would like them to be:

```
cart_item = CartItem()
my_form = ProductAddToCartForm(request, request.POST, instance=cart_item)
if my_form.is_valid():
    cart_item = my_form.save(commit=False)
    cart_item.cart_id = get_cart_id_function()
    cart_item.product = Product.objects.get(slug=product_slug)
    cart_item.save()
```

Here, we create a new empty cart item, an instance of the "Add To Cart" form that's bound to our POST data and cart_item object, check if the form is valid and, if so, populate the cart_item object with the values from our form with the save() method and commit set to False. Then, before actually saving the value to the database, we set the cart_id and the product.

In this particular case, we don't save very much code by using ModelForm instead of just leaving our form and model classes decoupled, the way we did in the last chapter. When we get to the order form on the checkout page, using this approach is going to save us a ton of work.

For the record, you can't validate a Django model in code the way you can a form.[5] There is no is_valid() method you can call on a model instance in order to ensure that the data it contains is consistent with the constraints of the model. So, any required model fields that you exclude from a form that you plan to update before saving the model, you'll need to keep track of and validate the data manually. This is somewhat error-prone, but for the small handful of fields we'll being using in our order form, it's a very tiny issue we can easily manage.

Secure HTTP Requests

In the first half of the chapter, we submitted our HTTP requests to Google Checkout using the Python urllib2 module. When we're submitting credit card data, it needs to be submitted securely over HTTPS. In order to do this, and in the interest of developing our Python skill set, we're going to shift gears away from the urllib2 module and use a different module for creating network connections.

To submit sensitive data, we're going to use the Python httplib module. This has a slightly different syntax, which we'll cover very quickly here. The following code block creates a secure connection to Authorize.Net's test site on port 443, creates and defines the method and path of the post at the remote site, adds some headers, sends the request, and then reads the response:

```
cn = httplib.HTTPSConnection('test.authorize.net',443)
cn.putrequest('POST','/gateway/transact.dll')
cn.putheader('content-type','application/x-www-form-urlencoded')
cn.putheader('content-length', len(data))
cn.endheaders()
cn.send(data)
response = cn.getresponse()
return response.read()
```

Don't worry that we haven't yet defined the variable called data. In our actual call, it will contain a URL-encoded version of our parameters to be processed. This code submits a POST request to https://test.authorize.net/gateway/transact.dll securely, over port 443.

---

[5] At the time I'm writing this (Django 1.1), model validation is currently in the works for future release.

We can actually refactor this code by taking advantage of the request() method on our HTTPSConnection object, like this:

```
cn = httplib.HTTPSConnection('test.authorize.net',443)
cn.request('POST', '/gateway/transact.dll', data, headers)
return cn.getresponse().read()
```

where the variable headers is a Python dictionary that defines our previous two request headers. The first block of code, while longer, can be useful in working through a request step-by-step for debugging purposes.

Credit Card Transactions

Before we jump into talking about integrating with a payment gateway, a little background is in order. There are a few types of transactions you can use when you're doing e-commerce, and which ones you choose to use will depend on your business requirements. The following are four terms you should be familiar with:

> *Authorization:* When you *authorize* an amount on a customer's credit card, you are checking to see if the customer has enough available credit on their account to cover the amount you are authorizing. This is useful when you want to check to see if the customer has the credit to pay for your transaction at the time of checkout, and then you want to charge them later, after you've shipped the order.

> *Capture: Capturing* funds actually initiates the transfer of funds from the customer's account into yours. Capture of funds happens after you've authorized them.

> *Void:* After an amount has been authorized, or authorized and captured, you have the option of *voiding* the transaction before it has been settled. That is, before the transfer of funds has occurred, if you void the transaction, the whole thing is called off.

> *Credit:* A *credit* can be issued against a previously settled transaction. So, after you've gotten the money from a customer, you can do a credit through the payment gateway in order to handle refunds.

Authorize.Net, the payment gateway that we're going to use to process our credit card transactions, makes this whole process pretty simple. After each initial call to their API with new credit card data, they'll issue a Transaction ID to us, which is a unique value we can use to reference that transaction in subsequent calls to the API.

So, we can perform an *authorization* via a call to Authorize.Net's API, and they respond with a success code and issue us a Transaction ID. Later, when we go to *capture* these funds, we can submit that Transaction ID to the gateway and they will associate our current capture with the authorization from before.

In our example, things will actually be a lot simpler. Authorize.Net allows for an authorization and capture of funds all in one go, so in this chapter, you don't need to handle the mess of authorizing first, capturing later. We'll simply perform one transaction when the user submits their order information to us.

Order Checkout by Django

The first thing we need to do before we jump into the code is to sign up for a test account with our payment gateway for processing credit card transactions. As I mentioned, we're going to be using Authorize.Net as our payment gateway, and you're going to need to sign up for an account before you can start really testing the checkout process we're going to implement.

Since some of you may read through the rest of this chapter before you actually jump in and start coding stuff, I would encourage you to go sign up for your test account now, before you start reading. Over the course of the past few years, I've signed up for a test account with Authorize.Net a few times, and each time it takes about a day before they approve my account and send along some credentials I can use to place test orders. So, I heartily recommend you sign up now, and by the time you actually get around to writing some code, you'll have some test credentials available.

Signing up for an Authorize.Net Test Account

You can sign up for an Authorize.Net test account at `http://developer.authorize.net/testaccount/`. As with Google Checkout, you're going to be required to provide some personal information, as well as some basic information about your company and a brief description of how you plan to use the account.

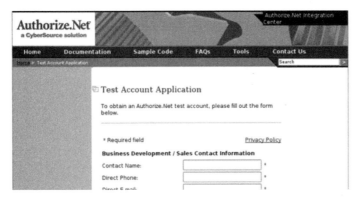

Figure 5-8. Signing up for a test account at Authorize.Net.

When you get the section that asks you for Type of Test Account, you want to select "Card Not Present (CNP)." Credit card transactions that occur over the Internet, when you can't easily verify that the person using the card actually has the card in hand, are referred to as Card Not Present transactions. CNP transactions are differentiated from Card Present transactions that tend to happen in retail stores where both the cardholder and the card are present because CNP transactions carry a higher degree of risk. They're more likely to be fraudulent.

Like Google Checkout, Authorize.Net is not entirely free. Before using this service, you should read up on the fees that apply for production accounts and make sure that you comply with the terms of service. Rest assured, however, while you're using the test account, you won't be charged any money. And, once your account is approved, Authorize.Net will send along a list of dummy credit cards you can use to place test orders.

After you've completed the sign-up and sent off the request, you can sit back and twiddle your thumbs while you wait for the acceptance e-mail to arrive in your inbox. No, wait, you can't, because we have a lot of work to do. Put that on the back burner for right now and let's get into coding our models.

Order Information Models

If you've come this far, there really isn't a whole lot of new concepts we're going to encounter in creating our order models. We're going to create two models for order information: Order and OrderItem.

Order will contain all of the information about the order that we need for processing, such as shipping, billing, and other contact information associated with the order. We'll also take the time to store the date, IP address, and reference the user if they're logged in. Until the next chapter, when we set up user accounts, all orders will be anonymous and not associated with accounts, but we'll set it up so we capture the information when it's available.

For the ID of each order, we'll default to the ID field set by the database. This might not be what you want, so feel free to create your own means of generating sequential order numbers.

Also, we're going to give our Orders a status field that will describe where the order is in our list of checkout step. This will be an enumerated type in our model definition that will have four values in the style of Python constant variables. Typically, constants in Python are defined with names in all uppercase characters, much like the variables we've created in settings.py. Defining the statuses on the model in this fashion allows us to make our code more readable by developers. Later, if we need to write a line where we are checking to see if an order is cancelled, we can write the following to start an if block:

```
if order.status == Order.CANCELLED:
```

This is much better than using a string in your if blocks. For example, code like this:

```
if order.status == 'Cancelled':
```

is much more prone to errors, since you might misspell the word "cancelled" or use an inconsistent casing strategy. Having the value of a cancelled order defined once, and using the values on the model definition to evaluate them, makes for much more robust code.

Each of the statuses is mapped to a corresponding integer value. The status will be stored in the database as an integer in a field that we'll call status, but when we refer to it in our user interface, we'll see the more user-friendly status text.

OrderItem will contain information related to each item in the cart. This will mostly just be a copy, item by item, of the CartItem model class we created in the last chapter. However, we will store the price of the product with each order item. That way, if the price ever changes in the Product model, we still have the price the product was at when the order was placed. OrderItem will have a foreign key reference to its parent Order instance.

Open the models.py file sitting in your checkout app directory and enter the following two model definitions:

```
from django.db import models
from django import forms
from django.contrib.auth.models import User
from ecomstore.catalog.models import Product
import decimal

class Order(models.Model):
    # each individual status
    SUBMITTED = 1
    PROCESSED = 2
    SHIPPED = 3
    CANCELLED = 4

    # set of possible order statuses
    ORDER_STATUSES = ((SUBMITTED,'Submitted'),
                      (PROCESSED,'Processed'),
```

```
                            (SHIPPED,'Shipped'),
                            (CANCELLED,'Cancelled'),)
    # order info
    date = models.DateTimeField(auto_now_add=True)
    status = models.IntegerField(choices=ORDER_STATUSES, default=SUBMITTED)
    ip_address = models.IPAddressField()
    last_updated = models.DateTimeField(auto_now=True)
    user = models.ForeignKey(User, null=True)
    transaction_id = models.CharField(max_length=20)

    # contact info
    email = models.EmailField(max_length=50)
    phone = models.CharField(max_length=20)

    # shipping information
    shipping_name = models.CharField(max_length=50)
    shipping_address_1 = models.CharField(max_length=50)
    shipping_address_2 = models.CharField(max_length=50, blank=True)
    shipping_city = models.CharField(max_length=50)
    shipping_state = models.CharField(max_length=2)
    shipping_country = models.CharField(max_length=50)
    shipping_zip = models.CharField(max_length=10)

    # billing information
    billing_name = models.CharField(max_length=50)
    billing_address_1 = models.CharField(max_length=50)
    billing_address_2 = models.CharField(max_length=50, blank=True)
    billing_city = models.CharField(max_length=50)
    billing_state = models.CharField(max_length=2)
    billing_country = models.CharField(max_length=50)
    billing_zip = models.CharField(max_length=10)

    def __unicode__(self):
        return 'Order #' + str(self.id)

    @property
    def total(self):
        total = decimal.Decimal('0.00')
        order_items = OrderItem.objects.filter(order=self)
        for item in order_items:
            total += item.total
        return total

class OrderItem(models.Model):
    product = models.ForeignKey(Product)
    quantity = models.IntegerField(default=1)
    price = models.DecimalField(max_digits=9,decimal_places=2)
    order = models.ForeignKey(Order)

    @property
    def total(self):
        return self.quantity * self.price
```

```python
@property
def name(self):
    return self.product.name

@property
def sku(self):
    return self.product.sku

def __unicode__(self):
    return self.product.name + ' (' + self.product.sku + ')'

def get_absolute_url(self):
    return self.product.get_absolute_url()
```

Most of this should look pretty familiar. The one new thing we're doing here is created our own four possible settings for the status field in the Order model, by naming them one a time, assigning each an integer value, and then listing all of them in a tuple. The actual status field is an IntegerField that will store the corresponding number, and we pass in a choices keyword argument to give the UI this list. We also specify a default, so that when an order is placed, it will be set to Submitted.

For your reference, here is what our statuses mean:

- Submitted: The credit card was valid and the order was saved. It is ready for us to process it.

- Processed: After submitted orders have been reviewed, we can mark them as processed, letting the shippers know that the order is ready to be shipped.

- Shipped: The order has been processed and approved by the administrator (maybe this is you), and so it can officially be prepared and shipped off to the customer by the shippers (this might also be you).

- Cancelled: Either by e-mail or phone, the customer contacted your company and decided they didn't want to go through with the whole thing.

You should change your own statuses to logical values that make sense for your own organization and its checkout process.

With this code in place, go ahead back to your shell and run manage.py syncdb in order to create the new database tables.

The Checkout Form

Now that we've just spent all that time setting up the multitudes of fields that our Order model requires, we're going to reap the benefit of a fairly lean form class for the checkout form. We're still going to do a few things to make sure that the checkout process goes all right, and that will involve a little bit of custom validation on our part. The first thing we can do is validate the credit card number that the user has supplied us. We can actually do this without submitting any call to Authorize.Net or any other gateway.

As it turns out, credit cards are not merely numbers that have been generated at random. For example, you can't just figure out a valid credit card number by taking your own credit card number and incrementing the last digit by one, like you can with most sequences of numbers. You can verify whether or not a credit card number is valid by using a checksum.

This is known as the Luhn algorithm.[6] In order to validate a card number, start at the right of the sequence of numbers and double the value of every second one (so, an "8" would become "16"). Then, take the sum of all of the digits (the aforementioned "16" would be "1+6," or "7"). If the sum of the result is divisible by 10, you have a valid credit card number. (Strictly going by the checksum, of course. It doesn't mean the customer actually has a valid credit card.)

This checksum doesn't afford any kind of security in the cryptography sense of the word, but it is handy for catching little typos before you actually submit to the payment gateway. And fortunately, there is already a Python function[7] defined by the community that we can use for our own validation.

We'll also verify that the phone number the customer has provided is at least 10 digits in length. You might have noticed when we defined our model that the field for phone number is of type CharField and not PhoneNumberField. I've opted to go this route so that we don't run into issues when we start getting orders in from Canada, Mexico, or elsewhere, where the format of the phone number might be quite different from one in the United States.

Note Although I won't cover the material here, Django actually does come equipped with a module call localflavor to handle capturing form information in other countries: http://docs.djangoproject.com/en/dev/ref/contrib/localflavor/.

Our forms file also needs to build some custom drop-down menus for the months of the year, a list of years from the current year to 12 years in the future, and a list of possible credit card types. We'll implement these as separate functions that our form can references in short order.

So, in the checkout app directory, create a new file called forms.py and insert the following code into it:

```
from django import forms
from ecomstore.checkout.models import Order
import datetime
import re

def cc_expire_years():
    current_year = datetime.datetime.now().year
    years = range(current_year, current_year+12)
    return [(str(x),str(x)) for x in years]

def cc_expire_months():
    months = []
    for month in range(1,13):
        if len(str(month)) == 1:
            numeric = '0' + str(month)
        else:
            numeric = str(month)
        months.append((numeric, datetime.date(2009, month, 1).strftime('%B')))
    return months
```

[6] http://en.wikipedia.org/wiki/Luhn_algorithm

[7] http://code.activestate.com/recipes/172845/

```python
CARD_TYPES = (('Mastercard','Mastercard'),
              ('VISA','VISA'),
              ('AMEX','AMEX'),
              ('Discover','Discover'),)

def strip_non_numbers(data):
    """ gets rid of all non-number characters """
    non_numbers = re.compile('\D')
    return non_numbers.sub('', data)

# Gateway test credit cards won't pass this validation
def cardLuhnChecksumIsValid(card_number):
    """ checks to make sure that the card passes a luhn mod-10 checksum """
    sum = 0
    num_digits = len(card_number)
    oddeven = num_digits & 1
    for count in range(0, num_digits):
        digit = int(card_number[count])
        if not (( count & 1 ) ^ oddeven ):
            digit = digit * 2
        if digit > 9:
            digit = digit - 9
        sum = sum + digit
    return ( (sum % 10) == 0 )

class CheckoutForm(forms.ModelForm):
    def __init__(self, *args, **kwargs):
        super(CheckoutForm, self).__init__(*args, **kwargs)
        # override default attributes
        for field in self.fields:
            self.fields[field].widget.attrs['size'] = '30'
        self.fields['shipping_state'].widget.attrs['size'] = '3'
        self.fields['shipping_state'].widget.attrs['size'] = '3'
        self.fields['shipping_zip'].widget.attrs['size'] = '6'
        self.fields['billing_state'].widget.attrs['size'] = '3'
        self.fields['billing_state'].widget.attrs['size'] = '3'
        self.fields['billing_zip'].widget.attrs['size'] = '6'
        self.fields['credit_card_type'].widget.attrs['size'] = '1'
        self.fields['credit_card_expire_year'].widget.attrs['size'] = '1'
        self.fields['credit_card_expire_month'].widget.attrs['size'] = '1'
        self.fields['credit_card_cvv'].widget.attrs['size'] = '5'

    class Meta:
        model = Order
        exclude = ('status','ip_address','user','transaction_id',)

    credit_card_number = forms.CharField()
    credit_card_type = forms.CharField(widget=forms.Select(choices=CARD_TYPES))
    credit_card_expire_month =
forms.CharField(widget=forms.Select(choices=cc_expire_months()))
    credit_card_expire_year =
forms.CharField(widget=forms.Select(choices=cc_expire_years()))
    credit_card_cvv = forms.CharField()
```

135

```
    def clean_credit_card_number(self):
        cc_number = self.cleaned_data['credit_card_number']
        stripped_cc_number = strip_non_numbers(cc_number)
        if not cardLuhnChecksumIsValid(stripped_cc_number):
            raise forms.ValidationError('The credit card you entered is invalid.')

    def clean_phone(self):
        phone = self.cleaned_data['phone']
        stripped_phone = strip_non_numbers(phone)
        if len(stripped_phone) < 10:
            raise forms.ValidationError('Enter a valid phone number with area code.(e.g.
555-555-5555)')
        return self.cleaned_data['phone']
```

There are a few helper functions here we've defined before we even get to the form. Let's run through these before we get to the form class itself.

cc_expire_years() generates a list of years that we can use for our credit card expiration year drop-down. We take the current year as a seed, create a list that goes out 12 years into the future, and then return a Python list comprised of a tuple for each year. The final line of this function uses a Python *list comprehension* to build the result. The output of calling this function is, at the current date:

```
[('2009', '2009'), ('2010', '2010'), … ]  # and so on
```

cc_expire_months() is a little more involved, and creates a Python list of tuples to represent each month of the year, where each tuple contains a two-digit string and the name of the month. We get the full name of the month by iterating through each ordinal value for each month and calling the strftime('%B')[8] on the first day of each month, which returns the full name of the month. Calling this function returns this (abbreviated) list:

```
[('01', 'January'), ('02', 'February'), … ] # etc
```

The CARD_TYPES is just a hard-coded tuple of tuples that contains the types of credit cards that our site will accept for payment. Incidentally, all of these card types have numbers that can be safely validated with the Luhn algorithm.

The function strip_non_numbers() takes a string, strips out all characters that aren't numbers, and returns just the numbers as a string. We do this with the use of the Python regular expression module, finding all non-numeric digits and replacing them with an empty string. We're going to use this when we validate our credit card numbers and phone numbers.

The final helper method is the cardLuhnChecksumIsValid(), which takes a credit card number and returns true if the card conforms to the Luhn mod 10 validation. Feel free to try and decode that little Python gem the next time you're sick of Sudoku and want a *real* challenge for your brain.

Now, we get to our CheckoutForm class. This is a subclass of ModelForm, so, by virtue of being hooked up to the Order model in the inner Meta class, will have all of the fields in the Order model. First of all, I wanted to explicitly set the size attribute of each of the form fields, so I can explicitly control the appearance of each field. The input asking for a state code, for example, makes more sense if it only appears to be a couple of characters long.

So, we override the form's default constructor to manipulate the form fields. I first loop through all of the fields and give each one an explicit size attribute with a value of 30. Then, I evaluate each of the others, giving them a custom size value that makes sense, given the type of input we're asking the user for.

---

[8] The benefit of using the strftime() Python function is that it's automatically localized for other regions if you're using Python locales (http://docs.python.org/library/time.html#time.strftime).

The inner Meta class, on top of specifying the corresponding model class, also has an exclude value. We provide exclude with the list of values that we want to exclude from the form. We don't, for instance, want to allow the customer to submit their own IP address. We'll set this later, before we save the order. The values we've excluded from the form will also not be validated when we call the is_valid() method on our instance of the form. So, even though these fields are required by the model, we can accept the form as valid even though they will be blank values when the customer submits an order form.

Next, we add five fields to the form that allow us to capture credit card information. These weren't part of the model because, for security reasons, we're not going to store customer credit card information in our database. However, we still need to have the customer submit this information to us with the rest of the order information so we can charge them for the stuff we're selling.

Notice that three of the fields for credit cards are actually going to be rendered in our form as drop-down menus with values we are pulling from three of the helper methods we created previously.

Lastly, inside the form class, we specify two custom clean_field_name() methods to check that the data the user has provided conforms to the rules of the model. In both of these, we strip all the non-numeric digits from the values entered by the user and run own our validation. We just make sure that the phone number is at least 10 digits in length, and that the credit card number is valid per the Luhn mod 10 algorithm.

And that's it for the form. In just a second, when we get around to coding up the template for the checkout process, you'll see just how much more the use of a ModelForm is helping save us oodles of time.

Authorization and Capture

Now, let's create the code that actually calls the Authorize.Net API and gets you money when a customer checks out. As soon as you get the e-mail back from Authorize.Net letting you know that they've approved your developer test account, you should see a list of logins, passwords, and other things. The two you want to take note of are the API Login and the Transaction Key, which are the two values you'll need to provide when making test calls.

Open your project's settings.py file and add the following configuration values:

```
AUTHNET_POST_URL = 'test.authorize.net'
AUTHNET_POST_PATH = '/gateway/transact.dll'
AUTHNET_LOGIN = [your login here]
AUTHNET_KEY = [your transaction key here]
```

Obviously, you're going to want to insert your own valid API Login and Transaction key into the preceding lines of code. Keep that e-mail handy once you have it because it contains test credit card values that you'll need to use when submitting test orders.

Inside your checkout app directory, create a new file and call it authnet.py. This file will contain one function that performs a single authorization and capture of funds:

```
from ecomstore import settings
import httplib
import urllib

def do_auth_capture(amount='0.00', card_num=None, exp_date=None,card_cvv=None):
    delimiter = '|'
    raw_params = {
                    'x_login':settings.AUTHNET_LOGIN,
                    'x_tran_key':settings.AUTHNET_KEY,
                    'x_type':'AUTH_CAPTURE',
                    'x_amount':amount,
                    'x_version':'3.1',
```

```
                    'x_card_num':card_num,
                    'x_exp_date':exp_date,
                    'x_delim_char':delimiter,
                    'x_relay_response':'FALSE',
                    'x_delim_data':'TRUE',
                    'x_card_code':card_cvv
                    }
    params = urllib.urlencode(raw_params)
    headers = { 'content-type':'application/x-www-form-urlencoded',
                'content-length':len(params) }
    post_url = settings.AUTHNET_POST_URL
    post_path = settings.AUTHNET_POST_PATH
    cn = httplib.HTTPSConnection(post_url,httplib.HTTPS_PORT)
    cn.request('POST',post_path,params,headers)
    return cn.getresponse().read().split(delimiter)
```

Our single function, do_auth_capture(), is the one that makes sure you are rewarded for all of your hard work with what is hopefully a steady paycheck. Let's have a look at what it's doing.

First, we specify a delimiter character. When Authorize.Net returns back the results of the transaction, it will separate them with the character or group of characters that we specify. Using the pipe (|) character is pretty safe since the response data should never contain one of these.

Next, we specify all of the parameters that we're going to post with our request. This includes the API credentials, such as API Login and Transaction Key, credit card information, and the amount we want to capture from the customer's account. We also specify the type of transaction, which in this particular case, is 'AUTH_CAPTURE'.

We then URL-encode our parameters for the actual post request, which merely gives them the typical URL format: x_login=api_login_here&x_tran_key=transaction_key_here&. And so on. URL encoding in this fashion also converts certain URL-illegal characters to their two-digit hexadecimal equivalents prefaced by the % character. The most common example of this is the space character, which is not allowed in URLs but is represented by %20 instead.[9]

We then prepare a dictionary of headers for the request and set two variable with the URL and path to which we're going to post. Then we get to the few lines that actually handle the connection, request, and reading of the response.

The response will come back delimited by the same character we specified in our request. There are quite a few parameters that it sends back, but we're only going to worry about two of them: the first one, which is the response code, and the seventh one, which is the unique Transaction ID that identifies this transaction to any future calls to the API (such as issuing a void or a credit transaction against an order).

So, the response we get back will be a string that looks like this:

```
'1|1|1|4… #etc'
```

We call the split() method on this string, passing in the delimiter, so that we get a Python list of these values returned to us:

```
['1','1','1','4', …]  # etc
```

For more on the response that Authorize.Net returns to you after each transaction attempt, refer to the Advanced Integration Method (AIM) Implementation Guide, which you can download at http://developer.authorize.net/guides/. For now, I'm going to cover the few points that we're going to take advantage of in our processing code.

---

[9] See http://www.w3schools.com/TAGS/ref_urlencode.asp for a thorough listing of character encodings. Not all of these character need to be encoded in every URL.

Order Processing

Now let's prepare the module that will actually handle a good deal of the logic and will be called directly by our views. Open up the checkout.py module we created earlier in the chapter, with the lonely get_checkout_url() function in it. Alter that function and add the following two to the file:

```python
from ecomstore.checkout import google_checkout
from ecomstore.cart import cart
from ecomstore.checkout.models import Order, OrderItem
from ecomstore.checkout.forms import CheckoutForm
from ecomstore.checkout import authnet
from ecomstore import settings
from django.core import urlresolvers
import urllib

# returns the URL from the checkout module for cart
def get_checkout_url(request):
    return urlresolvers.reverse('checkout')

def process(request):
    # Transaction results
    APPROVED = '1'
    DECLINED = '2'
    ERROR = '3'
    HELD_FOR_REVIEW = '4'
    postdata = request.POST.copy()
    card_num = postdata.get('credit_card_number','')
    exp_month = postdata.get('credit_card_expire_month','')
    exp_year = postdata.get('credit_card_expire_year','')
    exp_date = exp_month + exp_year
    cvv = postdata.get('credit_card_cvv','')
    amount = cart.cart_subtotal(request)
    results = {}
    response = authnet.do_auth_capture(amount=amount,
                                       card_num=card_num,
                                       exp_date=exp_date,
                                       card_cvv=cvv)
    if response[0] == APPROVED:
        transaction_id = response[6]
        order = create_order(request, transaction_id)
        results = {'order_number':order.id,'message':''}
    if response[0] == DECLINED:
        results = {'order_number':0,
                'message':'There is a problem with your credit card.'}
    if response[0] == ERROR or response[0] == HELD_FOR_REVIEW:
        results = {'order_number':0,'message':'Error processing your order.'}
    return results

def create_order(request,transaction_id):
    order = Order()
    checkout_form = CheckoutForm(request.POST, instance=order)
    order = checkout_form.save(commit=False)
    order.transaction_id = transaction_id
```

139

```
        order.ip_address = request.META.get('REMOTE_ADDR')
        order.user = None
        order.status = Order.SUBMITTED
        order.save()
        # if the order save succeeded
        if order.pk:
            cart_items = cart.get_cart_items(request)
            for ci in cart_items:
                # create order item for each cart item
                oi = OrderItem()
                oi.order = order
                oi.quantity = ci.quantity
                oi.price = ci.price  # now using @property
                oi.product = ci.product
                oi.save()
            # all set, empty cart
            cart.empty_cart(request)
        # return the new order object
        return order
```

There's a lot going on in these three functions. The first one we've merely changed so that it returns the location of the checkout page (which we haven't created yet) by using the urlresolvers module.

The second function, process(), will be called by our view when we've determined that our order checkout form is valid to actually process the credit card. We first set up four constants that represent the four possible response codes we might get from our API call. "Approved" means that all is hunky-dory, and we're going to get our grubby little paws on their money without any issue. "Declined" means that the customer's credit card was processed unsuccessfully, and the last two, "Error" and "Held For Review" are basically error codes that let us know something went wrong.

Next, we extract out the credit card data from the form post data and get the subtotal of the cart, which is the amount that we're going to charge the customer. We then call our do_auth_capture() function we set up in the last section, returning the Python list with all the information about how the transaction went. We look at the response code in the first index of the list:

response[0]

We compare this against our list of possible responses. If the status is approved, we get the Transaction ID out of the response, call the function to create our order, and prepare a Python dictionary called results, with two entries to return to the user interface for processing. The other three transaction codes also build a Python dictionary with the same two entries, which will have different values based on the results of our API call, and our view will handle them differently.

Lastly, the create_order() function simply walks through the process of creating an instance of the Order model from the form we created earlier. Then, before we actually save the order, we update a few of the values on the model, namely the remote IP address, the current user (None for now), and the status of the order, which is set to Submitted by default.

If the order was saved correctly, then we loop through all of the items in the cart and create an instance of OrderItem for each one, hooking it into the new Order instance and saving each one in turn. Then, we empty the cart, clearing the session of the items that the user just purchased. Obviously, we only want to empty the cart after we're certain that they've given us valid checkout information, so this happens very late in the overall checkout flow.

We are calling a function in our cart.py module that doesn't yet exist, which is for clearing the customer's shopping cart. Open up cart.py in your cart app directory and add the following two methods:

```
def is_empty(request):
    return cart_item_count(request) == 0
```

```
def empty_cart(request):
    user_cart = get_cart_items(request)
    user_cart.delete()
```

The first one returns a simple True or False we can use to check if the cart is empty, which, I promise, we *will* use when we get to our checkout view function. The second one is the function we call when we're ready to wipe out the objects in the user's cart.

Checkout Views and URLs

Right now, when the customer hits our cart page, they are still presented with the Google Checkout button that redirects them away from our site in order to checkout. With this new code in place, we're ready to change that. Let's make the few changes that will enable checkout on our own site.

First, let's change the button in the cart.html file. You can comment out the large and unsightly bunch of code that generates the Google Checkout button and replace it with the following input:

```
<input type="submit" name="submit" value="Checkout" alt="Checkout" />
```

Because the view function for the cart is calling the get_checkout_url() function, and because we altered this function in the last section, we don't need to make any changes to the cart view function.

However, it is high time that we set up the two URLs and views that we need for checkout. We're going to need two views for our checkout process: a checkout order form page, and a receipt page displaying the order information and communicate to the customer that we've processed their order successfully. You'll notice that we are not going to create a "Confirm your order" page, which generally sits between the order form and receipt page, and allows the customer to review their order information before submitting it. We're not going to include this step in this book to keep the example simple, but you should probably do your own research to see if your customers would appreciate a confirmation page when going through the checkout process.

Create a new urls.py module inside your project's checkout app directory and enter the follow two URL definitions into it:

```
from django.conf.urls.defaults import *
from ecomstore import settings

urlpatterns = patterns('ecomstore.checkout.views',
    (r'^$', 'show_checkout', {'template_name': 'checkout/checkout.html',
        'SSL': settings.ENABLE_SSL }, 'checkout'),
    (r'^receipt/$', 'receipt', {'template_name': 'checkout/receipt.html',
        'SSL': settings.ENABLE_SSL },'checkout_receipt'),
)
```

Notice that these two URLs are both set up to take advantage of the SSL Middleware we hooked up earlier in the chapter. When we deploy and set the ENABLE_SSL value to True, these two URLs will be served securely over HTTPS.

Now, crack open the views.py module inside your checkout app directory and add the following list of imports and two view functions:

```
from django.shortcuts import render_to_response
from django.template import RequestContext
from django.core import urlresolvers
from django.http import HttpResponseRedirect

from ecomstore.checkout.forms import CheckoutForm
```

```python
from ecomstore.checkout.models import Order, OrderItem
from ecomstore.checkout import checkout
from ecomstore.cart import cart

def show_checkout(request, template_name='checkout/checkout.html'):
    if cart.is_empty(request):
        cart_url = urlresolvers.reverse('show_cart')
        return HttpResponseRedirect(cart_url)
    if request.method == 'POST':
        postdata = request.POST.copy()
        form = CheckoutForm(postdata)
        if form.is_valid():
            response = checkout.process(request)
            order_number = response.get('order_number',0)
            error_message = response.get('message','')
            if order_number:
                request.session['order_number'] = order_number
                receipt_url = urlresolvers.reverse('checkout_receipt')
                return HttpResponseRedirect(receipt_url)
        else:
            error_message = 'Correct the errors below'
    else:
        form = CheckoutForm()
    page_title = 'Checkout'
    return render_to_response(template_name, locals(),
context_instance=RequestContext(request))

def receipt(request, template_name='checkout/receipt.html'):
    order_number = request.session.get('order_number','')
    if order_number:
        order = Order.objects.filter(id=order_number)[0]
        order_items = OrderItem.objects.filter(order=order)
        del request.session['order_number']
    else:
        cart_url = urlresolvers.reverse('show_cart')
        return HttpResponseRedirect(cart_url)     return render_to_response(template_name,
locals(), context_instance=RequestContext(request))
```

First, when someone first accesses the checkout page, we check to see if their cart is empty. If it is, we redirect them right back to the cart page, where they are presented with their empty cart. Since the only way to get to the checkout page is to click the "Checkout" button on the cart page, which will *only* show up if you have stuff in your cart, this is not likely to happen to anyone. It's a good measure to prevent anyone from trying to checkout with an empty cart.

Next, if the page is being accessed with a typical GET request, we display the empty cart form. However, if it's a POST, we assume that the user is trying to submit their information and place an order. Within this code block, we check to see if the form submitted has valid data in it. If not, the processing doesn't occur and we redisplay the form with the error messages on it, for the customer to correct before they re-submit it.

If the form doesn't have any validation errors in it, we pass along our request to the process() function in our checkout module. We parse out the order number of the response dictionary that the function sends back to us.

If there was any problem processing the order, the order number will have a value of 0, and we'll redisplay the form with any error message returned to us by the process() function.

If the order number is a valid number other than zero, we can assume that the billing information was processed correctly and redirect the user to the receipt page. Before doing so, we store the order number in the customer's session we so can pull up the details of the order for display on the receipt page.

In the receipt() view function, we attempt to retrieve the order number from the customer's current session. If it finds the number, we retrieve the order information, which we'll display on the receipt page. If it doesn't, we assume that somebody who didn't just place an order just entered the receipt page URL manually. Just like the checkout page and a customer with an empty cart, we'll redirect a customer with no order number to the cart page.

Notice that in the receipt() function, we also explicitly delete the order_number session variable if we find it in the user's session. It's best to clean house and remove session variables as soon as you no longer need them. Session information is stored in your database, and can grow quite large if left unchecked. If the table gets too large, it may hinder the performance of your site.

Incidentally, if you want to purge *all* of your old session information, you can use the Django-provided command inside your system's shell:

```
$ python manage.py cleanup
```

This removes any session records that have an expire_date set to some point in the past.

Checkout Template and Order Form

Now, I'm going to take a different approach to constructing our checkout page. It will display an order, which will just end up being a rendered instance of the CheckoutForm we created earlier. However, we're not going to simply call the as_p() on our form instance and let Django cough up the entire form automatically for us. We want to retain as much control over the appearance of the form as we can, because it's likely to get the very rapt attention of management when sales start to drop. As a result, your order form page is likely to go through several redesigns. In anticipation of this, we're going to create it by hand.

However, we don't want to create the whole thing *completely* by hand. We don't want to have to build each and every form element by hand, because we'd be repeating ourselves across several fields of the form.

So, we're going to strike a comfortable balance between the two. Each field of the form will be rendered using our own custom inclusion tag, which we're going to create right now. Inside your project's templates/tags directory, create a new file and call it form_table_row.html. Put the following HTML and Django template code into it:

```
<tr>
    <th>
    {% if form_field.field.required %}*{% endif %}
    {{ form_field.label_tag }}
    </th>
    <td>
    {% if form_field.errors %}
        <ul class="errorlist">
        {% for error in form_field.errors %}
            <li>{{ form_field.label }}: {{ error }}</li>
        {% endfor %}
        </ul>
    {% endif %}

    {{ form_field }}
    </td>
</tr>
```

143

As you can see, each field of our form will be in its own table row, with two columns: the first for the label element related to the input, and the second for the actual input element. If you look closer, there are two other things going on here. First of all, we're listing the form errors related to each field right above the input that's asking for them. So, a bright red message will be displayed right above any fields that have validation errors, right where the customer can easily find them and correct them.

But have a look at the line reading {% if form_field.field.required %}*{% endif %}. Typically, forms on the Internet have their fields that are required marked by an asterisk (*). This generally requires that the creator of the form and the person responsible for maintaining the database (in smaller organizations, these two people might be one and the same) have to get together, figure out which fields are required, and then the form developer puts an asterisk next to each field that's required.

In our case, though, the model class contains information about the database constraints. It knows which fields are required and which are not. And because our form class is based directly on the model, we can actually use this {% if %} block so that the asterisk character shows up next to the name of each required fields *all on its own*. It happens automatically, saving us the headache of updating the template if the model definition ever changes.

Of course, for this inclusion tag to work, we need to create the actual function definition so that our template can load and use the tag. Create a subdirectory in your checkout app directory called templatetags, and create the obligatory __init__.py file, as well as a module called checkout_tags.py. Enter the following code into checkout_tags.py:

```
from django import template

register = template.Library()

@register.inclusion_tag("tags/form_table_row.html")
def form_table_row(form_field):
    return {'form_field': form_field }
```

Now, when we use this tag in our checkout order form template, we just need to pass in the field on the form that we want to have rendered.

So, let's get to the last step: the creation of the templates themselves. Inside your templates directory, create a new subdirectory called checkout that will house all of the template files for our app. Create two files in here: checkout.html and receipt.html. Open checkout.html and enter in the following template code:

```
{% extends "catalog.html" %}

{% load checkout_tags %}

{% block content %}
<h1>Checkout</h1>{% if error_message %}
    <ul class="errorlist">
        <li>{{ error_message }}</li>
    </ul>
{% endif %}
<form action="." method="post">
    <fieldset class="checkout">
        <legend>Contact Info</legend>
        <table>
        {% form_table_row form.email %}
        {% form_table_row form.phone %}
        </table>
    </fieldset>
```

```
        <fieldset class="checkout">
            <legend>Shipping Info</legend>
            <table>
            {% form_table_row form.shipping_name %}
            {% form_table_row form.shipping_address_1 %}
            {% form_table_row form.shipping_address_2 %}
            {% form_table_row form.shipping_city %}
            {% form_table_row form.shipping_state %}
            {% form_table_row form.shipping_zip %}
            {% form_table_row form.shipping_country %}
            </table>
        </fieldset>
        <fieldset class="checkout">
            <legend>Billing Info</legend>
            <table>
            {% form_table_row form.billing_name %}
            {% form_table_row form.billing_address_1 %}
            {% form_table_row form.billing_address_2 %}
            {% form_table_row form.billing_city %}
            {% form_table_row form.billing_state %}
            {% form_table_row form.billing_zip %}
            {% form_table_row form.billing_country %}
            </table>
        </fieldset>
        <fieldset class="checkout">
            <legend>Credit Card Info</legend>
            <table>
            {% form_table_row form.credit_card_number %}
            {% form_table_row form.credit_card_type %}
            {% form_table_row form.credit_card_expire_month %}
            {% form_table_row form.credit_card_expire_year %}
            {% form_table_row form.credit_card_cvv %}
            </table>
        </fieldset>
        <table>
        <tr>
            <th colspan="2"><input type="submit" value="Place Order" class="submit" /></th>
        </tr>
        </table>
    </form>

{% endblock %}
```

As you can see, from a very high level, we're arranging our form into different sections using HTML `fieldset` elements, each of which has a legend to describe the groupings and a table, inside of which we use a `{% for_table_row %}` tag for each of the fields we want to display on our form. Each tag will render an HTML table row element, with the label, input, and an area for error messages if the form is submitted with any validation errors.

Above that, we also define a small `{% if %}` block that checks for the presence of the `error_message` variable and displays it to the user.

Now open `receipt.html` and enter the following simple template code:

```
{% extends "catalog.html" %}

{% load catalog_filters %}

{% block content %}
    <table id="receipt">
        <caption>Your order has been placed!<br /><br />
            Your Order Number is: {{ order.id }}
        </caption>
        <thead>
        <tr>
            <th scope="col">Name</th>
            <th scope="col">Price</th>
            <th scope="col">Quantity</th>
            <th class="right" scope="col">Total</th>
        </tr>
        </thead>
        <tfoot>
            <tr>
                <td colspan="4" class="right" style="height:30px;">
                Order Total: {{ order.total|currency }}
                </td>
            </tr>
        </tfoot>
        <tbody>
        {% for item in order_items %}
        <tr>
            <td>{{ item.name }}</td>
            <td>{{ item.price|currency }}</td>
            <td>{{ item.quantity }}</td>
            <td class="right">{{ item.total|currency }}</td>
        </tr>
        {% endfor %}
        </tbody>
    </table>
{% endblock %}
```

This is just a basic table that lets the customer know that their order was placed successfully, as well as a summary of their order in a simple table.

One last thing before we take this for a test run in a browser. Open your `css.css` file and enter the following few styles for the checkout form:

```
fieldset.checkout{
    padding-bottom:15px;
    margin-bottom:15px;
}

fieldset.checkout legend{
    font-weight:bold;
    color:Black;
    margin-left:15px;
}
```

```
fieldset.checkout table{
    border-collapse:collapse;
    width:100%;
}

fieldset.checkout table th{
    text-align:right;
    width:200px;
    font-weight:normal;
}

fieldset.checkout input {
    font-family:Courier;
    font-size:Large;
}

table#receipt{
    width:100%;
    border-collapse:collapse;
}
```

So let's have a look at this site in a browser. Go ahead and run `manage.py runserver` and view the site in a browser. Add a product or two to your shopping cart, and then click the new checkout button. You should be taken to the checkout page, and should appear as it does in Figure 5-9.

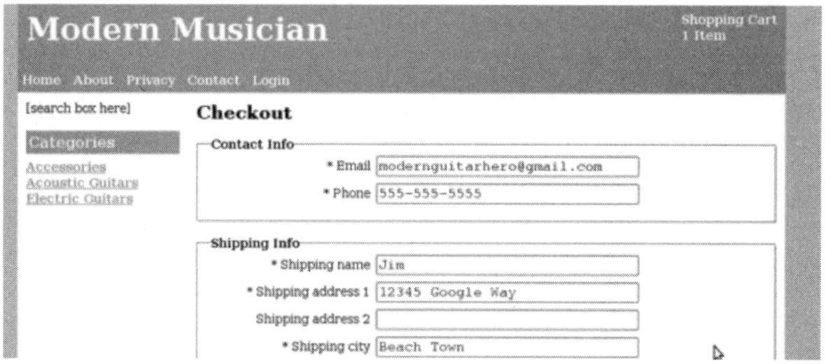

Figure 5-9. The order form on the checkout page.

In case you were wondering, yes, that font on the checkout form is Courier. I've chosen this because it's a monospaced font, which means that all letters get the same amount of horizontal space. I used to work for a company that did checkout forms, and I used to key in the company's address in order to place test orders on our sites. The name of the street was "Castilian Dr." Let's have a look at that in an itty-bitty font; I want you to tell me if I spelled it correctly:

```
Castilian Dr
```

My guess is that you had to take a closer look to see if I got the right number of letters, and the correct ones. I had to squint almost every time to make sure that I spelled it correctly. (I'm not sure why I did that, they were just *test orders*, after all.) But as I'm writing this, I'm about to turn 27. I don't have perfect vision, but if *I'm* struggling to make sure I spelled that street name correctly, then I'm sure there are some people who wouldn't have a prayer at reading that text very easily.

It may be ugly as sin, but it's convenient for the widest range of people. I doubt very much that the font on the checkout form is going to disgust anyone so much that they'll stop the checkout process, so the best thing you can do is at least choose one that proves the most readable for the widest range of people.

Go ahead and completely fill out the order form. When you get to the billing information, use one of the test credit card numbers that was sent to you in the Authorize.Net e-mail you got when your account was approved. You can try leaving a few required fields blank, or submitting too few digits for the phone number, in order to test the validation.

If you get an error when submitting one of these test cards about your credit card not being valid, you might need to comment out the lines of code that validate the card number with the Luhn mod 10 algorithm, as it's possible that the test credit card numbers don't pass this checksum.

When you finally click the "Place Order" button with valid order information, you should be redirected to a receipt page that looks something like Figure 5-10.

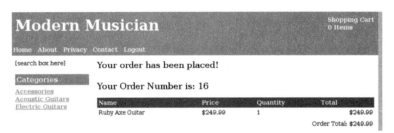

Figure 5-10. The receipt page, thanking the customer profusely for the order.

Now, we can check to make sure that this order was placed correctly by going to the Authorize.Net site. Take a quick mental note of the time you submit the order for processing, then, go back to the e-mail from Authorize.Net mentioning that they approved your application. Find the two values labeled "Login" and "Password" in this e-mail. These are the credentials you're going to use to log in to the developer test site.

Go to https://test.authorize.net/ (or the link provided for you in the e-mail) and log in using your test account Login and Password, and then click on Reports. Now, it's very likely the test account credentials you're using are not being used by only you. They're shared with other developers with test accounts, so the list of transactions you might see in the date and time drop-down might not all correspond to times you placed test orders. If you made a note of the time you placed your test order, it will help you determine which date and time to choose when running the list of transactions.

Once you find a transaction that matches the time you placed your test order, click "Run Report" and you should get a list of transactions, one of which should be the one you placed, for the same amount of your order and the same test credit card value, as depicted in Figure 5-11.

Figure 5-11. The transaction list by date/time on Authorize.Net.

Click on the transaction ID to view the details of the order, including the date, amount, and the type of transaction. You'll also notice that this interface has a "Refund" button that you can use to refund the customer's money. If this weren't just a test order, and you needed to issue a refund, you can easily do so through the Authorize.Net web site.

Notice that there are lots of other empty fields related to customer information, such as billing and shipping information, which are blank in this screen. Optionally, we could have submitted these values with the rest of the parameters when we submitted the credit card details for processing. For simplicity in our example, we did not list each and every one of them. However, you are free to go back and easily send more information to Authorize.Net.

If nothing else, you might consider sending along the billing ZIP code, as Authorize.Net verifies this value against the rest of the billing information, giving you a little more verification, and insurance against fraudulent orders being placed on your site.

Order Administration

That last piece of the puzzle is to enable our staff to actually browse orders and fulfill them as they come through. We're going to hook in our `Order` and `OrderItem` models to the Django admin interface, so that we can browse through them easily, finding them by status or date, or by the customer name or e-mail.

Create a new file called `admin.py` inside your `checkout` app directory, and put the following code into this file:

```
from django.contrib import admin
from ecomstore.checkout.models import Order, OrderItem

class OrderItemInline(admin.StackedInline):
    model = OrderItem
    extra = 0

class OrderAdmin(admin.ModelAdmin):
    list_display = ('__unicode__','date','status','transaction_id','user')
    list_filter = ('status','date')
    search_fields = ('email','shipping_name','billing_name','id','transaction_id')
    inlines = [OrderItemInline,]

    fieldsets = (
                ('Basics', {'fields': ('status','email','phone')}),
```

```
            ('Shipping', {'fields':('shipping_name','shipping_address_1',
            'shipping_address_2','shipping_city','shipping_state',
            'shipping_zip','shipping_country')}),
            ('Billing', {'fields':('billing_name','billing_address_1',
            'billing_address_2','billing_city','billing_state',
            'billing_zip','billing_country')})
            )
admin.site.register(Order, OrderAdmin)
```

Here, we're taking a slightly different approach to how we're hooking the models in. The details about an order should be shown completely on one page. That is, an Order should be displayed with contact, billing, and shipping information on a single page with all of its corresponding OrderItems, instead of splitting the two apart.

So, we're using one feature of the Django admin interface that allows us to display (and edit) models that are related to the current model instance with a foreign key or many-to-many relationship. Because the OrderItem model has a foreign key relating to the Order model, we can enable our admin interface to show the OrderItems along with each Order.

First, we create a class that inherits from one of the InlineModelAdmin classes. There are two possible values we can use here: TabularInline and StackedInline. We're going to go with the latter, and create a class called OrderItemInline. We reference the model that we want displayed inline. When we configure this, we have the option of leaving empty forms on the page, so that new OrderItems can be created for the Order. Because we don't need this functionality, we've also set the extra field to zero.

Then, when we hook in the Order model via the OrderAdmin class, we use two new tricks. We hook in the OrderItemInline class with the inlines field. This will ensure that the related OrderItem instances will be displayed on each Order page.

Also, we're using a new property called list_filter, and specifying two fields on the Order model. With this in place, we'll be able to browse orders by their status and date fields, easily drilling down to find the particular order we're looking for. On top of this, we've specified a few fields as search_fields, so that the Orders on the admin interface will be findable by searching for text that matches any one of these fields.

We're also partitioning up the sections of our Order for display in the admin interface via the use of the fieldsets property. This allows us to break up the details of the Order in logical groupings so that the information is organized and easier to read at a glance.

Once you've gotten this code in place, log in to the administrative interface. You should see a new section under your admin home page interface entitled "Checkout," with a link to browse the orders on your site. Click on it, and you should be presented with a list of each of your test orders, like the one you see in Figure 5-12.

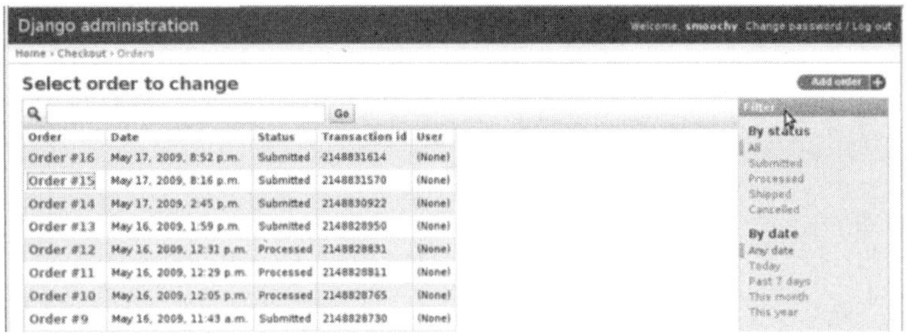

Figure 5-12. List of test orders placed on the site.

Click on one of these orders, and you should be taken to a page listing the details of the order. Toward the bottom, you'll see the list of the items that were included in the order, as in Figure 5-13.

Figure 5-13. *List of items included in the customer order.*

This will do nicely. Now, as the order moves down the checkout process, you can update the status of each order as need be, moving each one along from "Submitted" to "Processed," and finally to "Shipped" (or, you might have customized these steps for your own process). The shippers in your warehouse can use the admin interface to view the details about each order, allowing them to prepare parcels for shipment.

It's important to point out that the creators of Django caution against using the admin interface for too much. It's really handy for basic data entry, but it really wasn't built to do all kinds of crazy order-processing capabilities. The admin interface makes a nice placeholder for organizations that don't want to develop their own large custom solution right away.

Just remember that if you find yourself trying to develop a way for the Django admin interface to print up shipping labels, you've probably reached the point where you should consider rolling your own administrative interface for order processing.

Now that things are working with our test credentials, switching over to processing real payments with Authorize.Net is extremely simple. You just need to get your hands one some actual credentials for a production account, and you submit your transactions to `secure.authorize.net` as the host value.

Summary

This chapter was very Python-intensive, and full of new little tricks and tips for integrating our site with the payment gateways, but it was well worth the trouble. Now we have a fully functional site, which, once we flip the switch and make our order processing live, we can use to generate actual revenue. No matter whether you've hooked into Google Checkout or Authorize.Net, now that you have worked your way through this chapter, you now have a site that's ready to run as an e-commerce site.

The material in this chapter makes heavy use of Python's networking programming capabilities. If you're interested in learning more about how you can use Python for network programming, check out *Foundations of Python Network Programming*, by John Georzen (Apress, 2004). It's an excellent and comprehensive guide to the subject matter.

In the next chapter, we're going to hook in the Django authentication system provided to us by the framework, so our users will be able to sign up for customer accounts, reuse their billing and shipping information across multiple orders, and view their order history right on our site.

CHAPTER 6

■ ■ ■

Creating User Accounts

One thing we can offer our customers is the ability to create an account, giving them a username and password so that we can track information about our customers and help personalize their user experience. As a part of the traditional user experience, many sites display a message when you log in that reads, "Welcome, [your name here]!"? We're going to do that in this chapter, and Django actually provides a User model, login view functions, URL patterns, and forms that help make the development of user pages very quick and easy, without the need to worry about all that session junk ourselves.

Another benefit to user accounts is that it allows users to store their billing and shipping address information with a user account, so they can place multiple orders on our site without having to enter this information more than once. We'll look at how to store this information with the use of Django user profiles, which let you hook up as much information to the default Django User model, even though we're not going to edit a single line of the User model code.

We'll also look at how to restrict access to some pages, but not others. When we create the order history and order details pages, which we'll make available to registered users who want to view their past orders, we'll see how the use of Python decorators makes this a breeze.

Making Friends with the Source

Up until this point in the book, I've referenced the Django source code a handful of times to illustrate a few of my points. You might have followed along at home, digging down into your computer's PYTHONPATH and cracking open the files to look under the hood.

If you've avoided peeping at the Django source code until now because you're afraid of what you might find staring back at you, you're now out of luck. Fortunately, in this chapter, we don't have a whole lot of work to do, because the creators of Django have done a lot of the grunt work and the heavy lifting. Before we can look into that plumbing, however, we need to look it over and get a sense of what's there.

This isn't as foreboding as it sounds. As one example, here is the code for the login view, which is a part of the Django 1.1 web framework source code. You can find it on your own system under your Django installation directory, in /path/to/django/contrib/auth/views.py:

```
def login(request, template_name='registration/login.html',
        redirect_field_name=REDIRECT_FIELD_NAME):
    "Displays the login form and handles the login action."
    redirect_to = request.REQUEST.get(redirect_field_name, '')
    if request.method == "POST":
        form = AuthenticationForm(data=request.POST)
        if form.is_valid():
            # Light security check -- make sure redirect_to isn't garbage.
```

```
            if not redirect_to or '//' in redirect_to or ' ' in redirect_to:
                redirect_to = settings.LOGIN_REDIRECT_URL
            from django.contrib.auth import login
            login(request, form.get_user())
            if request.session.test_cookie_worked():
                request.session.delete_test_cookie()
            return HttpResponseRedirect(redirect_to)
    else:
        form = AuthenticationForm(request)
    request.session.set_test_cookie()
    if Site._meta.installed:
        current_site = Site.objects.get_current()
    else:
        current_site = RequestSite(request)
    return render_to_response(template_name, {
        'form': form,
        redirect_field_name: redirect_to,
        'site_name': current_site.name,
    }, context_instance=RequestContext(request))
login = never_cache(login)
```

If you've been working through the examples in this book so far, this should look very familiar. We could have written that ourselves. Sure, there may be a couple of variables here that you might not understand, because this function is out of context and there are import statements missing, but you get the gist of what it's supposed to do. And more importantly, it works, and it works well, so we're going to take full advantage of it.

Before we jump in, navigate to the contrib/auth directory in your Django installation and have a look at the files in there. You'll see the typical files for views, models, URL patterns, forms, and the admin hookup module. I'd strongly encourage you to have a look at all of these before we jump in. You don't have to—you are free to work through the rest of this chapter, adding in the bits to handle user authentication, and just accept that it works for you.

But, don't be shy. I even set up a symbolic link to my Django installation in my system's HOME directory, so I can easily jump right into it.

Hooking Into Django's Authentication

Django's authentication app that comes out of the box does quite a bit, but it doesn't do everything. As one perfect example of this, the login URLs are not at all aware of the SSL Middleware that we hooked up in the last chapter, but we would like to secure the login pages so that user passwords can't be sniffed over the network. We might not be storing credit cards yet, but we might eventually do that.

One thing that you should really *never* consider doing is modifying the Django source code itself. You're permitted to do this; Django is open source and you are free to modify as you need. However, I would strongly advise that you *don't* do this because if you ever want to upgrade, it's going to be a nightmare. You're going to have to have a system in place to track the changes that you've made to the source code to ensure that they don't get squashed when you do the upgrade.

Also, when it comes to the deployment phase, it helps if you can just use the Django source, as it's provided to you by the Django developers, as it is. That way, you don't have to worry about creating your own install package to make sure that production machines have the code they need. Just keep your own custom changes inside your project, within your control.

MONKEY-SEE, MONKEY-PATCH

Because Python is a dynamically typed programming language, you actually can make edits to the source code without altering the code in the actual source files.

One common example is the need to add an additional field to the Django User model, which stores user registration information. Let's say you want to add a DateTime field to store each user's birthday. You could use the following code in your project file to add the field to the model, prior to running manage.py syncdb:

```
User.add_to_class('birthday', models.DateTimeField())
```

Modifying the User model class is this fashion is known as *monkey patching*. Monkey patching takes advantage of the fact that Python is interpreted rather than compiled like other languages, such as C# or Java. This allows you to do things in Python that aren't possible in these other languages, such as altering class definitions right in your code. Interpreted languages, such as Python, allow the so-called "duck typing,"[1] which means your code is not so much concerned about *what* the class is so much as *what it can do*.

That said, in this particular case, there's really no reason to edit the User model in order to hold additional information, as Django provides user profiles that allow you to store additional user information. We look at user profiles later in this chapter.

So how are we going to merge the two? We're going to create our own Django app in our project to handle the authentication parts that we want to customize, and override the settings we want inside this app. We won't change the source code, but it will let us have fine-grained control over the degree to which we are using Django and our own custom code.

One downside to relying on the Django source for so much is that your project is at the whims of the upgrade changes that will be made by Django's developers in future releases. If they decide to change the login form in the source, and then you upgrade all of your machines, your login page is going to change and it may not be immediately apparent *why*.

For the purposes of our little site, this isn't too big of an issue. On top of this, the guys who created Django are pretty sharp cookies, if you ask me. They're not likely to make any drastic changes unless it really is an improvement, or they've got a darned good reason (although I suppose you never know... a benevolent dictator is still a dictator).

First of all, most of the things we need to do to hook up Django's built-in authentication system ha already been done. We hooked up the app and ran manage.py syncdb back in Chapter 3, and we've already hooked up the middleware that will handle authentication with each HTTP request. The only thing left to do is add in the URL entry to our project's urls.py module.

Open up your urls.py file and add the following lines to your list of patterns:

```
(r'^accounts/', include('accounts'urls')),
(r'^accounts/', include('django.contrib.auth.urls')),
```

On top of this, all of the Django authentication views that we've just tapped into return templates that are in a template subdirectory called registration. The Django source actually ships with these templates, which are used by the admin interface, and you can view them in your Django installation, under django/contrib/admin/templates/registration.

As one example, your application will return password_change_form.html if you use that view without creating your own template. However, when we get around to creating our own "Change

---

[1] http://en.wikipedia.org/wiki/Duck_typing

Password" page, we'll simply create a template file called password_change_form.html in our own project's registration subdirectory in templates, configure it to inherit from our site's templates to give it our look and feel, and this will override the Django one. Then, when this view is loaded, it will render our local template instead.

Creating the Login & Registration Pages

The first thing we're going to do is create three pages. The first will be our login page with the form that will take a username and password, letting registered users authenticate themselves. The second is the registration page that will let customers create user accounts on the site. The last one will be a "My Account" page, which will have a link to a page where the customer can set up their billing and shipping information to use with orders (which we'll create in the next section), a summary of the customer's past orders, and a link to a "Change Password" page.

So, hop down into your shell and let's start getting our hands dirty. Run the following in the root of your project to create the new accounts app:

```
$ python manage.py startapp accounts
```

Make sure that you add this new accounts app to your INSTALLED_APPS tuple in your settings.py file.

This is the app we're going to use to contain all of our custom settings, most of which will just be overriding the Django defaults. As one example, we're going to override the URL pattern for the login view, so that we can set the SSL keyword argument to True and ensure that user logins will be secure.

The first thing we're going to do is create the login, the registration, order details, and the My Account pages. Let's create a new file inside our new accounts app directory called urls.py, and add the following three URL definitions:

```
from django.conf.urls.defaults import *
from ecomstore import settings

urlpatterns = patterns('ecomstore.accounts.views',
    (r'^register/$', 'register',
        {'template_name': 'registration/register.html', 'SSL': settings.ENABLE_SSL },
'register'),
    (r'^my_account/$', 'my_account',
        {'template_name': 'registration/my_account.html'}, 'my_account'),
    (r'^order_details/(?P<order_id>[-\w]+)/$', 'order_details',
        {'template_name': 'registration/order_details.html'}, 'order_details'),
    (r'^order_info//$', 'order_info',
        {'template_name': 'registration/order_info.html'}, 'order_info'),
)

urlpatterns += patterns('django.contrib.auth.views',
    (r'^login/$', 'login',    {'template_name': 'registration/login.html', 'SSL':
settings.ENABLE_SSL }, 'login'),
)
```

You see four view functions, for the registration, Order Details, My Account, and Order Info pages, which will reside inside our project's accounts app directory. The last view, for the login page, is elsewhere in the Django source code. So, we've split them apart into two separate urlpatterns definitions, so that we can preface each one with a different path to view functions on our system. Notice that, when we define the second one, we use the += operator to simply add more URL entries to the first one.

Notice that in the order_details URL entry, we are again using a named parameter called order_id, which will be a visible part of the URL and will determine for which order the page should load details. The order_info URL will not be used until the second half of the chapter. I'm just including it here so when we include the link to the Order Info page in our templates, we won't get an error looking up the URL entry.

In this case, the login view is already written for us, so let's go further up the chain and create the template file for that page. If you glance back at the code for the login view at the beginning of the chapter, you should see that the view function is looking for a file called login.html, in a directory called registration. Go ahead and create the registration subdirectory inside your project's templates directory if you haven't done so already, and create the login.html file inside it. Add in the following code for the login page:

```
{% extends "catalog.html" %}

{% block content %}
{% if form.errors %}
    <ul class="errorlist">
        <li>You entered an invalid username or password.</li>
    </ul>
    <br />
{% endif %}
<form method="post" action="{% url django.contrib.auth.views.login %}">
<table summary="Login" id="login">
    <caption>Login</caption>
    <tr>
        <td>{{ form.username.label_tag }}:</td>
        <td>{{ form.username }}</td>
    </tr>
    <tr>
        <td>{{ form.password.label_tag }}:</td>
        <td>{{ form.password }}</td>
    </tr>
    <tr>
        <td colspan="2" class="right">
            <input type="submit" value="Login" />
        </td>
    </tr>
</table>
<input type="hidden" name="next" value="{{ next }}" />
</form>
{% endblock %}
```

Lastly, there is one definition inside the Django source, in the global_settings.py file we looked at in Chapter 4 in order to determine how long sessions would persist on our site. There are three definitions related to the login pages, one of which we need to override in our local configuration file. Open your settings.py file and add the following line of code:

```
LOGIN_REDIRECT_URL = '/accounts/my_account/'
```

This is the page the user will be redirected to after they log in, which in this case, we've set to the My Account page. So, if the user clicks the "Login" link we're going to create a moment and logs in using the login form, they will be sent to the My Account page by default.

Next, let's set up the views for the registration, so that new customers can easily set up a user account with us. In this case, the form class has already been created for us, but we need to create a view

157

function and a template for this page. Open the `views.py` file in your `accounts` app directory and add in the following function for the registration page:

```python
from django.contrib.auth.forms import UserCreationForm
from django.template import RequestContext
from django.shortcuts import render_to_response, get_object_or_404
from django.core import urlresolvers
from django.http import HttpResponseRedirect

def register(request, template_name="registration/register.html"):
    if request.method == 'POST':
        postdata = request.POST.copy()
        form = UserCreationForm(postdata)
        if form.is_valid():
            form.save()
            un = postdata.get('username','')
            pw = postdata.get('password1','')
            from django.contrib.auth import login, authenticate
            new_user = authenticate(username=un, password=pw)
            if new_user and new_user.is_active:
                login(request, new_user)
                url = urlresolvers.reverse('my_account')
                return HttpResponseRedirect(url)
    else:
        form = UserCreationForm()
    page_title = 'User Registration'
    return render_to_response(template_name, locals(),
        context_instance=RequestContext(request))
```

This single view contains a lot of the main functions that Django provides if you want to interact with the authentication of your users at a somewhat lower level. This takes data from a POST on your registration template and, if it validates per the rules of the form, saves the instance of the user to the database and retrieves the values from the username and password fields. Then, we call the `authenticate()` function, which takes the username and password as keyword arguments. If the user has been saved properly, this function returns the user instance. If not, it will return None.

Provided that `authenticate()` returns a valid user instance, we then call the `login()` function, which takes the current request object and the user instances as arguments. This gives the user a session on the site, effectively logging them in, right before we redirect them to the My Account page, where they'll be greeted with our "Welcome, [username]!" message.

There is a difference between the `authenticate()` function and the `login()` function, even though the two sound the same in concept. `authenticate()` checks to see if there is a corresponding instance of User in the database that matches the supplied username and password. `login()` takes a User instance and creates a session for you that persists the user's login across page requests. `login()` basically saves you from having to call `authenticate()` every time you want to make sure the user is who they claim to be, and lets you perform this check once, when they register or log in.

Next, we need to create the template file for the sign up page. Create a file called `register.html` inside your `templates/registration` directory and put the following code into it:

```html
{% extends "catalog.html" %}

{% block content %}
    <form action="." method="post">
        <table summary="Register" id="register">
```

```
            <caption>Sign Up For Your Account</caption>
            {{ form.as_table }}
            <tr>
                <th></th>
                <td>
                    <input type="submit" name="submit" value="Register" />
                </td>
            </tr>
            </table>
        </form>
{% endblock %}
```

This template simply displays the UserCreationForm, rendered as an HTML table. The validation of the three fields is encapsulated in the form class itself, so there's no more we need to do in order to get the page working.

■ **Note** For now, there is no minimum length required for a password. When we discuss security in Chapter 12, we're going to revisit the registration page and change it so that there are constraints on the length and strength of the password.

Let's create links to these pages in our navigation, as well as a link that will let any logged-in user easily and quickly log out, no matter what page they're on. Open your navigation.html file in your project's tags folder and let's add some additional links:

```
<ul>
    <li><a href="{% url catalog_home %}">Home</a></li>
    <li><a href="/about/">About</a></li>
    <li><a href="/privacy-policy/">Privacy</a></li>
    <li><a href="/contact/">Contact</a></li>

    <li>
        <a href="{% url my_account %}">My Account</a>
    </li>
</ul>
<div class="fr">
<ul>
    <li>
        {% if user.is_authenticated %}
            <a href="{% url django.contrib.auth.views.logout %}">Logout</a>
        {% else %}
            <a href="{% url register %}">Sign Up</a>
            </li>
            <li>
            <a href="{% url django.contrib.auth.views.login %}">Login</a>
        {% endif %}
    </li>
</ul>
</div>
<div class="cb"></div>
```

Now the navigation will have a link to the My Account page. We've also created a set of links at the far right of the navigation bar that will change depending on whether or not the user is logged in. If they are authenticated, the link to log out will be displayed. If they are not logged in, we will show a Sign Up link to the registration page, and a Login link to the login page.

One last thing we're going to do: after the user clicks the Logout link, they will be redirected to page letting them know they're logged out, and we're going to make this page now. Create a template called logged_out.html inside the registration directory in templates, and add this simple code to it:

```
{% extends "catalog.html" %}

{% block content %}
    <h1>You've Logged Out!</h1>
{% endblock %}
```

There's not a lot going on here, but you might consider taking this opportunity to show newly logged-out users some interesting product recommendations, like those flagged as "featured" in the database. For now, this simple confirmation page will work for us.

Unfortunately, these pages are not going to work until we create the My Account page, since this is where newly registered and logged-in users end up getting redirected. Let's create that page now.

The My Account Page

The My Account page for customers will have links to pages with details about each of their past orders placed on our site, a link to a page where they can change the password on their account, and a link to the page where they can set the billing and shipping information they want used in their orders. The final result will be something that looks like Figure 6-1.

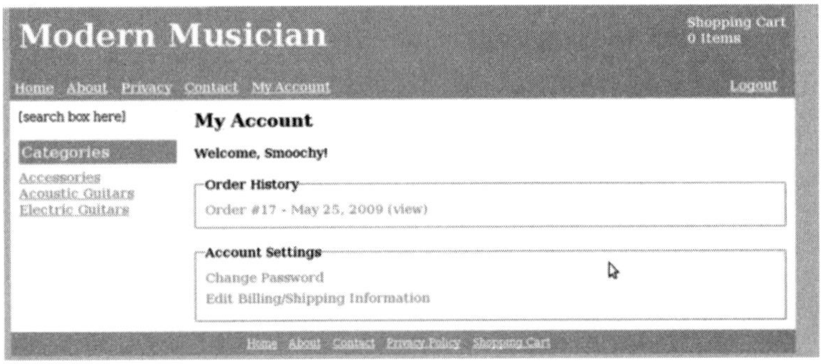

Figure 6-1.Where we're headed: the final My Account page.

The one key difference we'll need to take into consideration when designing our My Account page is that access to this page will be restricted to only customers that have a user account and are currently logged in. If they try to access this page but are not logged in, we will redirect them to the login page. From here, if they log in successfully, we'll redirect them back to where they were.

This flow is typical on the Internet. If you need to authenticate a user before letting them get to something, you want to ensure that you send them right back where they were before they logged in, so they don't need to click the Back button a bunch of times through a bunch of pages they went through while logging in.

Django makes this easy. There is a Python decorator we can put on each view that we want to be restricted only to users that are logged in. If they are not logged in, they are sent to the login page where, if they successfully authenticate, are then sent back to the page they tried to get to.

Back in your accounts app's view.py module, add the following import statements and view for the My Account page:

```
from ecomstore.checkout.models import Order, OrderItem
from django.contrib.auth.decorators import login_required

@login_required
def my_account(request, template_name="registration/my_account.html"):
    page_title = 'My Account'
    orders = Order.objects.filter(user=request.user)
    name = request.user.username
    return render_to_response(template_name, locals(),
        context_instance=RequestContext(request))
```

Through the use of the @login_required decorator, only authenticated users will be able to access the my_account() view function. Now that we have the view in place, let's create the template file. Inside the registration directory, create the my_account.html template file and, per the usual, put in the following template code:

```
{% extends "catalog.html" %}

{% block content %}
<h1>My Account</h1>
<strong>Welcome, {{ name|capfirst }}!</strong>
<br /><br />
<fieldset class="my_account">
    <legend>Order History</legend>
    {% for order in orders %}
        <a href="{{ order.get_absolute_url }}">
        Order #{{ order.id }} - {{ order.date|date }}  (view)
        </a>
        <br />
    {% empty %}
        You have no past orders.
    {% endfor %}
</fieldset>
<hr />
<fieldset class="my_account">
    <legend>Account Settings</legend>
    <ul>
    <li><a href="{% url django.contrib.auth.views.password_change %}">Change
Password</a></li>
    <li><a href="{% url order_info %}">Edit Billing/Shipping Information</a></li>
    </ul>
</fieldset>
{% endblock %}
```

In order to get this formatted properly, there is a little bit of CSS we need to add. But, before we get to that, have a look at the loop that's rolling out the list of past orders. There is a new syntax we're using here in our {% for %} loops:

```
{% for item in item_list %}
    <!-- iterate through results -->
{% empty %}
    <!-- display if item_list has zero items -->
{% endfor %}
```

If you're using Django 1.1 or above, you can use the {% empty %} tag inside your {% for %} loops in order to make your loops more concise. The alternative to this, in case you're using an older version of Django, is just to nest your {% for %} loop inside an {% if %} block that evaluates whether or not there are any items in your list. If it's empty, you can put the content you want to show up in the {% else %} block. We used the latter approach on the shopping cart page when iterating through the items in the user's cart.

There is one last missing piece of this puzzle. Right now, our Order model does not have a get_absolute_url() method defined on it. Now that we have a URL entry, go ahead and add this method definition to the Order model:

```
@models.permalink
def get_absolute_url(self):
    return ('order_details', (), { 'order_id': self.id })
```

Of course, before we go any further, let's add the following CSS styles to our stylesheet:

```
table#register{
    width:100%;
}
table#register th, td{
    vertical-align:top;
}
fieldset.my_account{
    padding:10px;
}
fieldset.my_account legend{
    font-weight:bold;
}
fieldset.my_account ul{
    list-style:none;
}
fieldset.my_account ul li{
    margin-bottom:5px;
}
```

While this gets us pretty close to where we want to be, we're still missing the Change Password and Order Details pages, which we can easily go ahead and create now.

The Change Password Page

The Change Password page is pretty simple to create. The URL and the view function are both provided for us, so all we need to do is create the template file that the view function needs. Inside the templates/registration directory, create two files called password_change_form.html and password_change_done.html. Open the first one and add the following template code:

```
{% extends "catalog.html" %}

{% block content %}
<form action="." method="post">
    <table>
    <caption>Change Password</caption>
        {{ form.as_table }}
        <tr>
            <td colspan="2" class="right">
            <input type="submit" name="submit" value="Change" />
            </td>
        </tr>
    </table>
 </form>
{% endblock %}
```

Then, in the second template for displaying a message to the user confirming that their password was changed, add in the following:

```
{% extends "catalog.html" %}

{% block content %}
<h1>Password Changed</h1>
Your password has been changed successfully.
<br /><br />
<a href="{% url catalog_home %}">Continue Shopping</a>
{% endblock %}
```

This is pretty straightforward, with the templates just using what's already provided to us. The only minor customization is the Continue Shopping link to the homepage. Once again, this could be something else that helps convince your users that there are other products on your site that they just cannot live without purchasing from you.

The Order Details Page

Each order that a logged-in user has placed on our site will be tied to that user, so if they would like to return and see the details of their order, like dollar total or the products purchased, they can come back and get to the details from their My Account page. This will pretty much be a clone of the receipt page we're showing to the user after they place an order, but it could be made to be more complex and show more details. We will not allow the user to edit the order on this page. It will be a read-only summary.

First, let's create the view function inside your views.py module:

```
@login_required
def order_details(request, order_id, template_name="registration/order_details.html"):
    order = get_object_or_404(Order, id=order_id, user=request.user)
    page_title = 'Order Details for Order #' + order_id
    order_items = OrderItem.objects.filter(order=order)
    return render_to_response(template_name, locals(),
        context_instance=RequestContext(request))
```

Again, access to this particular view has been restricted only to logged-in users. If the user requests details about an order that was not placed by them, the order will not be found by the filter() function and a 404 Not Found error will be returned instead.

Next, inside the registration directory for templates, create a new file called registration/order_details.html and enter in the following code, which does little more than simply list the details about the order:

```
{% extends "catalog.html" %}

{% load catalog_filters %}

{% block content %}
    <table id="receipt">
        <caption>
            Details for Order # {{ order.id }}
        </caption>
        <thead>
        <tr>
            <th scope="col">Name</th>
            <th scope="col">Price</th>
            <th scope="col">Quantity</th>
            <th class="right" scope="col">Total</th>
        </tr>
        </thead>
        <tfoot>
            <tr>
                <td colspan="4" class="right" style="height:30px;">
                Order Total: {{ order.total|currency }}
                </td>
            </tr>
        </tfoot>
        <tbody>
        {% for item in order_items %}
        <tr>
            <td>
                <a href="{{ item.get_absolute_url }}">
                    {{ item.name }}
                </a>
            </td>
            <td>{{ item.price|currency }}</td>
            <td>{{ item.quantity }}</td>
            <td class="right">{{ item.total|currency }}</td>
        </tr>
        {% endfor %}
        </tbody>
    </table>
{% endblock %}
```

It's nothing fancy, but it will let users view the details about their past orders. Now all we need to do is create logic in our checkout process that will associate orders placed with registered users if they are logged in during the checkout process. Let's set this up inside our checkout.py module that we created in the last chapter. In the create_order() function, add the following two lines that link the order we're creating with the user, if they are authenticated when they place they order:

```
order.user = None
if request.user.is_authenticated():
    order.user = request.user
```

Now, if you try placing an order while you are logged in, the order should show up under the "Order History" section in the My Account page.

We've got a lot of additional functionality in our site now, with login, registration, and pages that let a user peruse their past orders and change their password, without a whole lot of work. Now, we're going to look at storing our own custom list of information about each customer, extending the User model with Django's own built-in user profile mechanism.

Django User Profiles

If you've been playing along at home, dutifully coding up what we did in the last chapter when we created the checkout system, you're probably completely sick of entering dummy order information, time after time, in order to test your code and make sure that it's working. There are a couple of solutions to this problem. The first is automated testing, which we can actually do with Django pretty easily, but that's a topic for another chapter (see Chapter 14 for more on the Django testing suite).

The second option is a convenience we can afford not only to ourselves, but to our customers as well: let registered users store contact, shipping, and billing information as a part of their account. When the authenticated user goes to check out, we'll display these values as the defaults on the checkout form, sparing them the mindless and frustrating task of having to key in this information each and every time they place an order.

Storing all of these extra fields with each user is not something that we should take lightly. The User model is part of the Django source code, which, as we've already determined, we shouldn't be editing. Fortunately, Django comes equipped with a very powerful and flexible solution: profiles. We define a class that has a foreign key relationship to the User model, create a few fields inside this model, and then designate the model as a user profile in our settings.py file so the whole thing is really super official.

So, without further ado, let's implement this and save our customers some typing.

Abstract Base Classes

If we examine the list of fields in our Order model that we want to store with each user, you'll find that there are more than a dozen fields we want to copy verbatim from the Order model to this new profile model. While we could create a new model and just copy-paste the fields over from the Order model, there actually is a slightly better way of approaching this problem, through the use of Django abstract base classes.

It's possible to create a Django model that will never have its own table in your database. Instead, other model classes may subclass from this model, inheriting all of its fields, so that you are free to use the same field definitions across as many models as you'd like. All you need to do is declare the base model as an abstract one.

Looking back at our Order model, let's re-imagine the solution we created in the last chapter. We can easily cut the sixteen or so fields out of the Order model and put them into an abstract base class. Then, we'll change the Order model so that it inherits from this abstract model definition, so that those fields in the base class are still part of the Order model. Then, we can create our profile model and inherit from the same base class, and just by virtue of object-oriented magic, it too will have the same 16 fields. Figure 6-2 sums up the process quite nicely.

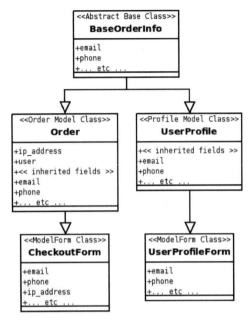

Figure 6-2. The use of an abstract base class for order information.

So, let's take a moment and refactor the model definitions we created in the last chapter. Open your models.py module in the checkout app, cut the definitions you want to store with the user profile out of the Order model, and put them into another class definition at the top of the file, above the Order and OrderItem models, like so:

```
class BaseOrderInfo(models.Model):

    class Meta:
        abstract = True

    #contact info
    email = models.EmailField(max_length=50)
    phone = models.CharField(max_length=20)

    #shipping information
    shipping_name = models.CharField(max_length=50)
    shipping_address_1 = models.CharField(max_length=50)
    shipping_address_2 = models.CharField(max_length=50, blank=True)
    shipping_city = models.CharField(max_length=50)
    shipping_state = models.CharField(max_length=2)
    shipping_country = models.CharField(max_length=50)
    shipping_zip = models.CharField(max_length=10)

    #billing information
    billing_name = models.CharField(max_length=50)
    billing_address_1 = models.CharField(max_length=50)
    billing_address_2 = models.CharField(max_length=50, blank=True)
```

```
billing_city = models.CharField(max_length=50)
billing_state = models.CharField(max_length=2)
billing_country = models.CharField(max_length=50)
billing_zip = models.CharField(max_length=10)
```

The abstract = True in the inner Meta class designates this model as a base class that will never get its own data table, and should not normally be instantiated in our Python code. Following this example, change the Order model class definition so that it inherits from this new BaseOrderInfo class:

```
class Order(BaseOrderInfo):
    # etc.
```

Provided that you've cut all of the fields out of the Order model properly, you should be able to run manage.py syncdb without any effect. At this point, for practical purposes, your model definition hasn't really changed at all. You've merely shifted the information around into another class.

Make sure that you don't move the user field from the Order class into the base class. While user will be a field used as a ForeignKey in both the Order and the profile models, the declaration will be much different in the profile model, in that only one profile will be allowed per user instance. While a user can have many orders (and we sure hope our users have many, many orders apiece!), we'll constrain the database so that only one profile can be created per user. This will be very much like a one-to-one relationship.

This really doesn't leave much work for us to do for creating the user profile model. Open the models.py module inside your new accounts app and create the following model definition:

```
from django.db import models
from django.contrib.auth.models import User
from ecomstore.checkout.models import BaseOrderInfo

class UserProfile(BaseOrderInfo):
    user = models.ForeignKey(User, unique=True)

    def __unicode__(self):
        return 'User Profile for: ' + self.user.username
```

The only strange thing we're doing here is adding the unique=True keyword argument to the user field definition, which effectively constrains the database to only allow one instance of the UserProfile class per user. And because we're inheriting from the BaseOrderInfo class, this profile model will have all of those other fields of data that we want to store regarding order information.

One last thing: open up your settings.py file and add the profile model as a profile module to your project:

```
AUTH_PROFILE_MODULE = 'accounts.userprofile'
```

This is the name of the app that contains the model definition, and the name of the model itself, all in lowercase. With this definition in place, run manage.py syncdb from your shell, in order to create the new user profile table. Once the table is created, we can move on to creating our UI and other logic to handle the user profile data.

The Order Info Page

The first thing we need is a means of capturing the information the user wants to enter for their contact, shipping, and billing information. For this, we're going to need to create a form class. Since our form is based strictly on data that's part of one of our models, we're going to subclass ModelForm. Create a file called forms.py inside the accounts app and add in:

```
from django import forms
from ecomstore.accounts.models import UserProfile

class UserProfileForm(forms.ModelForm):
    class Meta:
        model = UserProfile
        exclude = ('user',)
```

As before, we've just tied in the name of the model and excluded the one user field, so that the user editing the form can't manipulate the value in this field. Now, we need functions for retrieving our user profile data, and setting it after they've entered it into our little form. Inside the accounts app, create a new file called profile.py, and enter in the following two function definitions:

```
from ecomstore.accounts.models import UserProfile
from ecomstore.accounts.forms import UserProfileForm

def retrieve(request):
    ''' note that this requires an authenticated
    user before we try calling it '''
    try:
        profile = request.user.get_profile()
    except UserProfile.DoesNotExist:
        profile = UserProfile(user=request.user)
        profile.save()
    return profile

def set(request):
    profile = retrieve(request)
    profile_form = UserProfileForm(request.POST, instance=profile)
    profile_form.save()
```

These two lean functions act as simple getter and setter methods (not in the official Python sense) for the user profiles. retrieve() tries to get the profile of the currently authenticated user. If the profile has never been created for the user and it's not found, we catch the DoesNotExist exception and take that opportunity to create and save the profile instance for the user. Note that, before we call this function out in the wild, we need to make sure we are dealing with an authenticated user via the user.is_authenticated() method.

The second method, set(), retrieves the profile of the current user, binds the data that comes in from a POST request to the user's instance of their profile data, and saves it to the database. This should also only be called if the user is logged in, since without an authenticated user, calling the retrieve() method will cause an error.

Next, we just need to create the view function that will pull all of this together. Add the following view to the accounts/views.py module:

```
from ecomstore.accounts.forms import UserProfileForm
from ecomstore.accounts import profile

@login_required
def order_info(request, template_name="registration/order_info.html"):
    if request.method == 'POST':
        postdata = request.POST.copy()
        form = UserProfileForm(postdata)
        if form.is_valid():
```

```
            profile.set(request)
            url = urlresolvers.reverse('my_account')
            return HttpResponseRedirect(url)
    else:
        user_profile = profile.retrieve(request)
        form = UserProfileForm(instance=user_profile)
    page_title = 'Edit Order Information'
    return render_to_response(template_name, locals(),
context_instance=RequestContext(request))
```

Now, since we have the URL already in place from the first half of the chapter, the only thing we need to do now is create the corresponding template file. Create order_info.html in the templates/registration directory and add in the following template code:

```
{% extends "catalog.html" %}

{% block content %}
<h1>Edit Order Information</h1>
{{ response }}
{% if error_message %}
    <ul class="errorlist">
        <li>{{ error_message }}</li>
    </ul>
{% endif %}
<form action="." method="post">
    <table>
        {{ form.as_table }}
    </table>
    <table>
    <tr>
        <th colspan="2">
            <input type="submit" value="Save Information" class="submit" />
        </th>
    </tr>
    </table>
</form>
{% endblock %}
```

In the interest of saving space, and making sure the template code doesn't stretch out over two pages, I decided just to render the form as an HTML table. However, in the source code you can download from the Apress web site, I reused the {% form_table_row %} inclusion tag from the last chapter.

Updating the Checkout Page

Now that registered users can store order information, we need to hook this new functionality into the checkout flow. The first thing we need to do is bind the stored order information to the checkout form if the customer is authenticated. This will require just a small tweak to the show_checkout() view function. Crack open the views.py module and add the following to the else block, if the request is not a POST:

```
error_message = 'Correct the errors below'
    else:
        if request.user.is_authenticated():
```

169

```
        user_profile = profile.retrieve(request)
        form = CheckoutForm(instance=user_profile)
    else:
        form = CheckoutForm()
page_title = 'Checkout'
```

Then, we need to update the create_order() function so that if an order is placed successfully and the user is logged in, we'll do them the favor of automatically storing the information in the user profile too. That way, the next time they place an order on our site, we will already have their past order information stored.

Inside the checkout.py module, add the following to the create_order() function, just before the return line:

```
cart.empty_cart(request)
    # save profile info for future orders
    if request.user.is_authenticated():
        from ecomstore.accounts import profile
        profile.set(request)
    # return the new order object
    return order
```

Notice that here, I've chosen to do an import in the middle of the function. While this isn't typically the way I code my Python, I used it in this example just to be more concise.

There's one last touch I'm going to add to the checkout template before moving forward. In case a customer with an account navigates to the checkout page without being logged in, we still want to afford them the opportunity to log in and use their existing order information we've stored with their account.

Remember that when an anonymous user tries to access a page that requires a valid login, we redirect to the login page. After this, if they provide valid login credentials and are authenticated, the login page redirects them back to the page they were trying to access before they were redirected. It does this by sticking the path of the page into the URL of the login page. Therefore, this URL for the login page:

```
http://www.example.com/login/?next=/accounts/my_account/
```

will redirect back to the My Account page once the user successfully logs in. We can take advantage of this and easily construct a link to the login page from the checkout page that will encourage the customer to log in to their account if they have one. Then, once they are authenticated, the login page will send them back to checkout page, now authenticated, with their order profile information now bound to the checkout form.

At the top of the checkout.html template, above the h1 element, put the following block of code:

```
{% if not request.user.is_authenticated %}
<div class="fr">
    <a href="{% url login %}?next={{ request.path }}">
    Have an account?<br />Sign in now!
    </a>
</div>
{% endif %}
```

Now we have a link that will display if the user is not logged in, informing them they can log in before they start filling out the order form.

This little block of code would make a perfect inclusion tag. Notice that we might use this in several other places on our site, where you might need to display a link to the login page that will redirect the user back to this page after they've logged in. The only thing that might change is the text of the link. Feel free to move this out of your checkout template and into a custom Django template tag that you can use elsewhere.

Summary

We did a lot in this chapter, even though we weren't really required to write a lot of our own code. As a matter of fact, there's little in this chapter you couldn't have gleaned from the online documentation on your own. However, that doesn't make what we just did any less important: our e-commerce module now has an authentication system, complete with login and registration pages, as well as the ability to store customer order information so they don't need to wear their wrists out entering with each and every order they place on our site.

After you take the whole thing for a test drive, you might find that the Django defaults don't entirely suit you. This is pretty likely, actually, since the Django authentication system was certainly never designed to be all things to all people. It's just supposed to be most things to those people who want to save oodles of development time getting a fully functional site up and running. Even if it's not 100% of what you feel your site requires, it should already be most of the way there.

In the next chapter, we're going to create new models to deal with our product images, to tempt our customers with shiny pictures of the stuff we're hoping they buy.

CHAPTER 7

■ ■ ■

Product Images

Every now and then, I'm surfing the Internet, price shopping for a particular item using Google Shopping (which used to be called "Froogle," until they realized that people weren't able to figure out what the heck "Froogle" was or how it was supposed to be used) or some other comparison-shopping engine. Now, the stuff that I'm shopping for is pretty standardized. Most of what I buy is computer books, and for the most part, if the site has the ISBN number correct, you can probably order it and you'll get the book you were hoping to get.

Most of the listings have an image for each product, and some do not. I don't remember ever clicking on an item that didn't have a product image listed. Standardized or not, I never really feel comfortable paying for something on an e-commerce site unless they're willing to show me a picture of exactly what I'm purchasing.

Having product pictures on your site is of utmost importance. You want to show customers what they're looking at on each product page. We're visual creatures, and you want to give the shoppers on your site a visual foothold for your products. It gives people a good feeling and makes them feel more comfortable with you as a seller.

This is important in other places besides the product page. Whenever you list products on category pages, search results, wish lists, or cross-sells, you'll want to make sure you show a thumbnail of each product so that people have some impression of what they're about to click through to. While you *can* list more products without allocating the space for a thumbnail image, having fewer products with thumbnails is almost always better than a longer list of just hyperlinked product names.

In addition to this, you should make them really *good* images. Even if you have access to stock photos that you're legally allowed to use on your site, you probably should take your own if the stock ones you have are low-resolution, grainy, and unclear in any way. You want them to be as high quality as you can manage.

In this chapter, we're going to add new fields to our `Product` model in order to handle product pages and thumbnail images. We'll look at how Django makes handling images easy with the `ImageField` you can use on your models, which transparently handles the uploading of images to the file system and then stores the path to the image in the database.

Dealing with Images

Images tend to be very large in size. For this reason, it's generally a bad idea to store images directly inside your database. Although it is possible, this can result in a massive amount of data in a single field, which your database then has to read out and send back to you with each request you make for a product or group of products. This can result in a great deal of overhead for a simple read request.

Obviously, this isn't an ideal solution for performance reasons. A much more common approach is to store the actual image on the file system, and store the *path* to the image on the file system in the database, as a string field. Later, when you render your HTML page, you use the path in the src attribute of your img tag, and let the browser load the image from the file system using the provided path.

Before getting started, we're going to quickly introduce the model field that Django uses to store images, and then take a look at the Python Imaging Library, one of the most popular libraries for editing images files in Python. Then, we'll edit our Product model to accommodate some new images.

Django Image Fields

When we first created the Product model in Chapter 3, we merely created an image field that stores the string name of the image file. Our templates contain the link to each image, using the MEDIA_URL in settings.py, the name of the file, and the relative path to the file inside our media directory. This approach has worked fine for us so far, but it has a couple of drawbacks. First, we are repeating ourselves, by having to hard-code the path to the image files in each template where we're referencing them.

Second, it really doesn't afford us ease of adding images to each product. In order to set a product image, we need to upload it ourselves to the correct directory or directories, and then set the name of the file by editing the field in the corresponding product model. This is pretty simple on a development machine, where you likely have direct access to the folder where your images reside. However, when you deploy this to a hosting environment, you then need FTP access or some other means of transferring the images to the remote site.

While this works, it's a little clunky and makes things much more difficult than they need to be. Django comes equipped with a solution that makes dealing with image files very simple: a field type called ImageField that you can use in your models. The field in the database stores a string that contains a path to the image, relative to the MEDIA_URL value you have specified in your settings.py file.

In this chapter, we're going to edit the fields in our model, and add some new ones for product images.

Installing the Python Imaging Library

Using ImageFields on models requires installation of the Python Imaging Library[1] (PIL). The PIL is a powerful library that allows you to do complex image processing and manipulation in your Python code, using several different types of files. While we're not going to delve too deep or do anything too complex with it, I encourage you to have a look at the documentation to get a sense of its capabilities if you're a Python developer.

You'll need to download the appropriate files and install this on your system. There are installation packages available for Windows, tars for Unix systems, and a Debian package is available for Ubuntu Linux users.

Database Changes

The first thing we need to do is make a small handful of edits to the product database table. In order to do this, we're going to have to get our hands dirty and make the edits directly inside MySQL.

First, drop into MySQL using the dbshell command:

```
$ python manage.py dbshell
```

---

[1] http://www.pythonware.com/products/pil/

Now, execute the following command to remove the existing image field from the `products` database table:

```
mysql> ALTER TABLE products DROP image;
```

Now we're going to add three new columns to the `products` table. We're going to add two new fields to the database that will map to `ImageField`s in our product model that we're going to add in the next section. Each of these fields expects a database column that holds a string of type `varchar(100)`, so we're going to create two of these. Also, we're going to add another `varchar(200)` field for holding an image caption.

Execute these three commands to add three new columns:

```
mysql> ALTER TABLE products ADD image varchar(100);
mysql> ALTER TABLE products ADD thumbnail varchar(100);
mysql> ALTER TABLE products ADD image_caption varchar(200);
```

Naturally, these examples are MySQL-specific, so they won't work for PostgreSQL. However, if you're using PostgreSQL as your database, I imagine you're a real database wizard and you have a pretty good grasp of the syntax you would use to make these edits.

RAILS MIGRATIONS FOR DJANGO?

If you're coming from a Ruby on Rails background, or if you get nervous making direct edits to the database whether from the command line or the MySQL-Admin tool, you may be wondering if there isn't a way to handle database alterations using *migrations*.

Rails migrations allow you to write database alterations, such as adding and removing tables or columns, in Ruby code. You can then run the migration and it will make the change or batch of changes included in the migration to your database all at once. Not only this, but Rails generates an "up" and "down" version of each migration, which makes reverting changes a cinch as well.

As it happens, there is a solution out there in the wild that's quite helpful for dealing with these situations called *dmigrations* that mimics this very well. You can download the code and read the documentation for it at:

```
http://code.google.com/p/dmigrations/
```

Handling database schema evolutions in an automated fashion is especially helpful when there is more than one developer working on a project, as it allows you to easily propagate database changes to each developer, who may be working on a copy of the project on their own development machine.

As great as this feature is for development projects, I opted not to use them in this book for a couple of reasons. First, it requires MySQL. Secondly, I wanted the examples throughout the book not to be reliant on a third-party tool. That doesn't mean they won't save you oodles of development time.

Editing the Model

Now, we just need to make the actual change to the Product model class so that the new image field is included. Open up `models.py` inside `catalog` and remove the following field from the `Product` model:

```
image = models.CharField(max_length=50)
```

Then, add the following three field definitions to it:

```
image = models.ImageField(upload_to='images/products/main')
thumbnail = models.ImageField(upload_to='images/products/thumbnails')
image_caption = models.CharField(max_length=200)
```

Each product now has two image fields on it, one called `image` for the product page, and the other called `thumbnail`, which we'll use just about anywhere else we list products. Each `ImageField` takes one required argument, `upload_to`, which specifies the directory in which Django will save the image file after it's uploaded. The two directories we've listed here should already exist, since we created them to hold images in Chapter 3.

However, the `upload_to` part of the path is only one half of the path to the image on your server. The rest of the path is specified in your `settings.py` file. Open the `settings.py` file, find the `MEDIA_ROOT` variable, and set it to the following:

```
MEDIA_ROOT = os.path.join(CURRENT_PATH, 'static')
```

This takes advantage of the `CURRENT_PATH` constant we set earlier, so this line resolves to `/path/to/your/project/static/` on your system. When you upload an image file on an `ImageField`, Django concatenates the `MEDIA_ROOT` setting, the `upload_to` argument, and the name of the file to resolve where on your system it should save the file.

As one example, if you were to upload a product image called `slony.jpg` using the `image` field on our Product model, Django would put it all together and the file would be saved to:

```
/path/to/your/project/static/images/products/main/slony.jpg
```

Naturally, the thumbnail will end up in the other directory. This is exactly what we want. One last thing worth pointing out is that if you try to upload an image that has the same name as an image that's already in the specified directory, Django will alter it by adding an underscore character after the name before it saves it to the file system. This will be done any number of times to avoid name clashes, meaning that you could end up with image files with names containing hundreds of underscores. So, you don't need to worry about overwriting existing images because of a name clash.

Lastly, there is a text field for holding an image caption field, so we can put a brief blurb of text just below each photo. This was originally in my mockup of the product page that I created in Chapter 3.

Adding a New Image

So, get your test server up and running at localhost if it's not already running, log into the admin interface (at `/admin/`), and click the "Add Product" link. Optionally, you could just edit an existing one and add a new product image to it.

Below the form with the fields for filling our product data, you should see the new fields for adding images. There are two file input fields for each `ImageField`. It should bear a very strong similarity to Figure 7-1.

Figure 7-1. The new form for adding images to products.

Go ahead and add an image, thumbnail, and caption to one of your products now, even if you're doing nothing more than re-uploading the images that you already have stored for one of your products. Just specify all of the files and then click the "Save" button just as though you had made edits to any of the other fields. This is good to test the upload and make sure that the images are being written to the correct directory.

■ **Note** For the purpose of this example, I'm assuming here that you're working on a local development machine using the Django development `manage.py` runserver command. In this case, you're unlikely to run into problems, but if you're making this change to a site in production, you need to make sure that your web server has write permissions to these directories.

In the next section, we're going to make some quick changes to our templates so that the user interface will use the new fields on the `Product` model instead of the existing `image` field.

Image Template Changes

Now that the product images are being handled by the `Product` model form in the admin interface, we need to tweak our existing templates so that they use the new fields on the model. Inside your project's `templates/catalog` directory, open up `category.html` and have a look at the `{% for %}` loop we're using to iterate through the list of products. We've put the `<div>` containing the HTML for the product thumbnail right in this template:

```
<div class="product_thumbnail">
        <a href="{{ p.get_absolute_url }}">
          <img src="{{ MEDIA_URL }}images/products/thumbnails/{{ p.image }}
            alt="{{ p.name }}" class="bn" />
          <br />
          {{ p.name }}
        </a>
      </div>
```

177

While this works just fine, we're now acutely aware of the fact that we'll need to use this thumbnail HTML in other places on our site, and not merely inside the `category.html` file. This sounds like a good candidate for getting its own template file that we can load wherever we need.

Create a new file inside `templates/tags` and call it `product_thumbnail.html`. Inside this file, just copy over the existing HTML for the `div` with the class of `product_thumbnail` from the category template. You can comment out this `div` from `category.html` or just remove it altogether.

Now, with this new template file open, let's have a look at the following line:

```
<img src="{{ MEDIA_URL }}images/" … blah blah … />
```

This looks much longer than it really needs to be. We simply need to be able to get at the URL location of the thumbnail we just uploaded. To enable this, change the image tag line to the following:

```
<img src="{{ p.thumbnail.url }}" alt="{{ p.name }}" class="bn" />
```

Much simpler. You simply call the `url` property on the `ImageField` and you get back the corresponding path to the thumbnail.

Of course, you need to add this new template back into your `catalog/category.html` file in order to include the product thumbnail in your category pages. Inside this template file, where you removed the `product_thumbnail` div, add the following line:

```
{% include 'tags/product_thumbnail.html' %}
```

Now that we've refactored out the product thumbnail for use in multiple places, that just leaves a quick edit to the product page template to call on the new caption field we just created, as well as the new image file. Change the image tag in `catalog/product.html` to read:

```
<img src="{{ p.image.url }}" alt="{{ p.name }}" />
```

and add the following line below the image tag, but inside the `product_image` div element:

```
{{ p.image_caption }}
```

That's it! We're now dealing with product images with full-blown Django style. Make sure that you include a descriptive `alt` attribute to each image on your site, as people who have images disabled in their browsers or vision impairments won't be able to see the images, and will fall back on this text.

Summary

This short and simple chapter added a very important part of your site: product images. People will more often than not make buying decisions based on what they can see, so it's imperative that you make the effort to add quality images to each of your products. Even though search engines can't index the content of an image, remember that you need to optimize your site for your customers as well, and they'll want to see what they're buying.

In the next chapter, we're going to add a very large, mission-critical feature to our site: product search. While our site is equipped with very simple navigation, this will not be sufficient as our product catalog grows in size and each customer is forced to wade through hundreds of products. Since each product has a name, descriptive text, and meta tag data stored along with it, we're going to leverage this content so that our customers can get products matching search keywords.

CHAPTER 8

■ ■ ■

Implementing Product Search

Business on the Internet since it started becoming commonplace has been dominated by a single concept: *search*. As the World Wide Web became more widespread and the number of web sites out there started exploding, increasing into the millions, enterprising computer minds realized that there was good money to be made in organizing the sheer volume of content on the web so that it would be accessible by the average person. New search engines popped up left and right, all trying to make a business of searching on the web. Of course, during this time, Google was founded, and since then their name has become synonymous with searching on the web.

Customers will come to your site looking for stuff to buy and, depending on your site and the type of product you're selling, some of them probably won't even use the list of categories that we've put in the sidebar for them. They're just going to go right for the search box, type in what they want, and click away, waiting for it to come up.

In this chapter, we're going to implement search, and set a very basic algorithm that will match search keywords to the products in our database. We'll also look at how Django helps give us results using custom model manager classes, a special pagination class to allow us to spread large amounts of results across multiple pages, and look at how the Django ORM API lets us construct complex queries, all in Python code.

Instant Search

For the moment, I'm going to assume that you have no interest in hearing me drone on about the Django features that are going to make our search results really spiffy and clean. I'm going to imagine that you're sitting on top of a looming deadline with some software manager breathing down your neck and you *just don't care* about anything but getting the search functionality implemented in under 10 minutes.

Have it your way.

In order to create basic search functionality, you need two things. First, you need a search form nestled somewhere on your site, preferably on every page, so that users can easily enter some search text and click a button. Second, you need a page that lists the products that have fields containing text that is similar to the search text the user entered.

This can be achieved very easily. The following is a hand-coded form that will let the user enter some search text and click a button:

```
<form method="get" action="/search/results/">
    <label for="q">
    <input type="text" name="q" id="q" />
    <input type="Submit" value="Search" />
</form>
```

If the user enters "guitar tiddlywinks," the site will make a GET request to this path on your site:

```
/search/results/?q=guitar+tiddlywinks
```

All we need to now is to create a view function that can handle this request. It just needs to get the search text out of the URL and do a fairly simple lookup on our Product model. Here is a simple view function (less import statements) that will give us roughly what we're looking for:

```
def results(request):
    search_text = request.GET.get('q','')
    results = Product.objects.filter(name__icontains=search_text)
    return results  # via render_to_response, of course
```

While it lacks a lot of finesse, this does return a listing of matching products that we can iterate through on our template. It retrieves products using the icontains field lookup keyword argument. We'll cover the syntax of these in more detail in the next section, but evaluating the preceding query effectively executes the rough equivalent of the following SQL statement:

```
SELECT * FROM products WHERE name LIKE '%search_text%';
```

It does a case-insensitive comparison of the search text and the product name. If the product name contains the search text anywhere in it, it's a match.

From these humble beginnings, we can refine our approach and create something a little more compelling, and more appropriate for our customers.

Search Requirements

While the form and view that we created in the previous section would work just fine with a template that lists out all of the results to our users, there are a few drawbacks to the simple, 10-minutes-or-less approach. First of all, the results aren't quite as accurate that they could be. We have a product on our sample site called the "Ruby Axe Guitar," which would be returned with the search results if the user enters "ruby," or "ruby axe," or "axe guitar." If the user enters these keywords out of order, like if they do a search for "guitar ruby," the Ruby Axe Guitar won't be in the search results because our freeze-dried solution doesn't find that exact phrase in the product name.

More importantly, there are many other fields stuffed with content and keywords besides the product name. We have description, meta keywords and descriptions, and a SKU field on our product, each of which we should check to see if there is a match.

Before we get into matching more than one field and deal with search text that has multiple words, let's take a quick look at the queries we've been doing on our models so far.

Model Managers

As we have seen, Django helps you reduce the amount of repetitive code that you need to write. When writing queries, one feature that can significantly help you in creating queries is the ability to create Django model Manager classes.

To see this, let's take an example of querying for product data. To get all of the products on our site, we can easily create a query like this:

```
Product.objects.all()
```

This query will return a list of all the Product model instances we have stored in our database. However, whenever we're calling a query to load a list of products on our site, we always apply a filter to the results to make sure that the products we get back are all marked as "active" in the database:

```
Product.objects.filter(is_active=True)
```

So far, we've done this in a couple of places. The category list in the navigation at the side of each page is being loaded via a context processor, using a call much like the preceding one. Unfortunately, as the site grows over time, this kind of code will end up being repeated in several places, which is a little silly, since all we're really doing is applying a filter to the model.

The call to objects on the model is actually a call to the model's default Manager class. By default, all models have a Manager class called objects that maps to every record in the table for that model. However, it's possible to override the default Manager and create our own, to customize the records that are returned. Since we're going to be querying our Category and Product classes in several places, and filtering them to include only the active records, let's create custom Manager classes for each.

Enter the following class definition into models.py, directly above the Product model class:

```
class ActiveProductManager(models.Manager):
    def get_query_set(self):
        return super(ActiveProductManager, self).get_query_set().filter(is_active=True)
```

Then, inside the Product model class, add the following two lines to hook up the new Manager class:

```
objects = models.Manager()
active = ActiveProductManager()
```

With the active Manager class in place, the following query on the Product class is now legal and returns on those products marked as active:

```
Product.active.all()
```

Hooking up your own customer model manager class is useful, but whenever you do it, you need to make sure that you also include an explicit declaration of the default objects manager. This is because as soon as you add your own custom manager, Django no longer provides the objects manager by default. Since parts of our web project still depend on objects, we need to make sure it's still available. The perfect example of this is our admin interface, where we still want to be able to access and edit products and categories, whether or not they're active.

Before moving on, let's add the same enhancement to the Category model class. Just above that model, add the following class definition:

```
class ActiveCategoryManager(models.Manager):
    def get_query_set(self):
        return super(ActiveCategoryManager, self).get_query_set().filter(is_active=True)
```

And then, inside the Category model class, add these two lines to hook in the new manager class, as well as provide the default:

```
objects = models.Manager()
active = ActiveCategoryManager()
```

Now, wherever on your site you've made the call on the objects manager of the Category class that filters out the inactive ones, you can update it with a call to the active manager class. Go ahead and open the catalog_tags.py file now and edit the category_list() function definition.

Custom manager classes are quite useful in Django, but it is possible to misuse them. In our case, we want to get at only active product records, and using a manager to get back only the rows we want makes logical sense. You don't want to use managers to retrieve or manipulate the data returned from a single record. In those cases, you would just use a method on the model class definition, much like our `get_absolute_url()` methods.

Complex Lookups with Q

Django has some pretty useful mechanisms for building queries. Even though all of the raw SQL is abstracted away behind the Django's ORM, we still have a lot of options for tweaking and tuning the queries we make in order to get exactly the results that we want. Have a quick look back at the example we did in the last section to get products with names matching the search text:

```
results = Product.objects.filter(name__icontains=search_text)
```

You can filter out the results using several different methods. The construction of these special keyword arguments to a filter take the format of a field name on a model, followed by two underscores, and then one of the keywords Django provides in order to determine the value of the argument is matched against the corresponding field on the model.

There are a handful of different keywords you can use to create these queries: `contains`, `exact`, `startswith`, and `endswith`. All of these do exactly what they sound like, and each one can be prefaced with a lowercase letter i in order to make the comparison case-insensitive. `icontains` is by far the most useful, as it does a case-insensitive match to see if the value passed in matches any portion of the field. Of course, with that power comes a performance tradeoff; `icontains` is also the most computationally expensive of the comparison operators.

Now the question becomes, how do we use all of these to create a query that will match more than one field? In our first, overly simplistic example, we merely matched the product name, which, while useful, doesn't take advantage of the gobs of content I'm sure you generated for each of your products, such description, for example.

Django allows you to chain together your filters, using the following syntax:

```
Product.active.all().filter(name__icontains=text).filter(description__icontains=text)
```

You can chain together as many filters on as many fields using this syntax as you would like. However, this is not what we're looking for. The problem with this code is that it is much too exclusive. When it's evaluated, it's going to look for products that have the search text in the name AND the description AND any other fields that we add to the filter chain. It's possible that a product will contain "ruby" in its name, but if by chance the word "ruby" is not in the description, then the product will not be a match. This is, of course, not the behavior that a user searching would expect.

What we would like to do is query out results from products using a more inclusive means. We want products to match if the *name* contains "ruby" OR the *description* contains "ruby," and so forth, through all of the fields, so that if any one of them contains the word "ruby," the product will match the query.

The easiest way to do this in Django is using a series of Q objects, which permits you to make the same type of queries using the `icontains` keywords, but gives you the option of which operator you're going to use. So, you can specify OR instead of AND. For example, to refactor the preceding query to include products where the search keyword exists in any of the fields we specify, we can use the following code:

```
Q(name__icontains=word) | Q(description__icontains=word) | Q(… etc …)
```

The pipe character (|) is the OR operator in this case. You have the option of using the ampersand character instead (&) if you would like to filter out the query results using the AND syntax, similar to the results we were getting from chaining together the filters previously.

Now we just need to evaluate which fields on the Product model we want to match up with our search terms. The product name and description are a given. We might as well include the content of the meta keywords and description tags as well, since they might contain relevant information about the product. Let's also include the brand name, since people might include the brand name of the product in their search. Lastly, some people might do a search for a product based on the SKU number, so we'll return a product if the search term happens to match the SKU exactly.

The following block of code will achieve this result nicely:

```
word = 'ruby'
products = Product.active.all()
products = products.filter(Q(name__icontains=word) |
Q(description__icontains=word) |
Q(sku__iexact=word) |
Q(brand__icontains=word) |
Q(meta_description__icontains=word) |
Q(meta_keywords__icontains=word))
```

The last piece of this is to make sure that we can do this for each word that a user enters in their search query. For example, this example assumed that the user entered a single word, "ruby," in the search box. This is fine, but remember, one thing we need to do is make sure that our search algorithm can handle multiple words, so that a query such as "guitar ruby" will still return the Ruby Axe Guitar, even though none of the fields listed contain the specific phrase "guitar ruby."

Python makes this very simple. All we need to is split the query up use the built-in `split()` method on the search text the user has entered. Inside a Python shell, this looks like:

```
>>> search_text = 'guitar ruby axe'
>>> search_text.split()
['guitar','ruby','axe']
```

This returns a list of words, which we can iterate through and perform the previous query on each individual word in the search phrase.

Search Results Pagination

That last thing we need to do before we start implementing search is determine how we're going to split large amounts of results up into multiple pages. Basic search works for a smaller site, but sooner or later, your site may grow to have hundreds or even thousands of products. If the user enters a really common search term, such as "guitar," your site might potentially be forced to build a very large search results page that contains over a hundred product thumbnails. After they do so, they'll be forced to sit there and wait as your server struggles to build this massive page, send it to them, and then they have sit there as every last thumbnail image loads.

This is completely unacceptable, but fortunately, there is a solution in Django that makes the process of spreading result sets across multiple pages very simple: the `Paginator` class. The Django `Paginator` class allows us to restrict the number of results we query for to a certain number per page, allows us to fetch only one page worth of results at a time, and even provides properties that make it extremely simple to build a series of HTML links that will let the user easily navigate through the pages of results.

The use of a `Paginator` object is fairly straightforward and easy to grasp if you're a Django developer. To create one, simply pass in an iterable list of objects and the number you want to appear to per page:

```
pager = Paginator(Product.active.all(), 20)
```

Then, if you want to get the results for the second page, which, given 20 products per page, would be results 21-40, you can make the following call:

```
second_page = pager.page(2)
```

The actual code we'll put together will be much more dynamic, and we won't declare a separate variable for each page (e.g., second_page).

One more thing: a lot of sites include a count of the total number of results found on the search results page. This is a simple enough operation; you just assign the result of the following code to a variable and then display it on your page somewhere:

```
matching.count()
```

For the example search results page in this book, we're not going to include the count of total results in the template. However, if you'd like to show this to your customers, it's just a simple variable to include in the template.

Implementing Search

Now that we've got the little bits worked out, we just need to put all of these things together so that our site in searchable. In this section, we're going to create a model to store the phrases that our customers are searching for on our site. Then, we'll create the search form class for our interface. Then, we'll write the code that will take our search text and retrieve the matching product results for each keyword entered. To top it all off, we'll end by creating the view function and template for the search results pages, which will include logic for keeping search results pages lean by spreading large numbers of results out across more than one results page.

First, let's create a new app to house all of this glamorous new search code that we're going to create:

```
$ python manage.py startapp search
```

Don't forget to add this new app to the INSTALLED_APPS section of your settings.py file.

Now, the first thing we tend to do is start with the models, but in this case, we're not going to be using any models, are we? Actually, in the interest of keeping our thumbs on the pulse of our customers, we are going to create a very slim model that will store the searches that each customer enters on our site. The marketing people will thank you, even if, at the moment, you don't have any marketing people. And if you're a developer, and you have marketing people, giving them a massive list of searches that have been entered on your site is a good way to keep them occupied and off your back, so they don't bug you quite as often about other stuff.

In your models.py file in the new search app, add the following simple model definition:

```python
from django.db import models
from django.contrib.auth.models import User

class SearchTerm(models.Model):
    q = models.CharField(max_length=50)
    search_date = models.DateTimeField(auto_now_add=True)
    ip_address = models.IPAddressField()
    user = models.ForeignKey(User, null=True)

    def __unicode__(self):
        return self.q
```

Now, in the interest of actually being able to view these stored search phrases, create an `admin.py` file and add the following code to it:

```python
from django.contrib import admin
from ecomstore.search.models import SearchTerm

class SearchTermAdmin(admin.ModelAdmin):
    list_display = ('__unicode__','ip_address','search_date')
    list_filter = ('ip_address', 'user', 'q')
    exclude = ('user',)
admin.site.register(SearchTerm, SearchTermAdmin)
```

Now you can view each individual stored search through the admin interface, and drill down through the results by search term, user, or IP address where the search originated from. It's a very half-baked means of aggregating what will end up being a large amount of data, but it's quick and dirty. The important thing is that the data is there, so that it's available when you need to use it, regardless of how or when that is.

Remember that you need to run `manage.py syncdb` to create the corresponding database table.

The Search Module

Now, let's create the code that actually handles the queries. Create a new file called `search.py` inside the new app and add the following code to it:

```python
from ecomstore.search.models import SearchTerm
from ecomstore.catalog.models import Product
from django.db.models import Q

STRIP_WORDS = ['a','an','and','by','for','from','in','no','not',
               'of','on','or','that','the','to','with']

# store the search text in the database
def store(request, q):
    # if search term is at least three chars long, store in db
    if len(q) > 2:
        term = SearchTerm()
        term.q = q
        term.ip_address = request.META.get('REMOTE_ADDR')
        term.user = None
        if request.user.is_authenticated():
            term.user = request.user
        term.save()

# get products matching the search text
def products(search_text):
    words = _prepare_words(search_text)
    products = Product.active.all()
    results = {}
    results['products'] = []
    # iterate through keywords
    for word in words:
        products = products.filter(Q(name__icontains=word) |
```

```
            Q(description__icontains=word) |
            Q(sku__iexact=word) |
            Q(brand__icontains=word) |
            Q(meta_description__icontains=word) |
            Q(meta_keywords__icontains=word))
        results['products'] = products
    return results

# strip out common words, limit to 5 words
def _prepare_words(search_text):
    words = search_text.split()
    for common in STRIP_WORDS:
        if common in words:
            words.remove(common)
    return words[0:5]
```

First, this code defines a STRIP_WORDS constant, a list of very common words that we can just as easily remove from the actual search text before we perform the search with little risk of affecting the quality or accuracy of the results themselves.

The first function definition just stores the search query in the database, so long as the result itself is at least three characters in length. If someone searches for the letter "s" for some reason, it will be of little use or interest to us, so we're only going to take the trouble to store the phrase if it's at least one full word.

■ **Note** Later, in Chapter 10, we're going to add some JavaScript to the search form that will prevent our customers from submitting searches that are shorter than three characters in length.

Jump ahead to the last function for a second: _prepare_words(). This code block simply takes the search text, splits it into a Python list of each individual word, strips out the common ones we defined in STRIP_WORDS, and then returns the list of words. If there are more than five words remaining after we've stripped out the common words, we return only the first five. This is mostly so that longer queries, if any customer actually enters more than five keywords for a search, will not overly degrade performance of the search query. While we've set the value at a maximum of five, you're welcome to adjust this as you need.

The middle function, products(), is the one that we'll call in order to get back the products matching the search text per our rules. First, it passes the search text into the _prepare_words() function to get the search keywords as a Python list. Next, we create a list of all the products on the site using the active Product manager class, as well as declare an empty Python dictionary to hold our result set. Then, we iterate through the list of keywords and create a filter, using a Django Q object on each of the fields in which we're looking for the search keyword.

After creating this filter for each object, we add this query to the results dictionary using Python's built-in update() method. Notice that the results dictionary does not contain an entry for each product. Instead, it has only has one entry, called products, which contains the QuerySet describing the query we're about to send to the database. Then, finally, we return the results dictionary to the calling code.

The database optimization people out there might be a little concerned about the performance impact of retrieving all the product results and then applying all of these filters to them, one at a time, for up to five separate words. The amazing thing about the function that builds up this query is that it only ever performs a single SQL query. Just one. Don't believe me? We can view the raw SQL of our function using the `connection` module. Drop into a Python shell from inside your project's root directory and type in the following:

```
$ python manage.py shell
>>> from ecomstore.search import search
>>> from django.db import connection
>>> connection.queries
[ ]
>>> search.products('ruby axe guitar')
{'products': [<Product: Groovy-Guitar>, <Product: Ruby Axe Guitar>]}
>>> len(connection.queries)
```

This is the great thing about building queries dynamically with Django's syntax. You can take as long as you'd like building them, but until you call for the function to evaluate the results, say, for displaying them in one of your templates, your query doesn't hit the database.

In the course of refining your own search query, the `django.db.connection` object can be immensely helpful, allowing you to view the raw SQL output that the Django ORM is sending to the database just by calling the `queries` object and viewing the list it returns.

Search Template Tags

Before we jump in and create the view function and template to house the product search results, we're going to create a couple of template inclusion tags. First, we need to create the search box that will appear in the column on the left side of every page of the site. We're also going to create a tag that will handle the pagination controls on the results pages, so that if there is more than one page of search results, the user will be able to click around to the other pages.

First, let's code up the `form` class for our search box. Create a new file called `forms.py` inside your search app directory and enter the following `form` class definition into it:

```
from ecomstore.search.models import SearchTerm
from django import forms

class SearchForm(forms.ModelForm):
    class Meta:
        model = SearchTerm

    def __init__(self, *args, **kwargs):
        super(SearchForm, self).__init__(*args, **kwargs)
        default_text = 'Search'
        self.fields['q'].widget.attrs['value'] = default_text
        self.fields['q'].widget.attrs['onfocus'] =
            "if (this.value=='" + default_text + "')this.value = ''"

    include = ('q',)
```

This simple search form, which is tied into the `SearchTerm` model we defined earlier, merely contains a single field from the model: the q field. When the form is rendered, the text "Search" will appear if the form is unbound. When the user clicks into the search box, the text will disappear if it reads "Search" so that the user can enter new search text. However, we've defined it so that it won't clear the box if the user clicks on it and it contains search text.

Now, we're going to define the functions that handle the two template tags. Create a new directory inside your project's search app called templatetags, and create two files: __init__.py and search_tags.py. Open the latter file and enter in the following code:

```python
from django import template
from ecomstore.search.forms import SearchForm
import urllib

register = template.Library()

@register.inclusion_tag("tags/search_box.html")
def search_box(request):
    q = request.GET.get('q','')
    form = SearchForm({'q': q })
    return {'form': form }

@register.inclusion_tag('tags/pagination_links.html')
def pagination_links(request, paginator):
    raw_params = request.GET.copy()
    page = raw_params.get('page',1)
    p = paginator.page(page)
    try:
        del raw_params['page']
    except KeyError:
        pass
    params = urllib.urlencode(raw_params)
    return {'request': request,
            'paginator': paginator,
            'p': p,
            'params': params }
```

The first function takes the current request objects as an argument. If the search box detects the presence of a submitted query in the URL, then it binds the form to that search text, rendering the search string inside the form. Otherwise, it will fall back on the default text "Search" we specified in the form class.

The second function definitions takes two arguments, the current request object and the current paginator object, which we're going to create inside the view function in a moment. This function does quite a bit; we need to copy the parameters in the URL out so we can use them later to build the hyperlinks in our pagination tag. From these, we pull out the current page number if it exists in the URL. If it's not in the URL, we just default to page one. We then retrieve the current page object from paginator.

Then, for the pagination hyperlinks, we get rid of the page in the URL parameters, if it exists, and then URL-encode the remaining parameters. In most cases, this will merely be the q parameter, but we're going to keep things flexible, in case we ever need to add other parameters to the results pages.

Now, these two template inclusion tag functions depend on the existence of their corresponding template files, which we're going to create now. Inside your project's templates/tags directory, add two files. First, create search_box.html and add the following code to the file:

```html
<form id="search" action="{% url search_results %}" method="get">
<h3><label for="id_q">Search</label></h3>
    <div style="text-align:right;">
    {{ form.q }}
        <input type="submit" value="Search" />
    </div>
</form>
```

Then, create the `pagination_links.html` file and enter into it the following template code:

```
{% if p.has_other_pages %}
    {% if p.has_previous %}
        <a href="{{ request.path }}?{{ params }}&page={{ p.previous_page_number }}">
            &laquo; Previous
        </a>
    {% else %}
        &laquo; Previous
    {% endif %}
    | Page {{ p.number }} of {{ paginator.num_pages }} |
    {% if p.has_next %}
        <a href="{{ request.path }}?{{ params }}&page={{ p.next_page_number }}">
            Next &raquo;
        </a>
    {% else %}
        Next &raquo;
    {% endif %}
{% endif %}
```

The `pagination_links.html` template file takes advantage of a number of different methods that the Paginator class offers us. First, the contents of the entire template are encompassed by an `{% if %}` block so that the links will only appear if there are pages other than the current one on our Paginator instance. Then, we check to see if a previous and a next page are available and, if they are, render some "Previous" and "Next" hyperlinks that link to their respective pages. If these are not available, they are simply rendered as text. Between both of these, we display the current page number and the total number of pages, with a line that reads with the familiar: "Page 1 of 5."

Search View and Template

Now that we've taken care of the underlying structure, we can come back to the surface and create the templates needed to put this new search functionality into action. First, let's define one constant variable. Open your project's `settings.py` file and add the following line someplace:

```
PRODUCTS_PER_PAGE = 12
```

This number can be anything you'd like. At the moment, the CSS for our product thumbnail divs should automatically restrict the number of thumbnails per row to four, so any multiple of four should return a number of results that has full rows.

Next, open `views.py` in the search app and let's add the code for the view function, which will actually make the query and return the result set to the user:

```
from django.shortcuts import render_to_response
from django.template import RequestContext
from django.core.paginator import Paginator, InvalidPage, EmptyPage
from ecomstore.search import search
from ecomstore import settings

def results(request, template_name="search/results.html"):
    # get current search phrase
    q = request.GET.get('q', '')
    # get current page number. Set to 1 is missing or invalid
    try:
```

```
        page = int(request.GET.get('page', 1))
    except ValueError:
        page = 1
    # retrieve the matching products
    matching = search.products(q).get('products')
    # generate the pagintor object
    paginator = Paginator(matching,
                          settings.PRODUCTS_PER_PAGE)
    try:
        results = paginator.page(page).object_list
    except (InvalidPage, EmptyPage):
        results = paginator.page(1).object_list
    # store the search
    search.store(request, q)
    # the usual…
    page_title = 'Search Results for: ' + q
    return render_to_response(template_name, locals(),
        context_instance=RequestContext(request))
```

There's quite a bit of code here for a single view, so let's walk through what's happening. First, we get the page number and the search text out of the URL. We try to parse the page number into an integer, falling back on page one if there's any kind of error. If there isn't a page number, we also just default to page one.

Then, we get back the results from running the query function we constructed earlier and use that to create a new Paginator instance. Using the page number we just parsed out, we get the current page on the paginator object and retrieve the corresponding object_list, which is our list of matching products. We store the search term and then return the current template back to the user.

Next, we need to hook up the URL. Create a new file called urls.py inside your new search app and add the following code:

```
from django.conf.urls.defaults import *

urlpatterns = patterns('ecomstore.search.views',
    (r'^results/$','results',{'template_name': 'search/results.html'}, 'search_results'),
)
```

Then, inside of the urls.py file in the root of your project, add the following line to urlpatterns:

```
(r'^search/', include('search.urls')),
```

Of course, we haven't yet created this template, so let's add this file so our customers actually get to see the product search results. Inside your templates directory, create a new subdirectory and call it search, to correspond to our new app, and create a new file called results.html:

```
{% extends "catalog.html" %}

{% load search_tags %}

{% block content %}
    <h1>Search Results for: '{{ q }}'</h1>
    {% for p in results %}
        {% include 'tags/product_thumbnail.html' %}
    {% empty %}
        No products were found matching those search terms.
```

```
    {% endfor %}
    <div class="cb"> </div>
    {% pagination_links request paginator %}
{% endblock %}
```

You might consider adding some other content in the event that there are no matching search terms, such as featured products or other recommended items. (We look at making product recommendations in the next chapter.)

There's only one last piece that we need to add, and that is the search box itself, in the left column, so that customers can perform searches from every page on the site. Open your site's catalog.html template, and add the line at the top (but below the extends directive) to load the new search tags:

```
{% load search_tags %}
```

And then, find the placeholder text in square brackets:

```
[search box here]
```

and replace it with the new search box tag, passing in the current request object:

```
{% search_box request %}
```

Now we've got search enabled on our site. A search box will appear on each page, and if the user enters some text and clicks the search button, they'll be taken to a results page with a list of product thumbnails matching their query.

If you don't have that many products on your site just yet, and would like to test that the product pagination is working correctly, just change the PRODUCTS_PER_PAGE variable to something much lower, like 1 or 2, and try performing a search then. Provided you have more than one or two products and your query matches more than this, you should be able see the pagination links in action.

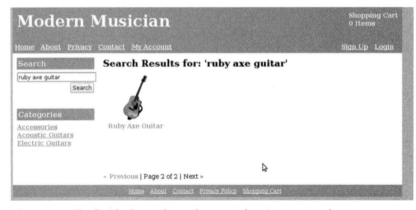

Figure 8-1. The finished search results page, showing one product per page.

Also, you might be interested in seeing the raw SQL output that your query is sending to the database. To do this, just add the following bits of the code to the results() view function, below where you make the call to create the results QuerySet:

```
search_query = results.query
```

Then, in your results template, just output the variable {{ search_query }} somewhere below your results. It will allow you see the actual SQL that is running to fetch the search results.

Third-Party Search Solutions

Our search solution works very nicely for a small- to medium-sized e-commerce site, as it will find accurate results and run quickly enough. As your product catalog grows, however, you may need to adjust and upgrade your search algorithm in order to accommodate it.

The solution we implemented does have a couple of limitations. Most notably, it doesn't match words based on singular and plural variations. For example, a search for "rubys" or "rubies" would not match the Ruby Axe Guitar, even though we have entered some variation of the word "ruby," which is contained in the product name field.

For more complex cases such as this, you may want to implement a solution that includes a full-text search ,which is supported by the MySQL and PostgreSQL database engines. One very good solution to look into is django-sphinx[1], which allows you to hook the Django ORM and your models into the Sphinx[2] full-text search engine.

django-sphinx does require you to download and compile the Sphinx source code. If this freaks you out, you may consider using the Haystack[3] search package for your Django app instead. Haystack is a search solution implemented completely in Python that you can hook into your models.

Summary

In this chapter, we created a working internal search solution for the products on our site. In the process, we got a look at some of the little extras that Django affords developers to help us make our site more scalable. The Paginator class is an extremely useful tool for dealing with large amounts of query data. You might consider going back now and adding pagination controls to the category pages. We also got a look at the use of custom model Manager classes in order to reduce repetition in our ORM queries.

Now that we're collecting various types of data from different places on the site, we're going to look in the next chapter at how we can put it to good use, by using it to make product recommendations to our customers.

---

[1] http://code.google.com/p/django-sphinx/

[2] http://www.sphinxsearch.com/

[3] http://haystacksearch.org/

## CHAPTER 9

Intelligent Cross-Selling

Our ability to communicate effectively hinges on our ability, as a species, to recognize patterns. In verbal communication, our brains are interpreting auditory signals and breaking them down into patterns that allow us to decipher the message being conveyed by the speaker. It's interesting to contemplate the exact origin of human speech. It may have been a caveman who noticed a large saber-toothed cat sneaking up on his fellow caveman brother from a distance, and felt the need to yelp aloud about the impending cat-attack to warn him. We make little chicken scratches on pieces of paper and other people are able to read these chicken scratches because they're able to recognize patterns in the writing. Unless, of course, you're dealing with a prescription from a doctor, in which case you need an advanced Pharmacy degree in order to determine exactly what the heck to the doctor wrote on that little piece of paper.

Fortunately, we have advanced beyond the need to warn fellow peers about the dangers of tar pits or Wooly Mammoth stampedes. However, your survival as an online merchant does still depend largely on your ability to communicate with your customers. You need to be able to discern patterns in their shopping behavior, by looking at exactly how they are using your site, and then use any information they provide you to your own advantage by helping talk to them as individuals.

In this chapter, we're going to build the home page. While we haven't created every aspect of our site, we've got enough data to go on that we can create product recommendations based on a user's browsing habits. We're also going to help them while they're browsing our site by setting up intelligent product cross-sells on each product page.

The name of the game is always increasing revenue. Since this hinges on our ability to talk to each customer, with as personal a touch as we can manage, let's look at what our customers are saying to us already.

Product Page Recommendations

Whether or not you've considered it yet, the customers shopping on your site are providing you with quite a bit of information about themselves. Sure, you may not know their name or where they live quite yet, but as soon as they hit your site, they are giving you some feedback about what kind of person they are. It's up to you to recognize what information they're providing, and how best to use this information in order to help them use your site more effectively. In this way, we hope to increase the value our site is providing the customer, enhance their shopping experience, and hopefully get more sales revenue out of each customer.

So what are our customers telling us? Think about the ways in which your customer currently interacts with your site. They can browse categories, browse products, add products to a shopping cart, place orders, and search the product catalog. There is actually quite a lot that we can do with this data, even though it's a fairly short list. Let's look at each of these one at a time, starting with what we can do on the product page itself.

Order-Based Filtering

One option we have in creating product recommendations is to create relationships between products manually. We could create a new "relationship" model and make recommendations based on the products that we specify by hand. However, this approach is tedious and won't scale as the number of products we have on our site grows very large.

The easiest thing for us to do is look at our order history. A customer can create an order with more than one item. It makes perfect sense, then, that if a customer ordered a Backwater Boondocks Banjo along with a set of Superior Brand Banjo strings, other customers who view the Backwater Boondocks Banjo might be interested in that same set of Superior Brand Banjo strings. It stands to reason that we should display that set of banjo strings on the banjo page since there's a high probability that future customers might also want to purchase this product as well. If you were to label these product recommendations on the product page, you might use the text: "Also purchased with this product…"

Doing this in code is a pretty simple process. We merely need to look up any orders that included the given product we're interested in evaluating. Say we're looking up cross-sells for the Ruby Axe Guitar:

```
my_product = Product.active.filter(name="Ruby Axe Guitar")
orders = Order.objects.filter(orderitem__product=my_product)
```

Then, we look up any order items that we in those same orders, but that were not the Ruby Axe Guitar:

```
order_items = OrderItem.objects.filter(order__in=orders).exclude(product=my_product)
```

From this, we just need to get the associated products from the list of order items. We call the distinct() method on the result set in order to eliminate any duplicates:

```
products = Product.active.filter(orderitem__in=order_items).distinct()
```

It makes the most sense to retrieve these product recommendations as a method we can call on a model instance. Open models.py and add this method to your Product model:

```
def cross_sells(self):
        from ecomstore.checkout.models import Order, OrderItem
        orders = Order.objects.filter(orderitem__product=self)
        order_items = OrderItem.objects.filter(order__in=orders).exclude(product=self)
        products = Product.active.filter(orderitem__in=order_items).distinct()
        return products
```

Notice that we're doing the import of the Order and OrderItem models down in the method instead of at the top of the file. In this particular case, that's intentional. You see, the OrderItem model is dependent on the Product model itself, which we import at the top of the file. If we try to import the OrderItem model at the top of the file that contains the Product model, we get an import error, since we have a series of imports that result in a circle. For example, let's say you have class A in one module called A and class B in another module called B. Module A imports class B, and module B import class A. What we have here is a circular dependency, and when this code is run, Python gets very confused about what it's supposed to do. These kinds of situations result in runtime errors that are very difficult to track down in your code. The best solution is to either change where you are performing the import statement in your code, or move stuff around into different modules.

Customer-Based Order Filtering

Of course, a much more powerful approach would be to look at all of the registered customers on the site and see which of them have purchased the product we're currently viewing. Then, for each customer, query out all of the other products each customer purchased across *all* of their past orders. We can recommend these products, as other customers might potentially be interested in purchasing them as well.

This is a much more fine-grained and accurate approach to gauging similarities between products, since it's possible for a user to place several orders on a site over time, perhaps only ordering one product in each order. By looking at all of the products a user has ever ordered, we have access to a much larger scope of a given user's preferences that isn't merely confined to the data of a single order. Results from this approach could be labeled with the text: "Customers who purchased this product also purchased…"

Generating customer-based recommendations is fairly straightforward. First, we just need to query out all of the users who have bought the current product:

```
my_product = Product.active.filter(name="Ruby Axe Guitar")
users = User.objects.filter(order__orderitem__product=my_product)
```

Notice the long string of model names inside the filter, delimited by two underscore characters; this single line of code is performing several joins across four tables, going from users' orders, to the items in each order, to the product associated with each item. That's a whole lot of work being performed at the database level without a whole lot of work on our part.

Then, we get a list of all of the items that customer has ever ordered on our site (excluding the current product, of course):

```
items = OrderItem.objects.filter(order__user__in=users).exclude(product=self)
```

Then, we just need to get a list of the distinct products we find listed in this batch of order items:

```
products = Product.active.filter(orderitem__in=items).distinct()
```

Putting this all together, we end up with the following method definition, which you can add to your Product model just like the order-based one:

```
def cross_sells_user(self):
        from ecomstore.checkout.models import Order, OrderItem
        from django.contrib.auth.models import User
        users = User.objects.filter(order__orderitem__product=self)
        items = OrderItem.objects.filter(order__user__in=users).exclude(product=self)
        products = Product.active.filter(orderitem__in=items).distinct()
        return products
```

So, now we have two methods, both of which retrieve product recommendations based on past order history. Which one you choose to use will depend on the texture of your customer base. If there are a large number of anonymous orders that contain multiple items, the first cross-sell method makes the most sense. If there are more registered users than not, you'll want to use the latter method.

A Hybrid Approach

Of course, we have two separate methods that get product recommendations in two slightly different ways, and while we can use either one, we really shouldn't *have* to choose between the two of them. With a bit of refactoring, we should be able to easily combine the two methods and get product recommendations based on both systems.

With a quick revisit to the Q object we introduced in Chapter 8, we can easily aggregate the results from both of these approaches. The following method does both at the same time, in much the same way. We get both the list of orders that contained the current product, as well as users that have bought the current product. Then, using two custom Q objects, we filter out the order items based on the two criteria. Then we request the products just the same way that we did in the last two methods and return that result set to the calling function.

The following method is our hybrid approach:

```
def cross_sells_hybrid(self):
        from ecomstore.checkout.models import Order, OrderItem
        from django.contrib.auth.models import User
        from django.db.models import Q
        orders = Order.objects.filter(orderitem__product=self)
        users = User.objects.filter(order__orderitem__product=self)
        items = OrderItem.objects.filter( Q(order__in=orders) |
                    Q(order__user__in=users)
                    ).exclude(product=self)
        products = Product.active.filter(orderitem__in=items).distinct()
        return products
```

Feel free to add this method to your product model for your use. In order to use any of these inside your catalog/product.html template, just add the following below the product details on the product page, but above the product description:

```
</form>
    <div class="cb"><br /><br /></div>
    <h3>Related Products</h3>
        {% for p in p.cross_sells_hybrid %}
            {% include 'tags/product_thumbnail.html' %}
        {% empty %}
            No related products.
        {% endfor %}
    <div class="cb"><br /><br /></div>
    <h3>Product Description</h3>
```

You can use any one of these three methods that returns the most accurate results given your current site. In the early stages of an initial launch, before you have any order history, you might try something a little simpler, such as just recommending other products that are in the same category. Then, once you have some data to go on, switch over to one of the more complex methods.

Home Page Recommendations

Now let's turn our focus away from the product page and have a look at the home page. Customers that come to your site and end up on the home page can be grouped into two main categories: first-time customers that have never been to your site before, and customers that have been to your site before. The first group is pretty easy to deal with; you just list your "featured products."

However, once a customer has come to your site, whether or not they've logged in and created an account, they are providing you with some pretty useful information. They may be searching for things on your site, adding stuff to their shopping cart, or looking at product pages that are of interest to them. You can use this information to show them products that might be of interest to each of them individually.

Take the search box on our music site. Once we've gotten John Q. Fratboy to navigate into our site to our landing pages, and we've convinced him that we're the best musical instrument site on the web, he's apt to go right for the search box and start entering little blobs of words, looking for those radical acoustic guitar strings he wants, so he can play Jack Johnson songs with too much cologne on, and hopefully charm the ladies hanging around beneath the trees outside the dorms.

The main point is that we should be tracking John's every search so that we can later determine that he was looking for acoustic guitar strings, so later, we can show him product recommendations directly related to that.

Tracking Each User

So now we've got to figure out how to store and retrieve the searches that any given user has entered on our site. At the moment, we store the IP Address and the User instance of any authenticated user with each search term, but not every user will be logged in and a single IP Address doesn't necessarily correlate with a single user. Think about a bunch of people using wireless Internet at their local Starbucks, all using the same Internet connection. If they're all shopping our site at once, all of their requests will come from the same IP.

So, to solve this problem, we're going to create a unique tracking ID for each user that navigates to our site, and write this information into their session, very similar to how we set up cart IDs in Chapter 4. Because this information may be used for more than just the search functionality, we're going to start storing new code for managing tracking information inside a new app called stats:

```
$ python manage.py startapp stats
```

Inside this app, create a new file called stats.py and enter the following lines of code for retrieving and generating new tracking IDs in each user's session:

```
import os
import base64

def tracking_id(request):
    try:
        return request.session['tracking_id']
    except KeyError:
        request.session['tracking_id'] = base64.b64encode(os.urandom(36))
        return request.session['tracking_id']
```

In effect, this code does the same thing as the code that we used to generate and retrieve cart IDs in Chapter 4, but we are doing a few things differently. First, we try to get the value of a session variable called tracking_id from the session object, and return it if it exists. If the value is not found in the session because the customer is new and we haven't written this value yet, then we catch a KeyError exception, which will occur if a key with the name tracking_id doesn't exist in our session dictionary.

Handling a missing dictionary value in this manner is fairly common in Python programming, although I find it a bit strange. Any new customer will not have a tracking ID set yet, so this particular KeyError is not that *exceptional*. We *expect* any new customer not to have this set, so when we try to access it and get the exception, it's not really an exception in the purest programming sense of the word because we haven't encountered a condition that indicates a true application error.

However, my own opinions aside, I don't really have any problem with the exception-based approach. At least we're not raising it at the same time, so it's not getting logged to our database as an error we'll need to examine later. It's concise, and it works. If you prefer the approach we took in Chapter 4, of checking for existing values in the session dictionary using the get() method and then addressing a missing value with an if-else block, you can use that here as well.

In either case, if we find that the `tracking_id` is not there, we must create a new one. In this function, I've also taken a different approach to generating random strings of characters for the tracking IDs. Here, we use the `urandom` module to generate a random string of 36 bytes, and then base64-encode the result to generate the characters. In this case, the result will always be 48 characters long.

■ **Caution** The `urandom` module is good for generating random bytes, which we convert to character strings in this example. However, the use of `urandom` is potentially very slow. In addition, `urandom` actually uses a random number generator provided by the operating system, which is `/dev/urandom` on Unix systems and `CryptGenRandom` on Windows. On some operating systems, the random number generator used may be a locked resource, which might result in the blocking of web requests.

So, now that we're generating tracking IDs, we just need to put them to work for us. Let's make a quick edit to the `SearchTerm` model to add this new field that we plan to store along with each search, inside `search/models.py`:

```
tracking_id = models.CharField(max_length=50, default='')
```

Now, we need to jump down into our database and add this column to the `search_searchterm` table:

```
$ python manage.py dbshell
mysql> ALTER TABLE search_searchterm ADD tracking_id varchar(50);
Query OK, 174 row affected (0.00 sec)
Records: 174  Duplicates: 0  Warnings: 0
```

Lastly, we just need to make sure that we're storing this new tracking ID with each search. Add the following code to the `search.py` module, inside the `store()` function:

```
from ecomstore.stats import stats

def store(request, q):
    … etc …
    term.ip_address = request.META.get('REMOTE_ADDR')
    term.tracking_id = stats.tracking_id(request)
    term.user = None     … etc …
```

So now we're associating our stored searches with each individual browser that is accessing our site. We now have a small infrastructure for uniquely identifying each customer and tracking their behavior on the site.

Dealing with Searches

Now that we're collecting the searches associated with each individual customer, how can we use them to make some recommendations? First, we have no way of knowing just how many searches a customer might have entered over the course of using our site, so in the interest of prioritizing the data, we'll retrieve and use at most the last 10 searches the customer entered. While they might have entered more, we're going to assume that anything beyond the most recent 10 is irrelevant.

With the most recent 10 search strings, we're going to take a count of how often each word occurs in total, and then take the highest-ranking 3 words and perform a search using each of them. We'll construct a list of results from these three searches and return them to the user interface.

The first thing we're going to do is define a constant in our settings.py file. Whenever we get a list of products, we're going to place a limit on the number of results we're going to get. In order to make sure that the maximum number of results is a multiple of the number of products that will fit in a single row of product thumbnails, we're going to store the number of products per row in our settings file. Add the following line:

```
PRODUCTS_PER_ROW = 4
```

Now, inside stats.py, below the new tracking ID function, add the following imports and three function definitions:

```
from ecomstore.search.models import SearchTerm
from ecomstore.settings import PRODUCTS_PER_ROW

def recommended_from_search(request):
    # get the common words from the stored searches
    common_words = frequent_search_words(request)
    from ecomstore.search import search
    matching = []
    for word in common_words:
        results = search.products(word).get('products',[])
        for r in results:
            if len(matching) < PRODUCTS_PER_ROW and not r in matching:
                matching.append(r)
    return matching

def frequent_search_words(request):
    # get the ten most recent searches from the database.
    searches = SearchTerm.objects.filter(tracking_id=
        tracking_id(request)).values('q').order_by('-search_date')[0:10]
    # join all of the searches together into a single string.
    search_string = ' '.join([search['q'] for search in searches])
    # return the top three most common words in the searches
    return sort_words_by_frequency(search_string)[0:3]

def sort_words_by_frequency(some_string):
    # convert the string to a python list
    words = some_string.split()
    # assign a rank to each word based on frequency
    ranked_words = [[word, words.count(word)] for word in set(words)]
    # sort the words based on descending frequency
    sorted_words = sorted(ranked_words, key = lambda word: -word[1])
    # return the list of words, most frequent first
    return [p[0] for p in sorted_words]
```

Let's step through this chain of events from top to bottom. The first function is responsible for retrieving the products. First, it calls frequent_search_words() in order to get a Python list of the top three words that occurred with the highest frequency. This function retrieves the 10 most recent searches that the customer entered on the site, joins them together into a single string, and passes it into the sort_words() function. sort_words() splits the string into separate words. Then, we create a list that contains each word along with the frequency it occurred in all of the searches. We then sort the list and return the words, from highest to lowest frequency, back to `frequent_search_words()`, which takes the first three and sends them back to `recommended_from_search()`.

Back at the top, `recommended_from_search()` executes a simple product search for each of these three words. Through each of these, it appends the results onto a list called `matching`, so long as the number of results is less than the `PRODUCTS_PER_ROW` variable we just set.

View-Based Recommendations

Provided that we're giving the user enough information about the products in each thumbnail that they can easily determine which products they're interested in (let's hope we're doing this), we can assume that if one customer views the pages for products A, B, and C, then another customer who views product B might also be interested in products A and C. It makes sense that if we track the product pages that each customer chooses to view, we can determine similarities between our own products and make recommendations based on these.

So, let's create a model that will log product page views for each customer. Inside `models.py` in your new `stats` app, add the following model code:

```python
from django.db import models
from django.contrib.auth.models import User
from ecomstore.catalog.models import Product

class PageView(models.Model):
    class Meta:
        abstract = True

    date = models.DateTimeField(auto_now=True)
    ip_address = models.IPAddressField()
    user = models.ForeignKey(User, null=True)
    tracking_id = models.CharField(max_length=50, default='')

class ProductView(PageView):
    product = models.ForeignKey(Product)
```

Here, we've created an abstract base class for logging page views. This stores information that is common to any other types of pages we might want to track. For now, we've only created a single model to hold any data: `ProductView`. But later, if there is other information we want to track—say, if we wanted to track the categories that each customer views—we could easily create another model that inherits from `PageView`.

Now that you have the new model set up, run `manage.py syncdb` to create the new database table.

■ **Note** You might be thinking, "Sweet! Let's track *every single page* that every customer views so we can get a handle on what everyone is doing!" While this might sound like a good idea, hold off on that until later. In Chapter 11, we're going to look at how to use Google Analytics to track user page views.

Back inside `stats.py`, add the following imports and function definitions to handle getting product recommendations based on product page views:

```
from ecomstore.catalog.models import Product
from ecomstore.stats.models import ProductView

def log_product_view(request, product):
    t_id = tracking_id(request)
    try:
        v = ProductView.objects.get(tracking_id=t_id, product=product)
        v.save()
    except ProductView.DoesNotExist:
        v = ProductView()
        v.product = product
        v.ip_address = request.META.get('REMOTE_ADDR')
        v.tracking_id = t_id
        v.user = None        if request.user.is_authenticated():
            v.user = request.user
        v.save()

def recommended_from_views(request):
    t_id = tracking_id(request)
    # get recently viewed products
    viewed = get_recently_viewed(request)
    # if there are previously viewed products, get other tracking ids that have
    # viewed those products also
    if viewed:
        productviews = ProductView.objects.filter(product__in=
            viewed).values('tracking_id')
        t_ids = [v['tracking_id'] for v in productviews]
        # if there are other tracking ids, get other products.
        if t_ids:
            all_viewed = Product.active.filter(productview__tracking_id__in=t_ids)
            # if there are other products, get them, excluding the
            # products that the customer has already viewed.
            if all_viewed:
                other_viewed = ProductView.objects.filter(product__in=
                    all_viewed).exclude(product__in=viewed)
                if other_viewed:
                    return Product.active.filter(productview__in=other_viewed).distinct()

def get_recently_viewed(request):
    t_id = tracking_id(request)
    views = ProductView.objects.filter(tracking_id=t_id).values('product_id')
        .order_by('-date')[0:PRODUCTS_PER_ROW]
    product_ids = [v['product_id'] for v in views]
    return Product.active.filter(id__in=product_ids)
```

The last function, get_recently_viewed(), has a couple of uses. First, we'll list these products on the home page. On the off chance that a customer browses a few products on our site, leaves for a while, and then comes back, we'd like to be able to jog their memory and remind them of exactly what they were looking at. Notice that when we query out the results, we sort them by date descending, so the more recently viewed products will appear first. We're also using it to exclude products from the recommended product based on search, just so we don't end up duplicating recommendations.

The first function will be called from inside the product view to log each product that a customer views. We first check to see if the customer has already viewed that particular product and, if they have, we just update the date associated with the product view by calling save() on the view. This enables the sort to retrieve the more recently viewed items first. If the user hasn't yet viewed the product, we create and save a new ProductView model instance.

The recommended_from_views() function is the champion among these functions. We start with the recently viewed products and, from the list of them, get the list of ProductViews associated with those products. After we parse out the list of tracking IDs of those views, we get *all* of the products that are associated with those tracking IDs (not just the ones associated with the current customer). From these products, we get all of the ProductViews related to those products, *excluding* the products that were included in the "recently viewed" list we just fetched. Finally, we retrieve a distinct list of products associated with this list of product views.

That last thing you need to do is add the call to the log_product_view() function to your show_product() view function:

```
from ecomstore.stats import stats
stats.log_product_view(request, p)  # add to product view
```

Notice that if you were going to start logging page views all over the place, you wouldn't want to put the logging code inside the view function. Instead, you'd want to use a Django middleware class to handle this to keep the clutter out of your views. However, for this simple example, we can easily leave this one call inside our view.

Building the Homepage

Now, we have four distinct lists of products we can show to customers on the home page: featured products, recently viewed products, recommended based on product page views, and the recommended based on search terms. At the moment, each of these is designed to be a single row of thumbnails, each with a header. Since these will all be very similar, let's create a custom inclusion tag to display each of these.

Inside your catalog_tags.py file, add the following function for an inclusion tag:

```
@register.inclusion_tag("tags/product_list.html")
def product_list(products, header_text):
    return { 'products': products,
             'header_text': header_text }
```

This tag takes a list of products and some header text. What are we going to do with it? Create the associated product_list.html template file and add the following code:

```
{% for p in products %}
    {% if forloop.first %}
        <h3>{{ header_text }}</h3>
    {% endif %}
    {% include 'tags/product_thumbnail.html' %}
    {% if forloop.last %}
        <div class="cb"> </div>
    {% endif %}
{% endfor %}
```

This template iterates through the list of products we passed into the template, creating a thumbnail for each one. We're also leveraging two variables that are available inside of {% for %} template tag loops: forloop.first and forloop.last. In the first run through the loop, we add a header with the text we passed in to the template. On the last run through, we add a div element with a property of clear:both;. This is for style reasons: our product thumbnails have a property of float:left;. We added the clear div to ensure that any other nearby content doesn't wrap around the thumbnails, and instead appears below them.

Now, we just need to load all of the data from our new stats app inside the home page view function. First, since we might want to retrieve the featured products list from places other than the home page, we're going to create a new Manager class to handle this for us. Add the following class definition in the models.py module, above the Product class model:

```
class FeaturedProductManager(models.Manager):
    def all(self):
        return super(FeaturedProductManager, self).all()
            .filter(is_active=True).filter(is_featured=True)
```

Then, add this line below the objects and active managers inside the Product class:

```
featured = FeaturedProductManager()
```

With this in place, we can now turn our sights to loading the data in our view function. Open views.py inside the catalog app and add the following new lines of code:

```
from ecomstore.stats import stats
from ecomstore.settings import PRODUCTS_PER_ROW

def index(request, template_name="catalog/index.html"):
    search_recs = stats.recommended_from_search(request)
    featured = Product.featured.all()[0:PRODUCTS_PER_ROW]
    recently_viewed = stats.get_recently_viewed(request)
    view_recs = stats.recommended_from_views(request)
    … etc …
```

Now that we've taken the extra trouble to create the product_list.html inclusion tag, we can construct our home page by adding only four lines of code to the home page template (okay, five if you count the {% load %} directive at the top):

```
{% extends "catalog.html" %}

{% load catalog_tags %}

{% block content %}
<h1>Welcome to Modern Musician!</h1>
{% product_list recently_viewed 'Your Recently Viewed' %}
{% product_list view_recs 'Similar Products' %}
{% product_list featured 'Featured Products' %}
{% product_list search_recs 'Recommended For You' %}
{% endblock %}
```

Now, you can get the site up and running and see how you like what you see. To start with, clear the cookies and cache on your browser so you come to the site like a first-time, anonymous user. At this point, you should only see the "Featured Products" listed, as there is no other data about you available to the site yet. Try clicking on one of the products and then, using the navigation instead of your browser's Back button, click back to the home page. You should see the "Recently Viewed" list displaying the product you just viewed.

Click around the site a few places and run a few searches. See how each of these things affects the products you're seeing on the home page. When you're done with this, clear the cookies and cache in your browser again and try returning to the site as an anonymous user. Now that the site has some data about "another" customer (you, just a moment ago), the results you see the second time should be slightly different and, hopefully, a little more interesting.

Summary

This chapter took a very cursory look at the fairly complicated process of making product recommendations based on data you're collecting from your customers. While the examples in this chapter were relatively simple, recognizing patterns in your data and creating cross-sells from them is actually a very serious engineering matter. The difficulty is further compounded by the fact that as you create more and more complex algorithms for generating a recommendation engine, your product dataset is likely to grow and the processing you are doing to get cross-sells is likely to become a performance bottleneck. Indeed, scalable and accurate algorithms for this sort of thing are the stuff of highly successful sites such as Amazon.

The examples in this chapter should be tested with a representative dataset for performance considerations before you deploy them into production. While they make an interesting intellectual example, all of the queries and joins we did in this chapter incur a good deal of overhead that a highly trafficked site with hundred of products and thousands of records in the order history would not be able to handle. However, for a smaller site with a couple hundred products and few page views, these examples should work all right. We'll look at how to speed them up in Chapter 13 when we look at scaling the site for performance.

If you're really interested in delving a lot further into the world of machine intelligence, I highly recommend checkout out *Programming Collective Intelligence*, by Toby Segaran (O'Reilly, 2007). It's an extremely well-written overview of the subject matter, making some very difficult concepts very accessible to people who don't have degrees in mathematics. As an added bonus, all of the code samples are in Python!

In the next chapter, we're going to take our site into the realm of the new web era and add some whiz-bang pizzazz in the form of Ajax functionality. (Try to image Rod Sterling reading that sentence using his spooky voice and it actually sounds interesting). Read on, if you dare.

CHAPTER 10

■ ■ ■

Adding in Ajax

I imagine that, in the days before most programming languages included garbage collection, way back in the 1980s when people were working with C and Pascal, programming was a much more existential profession. People programmed computer applications that were never intended to be made public, working on programs that were only ever intended to be run on a small number of computers not connected to a big open network like the Internet. Much more time was spent on code to perform data processing and making a program *run* than went into the user interface.

Obviously, a lot of things have changed since then. A lot of software development has moved out of the basement and onto the web. Because of this, a lot of effort now goes into a user interface that is publicly available to anyone with a computer and a network connection. This means that development is a lot more engaging to developers these days because we're able to get visual feedback from our coding efforts a lot quicker than you could when people were coding up computer programs in C.

A large portion of increased interactivity via the web can be attributed to the rise in popularity of a technology called Ajax. Developers use Ajax to make their Web pages more dynamic and more responsive to a user's actions on the site. Don't worry, this has nothing to do with those Flash intros that cropped up all over pages in the late 1990s. It's far better than that. With Ajax, we can add dynamic functionality to the site, capturing input from the user and then updating the current page without having to reload the entire page.

And the great thing is, the work we do can be viewed by anyone with a computer and an Internet connection. It's a great time to be a web developer.

In this chapter, we're going to add two little functions to our site using Ajax. We're going to briefly discuss Ajax, what it can do for us, and how it works. We'll look at how we can use the jQuery JavaScript library in order to handle most of the Ajax details for us. Then, using these new concepts, we're going to set up a means for registered customers to write product reviews on the site and set up tagging functionality so that users can tag products with keywords.

The Ajax Pros and Cons

"Ajax" stands for Asynchronous JavaScript and XML, after two of the technologies that were primarily used in the initial implementations. However, the term "Ajax" itself has come to embody more than simply JavaScript working in conjunction with XML. Ajax represents an entirely different means of requesting data from a server than a typical web page. Whereas typical requests are made for entire pages of HTML, an Ajax request typically returns a smaller amount of data, which is then injected into the current page using the Document Object Model (DOM).

One of the main advantages of this is the ability to process data and requests with a great deal less bandwidth. When you make a request to any given web site for a certain page, the HTML is downloaded and rendered by the browser. Then, the browser makes a bunch of subsequent requests to the server for all of the extra components on that page, such as style sheets, JavaScript files, and any images. All put together, each of these subsequent HTTP requests for pictures and other static files can comprise a great deal of the overall load time for a page, although it's quite easy to forget this point in the era of high-speed Internet connections, which make it seem as though everything on an HTML page is downloaded in one fell swoop.

Ajax requests, on the other hand, are triggered by events within pages, and are able to send and retrieve data to and from the server without the need to incur all of this extra page overhead of downloading components. Remember that HTTP is stateless, so each HTTP request is independent. Imagine that you're a door-to-door salesperson selling some new kind of vacuum cleaner that you hitch to the back of your housecat, and let the cat clean the house for you. You knock on someone's door and, if the person living there doesn't want to buy the cat vacuum cleaner (hey, it's *their* loss), they shut the door on you, mid-sentence. You're cut off. The only way to get back in is to knock again.

Let's transfer this analogy to the context of the web: you would just need to refresh the page, and the new, updated page will be sent back to you. However, if all you want to do is update a small portion of the page, having to reload the entire page and everything on it can be overkill.

As one example, let's say you want to allow a user to reload the list of messages posted on a message board page by having the user click a "Reload" button somewhere on the page. Using Ajax, the new content could be loaded and the page could be updated, all without having to reload the entire page. This is all done using JavaScript, which can make requests to the server, parse out data it retrieves, and then update the part of the page with the new content. And you save the overhead of a page refresh.

The main problem with Ajax is that it's still dependent on the user of the site having JavaScript enabled in their browser. There's simply no guarantee that this will always be the case. Some of the people using your site may have JavaScript turned off. When you're programming an e-commerce site, there's generally one of two things that should keep you from going crazy and adding Ajax to everything:

- Content that is accessible only via JavaScript, like in DHTML navigation menus, cannot be crawled by search engines. If you use a good deal of content that is only available via Ajax events, then this content is invisible to spiders.

- Mission-critical parts of your site, like the checkout process, cannot rely on any JavaScript at all. The last thing you want to do is stop someone from buying stuff from your site.

I really can't give you firm advice about when you should be using Ajax functionality on your site and when you shouldn't. I will, however, offer one guideline that not only makes good business sense, but will also help save you countless hours of development time:

- Code for your customers and *not* for your fellow developers.

Stuff that is all Ajaxy and dynamic is admittedly very cool. I remember using Google Maps for the first time, and *it was superb*. However, you shouldn't preoccupy yourself with tasks that are mainly to add zing to your site without adding any value for your customers. Ajax, for all its wonders, does bring up a whole different slew of security issues that you need to consider, such as Cross-Site Scripting attacks (I'll cover those in Chapter 12). It can also make the content of your site less accessible to people who have JavaScript disabled in their browsers.

As I've been saying all along, you should be coding an application that best serves your customers, and that *might* include some Ajax functionality. By default, though, it's not necessarily a great idea. Imagine that you get the urge to code up a series of checkout pages that *slide* by the user as they go from page to page; yeah, that's cool, but are your customers even going to notice it? Do they care? Is the extra functionality *interfering* with anyone trying to check out? It all depends on your audience and their expectations. So far, in this book, I haven't used Ajax for other stuff, such as the checkout process or the shopping cart, merely because it's in your best interest not to use Ajax for anything mission-critical, and because Ajax and accessibility are, at the time I'm writing this, something of an oil and water combo. They don't mix well.

On the other hand, maybe working on this Modern Musician site we've been creating so far *without* any Ajax effects is leaving you yearning for some happier days. You're craving development with some flair. You want out of the basement. I understand, and I agree. Let's add some Ajax to a couple of areas to our site that shouldn't make or break it.

How Ajax Works

The way Ajax works is very simple in concept. JavaScript works client-side, allowing the developer to embed little blocks of code that execute in the user's browser, instead of server-side, where most of the processing occurs. Traditionally, JavaScript was used to create simple mouseover effects, or to check the validity of form data before it was submitted to the server for processing. The JavaScript was hooked up to HTML elements by using an attribute on the element with a value of the name of the function.

As one example, here is some JavaScript and HTML code that pops up a JavaScript alert box as soon as the mouse cursor hovers over the anchor tag on the page. While this doesn't really do anything useful, it demonstrates JavaScript in action:

```
<html>
    <head>
        <script>
        function alertBox(){
            alert('Hi!');    }
        </script>
    </head>
    <body>
        <a href="" onmouseover="alertBox();" >
            Hover Over Me
        </a>
    </body>
</html>
```

The really interesting thing about JavaScript is that it also has the ability to manipulate the elements on the page. The structure of an HTML page, the sum of all its elements and attributes, is known as the Document Object Model (DOM). You can use JavaScript to access the contents of an element based on its class or id attributes, add or remove elements from a page, and even inject new content into elements.

As great as this sounds, the potential of this functionality wasn't fully realized until a few years ago, when developers started to realize that JavaScript could initiate its own HTTP requests using the XMLHttpRequest object, an API of the DOM that is now implemented by every major browser. (IE 6 implements it slightly differently, but we'll work around that.) This means that, entirely using JavaScript, developers could fetch new data from the server and update the current page without the user needing to refresh the page.

As one potential example of this, take the product page form that we created in Chapter 4, which allows customers to enter a quantity and add an item to their shopping cart. After the customer clicks the "Add To Cart" button, a POST request is initiated back to the product page view, which processes the request, reloading the product page if there are any errors and redirecting the user to the cart page if the operation was successful. Instead of this, we could have simply initiated the Add To Cart request using JavaScript.

First, we'd get the quantity by traversing the DOM of the product page and getting the value of the input box. Then, we send the request to add the item to the user's shopping cart by creating a new XMLHttpRequest. Finally, if the operation was successful, we would then update the cart box at the top of the page, augmenting the number of items in the cart, and possibly displaying a quick message to the user letting them know that their cart has been updated. All of this could be done without have to refresh the current page, or redirect the user to a different page.

The reason that we didn't do this is because after the user has made the decision to add the current product to the shopping cart, it's only logical that we send them to the shopping cart. While this particular point is debatable, it makes sense that a customer will click the "Add To Cart" button only *after* they've finished with the current page, want to add it to the cart, and move on in the process, either by looking for other items or by checking out.

Even though we didn't do this earlier, rest assured that by the end of this chapter, you'll understand how to implement this functionality on your site.

jQuery for Ajax

Unlike other web frameworks, such as Ruby on Rails, Ajax functionality is not built directly into the Django web framework. For this reason, we have to fall back on creating our own Ajax requests. Creating a new Ajax request from within JavaScript, entirely from scratch, can be something of a tricky beast.

We're going to use the jQuery library in order to develop JavaScript and Ajax functionality for our site. There are several major JavaScript libraries out there, among them Dojo,[1] Prototype,[2] script.aculo.us,[3] MooTools,[4] and YUI.[5] While all of these are fine choices, I've opted to go with jQuery mainly because there is a lot of overlap between the Django community and the jQuery community. You're not in any way obligated to use jQuery; if there is another framework that strikes your fancy and you know how to make it work for you, use that instead.

Using a library for implementing Ajax has one big advantage over your own JavaScript: cross-browser compatibility issues are abstracted away beneath the implementation of the framework, allowing you to focus on implementing the Ajax feature at hand, instead of wrestling with differences between different browsers. It also has the added bonus of allowing us to perform visual effects with the newly loaded data. Often, this is a requirement because when you're performing Ajax requests, you need to provide sufficient visual feedback to the user, so that they know the button they've just clicked worked without any errors. Most of the major JavaScript libraries come with these effects built-in, and are pretty well-equipped to handle many of the visual tricks you'll want to use on your own site.

Getting jQuery

The jQuery JavaScript library is not a part of the Django web framework, so before you start using it, you'll need to download the file from the jQuery site. There are two versions available for download: a large development version, in which the code is nicely formatted so as to be readable by human beings, and a "minified" version, which is compressed and has all the extra whitespace removed from it. I highly recommended that you get the minified, gzipped version because it will drastically reduce the load time of your pages.

If you have a keen interest in peeking at the source code of the jQuery library, you can download the development version of it for right now, but make sure that when you deploy your site, you replace this with the minified version. You can download both versions at: `http://jquery.com/`.

---

[1] `http://www.dojotoolkit.org/`

[2] `http://www.prototypejs.org/`

[3] `http://script.aculo.us/`

[4] `http://mootools.net/`

[5] `http://developer.yahoo.com/yui/`

After you've downloaded the file, place the file inside your project's static directory alongside the CSS file. While you're in there, create a new file for holding the custom JavaScript code we're going to write and call it scripts.js. For performance reasons, you should be putting all of your scripts into an external .js file, instead of embedded in your page. Then, open your base.html template file and add the following two lines at the bottom of the file, just above the closing body tag, to include the two new files in your site:

```
<script type="text/javascript" src="{{ MEDIA_URL }}jquery-1.3.1.min.js"></script>
<script type="text/javascript" src="{{ MEDIA_URL }}scripts.js"></script>
</body>
```

These two script includes could have gone at the top of the page, inside the head tags, but to enable progressive rendering of the page, you should put all of your JavaScript includes as close to the bottom of the page as you can.[6] That way, when the page initially loads for the user, visible elements of the page will load first, followed by the JavaScript behavior elements.

jQuery Basics

One interesting feature of jQuery is how it attaches events to elements on a web page. Whereas using traditional JavaScript, you use the name of the event you want to trigger the action as an attribute and the name of the JavaScript function as a value, jQuery doesn't require you to add anything extra to your HTML elements. You simply attach events and functions to them based on their element type, class name, or ID.

This is nice because it allows you to use JavaScript in your web pages without needing to mangle up any of the HTML. Most of your web page code should already be marked up with CSS classes and IDs, so you can add lots of functionality without having to make any changes to your code. It's a clean separation of structure from behavior.

Before getting into making Ajax requests, let's look at how to reference elements in the DOM. We do this using the *jQuery object*, which uses the following syntax: jQuery(). This takes a CSS selector or element tag name as a parameter. So, to reference all the anchor tags on a page, you can use the following selection syntax:

```
jQuery("a");
```

In order to select the div element on a page that has an id of product_image, you'd use the following:

```
jQuery("#product_image");
```

If you want to select every element that has a class of product_thumbnail:

```
jQuery(".product_thumbnail");
```

And so on. You can even select all child elements of a parent element:

```
jQuery("#ul_list > li");
```

And if you just want to reference the first or the last child element:

```
jQuery("#ul_list").children(":first");
jQuery("#ul_list").children(":last");
```

---

[6] http://developer.yahoo.com/performance/rules.html

209

While these don't actually do anything in and of themselves, you can chain together other jQuery functions in order to do things with them. By this point, you should be familiar with how to create Django ORM QuerySets by stringing together `filter()` and `exclude()` functions in order to get at the results you want. jQuery actually works in a very similar fashion. As one example, if you want to add a CSS class called `visible` to an element dynamically, you would use:

```
jQuery("div#product_image").addClass("visible");
```

In the latter example, we've explicitly noted that the element in question is a `div` element.

THE JQUERY OBJECT VIA $ SYNTAX

Like a lot of other JavaScript libraries, jQuery allows you to select elements using `$()` syntax instead of `jQuery()`. However, in this book, I'm going to create my examples using `jQuery()` instead of the dollar sign alternative. The reason for this is that if you ever get to a point where you want to use another JavaScript library, such as MooTools or Prototype, in conjunction with your current jQuery code, your code won't get confused about which library the ambiguous `$()` function is referring to.

When you're working with the jQuery examples available on the Internet, you'll generally see the dollar sign syntax used instead of spelling out jQuery every time. Choose whichever you feel the most comfortable with.

There are quite a few things that you can do with an element once you have it selected, and `addClass()` is only one of many. While full coverage of jQuery is beyond the scope of this book, from these simple examples you should be able to grasp what we're doing in the rest of the chapter.

Right now, there is nothing to stop a user from clicking the "Search" button with no text in the search box. We didn't put any validation on the search box, so a blank submission is perfectly valid and should match every single product in your database. Of course, this isn't ideal, so let's require that the user enter some text.

We'll also go a step further and require them to enter something other than "Search," which is the default text in the search box. That way, if they just click the Search button without changing the default text, they won't get a list of products matching "Search." (You might want to change this if "Search" is something your users might actually search for.)

Open your new `scripts.js` file, where we're going to include all of our custom JavaScript code. In this file, add the following two function definitions:

```
function prepareDocument(){
    //code to prepare page here.
}

jQuery(document).ready(prepareDocument);
```

You need a point during the loading of each page at which you can attach each of the events to each element. Using jQuery, this is done by calling the ready() function on the document body. This is very similar to the window.onload, which is the customary means of firing up JavaScript functionality as soon as the document has loaded. The advantage to using jQuery's ready() function is that your events can fire as soon as the DOM is ready, instead of having to wait until the entire page and every component on it has loaded. In addition to this, there have been numerous problems in the past for developers in getting the window.onload event to behave consistently across major browsers, resulting in lots of different hacks to JavaScript examples. ready() solves these issues for you.

The ready() function takes the name of the function you want to run when the document is ready. Optionally, you could pass in an *anonymous* function, putting all your code directly in the ready() function:

```
jQuery(document).ready(function(){
    //code to prepare page here.
});
```

However, in the interest of keeping things separated logically, I chose to split the code that will attach the events in its own function.

Now, getting back to our search box problem, we don't actually want to attach any event to the search text box itself. Text boxes have events that fire when the user presses a key, when the user brings focus to the box, and so forth. However, none of these are appropriate for validating the search form input, since attaching an error to any of these events wouldn't really be appropriate.

What we really want to do is validate the text in the search box when the form is *submitted*. We can do this very easily, referencing the id of the search form. We'll attach an event that fires when this form is submitted and ensures that there is something (other than "Search") entered into the box. Otherwise, we'll pop up an alert letting the user know they haven't entered anything yet, and halt the submission of the form to the server.

The following code does this:

```
jQuery("form#search").submit(function(){
    text = jQuery("#id_q").val();
    if (text == "" || text == "Search"){
        // if empty, pop up alert
        alert("Enter a search term.");
        // halt submission of form
        return false;
    }
});
```

Place this code inside your prepareDocument() function, and this code will be attached to the search form as soon as the DOM is loaded and ready to use, on each page. Notice that if you call the val() function on an element, such as our search box text field, than you can obtain the value of that text box. This is very handy, and we will use it when we get around to sending data to the server, via Ajax, for processing.

JavaScript Object Notation

Typically, when using Ajax, you send an XMLHttpRequest object and the server returns XML that your JavaScript code parses through to get the data. You first got an introduction back in Chapter 5, when using XML to communicate with Google Checkout and Authorize.Net. In this chapter, we're not actually going to be using XML in our Ajax functions. Instead, we're going to use a different means of formatting data, called JavaScript Object Notation, or JSON, for short.

JSON is remarkably similar to a Python dictionary in the sense that it's little more than a glorified set of name-value pairs that can be nested, and the values themselves can be arrays or other complex data types. In general, they are more lightweight, requiring fewer bytes because they don't require opening and closing tags, like XML does. Instead, JSON syntax uses curly braces to denote context of variable definitions, with the variable name defined only once. Django comes equipped with modules for serializing Django ORM objects, as well as Python dictionaries, into the JSON format in order to transmit data in response to your Ajax client requests.

As an example, this view function will return all of the active products on the site, formatted as JSON:

```
from django.http import HttpResponse
from ecomstore.catalog.models import Product
from django.core import serializers

def get_json_products(request):
    products = Product.active.all()
    json_products = serializers.serialize("json", products)
    return HttpResponse(json_products,
        content_type='application/javascript; charset=utf-8')
```

Go ahead and put this data into one of your apps and give it a URL definition. Open the page in a browser and you'll see the JSON-formatted product data. Notice that we're setting the Content-Type header of the response to be application/javascript, which is how you specify that you're returning JSON data. Alternatively, you could have used the mimetype keyword argument.

■ **Note** When using the content_type argument in returning a JSON response, make sure you specify the charset as utf-8 and *not* utf8. The dash matters in some browsers, most notably IE 7.

In this example, we used the Django serializers module, which is intended specifically to format Django ORM objects. In order to format regular Python dictionaries, as we're going to do in the examples in this chapter, you'll instead use the simplejson module, which is part of the django.utils module.

Making Ajax Requests

Now, the meat and potatoes of the whole process: making Ajax requests from within your JavaScript. In order to make an Ajax request, we're going to use the post() function of the jQuery object. This particular function is actually a higher-level wrapper around the actual ajax() function that the jQuery library offers, which has slightly fewer options and allows the developer a little less control over how the request is processed, but it's very simple and perfect for what we're about to do.

The post() function takes four arguments: the URL to which we will post the request, any data we want to submit with the request (which can be a string or a collection of name-value pairs), a callback function that will execute on the client after we've gotten the response from the server (this is where we'll update the DOM), and the format that we expect the request to be in.

So, here is a very simple and hollowed-out example of the function we're going to write to add a new product review on the site:

```
function addProductReview(){
    // prepare data for request here.
    var data = { foo: bar };
    jQuery.post("/path/to/page/", data,
        function(response){
            // do something with "response" here.
        }
}, "json");
```

It's a simple as that. The biggest challenge you'll likely encounter in this whole process is figuring out how to use jQuery's syntax and functions to update the page after you get the response back from the server. That, and since you're using JavaScript, you have to remember to end each line with a semicolon or you'll encounter errors. (Which reminds me: ain't Python grand?)

Product Reviews

Before we jump into making any Ajax requests or writing jQuery code, we need to hook up the plumbing we need for the product reviews, the same way we would if we were doing the product reviews the old-fashioned, pre-Ajax way. We need to create a model to hold the reviews, as well as a form to capture them on the product page. By now, doing both of these is somewhat old hat, so we don't need to dwell on the specifics of this code.

You can create any fields that you like, but for our example, we're going to have a rating system where users must be authenticated in order to rate an item and submit a product review. The rating system will be from 1 to 5, with 5 being the highest rating. We'll put a Boolean field on the model, called is_approved, to allow us to turn reviews on or off at management's (that is, our) discretion, but by default, all submitted reviews will be enabled.

Review Model and Form

We're going to put the model inside the catalog app, below the Product model definition. While we're in there, we'll create a quick Manager class to handle the filtering of active ProductReview instances, and add a slim class to our admin.py file so that we can administrate the product reviews.

Inside models.py, add the following code:

```
from django.contrib.auth.models import User

class ActiveProductReviewManager(models.Manager):
    def all(self):
        return super(ActiveProductReviewManager, self).all().filter(is_approved=True)

class ProductReview(models.Model):
    RATINGS = ((5,5),(4,4),(3,3),(2,2),(1,1),)

    product = models.ForeignKey(Product)
    user = models.ForeignKey(User)
    title = models.CharField(max_length=50)
    date = models.DateTimeField(auto_now_add=True)
    rating = models.PositiveSmallIntegerField(default=5, choices=RATINGS)
    is_approved = models.BooleanField(default=True)
    content = models.TextField()

    objects = models.Manager()
    approved = ActiveProductReviewManager()
```

Then, inside your `admin.py` file, add the following code to hook the model into the admin interface:

```
from ecomstore.catalog.models import Product, Category, ProductReview

class ProductReviewAdmin(admin.ModelAdmin):
    list_display = ('product', 'user', 'title', 'date', 'rating', 'is_approved')
    list_per_page = 20
    list_filter = ('product', 'user', 'is_approved')
    ordering = ['date']
    search_fields = ['user','content','title']

admin.site.register(ProductReview, ProductReviewAdmin)
```

Now, in keeping with the simple Don't Repeat Yourself (DRY) style, we're going to create the form for the product review model by subclassing `ModelForm` and then including the relevant fields. Open the `forms.py` file inside your `catalog` app and add the following review form definition:

```
class ProductReviewForm(forms.ModelForm):
    class Meta:
        model = ProductReview
        exclude = ('user','product', 'is_approved')
```

Don't forget that you need to import the `ProductReview` model in order for this to run properly.

Template and View Changes

First, let's get things settled with our view function for the product page. We just need to query out the reviews for the current product, as well as create an instance of the new product review form. Open uviews.py in your `catalog` app and add the following two lines to the product view:

```
product_reviews = ProductReview.approved.filter(product=p).order_by('-date')
review_form = ProductReviewForm()
```

Remember that you need to add these two classes to the import statements at the top of the module.

Now we'll turn our sights on the interface. Again, there won't be much here that we haven't seen before, so most of this will be self-explanatory. Open your `catalog/product.html` template and add this code to the bottom of the page, below the section for the product description:

```
<div class="cb"><br /><br /></div>
    <h3>Product Reviews</h3>
        {% if request.user.is_authenticated %}
        <a id="add_review">Write a Review</a>
    <div id="review_form">
        <div id="review_errors"></div>
        <table>
        {{ review_form.as_table }}
        <tr><td colspan="2">
            <input type="hidden" id="id_slug" value="{{ p.slug }}" />
            <input type="submit" id="submit_review" value="Submit" />
            <input type="submit" id="cancel_review" value="Cancel" />
        </td></tr>
        </table>
```

```
    </div>
        {% else %}
            <a href="{% url login %}?next={{ request.path }}">
                Log in to write your own review.
            </a>
        {% endif %}
    <div class="cb"><br /><br /></div>
    <div id="reviews">
        {% for review in product_reviews %}
            {% include 'catalog/product_review.html' %}
        {% empty %}
            <div id="no_reviews">
                No product reviews yet.
            </div>
        {% endfor %}
    </div>
    <div class="cb"><br /><br /></div>
```

Notice that we're restricting the display of the product review form so that it's only available on the page to authenticated users. If the user isn't logged in, they are shown a hyperlink that links to the login page and will redirect them back to the current product page once they're logged in.

Also, you might notice that we've got an anchor tag on the page, with the text "Write a Review" that just had an id attribute and doesn't link to anyplace. The reasons for this will make more sense once we get to writing our jQuery code. By default, when the user is logged in, the product review form won't be visible, either. There will simply be the "Write a Review" link. If they click that link, *then* the product review form will reveal itself. Just by looking at the markup, it's a little tricky to tell what's going to happen by the time we're done.

Notice that we've created a separate include file for each product review that appears inside the {% for %} loop that iterates through all of the reviews for that given product. The next step is to create this template file. Inside templates/catalog, create a new file called product_review.html, and add the following bit of code to it:

```
<div class="review">
    Rating: {{ review.rating }}
    <strong>{{ review.title }}</strong>
    by {{ review.user.username }}
    <br />
    {{ review.content }}
    <br /><br />
    <hr />
</div>
```

The icing on the cake is to add the CSS code necessary to bring this part of the site to life:

```
#add_review{
    cursor:pointer;
}
.hidden{display:none;}
.visible{display:block;}
.new_review{background-color:Pink;}
```

There isn't much here; just a couple of classes to help us control the visibility of page elements, a style so that the newly added product review gets a flashy background color, and a style that makes our

215

cursor a "hand" when the user hovers over the "Write a Review" link. This is a little visual cue that lets the user know that they're supposed to click this link.

Now that this is out of the way, we can get down to the heart of the matter: the Ajax.

The Ajax Part of this Equation

Now that we have the back end and the interface set up, all we need to do is add the Ajax. The Ajax portion of this functionality is the gatekeeper between the database and the product page, acting as the middleman between the bottom and the top that will accept input, validate it, and return either an error message or a successful product review posting to the user.

Conceptually, nothing we're about to do is new. Much in the same way that we validated form data via a POST request and processed it accordingly, we're just going to take the data, send it to the server, and get a JSON response back, acting on *that* accordingly. The only differences are the extra step with the jQuery, and the fact that the code to process the reviews will get its own view function (instead of evaluating `request.method == 'POST'` right in the same product view, for example).

First, open `scripts.js` and add the following code to the `prepareDocument()` function, below the code we created to validate the search form contents, in order to attach events and behaviors to our new product review controls:

```
jQuery("#submit_review").click(addProductReview);
jQuery("#review_form").addClass('hidden');
jQuery("#add_review").click(slideToggleReviewForm);
jQuery("#add_review").addClass('visible');
jQuery("#cancel_review").click(slideToggleReviewForm);
```

These few lines are tying some other function definitions to the controls on the page. Notice that the `submit_review` button on the product page will handle the submission of the new reviews. This is the only really important one, as the rest merely control the visibility of the other elements on the page.

▓ **Note** The jQuery code we've included will be on every page, and so even the non-product pages will have these product template-specific scripts executed when they load. Because these elements don't exist on other pages, this might result in JavaScript errors in the browser. We're going to revisit this issue in Chapter 13, when we look at including JavaScript files on a per-template basis, as needed.

The flow of the controls in action will go something like this: when an authenticated user first navigates to a product page, they will be presented with a link reading "Write a Review" that, if clicked, will reveal the product review form and hide itself (we don't need to show the link anymore) at the same time. If the user clicks the Cancel button, we'll hide the review form and make the "Write a Review" link reappear.

Now, add the following function definition to complete this simple behavior:

```
// toggles visibility of "write review" link
// and the review form.
function slideToggleReviewForm(){
    jQuery("#review_form").slideToggle();
    jQuery("#add_review").slideToggle();
}
```

This function shows what's really going on here. In order to hide and reveal the elements, we're using jQuery's slideToggle() function, which slowly brings hidden elements into view, and visible elements out of sight, using a sliding vertical-accordion visual effect.

Now that both of these are in place, we just need to create our addProductReview() function. In order to see just how this is working hand-in-hand with your view function that we're going to create, you should look at them side by side, to see how the two interlock and pass data between one another.

First, have a look at the function for adding product reviews:

```
function addProductReview(){
    // build an object of review data to submit
    var review = {
        title: jQuery("#id_title").val(),
        content: jQuery("#id_content").val(),
        rating: jQuery("#id_rating").val(),
        slug: jQuery("#id_slug").val() };
    // make request, process response
    jQuery.post("/review/product/add/", review,
        function(response){
            jQuery("#review_errors").empty();
            // evaluate the "success" parameter
            if(response.success == "True"){
                // disable the submit button to prevent duplicates
                jQuery("#submit_review").attr('disabled','disabled');
                // if this is first review, get rid of "no reviews" text
                jQuery("#no_reviews").empty();
                // add the new review to the reviews section
                jQuery("#reviews").prepend(response.html).slideDown();
                // get the newly added review and style it with color
                new_review = jQuery("#reviews").children(":first");
                new_review.addClass('new_review');
                // hide the review form
                jQuery("#review_form").slideToggle();
            }
            else{
                // add the error text to the review_errors div
                jQuery("#review_errors").append(response.html);
            }
        }, "json");
}
```

Before I explain things, let me show you the view function we'll add to views.py in catalog that will end up at the /review/product/add/ URL defined in this JavaScript:

```
from ecomstore.catalog.models import Category, Product, ProductReview
from django.contrib.auth.decorators import login_required
from django.template.loader import render_to_string
from django.utils import simplejson
from django.http import HttpResponse

@login_required
def add_review(request):
    form = ProductReviewForm(request.POST)
    if form.is_valid():
```

217

```
        review = form.save(commit=False)
        slug = request.POST.get('slug')
        product = Product.active.get(slug=slug)
        review.user = request.user
        review.product = product
        review.save()

        template = "catalog/product_review.html"
        html = render_to_string(template, {'review': review })
        response = simplejson.dumps({'success':'True', 'html': html})

    else:
        html = form.errors.as_ul()
        response = simplejson.dumps({'success':'False', 'html': html})
    return HttpResponse(response,
                        content_type='application/javascript; charset=utf-8')
```

First, note that the view is decorated with the @login_required decorator, so that a user must be authenticated to successfully add a review. This will prevent the majority of bogus review submissions that would otherwise be made by anonymous users. After the user clicks the "Submit Review" button and calls the addProductReview() function, we create a variable called review that is populated with the content of the review form. Each of the fields of the product review form are accessed via their id attributes and assigned variables inside this one, effectively creating a set of name-value pairs that will end up in our POST data.

Next, the jQuery function makes a call to the view function, passing in the review data we just assembled. Jump down the view function: the first thing we do is bind all of this data from the request.POST dictionary to an instance of ProductReviewForm. Just as we would in a regular view function, we call is_valid() on the form to check and make sure that the data provided conforms to the database constraints of the model fields. If it is valid, we assign the new review its corresponding product and the current user.

Now, here's where things get interesting: Django provides a function called render_to_string(), which is very similar in concept to the render_to_response() function we've been using at the end of every view on our site. render_to_string() takes the name of a template file and a Python dictionary as parameters, and returns the rendered content of the template, with the dictionary variables inserted into the template, as a single string. We're going to take this bit of rendered HTML that render_to_string() just created for us, send it back to the jQuery function, and insert it into the page along with all of the other reviews.

The nice thing about this approach is that the HTML and variables are defined only in one place: the template file for the product reviews. We're spared the horrible clutter of building HTML on the fly in our jQuery code, an approach that is messy and more difficult to maintain. This has the added benefit of being much more secure, as the rendered string will escape any HTML that is entered by the user, but still interpret the HTML that's part of our template. This minimizes the risk of Cross-Site Scripting attacks.

Lastly, we return an HTTP response containing JSON to the Ajax request we've made. Our JSON response contains two variables. First, we assign a variable called success a value of True, so that we have some way of evaluating whether or not the form validated in our jQuery code, along with another variable containing the HTML we just created. If, on the other hand, the form didn't validate properly, we assign the errors of the form to the HTML variable and give success a value of False. In either case, the variables are serialized as JSON text using the simplejson module and returned to the jQuery with the appropriate Content-Type header set in the response.

This brings us back to the jQuery function, which is, per the last parameter of the post() function, expecting some JSON. We first evaluate if the operation was successful by checking the success variable. If it was, we first disable the Submit button in order to prevent duplicate submissions. Due to network latency, it may take a few seconds (even using Ajax) for the review to be processed and return anything to the client jQuery code. We don't want the user to start clicking the button a bunch of times when they get impatient, flooding our site with requests and possibly posting the same review more than once.

Next, if this is the first review for any given product, we wipe out the "No reviews" text in the div that will be present if there aren't any reviews yet. Then, we add the HTML of the new review to the top of the `reviews` div using the `prepend()` function. We give this new review the pink background color, so the user can plainly see that their new review was just added. Lastly, we slide the product review form out of sight.

On the other hand, if there were any errors, such as missing fields, we instead inject this error text inside the `review_errors` div above the product review form and let the user try again.

The last thing we need to do is add the URL definition to our `catalog` app's `urls.py` file. Open this baby up and add the following URL:

```
(r'^review/product/add/$', 'add_review'),
```

Once that's in place, there's nothing to stop our new review code from doing what we want it to, save for typos and the like. Let's be optimistic, assume it will work, and try it out.

Adding a Product Review

Now it's time to give our new product review form a little bit of testing to see if it behaves as we expect. Go ahead and bring up the site on your local machine and browse to your favorite product. Let's leave it a glowing review.

First, go to the product page to make sure that the "Log In To Write a Review" link works all right, sending you to the login page and then sending you back to the current product page. Make sure that the "Write a Review" link doesn't appear on the page until *after* you log in.

Once you've verified that, try clicking the review link and make sure that the review form slides into view. Try clicking the Submit button without filling out any fields and make sure that the page updates itself with the form errors. Then, fill out the form and submit it. If everything is valid, the review form should slide out of view and leave you with your newly added review showing up in the reviews section below, highlighted in our beautiful pink. (Even if you are using the orange and green theme I've been using, you'll probably want to *at least* change that pink to something else.)

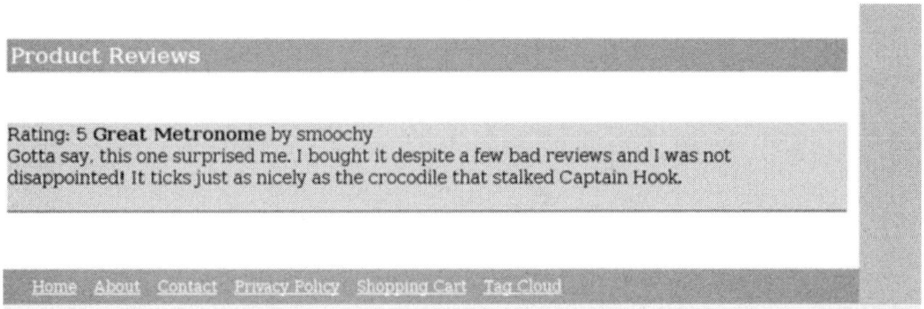

Figure 10-1. A newly added product review in pink.

If everything doesn't go quite as planned, look back over the code to see if there are any typos in the code you entered. Remember that when you build the review variable to submit to the site in your jQuery code, you don't need to enclose the name of each variable in quotes, as we're building a list of name-value pairs and *not* a Python dictionary. Check to make sure that you've entered the correct number of parentheses and curly braces, and that they open and close in the correct order.

For troubleshooting, I'd highly recommend using one of the excellent Firefox plug-ins, if you don't have them already. Firebug allows you to see the Ajax requests that are being made, and Tamper Data allows you to intercept and *manipulate* HTTP requests in action. If your response has an HTTP status code of 500, that means there is an error in the new view function you just created. If you're getting a 404, that likely means that your view function is not returning any kind of response.

In order to troubleshoot 500 errors with the view function, I recommend adjusting the code in your view so that you refer to request.GET instead of request.POST, and then try accessing the view just by typing the URL with any needed parameters in your browser. So, if you navigate to:

```
/review/product/add/?title=title&content=content&… (etc)
```

you should see the standard Django error page, with lots of information you can use to debug the issue, provided, of course, that DEBUG is set to True in your settings.py file. After you've found the problem, of course, you have to change the request.GET references back to POST.

If it's something else, like an error in your jQuery code, try viewing the errors in the built-in Firefox Error Console, where any syntax errors in your JavaScript syntax will be listed.

And there you have it. Our site now has some Ajax on it, as well as product review capabilities for registered users.

Product Catalog Tagging

While we could stop right there and move on to some other endeavors, we're going to add additional functionality to our site using this new-found Ajax functionality: product tagging. Allowing customers to tag your products is a great way to let customers interact with your product catalog, allowing them to contribute their own little bits of content. It's a very simple, easy-to-implement means of making the shopping process on your site slightly more social. You can also use these in fetching your search results and making product recommendations.

For now, we're going to display a list of tags on the product page, and permit authenticated users to tag products with new words. We'll set it up so that each product tag is a link that leads the user to a page listing all the products that were also tagged with that particular word. Finally, we'll create a page on our site that is one big product tag cloud, with the more frequently used words appearing largest, and the less frequently used ones appearing smaller.

Getting Django-Tagging

Fortunately, there's already a Django application on the Internet for our use in creating tagging functionality, so we don't need to do a lot of the basic work, such as setting up models, in order to get the tagging architecture in place. It's called django-tagging, and it provides an excellent interface, with lots of custom model managers that allow you to create, update, and retrieve tags related to each model or each model instance extremely easily.

The code is available for download at http://code.google.com/p/django-tagging/. If you're working with Django 1.1, as we have been in the rest of the book, you should check out the current development version (which is 0.3 at the time I'm writing this) using Subversion.

Once you've downloaded the django-tagging app, navigate into the directory and execute the usual python setup.py install to install the package on your system. You'll need to make sure that the package itself ends up somewhere on your Python path, such as in your system's site-packages directory. To test that it's been installed and is ready for you to use, jump into a Python interpreter and try the following import:

```
>>> import tagging
```

If you don't see any errors, you now have django-tagging on your system. In order to use this code in our project, we need to add this to our project's INSTALLED_APPS section. Inside of settings.py, add the following line to hook it up:

```
'tagging',
```

Then run `manage.py syncdb` in order to create the two new database tables that are required by the tagging package. Because the relations between your own models and the tagging models are defined by a many-to-many relationship, using an intermediate join table, there's no need to edit any of the fields on your existing models.

The one thing we *do* need to do is register any models you want to tag in your project with the tagging module. You can do this with a couple very short lines of code. Just import the `tagging` module into your `catalog/models.py` file, and then, below the `Product` model, register it:

```
import tagging

# Product model class definition here
try:
    tagging.register(Product)
except tagging.AlreadyRegistered:
    pass
```

And that's it. We can now tag products. The only thing we need to do is add template and view code. Before we do that, however, a quick word on how Django deals with your project's models.

Django Content Types

Now that you have the tagging package installed in your Django project, you're now set up to let your users tag *anything*. While we're just going to use it for tagging products, it's interesting that these two tagging models you just added to your project are flexible enough that you can tag any one of your own models. It does this by hooking into the Django contenttypes framework.

Whenever you add a new model to your project and run `syncdb`, an instance of `contenttype` is created and stored in your database. This is a means for Django to store information about your models, allowing you to write code that interacts with your database without the need to specify a model. This is useful in cases where you want to create relationships between models without making the dependent on specific models.

Take this tagging package that we just installed: there are two models, `Tag` and `TaggedItem`. The first model, `Tag`, stores the actual tag words that have been entered by your users. The other model, `TaggedItem`, is the join table that acts as the intermediary between the tags and all of your models. Stored in the `TaggedItem` model are three key pieces of information: the ID of the `Tag` model instance, the primary key of the tagged model instance, and the content type ID of the model instance that was tagged. The latter two items, the primary key and content type ID, point to a single model instance in your database. While it's possible for two different models instances of differing types to share the same primary key, the content type ID disambiguates the two.

When you created the `Product` model, imagine that it was assigned a content type ID of 2. When you go to tag the product that has an ID of 8, the `django-tagging` package will create a tag and associate with the model instance in the table with the associated content type ID *and* the given primary key. In this way, any given `TaggedItem` instance should only ever refer to a single model instance, but you're not constrained to having that instance only in a single table. It's a nifty little abstraction that enables you to do things more generically.

The Django contenttypes framework is already installed in your project, and the corresponding database tables for the models were created when we ran `syncdb` in order to create our first models back in Chapter 3. So, with the tables created, we're ready to start making template changes.

Enabling Product Tagging

Now let's turn to the product page and add the section where the tags will reside, along with a small form so that our customers can tag products. Again, we're going to constrain the form (and its corresponding view function) so that it's only accessible to authenticated users. Open the `product.html` template file in your project and add the following bit of code, below the description section but above the product reviews:

```
<div class="cb"><br /><br /></div>
    <h3>Product Tags</h3>

        <div id="tags">
            {% for tag in p.tags %}
                {% include 'catalog/tag_link.html' %}
            {% endfor %}
        </div>
        <br />
        {% if request.user.is_authenticated %}
            <label for="id_tag">Tag this product (must be at least three
characters):</label>
            <br />
            <input id="id_tag" type="text" />
            <input type="submit" value="Tag It" id="add_tag" />

        {% else %}
            <a href="{% url login %}?next={{ request.path }}">
                Log in to tag this product.
            </a>
        {% endif %}
    <div class="cb"><br /><br /></div>
```

Notice that this code relies on a new template include that we haven't yet created. Go ahead and create the `tag_link.html` file now, inside `templates/catalog`, and add the following code to it:

```
<a href="/tag/{{ tag.name }}/">{{ tag.name|slugify }}</a> 
```

Notice that in both of these cases, we're passing the tag name through the Django built-in `slugify` template filter. This converts all letters to lowercase, replaces spaces with dashes, and removes any leading or trailing whitespace. Basically, this does the same thing that the `SlugField` does on our models: ensures that the text is rendered in the link with only URL-legal characters.

Now let's turn back to our jQuery code file, and add the function we need there. We'll be following the same process as before in submitting the information to the server. The only difference is that this time, we only need to submit two values to the server, the new tag and the slug of the product that we want to tag. The product slug will come from the hidden `input` we created for our product review in the last section. If you skipped over that section and didn't add the product reviews, go back and copy that `input` element somewhere onto the product page now so that your jQuery will be able to get the slug from your page's DOM.

First, let's create the view function that will process newly submitted tags. In order to add new tags to a product model instance, we just call the `add_tag()` method on the `Tag` model's default `objects` manager class, passing in the model instance and the tag text that was entered, like so:

```
Tag.objects.add_tag(product, tag)
```

The second variable, tag, has to be a single word. In our code, we're going to split up multiple words and add them one at a time. For validation of input, we're merely going to check the length of the submitted string and make sure that it's at least three characters in length.

Inside your catalog app's views.py file, add the following view function:

```
import tagging
from tagging.models import Tag, TaggedItem

@login_required
def add_tag(request):
    tags = request.POST.get('tag','')
    slug = request.POST.get('slug','')
    if len(tags) > 2:
        p = Product.active.get(slug=slug)
        html = u''
        template = "catalog/tag_link.html"
        for tag in tags.split():
            tag.strip(',')
            Tag.objects.add_tag(p,tag)
        for tag in p.tags:
            html += render_to_string(template, {'tag': tag })
        response = simplejson.dumps({'success':'True', 'html': html })
    else:
        response = simplejson.dumps({'success':'False'})
    return HttpResponse(response,
                        content_type='application/javascript; charset=utf8')
```

The main difference between the last Ajax view function we created and this one is the fact that instead of merely returning the most recently added tag instance, we're returning all of the tags for the given product. In our jQuery code, we're going to clear out the entire contents of the element containing all of the product tags and reload all of them.

Now let's create the JavaScript function in our jQuery code to link the view function and the interface. First, add the following code to the prepareDocument() function to tie the functions to the elements on the product page.

```
//tagging functionality to prepareDocument()
    jQuery("#add_tag").click(addTag);
    jQuery("#id_tag").keypress(function(event){
        if (event.keyCode == 13 && jQuery("#id_tag").val().length > 2){
            addTag();
            event.preventDefault();
        }
    });
```

The first line simply attaches the name of the addTag() function to the add_tag button on the product page. The second item here attaches an event to the tag input box itself. Key code 13 corresponds to the Enter key on a user's keyboard. We're using it here to fire the addTag() function if the user types in a word and hits the Enter key, so they don't need to reach back to the mouse and click the "Tag It" button with the cursor. Enabling the Enter key to fire this event is much more natural than requiring the user to click the button. In this function, we check the length of the entered text, making sure that it's at least three characters in length.

Now, add the addTag() function definition to the file:

```
function addTag(){
    tag = { tag: jQuery("#id_tag").val(),
            slug: jQuery("#id_slug").val() };
    jQuery.post("/tag/product/add/", tag,
            function(response){
                if (response.success == "True"){
                    jQuery("#tags").empty();
                    jQuery("#tags").append(response.html);
                    jQuery("#id_tag").val("");
                }
        }, "json");
}
```

Next, we need to make sure that our view function can be found by our project when it makes the Ajax requests, so we need to add the following URL definition to the urls.py file in the catalog app:

```
(r'^tag/product/add/$', 'add_tag'),
```

The final piece we need to include is a slender CSS style definition in our style sheet to color the tag links:

```
#tags a{
    color:DarkOrange;
}
```

That's all we need. Now, you should be able to bring up the site, log in, and start tagging up products with your own keywords. One thing that is still missing is the results page that should come up each time you click on a particular tag link. Also, on sites where tagging functionality is enabled, it's common to have a single page that lists all the tags in use, using a "tag cloud," so users can browse the catalog by tags. In the next section, we're going to add these two pages.

Creating the Tag Cloud

Now let's create a new page on our site that will contain a tag cloud for all of our products. Like most of the tag clouds floating around the Internet, the font size of each tag will we "weighted," so that the more frequently used tags will appear with the largest font size and the least frequently used tags will appear smallest.

We're going to house all of the code and template files for this simple tag cloud in our catalog app, since this functionality ties in directly with the product catalog. We need to create two new pages: one for the tag cloud itself, and a second to list the products that are tagged with any given tag. Add the following two view functions to the views.py file:

```
def tag_cloud(request, template_name="catalog/tag_cloud.html"):
    product_tags = Tag.objects.cloud_for_model(Product, steps=9,
        distribution=tagging.utils.LOGARITHMIC,
        filters={ 'is_active': True })
    page_title = 'Product Tag Cloud'
    return render_to_response(template_name, locals(),
        context_instance=RequestContext(request))

def tag(request, tag, template_name="catalog/tag.html"):
```

```
products = TaggedItem.objects.get_by_model(Product.active, tag)
return render_to_response(template_name, locals(),
    context_instance=RequestContext(request))
```

In order to retrieve all of the tags for a given model, you can simply call the `cloud_for_model()` method on the `Tag` model's default manager class, passing in the name of model. We pass in two additional keyword arguments named `steps`, which takes an integer value, and `distribution`, which takes one element of the `tagging.utils` enumeration. Both of these values are used to annotate each tag with a numerical value we can use in our templates to set the font-size property of each tag. Since we've used a value of 9, the least frequently used tags will have a `font_size` value of 1, while the most frequent will have a `font_size` value of 9.

Now, create a new template file called `catalog/tag_cloud.html` and add the following code to it:

```
{% extends "catalog.html" %}

{% load tagging_tags %}

{% block content %}
    <h1>Product Tag Cloud</h1>
    {% for tag in product_tags %}
        <a href="/tag/{{ tag.name }}/" style="font-size:
            {{ tag.font_size|add:"11" }}px;">{{ tag.name|slugify }}</a> 
    {% endfor %}
{% endblock %}
```

Notice that we're setting the font size directly in each link, via the `style` attribute. In order to set `font size` to a reasonable value, we're augmenting the `font_size` attribute of each tag by 11, so that infrequent tags have a `font size` of 12px, while larger ones will have a `font size` of 20px. You might want to tweak these values to get the tag cloud looking the way you want it to.

Finally, create a new template file call `tag.html` to correspond with the results page for each tag. Until now, the links on the product page haven't gone anyplace. If you clicked on one, you should have just gotten a Django 404 Page Not Found error page. Instead of this, we want to list product thumbnails for all products tagged with a given tag. Inside this new template file, add the following template code:

```
{% extends "catalog.html" %}

{% block content %}
    <h1>Products tagged with: '{{ tag }}'</h1>
    {% for p in products %}
        {% include 'tags/product_thumbnail.html' %}
    {% endfor %}
{% endblock %}
```

Of course, we just need to add a couple of URL definitions to the `catalog` app so that these pages are accessible to our browser and not just our IDE:

```
(r'^tag_cloud/$', 'tag_cloud', {'template_name': 'catalog/tag_cloud.html'}, 'tag_cloud'),
(r'^tag/(?P<tag>[-\w]+)/$', 'tag', {'template_name': 'catalog/tag.html'}, 'tag'),
```

Go ahead and add a link to the product tag cloud page to your site's footer so that your customers can click on it and Google can crawl it. If you bring up the tag cloud in your browser, you should see it as a set of links. If their usage frequency varies between different tags, then the font size of the tags should vary in proportion to their use.

Figure 10-2. *The tag cloud for our product catalog.*

One thing you'll notice about our tag solution is that we're hard-coding the URL for the tag results page in each place that a tag link occurs on our site. This is, of course, in stark contrast to the cleanliness of the get_absolute_url() method we added to each of our other models that allows us to define the URLs in a single place, without any repetition. In this case, we've broken our rule and made things slightly less DRY by doing this. If this really bothers you, you should be able to subclass the Tag class with your own custom model class, add a get_absolute_url() method to it, and use that class instead. For such a small example, I didn't feel it was necessary to go this extra step, but remember that object-oriented programming affords you the ability.

JavaScript Finishing Touches

Now that we've added this new functionality, and our site has officially entered the "Web 2.0" with some style, there are a couple of small things we can add to our site in order to help the user out. First of all, testing the Ajax calls on our local development machine is pretty simple. When you logged in and created the first product review to test the new Ajax submission code, you probably entered something really unique like "title here" for the title of the review and "blah blah blah" for the content and then hit the Submit button. And in a flash, the new review was added to the top of the list of product reviews right below it, and everything seems to be working just as you want it to.

There's still a small problem with the product review. In the real world of the Internet, we have to deal with a little issue called *network latency*. Developers almost always have high-speed Internet connections because it's critical to their livelihood. Without that cable modem, you wouldn't be able to reach the latest blog entries on Technorati about Google Wave or the Semantic Web or any other up-and-coming technologies that keep us geeks drooling. Unfortunately, not everyone has the luxury of high-bandwidth connections, and we have to tweak the experience to take them into account.

On top of this, the product reviews that people write are often longer than the mere "yada yada" you might have added for your simple test review. Have a look the reviews for a hot product like the book *The Da Vinci Code*, and you'll see that people are not lazy. *Au contraire*, a great many people are willing to write at length about their own opinions, often using lots of extra words to expound on their points. When these people come to your site, ready to talk about a product that they loved, and why they loved it, and how they bought eight of them because they wanted one for each of their *cats*, they might submit a large review. And because this would-be cat lover is still using dial-up, the connection is really slow and it might take our server a little bit longer than a few seconds to respond.

Fortunately, there is a very easy solution to this problem that we can add to our site with only a few lines of code. We're going to create a very simple box at the top of the browser window, which will appear with a "Loading…" status message, to let the user know that we've received their button click and that our web server is trying *really hard* to fulfill their request, but that it's just taking a moment. It's a polite way of giving the user feedback and asking them to be patient.

First, we're going to add some JavaScript to our prepareDocument() function that will insert the status box into the page when the document loads. While we could just stick this div element into the code of the page itself, it really doesn't belong there, and for practical purposes is just clutter. For this reason, we're going to rely on the jQuery itself to stick the actual HTML of the status box into the page:

```
function statusBox(){
    jQuery('<div id="loading">Loading...</div>')
    .prependTo("#main")
    .ajaxStart(function(){jQuery(this).show();})
    .ajaxStop(function(){jQuery(this).hide();})
}
```

Add the call to this function to the bottom of your prepareDocument() function so that it's called when each page loads. Now what we need to do is style this div element up with some CSS so that it's hidden initially, and so that it appears where we want it to.

```
#loading{
    display:none;
    position:fixed;
    top:0;
    left:45%;
    background-color:Pink;
    width: 200px;
    font-size:medium;
    color:Black;
    font-weight:bold;
    padding:2px;
    border:solid 1px Red;
    text-align: center;
    z-index:100;
}
```

Using postion:fixed; on the element allows us to position the status box at the top of the browser window, so that no matter where the user is on the page, whether at the top or scrolled down very far down the page, the box will appear top-centered in the browser. After the page is loaded, the status box will first be rendered with a display property of hidden. This box will reveal itself whenever an Ajax call is initiated in our code, and will again slip back into hiding after the processing of the Ajax response has been completed.

Figure 10-3. The "Loading..." status box at the top of our browser window.

The second thing you might consider adding is a warning message to the top of the site letting the user know that some parts of your site require JavaScript. This is not strictly necessary, and the solution we're going to use may be a little overbearing depending on your requirements, but it's a nice courtesy to let users know that they ought to have JavaScript enabled in their browser in order to use every aspect of your site.

First, add the following lines of code to your catalog.html file:

```
<a href="#content" class="skip_link">Skip to main content</a>
    <noscript>
        <div id="noscript">Some parts of {{ site_name }} require Javascript</div>
        <div id="noscript_padder"></div>
    </noscript>
    <div id="banner">
```

Then, in your CSS file, add the following styles to position and style these two new divs accordingly:

```
#noscript{
    position:fixed;
    top:0;left:0;
    width:100%;
    background-color:Red;
    color:White;
    font-weight:bold;
    padding:5px;
    text-align:center;
}
#noscript_padder{
    height:30px;
}
```

In the event that the site detects that a user has JavaScript disabled in their browser, a red bar will appear across the top of the page letting the user know that some parts of the site require that JavaScript be enabled in order for all parts of the site to function properly. Whether or not you decide to use this on your site is your decision, but it can be helpful to users when they reach a JavaScript-dependent area of your site,

228

they click on something, and then nothing happens. The important thing is that if several areas of your site are dependent on JavaScript, that you make use of the noscript tags to let your customers know.

Summary

In this chapter, we added a couple of very common features on e-commerce sites: product reviews and tagging functionality. On top of this, we did it with Ajax, and so now our little e-commerce site has some real flair on it. The techniques we used in this chapter could be applied to several other areas of your site. You might have a good idea of how you'd like to change the shopping cart so that adding products to the cart is Ajax-based.

As a matter of fact, that's a good exercise to try now that you understand how to use the jQuery library in order to make Ajax requests and update the current web page using the DOM. Make the "Add To Cart" button on the product page add items to a shopping cart at the side of the page.

In the next chapter, we're going to talk about a topic that's of paramount importance to any e-commerce site: search engine optimization. Just how well you architect your site for visibility in search engines such as Google and Yahoo! may make or break just how successful your site may be. The good news: so far, just doing everything the Django way, we've actually got a pretty good head start over other people. That doesn't mean there isn't lots more we can do to bring our site up in the rankings. So let's continue on and see what we can do to help Google find our site.

CHAPTER 11

■ ■ ■

Search Engine Optimization

There's a lot that goes into making a site successful. Despite the somewhat disparaging jokes I've made about people in marketing over the course of the book so far, I don't mean to trivialize their critical role in taking a web site from a lonely bunch of code on a developer's machine to a public place where (hopefully) lots of *actual human beings* will use it.

In this chapter, I'm going to talk about Search Engine Optimization (SEO). Optimizing your site for indexing with search engines is more of an ongoing process than just a single step in the development cycle. The process itself, however, should start in the planning phase, when you are making initial plans about the architecture of your site. It's monumentally more challenging to take an existing site and optimize it for search engines than to plan for this kind of thing from the start.

There are several aspects of marketing an e-commerce site that you should consider. You need to consider your marketing strategy as a whole; that is, how will people find your site? How will you get the word out about your new online store after it's launched? Will it be an online marketing effort using ad campaigns on other sites, an offline effort to promote the site by some other means, such the radio or magazines, or some combination of the two? Will you do any kind of e-mail marketing campaign that targets those people who have placed orders on your site? The specific answers to these questions will depend largely on the type of product that you're selling.

We're not going to cover these issues in the chapter. SEO is the process by which you make your site friendly to search engines such as Google or Yahoo!, so that they are able to crawl your site, index your pages, and add them to their Search Engine Results Pages (SERPs). Search engine optimization is a set of guidelines you can follow in the hopes that your site's pages appear as close to the top as possible in the results pages for people searching for relevant terms. This is an important *part* of your overall marketing strategy, but it shouldn't be the *only* part of your marketing strategy. In order to have a successful site, you should be doing other forms of marketing. However, in this chapter, we're going to cover only SEO and not other specific marketing techniques.

It's important also to note that, although we'll go over search engine optimization best practices, I can't guarantee that you will get good results in a timely fashion. There are a couple of reasons for this: first, while we have a pretty good idea of how search engines rank pages, the exact means by which search engines sort pages is not known by anyone (except for the search engine companies themselves). While we can base our strategies on the information that these companies give us, a lot of the whole process is simply shooting in the dark with some educated guesses, to test and see what works.

Lastly, when you enter into business in the online landscape, it's the same as entering into business in the real world in that you are probably up against a good deal of competition. While you may have a great idea to start a new computer company that will revolutionize the home computer market, this doesn't mean that you're going to be able to overtake Gateway or Apple simply because you plan to work really hard. The Internet is the same way. You might be starting an online business so that you can start selling books, but that doesn't mean you will necessarily be able to rise above Amazon.com, Google Books, or Barnes & Noble in the search engines results pages when a user enters the search term "books." If there is already well-established competition in the arena, it's a David and Goliath situation, and if you're just getting started, then I'm sorry, but for the time being, you're a huge underdog and you'll need to be patient about rising up in the search results.

Don't worry, it's not quite as gloom and doom as that. The approaches we're going to take in this chapter should help you get ahead of most of the other e-commerce companies out there. My only point is that it's important not to get inflated with unrealistic expectations before developing your strategy.

The good news is, whether or not you're aware of it, we've done things correctly thus far in the book. We're going to touch upon what we've created in this book so far, and I'll explain the logic behind those efforts. We'll look at how to create a very rudimentary SEO plan, and what kinds of strategies you should be working on to get your site positioned in the search engine results pages. Then, we'll go a bit deeper and discuss some additional things we can do in order to get our site indexed as quickly as possible, by creating a sitemap to submit to Google, as well as a product feed we can submit to Google Base to be included in Google's Shopping results.

We'll also look at how to use Google Analytics and the Webmasters tools to track how your customers are finding your site, how they're behaving on the site, and what kind of demographics they are in, so you can adjust your site design or overall marketing strategy to target your site's customers.

One final word about this chapter before I get into the details: throughout this chapter, I refer to "search engines" and "Google" somewhat interchangeably. At the time of this writing, Google still handles the majority of searches on the web, and most of the other major search engines now use some variation of Google's technology to drive their search results. For this reason, the two are conceptually equivalent for the purposes of this chapter. However, in the real world, there are lots of search engines that are not Google that you should be targeting in your marketing strategies as well. Keep this in mind as you read this chapter.

We're going to get started by going over the very basic tenets of SEO. Before you start reading, I would, of course, heartily encourage you to take a look at the Google's own authoritative SEO guidelines at: http://www.google.com/support/webmasters/.

The Importance of Inbound Links

In order to bring you all of those wonderful search results, Google indexes the content of pages on the web and stores a copy of each page on their servers. They do this using an automated network of computers, called *spiders*, that navigate around the web, following all hyperlinks they find and indexing all the pages they encounter. When you perform a search using Google, the pages matching your search terms are returned to you with the most relevant results returned first. It sorts the results using an algorithm of their own design, called the PageRank algorithm.

The primary mechanism behind the PageRank algorithm is the count and content of inbound hyperlinks from other sites to a page. The text of the anchor tags is a key component of where the page will rank in relation to all others. For example, if another page under a different domain links to a page on your site with the text "cheap electric guitars," then that page on your site is all the more likely to come up when someone searches for one, some, or all of those words.

The number of links into your site from external sites also matters a great deal. The more sites that link into pages on your site, the more important Google assumes that page is, and so the pages in your site are more likely to come up higher in the search results. You can think of each external page that links into yours as a "vote" for the importance of your page.

All of the major search engines now use a variation of the PageRank algorithm to determine how to sort the content that they've indexed. Even though we're going to focus on Google in this chapter, the techniques discussed in this chapter should help you in getting up in the results pages for all of the major search engines.

Unfortunately, while this is the most important factor in determining where your site ranks in the search engines, it's also the one we have the least amount of control over. If you know other people, friends who run web sites or have blogs, you should get as many of them to link to you as possible. One common thing that web sites do to encourage their fellow webmasters to link to them is provide some ready-made HTML anchor tag that people can copy and paste onto their own site. This is a pretty good idea in my mind; whenever you ask someone to do you a favor, you might as well make it *easy* for them to do it. And, as an added bonus, if you provide the HTML of the anchor tag for them, you can control what anchor text appears in the links.

Before doing this, you should have a list of keywords written up so you can determine the best possible keywords you can put into the anchor tags. We'll look at some tricks for generating a keyword list in the section "Generating a Keyword List" later in this chapter.

Content Is King

The second main factor that search engines examine when crawling your site is the content that they find on the pages in the form of text. Since search engine users search uses keywords, this is the most logical means of finding relevant pages: by analyzing all of the words on each page. While not as important as inbound links from external sites, it's the largest factor on your site over which you have complete control, so you should be careful to do everything right from the start.

First of all, because search engines are going to crawl your site, hopefully following all of the hyperlinks they find, you want to make sure that they can *find* all of the pages on your site that you want to have in the index. This makes sense for reasons other than SEO. If a customer is browsing your site, clicking around on various links, you want them to theoretically be able to access every page on your site.

In this section, we're going to review the content we've created for the pages of your site so far, and look at the reasons why we've structured things the way we have. Then, we'll cover to how to generate an appropriate keyword list, so that as you add new content to your site, you'll be able to use words and phrases that effectively target your customer base. We're also going to look at how you use HTML to give your content semantic meaning for search engine spiders, and avoid the potential pitfall of duplicate content.

Title and Meta Tags

There are several things that search engines look at on a web page to determine the nature of its content. Some things on your web page are weighed more heavily than mere text on that page. One key component of each page is the title tag text, which displays in the title bar of the browser, or in the tab of the window if you're using a tabbed browser.

In order to make the best use of the `title` tags, you should ensure that each page has unique title text. A lot of sites preface the title text on each and every one of their pages with the name of their site. However, unless you're really trying to brand your own company name very heavily, it makes more sense to include this in every page, but at the *end* of each `title` tag instead of at the beginning. This is the approach we've taken with our site so far in the book. Inside each view, we've specified a `page_title` variable that is inserted into the page's `title` element that is unique and describes the content of the page. The name of the site is appended onto the end of this text. In this way, the site name still appears inside every `title` tag, but the description of the content appears first.

Remember, it's not likely that people will be searching for the name of our site. Each of our product pages has the name of the product appearing first. This is much more likely to make each product page come up for a relevant search. If someone is searching for, and enters "ruby axe guitar" into Google, our product page has a much better chance of coming up if this is the first text that appears in the `title` tags. Having the site name at the end, however, is a great means of stamping your company name on each page.

Also of special importance are the `meta` tags in your site's head element. There are actually quite a few different kinds of header tags you can use to define the nature of the content on the page, but there are only two that matter enough that you should be including them inside every page: the `keywords` and `description` meta tags.

The keywords meta tag is intended to contain a comma-delimited list of keywords and phrases that help search engine spiders discern the type of content that appears on the page. Similarly, the description meta tag is supposed to contain a very brief description of the page's content. These aren't nearly as important as they once were, since early on in the history of the Internet webmasters realized it was pretty easy to "cheat" and lead users into spam sites simply by tweaking the keywords and description meta tags to give the appearance of legitimate content to search engines.

Consequently, they are no longer the primary means by which search engines determine the nature of the content on a page. Rather, they are now used in conjunction with all of the other factors mentioned so far, as two factors among many. It's still worth your while to make sure that they appear on every page, that they are unique to the page, and are accurate and up-to-date. While the content of both of these can be as long as you'd like, major search engines recommend a maximum of 200 characters for the description meta tag, and should not contain any HTML elements. These are a couple of reasons that we chose not to use the product description in the description meta tag: our product descriptions might be very long and may contain HTML tags. Regarding the keywords meta tag, you should keep the number of words and phrases for each page down to a small number, around three or so, so that the weight of each word or phrase is higher.

You just want to make sure that you don't overdo it. Major search engines, including Google, may penalize you for trying to overload your keyword meta tag with content. If you find yourself adding more than five keywords per page, you should probably stop and start focusing your efforts on creating content for the page instead, as it's more likely to help your site's rankings.

Keep in mind that the singular and plural versions of any given word are considered different keywords.

There are other areas of your site where the text is weighed more heavily than just text that appears in the body of the page. One example is header tags: the h1 through h7 elements that are rendered larger than normal text by browsers. Search engines also amplify the content of these tags, regarding their content as more important than mere text. For this reason, for the site we're creating in this book, we've put product names and category names into h1 elements on their respective pages, hopefully giving them a small "bump up" in the overall search results for searches containing similar words.

Another area is the alt text for image tags. You should be supplying descriptive alt text for your image tags for accessibility reasons, since not all users will be able to view the images, and in those cases, the browser will fall back on the alt text. However, it's also an excellent opportunity for you to put some descriptive keywords, such as the product name or other text, into the page in a place where search engines will take special note of it.

Keywords in URLs

This is an important element in your site's overall SEO: the contents of the URL for each page. This is key in giving search engines a sense of what kind of content is on any given page. They not only play a big role in helping search engines determine what is on the page, but when human users copy links to your pages and post them on forums around the Internet, the link itself is then self-describing, giving each person who views the link an idea of what it contains. Much more importantly, these links will automatically contain the product name, and this is certainly relevant and descriptive text.

Since spaces are illegal in URLs, the best delimiter you can use in order to separate different words is a dash, or hyphen, character. There are some people who say that it's better to use an underscore character to separate words in your URLs. I'm basing my conclusion on a blog post[1] by Matt Cutts, a software engineer at Google, in which he *recommends* that people use dashes instead of underscores.

Our site is already set up to use product names in the product page URLs by default, through the use of a Django SlugField on our models, which is created automatically for us from the name of the product.

---

[1] http://www.mattcutts.com/blog/dashes-vs-underscores/

You might be thinking that it would be a good idea to include category names in the product page URLs as well. This would be okay, but there's an important problem with that implementation: right now, products can potentially map to more than one category. In order to avoid getting penalized for duplicate content, each of your products should only have one page, and that page should only be available at *one* URL. I'll come back to this in the "Duplicate Content" section later in this chapter.

In my opinion, giving your products descriptive names and letting Django create the URLs by auto-populating the SlugField for each product is an excellent and simple solution that should help your site in its rankings. There is a balance you need to strike in determining what content your product page URLs ought to contain. While URLs containing loads of keywords will help just how relevant the site is for the search engines, URLs with an overbearing length are more difficult for your human users to type in.

Generating a Keyword List

Before you start pounding out the content for all of the pages on your site, you should determine what keywords you should be using to create the content on your site so that you can develop content directed at the users out there who are looking for your products. The first step in doing this is to determine what people are searching for that's relevant to the type of products that you're selling.

For our example, we're going to keep with the musical instrument site example, and determine what musicians are searching for online. The first step is to brainstorm a large list of keywords and phrases that we feel might be relevant to our site. We're going to use a tool that was created by Google to help us brainstorm some keywords that are related to people looking for musical instruments, sheet music, or other accessories, called Google Sets.

Google Sets[2] is little more than a form that lets you enter up to five keywords or phrases and, from these inputs, will generate a list of items that are closely related based on the content of other sites in Google's index. To begin, we're going to enter a few very basic terms related to the guitar. In three of the boxes, enter the following three things: "electric guitars," "metronome," and "sheet music." The three are very general, but should produce results that are all related to music. Click the "Large Set" button and let Google Sets generate the result set for you. You should see a lengthy list of words and phrases, all of which are clearly related to items that musicians might be looking for.

Jot down the ones that look relevant to your site's product line and repeat the process, changing one or all of the words you enter. After about 10 minutes of this, you should easily be able to compile a substantial list of words and phrases that relate to the content of your site.

■ **Caution** In creating your final keyword list for use on your site, you need to make sure that none of the keywords you use in your meta tags are trademarked or copyrighted terms. If you use a term that infringes on someone else's copyright, you can held liable for its use.

Once you have this list of keywords, it's now time to figure out which of them people are searching for. You can do this using the Google Adwords Keyword Tool.[3] The Keyword Tool allows you to enter a word or phrase, or a set of words and phrases. If your site is up live, you can instead just provide the URL for your site and the Keyword Tool will do a quick, live analysis of the content on your site and provide keywords and phrase suggestions based on the existing content of your site.

---

[2] http://labs.google.com/sets

[3] https://adwords.google.com/select/KeywordToolExternal

Google then analyzes these words and gives you a list of words and phrases that are related to the content you provided, as well as the frequency each one was searched for on Google in the most recent month and an average monthly frequency for the latest 12-month period. The top few results will be very generic terms such as "guitar" and although a lot of people search for the word "guitar," there are just as many web site owners fighting to rank for those words as well. For example, the chance of your site ranking very high for the word "guitar" is *extremely* slim. Most generic terms are going to be difficult to rank well for in the SERPs just because there are so many other people competing for these terms, and several already-established sites that have worked their way up in the rankings over time.

In most cases, you are better off narrowing your search terms down and using more of the less frequently searched terms. If you look further down the list, you'll start to see narrower terms such as "blues guitar." The more targeted you make your keywords, the better your site will rank in the search engine results. After you have found a narrower search term, you can use that term, or you can redo the process by typing that term into the keyword tool and running another list for that term to help you further narrow your keywords.

Based on the nature of your site, you should decide which ones you would like to use. Give a copy of this list to the person responsible for generating copy on your site, either for product descriptions, page content, or for other marketing materials, such as press releases. Don't force the use of your keywords where they aren't appropriate, or try to shove a bunch of them into your content just to make them more keyword-rich. Remember when it comes to page content, you're still trying to write for human beings first and for search engines second.

When it comes to creating the three to five keywords for each product, take these keywords into account. Do some basic research on each product. If you have a particular model of electric guitar that is popular amongst blues musicians, you might consider using "blues guitar" as a keyword instead of merely "electric guitar," as a means of targeting the customers who might be looking for an electric blues guitar.

The Duplicate Content Problem

Just as search engines can giveth, so too can they taketh away. Search engines do reward good practices by indexing the pages of your site and bringing them up in its results pages for relevant searches, but they are aware the people might try to "game" the system, and push their results up higher by manipulating the content on their page to be artificially more keyword-rich.

The first issue you need to be aware of related to duplicate content is a problem that is present on many sites as an innocent mistake. Take the homepage of typical site: it might be available at the four following URLs:

```
http://www.example.com/
http://example.com/
http://www.example.com/index.php
http://example.com/index.php
```

Now, these four links all point to the same file, so all four of the pages contain the same content. However, in the eyes of the search engines, the content at these four different URLs is four different, distinct pages that all happen to contain the same thing. From an SEO standpoint, this is a problem. Most major search engines, Google in particular, penalize sites for making the same content available across multiple pages.

The reason for this is that search engines don't want webmasters to have the same content on a bunch of pages on the same site, or to have the same site at multiple domains or subdomains. The pages don't have to be identical for search engines to regard them as duplicate content. If they find that the content of two pages has substantial similarities, those two pages could be penalized.

In our examples, notice that the homepage can be accessed at the slash and at index.php. This is not a problem for our Django site, as pages don't resolve to file names, and the home page is only accessible at one URL. However, the hostname of our site is ambiguous right now. When we deploy it in Chapter

15, it will be available at sitename.com and www.sitename.com. This is a problem, because potentially every page on the site could end up being available, indexed, and subsequently penalized because our site has duplicates of everything at two different hostnames.

As it stands right now, if we leave things alone, search engines will crawl our site and likely make a "best guess" about which hostname should be used. This process of search engines making the best guess is known as *canonicalization.* They will index the one that they determine is best, and make that one available in their search results. This doesn't solve the duplicate content problem, however.

The solution to this problem is to not leave things to chance, and to canonicalize the hostname ourselves. Before you launch your site, decide whether you want your site to be at sitename.com or www.sitename.com. Then, if a request comes in for the one that you don't want, force an HTTP redirect with a status code of 301 (which translates to "permanent redirect" in human terms) to the other hostname. With the 301 redirect in place, search engines will not index the hostname you don't want used, and if it does have the one you don't want in its index, the 301 redirect will phase it out to the other one over time. (I'm going to talk more about 301 redirects in "Content Relocation with Django Redirects" later in this chapter.) So now we're going to write some code to handle this hostname issue. We're going to structure it so that our site is available at the www-variety of hostname. Since this is something that is going to happen with every request on the site, it sounds like an excellent case to write our own Django middleware class.

First, create a new app for your project called marketing. This new app will contain all of the code related to SEO and marketing efforts in this chapter. Then, create a new file inside this new app called urlcanon.py. This is where we're going to put our middleware to handle any redirects to the incorrect hostname:

```
from django.http import get_host, HttpResponsePermanentRedirect
from ecomstore import settings

class URLCanonicalizationMiddleware(object):
    def process_view(self, request, view_func, view_args, view_kwargs):
        if not settings.DEBUG:
            """ only perform the redirect if not debug mode """
            protocol = 'https://' if request.is_secure() else 'http://'
            host = get_host(request)
            new_url = ''
            try:
                if host in settings.CANON_URLS_TO_REWRITE:
                    new_url = protocol + settings.CANON_URL_HOST + request.get_full_path()
            except AttributeError:
                if host != settings.CANON_URL_HOST:
                    new_url = protocol + settings.CANON_URL_HOST + request.get_full_path()

            if new_url:
                return HttpResponsePermanentRedirect(new_url)
```

This middleware uses a couple of configuration variables that we need to add to our settings.py file. Open that file and add the following to the bottom:

```
CANON_URL_HOST = 'www.django-ecommerce.com'
CANON_URLS_TO_REWRITE = ['django-ecommerce.com', 'modernmusician.com']
```

CANON_URL_HOST is the hostname of the site to which we will redirect our users. It's our *canonical* hostname explicitly spelled out. Optionally, you can specify a list of hostnames that, if detected, will be redirected to our canonical hostname. If the list is not present, then all requests not matching the canonical hostname are redirected.

To enable this on your site, you simply need to add this new class to your `MIDDLEWARE_CLASSES` section in `settings.py`:

`'ecomstore.marketing.urlcanon.URLCanonicalizationMiddleware',`

Now any requests that come into your site (that aren't on your local machine) for `sitename.com` will be redirected to `www.sitename.com`. Notice that this won't work if anyone is trying to access a particular subdomain.

■ **Note** The approach we've implemented here with the custom middleware class handles URL canonicalization at the application level. However, a more common approach is use the web server in order to handle this. For example, there is an easy way of handling this using Apache's `mod_rewrite`[4] module.

If you're the webmaster of your own e-commerce site, or *any* site, for that matter, the duplicate content problem is a serious issue that you need to take into consideration when designing the architecture of your site. It has other implications for what you should and shouldn't do to manage your content. For example, there's a very good reason that we didn't include the category name in the URL, even though it would have been a good way to include more keywords in the URL. The problem is that a product can be included in more than one category. So we hit a wall, since we need to maintain only one URL per product to avoid the duplicate content problem.

Often times, people running sites might try and have the same page on their site at more than one URL in the hopes of driving more traffic to their site. We could call this the "casting the net" strategy: throw out tons of web pages, many of them duplicates at different URLs, in the hopes that the sheer number of them will get more traffic to your site. It's a bad idea, for all kinds of reasons. Remember that the rank of your pages is driven by hyperlinks to your pages from other sites. The duplicate content issue aside, if other sites are linking to the same product on your site at five different URLs, then the link equity of that "single" page is diffused between five pages. You're *much* better off with the one page per product.

Semantic Web - Microformats & RDFa

When search engines crawl your site, they generally have the burden of trying to make order out of the chaos that is the HTML of your web site. This is not to say that your code is bad in any way, but creating a computer that scans and makes sense of a bunch of random HTML pages on the web is, even with today's tools, a fairly tricky prospect. Even if you get rid of all the HTML tags, you're left with a mess of text without any context to tell you anything useful about what kind of information it contains.

For this reason, many large search engines have started supporting microformats[5] and the Resource Description Framework in attributes (RDFa).[6] The use of microformats and RDFa is a means for you to mark up the contents of your web pages in such a way that you can convey to the search engine spiders what kind of information the pages contain, so they can use that information for indexing purposes, or even for use in their search results pages.

---

[4] http://httpd.apache.org/docs/2.0/mod/mod_rewrite.html

[5] http://www.microformats.org/

[6] http://www.w3.org/TR/xhtml-rdfa-primer/

The Yahoo! search engine has been using microformats in their search results since early 2008. More recently, in May of 2009, Google announced that they would begin supporting RDFa, as well as microformats, to adjust how they would display results to users in their SERPs.

According to Google, they will support both microformats and RDFa. They allow you to not only present content to users and search engines, but also to mark it up in such a way that search engines can determine what kind of content the markup contains. They even allow you to define relationships *between* two different types of content.

Let's take a quick look at one example of microformatted data. You might have noticed that the content we put into our "Contact" page in Chapter 4 was loaded with some funny-looking HTML. This was an example of microformats, using the hCard format for representing company contact information. Here is the markup that I entered for that page, which you can easily take and modify to match the information on your own site:

```
<div class="vcard">
  <div class="fn org">Modern Musician</div>
  <div class="adr">
    <div class="street-address">12345 Google Way Ave</div>
    <div>
      <span class="locality">Beach Town</span>,
      <abbr class="region" title="California">CA</abbr>
      <span class="postal-code">93456</span>
    </div>
    <div class="country-name">USA</div>
  </div>
  <div>Phone: <span class="tel">+1-555-555-1212</span></div>
  <div>Email: <span class="email">info@modernmusician.com</span></div>
</div>
```

Much more interesting than the contact page information, however, is that there is a specification for marking up product pages with semantic information. With a few simple additions to our product page, we can add RDFa-formatted markup so that search engines have a much better idea about the nature of the content on the page.

```
<div xmlns:v="http://rdf.data-vocabulary.org/#"
    about="{{ p.get_absolute_url }}" typeof="v:Product">
    <!--- code omitted -->
    <h1><span property="v:name">{{ p.name }}</span></h1>
    Brand: <em><span property="v:brand">{{ p.brand }}<span></em>
    <!--- code omitted -->
    {% for c in categories %}
        <a href="{{ c.get_absolute_url }}">
        <span property="v:category">
        {{ c.name }}
        </span>
        </a>
        <!--- code omitted -->
    {% if p.sale_price %}
        Was: <del>{{ p.old_price|currency }}</del>
        <br />
        Now: <span property="v:price">{{ p.price|currency }}</span>
    {% else %}
        Price: <span property="v:price">{{ p.price|currency }}</span>
    {% endif %}
    <!--- code omitted -->
```

```
    <h3>Product Description</h3>
    <span property="v:description">{{ p.description }}</span>
</div>
```

We've enclosed the product information inside a single div we just added, with the namespace information, about, and typeof attributes that describe the contents of the div as product information. Inside, we've added span elements with property attributes to label the product name, categories, brand, price, and description fields in the markup. One last thing you'll need to do before you deploy these additions into production is to change your web site's Document Type Declaration in your base.html template file to:

```
<!DOCTYPE html PUBLIC "-//W3C//DTD XHTML+RDFa 1.0//EN"
    "http://www.w3.org/MarkUp/DTD/xhtml-rdfa-1.dtd">
```

So should you use microformats or should you use RDFa in your site? Google claims that it doesn't matter, and that you can add either one to your site, based on the format with which you feel more comfortable as a developer. There are several other specifications for reviews, personal contact information, and pages where you list multiple products, such as search results or thumbnails. The examples in this section are just two very small examples of two specifications that are likely to become very important in the search engine marketing world in the coming years.

Launching the Site

At this stage of the game, we haven't yet deployed our site into production. You should still be developing your site on a local machine, and it's not available anywhere public yet. The techniques I'm going to describe in this section may seem a little premature, since there's a few of them you cannot do yet, such as submitting your URL to search engines, or signing up with Webmasters and Analytics. I included them here because they are very much a key part of the search engine optimization process and less related to deployment (which I'm going to cover in Chapter 15).

In spite of this, there are still a few things in this section you can do at this stage of the game. For example, you can create a robots.txt file and an XML sitemap for search engines, even though we haven't launched the site yet. I recommend that you read over this section and work through the development examples. However, you can safely ignore the tasks that are obviously meant to be done *after* deployment, and refer back to them later.

Submit Your URL

Once you throw your site out onto the Internet, chances are good that sooner or later, someone is going to post a hyperlink to it on their own site. Provided that *their* site is crawlable by search engines and is indexed, this means that sooner or later, the search engines are going to crawl, index, and presumably include your site's pages in their search indexes, so people will find you when they search for you. This is an awful lot to assume. Even if you are making some PR efforts to get your site linked to, and you're not leaving it to chance, it cannot hurt to tell the search engines about your site directly.

If you want to tell Google about your newly launched e-commerce site, all you need to is let them know yourself at the following URL: http://www.google.com/addurl/. Most of the other major search engines, such as Yahoo! and MSN, also have similar such pages where you can submit the URL of your homepage. Provided that you can click through to the rest of your pages from the home page via hyperlinks, this simple step should be enough to get the ball rolling.

If you're interested in seeing what pages of your site have been indexed and are now included in Google's search index, you can do this simple Google search:

`site:www.your-site.com`

Of course, you should change this to use your own hostname. Bear in mind that if any of your pages come up in the search results for this query, this doesn't necessarily mean that they are coming up very *high* in the SERPs. It just means that they are included in Google's search index, and should be included in the SERPs, even if they are on 25th page and probably won't be found by the majority of people. It's just a means of checking if Google has found and indexed your site yet.

robots.txt File

One very simple thing we can add to our site is a `robots.txt` file.[7] This plain-text file contains directives that a search engine spider should crawl, and what it shouldn't crawl, if any. Before a search engine spider visits your site, it will check for the presence of this file at the root of your project. If it finds this file, it will follow the directives that it finds in the file.

Why would you want to use something that excludes pages of your site from Google's crawlers? There are a few good reasons, generally involving the need to include duplicate content. Imagine that you have a page on your site that a user is supposed to view, and optionally, they can navigate to a separate page that contains a printer-friendly version of the same page. Obviously, you don't want to let Google include both of these in its index, as it may regard two separate pages as duplicate content and you may be penalized for it. Using a `robots.txt` file, you can tell Google and other search engines not to index the printable version.

It's worth noting that the use of a `robots.txt` file doesn't prevent an automated crawler such as Google from crawling the content you choose to exclude. Also, while Google and other major search engines tend to scrupulously follow the rules you set in your `robots.txt` file, other spammers that might be crawling your site for e-mail addresses are not under any legal obligation to listen to the directives in the file. If there's any content that you don't want made available to bots, you should restrict it some other way, such as making it available only to users who are logged in.

Even though we're not going to exclude any content on our site just yet, we are going to create a simple `robots.txt` file that tells the all search engines (actually, any robots at all) that they can crawl our site, and that they should include all the pages that they find. Inside your `marketing` app directory, create a `robots.txt` file and add just the following two lines to it:

```
User-agent: *
Disallow:
```

Now, we just need to make it available at the "root" of our site, so that it is available to search engines at: http://www.our-site.com/robots.txt. This is easy enough to do with a simple view function that returns this file, and a URL entry. Inside your marketing app's views.py file, add the following code:

```
from django.http import HttpResponse
from ecomstore.settings import CURRENT_PATH
import os

ROBOTS_PATH = os.path.join(CURRENT_PATH, 'marketing/robots.txt')
```

---

[7] http://www.robotstxt.org/

241

```
def robots(request):
    return HttpResponse(open(ROBOTS_PATH).read(), 'text/plain')
```

Then, add the following line inside of your `marketing` app's `urls.py` file:

```
(r'^robots\.txt$', 'robots'),
```

If nothing else, this file serves as a placeholder for any exclusions you may want to add to it later.

Sitemaps for Search Engines

Now that you've submitted your site to Google, you could sit back, relax, and wait for the traffic to start rolling in, followed closely by oodles of sales dollars as customers start buying your products. But, of course, we know that in the real world, this just won't do. In order to get the ball rolling with Google, we need to take a much more proactive approach to things.

One of the best things you can do right after launching a new site is to submit a sitemap to Google. A sitemap is a simple XML file that lists pages on your site individually, with optional values for how often your content changes. It gives search engine spiders a systematic means of crawling every page on your site, without having to just crawl the homepage and follow links, in the hopes that it will be able to find all the pages. It's a means of giving some order to the chaos that is the HTML soup of your site. Google's crawlers will examine the contents of this sitemap, and (hopefully) crawl all of the pages it contains.

Here is an example of an XML sitemap, which contains only a single page:

```
<?xml version="1.0" encoding="UTF-8"?>
<urlset xmlns="http://www.sitemaps.org/schemas/sitemap/0.9">
    <url>
        <loc>http://www.django-ecommerce.com/</loc>
    </url>
</urlset>
```

In order to add other pages, all you'd need to do is create other `url` elements inside the `urlset`. The `loc` element inside each one represents the absolute URL of the page you want indexed. You can learn more about the sitemaps specification at: `http://www.sitemaps.org/`.

In my experience, creating a sitemap and submitting it to Google is an excellent way of getting the pages of your site indexed fairly quickly. While creating a site where all pages can be reached via hyperlinks should be enough to get every page on your site indexed, often times it doesn't yield timely results. After submitting the URL of your site to Google, you may find yourself waiting weeks to get just a few pages indexed, and even longer for them to come up in search results pages.

There are still no guarantees, but the odds that most pages of your site will end up being crawled and indexed by Google in a timely fashion are greatly improved by creating a sitemap.

If you're still not convinced, it's worth pointing out that the creators of Django felt that sitemaps were important enough to include right in the framework itself. Consequently, creating an XML sitemap file for your e-commerce site is really easy. Without creating any templates, you just create a Python class that inherits from the Sitemap class, hook in the model classes containing the pages that you want in the sitemap, and then make it available via a URL entry.

Inside the new `marketing` app we created, create a new file called `sitemap.py`, and add the following code to it to define your sitemap:

```
from ecomstore.catalog.models import Product, Category
from django.contrib.flatpages.models import FlatPage
from django.contrib.sitemaps import Sitemap

class ProductSitemap(Sitemap):
```

```
    def items(self):
        return Product.active.all()

class CategorySitemap(Sitemap):
    def items(self):
        return Category.active.all()

class FlatPageSitemap(Sitemap):
    def items(self):
        return FlatPage.objects.all()

SITEMAPS = {'categories': CategorySitemap,
            'products': ProductSitemap,
            'flatpages': FlatPageSitemap }
```

To start, we're going to hook in three models: Product, Category, and FlatPage. The sitemap that will be created from this code will contain a link to each model instance, so each product, category, and flatpage will get its own entry. This works in conjunction with the get_absolute_url() method that is defined on each model in order to build the URL.

Before this will work, we need to make sure that the sitemaps app is included in our INSTALLED_APPS in settings.py:

```
'django.contrib.sitemaps',
```

You also need to make sure that you have the Django sites framework installed:

```
'django.contrib.sites',
```

In the admin interface, if you haven't done so yet, make sure you have the correct hostname specified in the Site model, in order for the URLs to be constructed to point back to your site. Make sure that you have this installed, and that the SITE_ID in your settings.py file is set to the correct value that matches the Site instance.

Now, in order to make your sitemap viewable, you just need to create a URL entry for it in the marketing app. Create a urls.py file in this app now and add the following URL definition to it:

```
from ecomstore.marketing.sitemap import SITEMAPS

urlpatterns += patterns('',
    (r'^sitemap\.xml$', 'django.contrib.sitemaps.views.sitemap', {'sitemaps': SITEMAPS }),
)
```

Have a look at the first argument for that sitemap URL entry. Notice that we're escaping the period (.) character with the backslash. This is because in regular expression syntax, periods have a special meaning. If we didn't escape it, then the period wouldn't be a literal period character in our expression. Instead, it would make our sitemap available at /sitemap[any URL legal character]xml. The period would still work... but only because it's one of many URL-legal characters that could have gone in that spot.

With that, pull up /sitemap.xml in your browser to test and make sure that it's working all right. If you view the source of the page, you should see an XML document that looks like the sample one earlier in this section. Check to make sure that the URLs are valid and point to real pages on your site.

One important final point about sitemaps before we move on: they are limited as far as the number of URLs you can include in them. At the time I'm writing this, Google has the maximum value set at 50,000 url elements in the urlset. For most small- to medium-sized e-commerce sites, this shouldn't be a substantial constraint.

We're going to submit this URL to Google in the "Google Webmasters" section later in this chapter.

Content Relocation

Sooner or later, after you've been in business for a while, you or the person you work for is going to start looking over the site and looking for ways to improve it. Naturally, this isn't a bad thing, but sooner or later, you may encounter the following simple problem: how to move content from one URL to another.

This isn't as easy as it sounds. Let's take one example: up until now, our Ruby Axe Guitar has been available at a URL with a slug of `ruby-axe-guitar`, and so far, that has worked *great* for us, because anyone searching for this on the Internet tends to find our site very easily when they go searching for that particular product name.

But, one day, we notice that people are also searching for "ruby axe electric guitar," because people know that it's an electric guitar. However, the product page on our site isn't coming up very high in the search results pages. As a solution to this, we decide to change the slug on our Ruby Axe Guitar to be `ruby-axe-electric-guitar` instead, so that URL will contain more keywords and it will have a better shot at getting hits when customers search for "electric guitar."

Now, changing this slug is the easy part. Remember that all of the hyperlinks to that product's page will be updated on our site automatically, as we're generating the links using the `get_absolute_url()` method on the Product model. However, this does not take into account hyperlinks to each product page on external sites that are beyond our control. Unbeknownst to us, a guitar player in a small up-and-coming heavy-death-squeak metal band in Finland named Teemu Ruotsalainen absolutely loves the Ruby Axe, raved about it in an entry on his blog a month ago, and linked to the product page for the guitar on our site. We don't want to lose this link-love, neither for human visitors nor for search engines.

Far more important, however, is how Google treats pages in its index that suddenly vanish. Once you've patiently let a product page climb in the search results, you don't want to have that product page suddenly disappear completely and return a 404 Page Not Found error, because Google will just remove that page from its index, and subsequently its results pages. Search engines have no way of knowing that you've relocated the page without you telling them explicitly, and if you do just yank a page from one URL and put it at another, you're going to lose all of that "search engine equity" that you've built up over time, so to speak.

The best way to handle this is to still handle incoming requests to the old URL, but respond to them with a 301 HTTP permanent redirect to the new page. This is like telling the search engines, "Hey, this page still exists, but it's over here now." It's like leaving a forwarding address with the post office when you move.

Django actually has a framework called redirects that is designed to let you permanently redirect old URLs to new ones. This is perfect for handling these kinds of cases where you want to move content to new URLs. That doesn't make relocating content a good idea; I think you're still better off leaving things the way they are and keeping the amount of content that you relocate to a minimum. You don't want to be moving every page on your site every few months just so you can keep stuffing more keywords into the URLs.

In order to install the `redirects` app, add this line to your `INSTALLED_APPS`:

```
'django.contrib.redirects',
```

Then, in your `MIDDLEWARE_CLASSES`, add this at the bottom:

```
'django.contrib.redirects.middleware.RedirectFallbackMiddleware',
```

Now, run `manage.py syncdb` from your shell to create the new database table. Now that the table exists, you should add the redirect first, *before* you change the slug on the product. The reason for this is that the redirect will only kick in if Django encounters a 404 error, which won't happen as long as the product page is still there. However, if you change the product first, before adding the redirect, there is a small gap of time during which the URL for the old page will return a 404 error. To prevent this, add the redirects first, and then change your content.

So, bring up the admin interface. Click into the redirects section and go to add a new redirect. Here, you just need to add the old path of the page you want to redirect from, and add the one you want to redirect to. Make sure that you've got the correct site selected from the sites framework. So, we want to move from here:

```
/product/ruby-axe-guitar/
```

to here:

```
/product/ruby-axe-electric-guitar/
```

Now the redirect is all set. You just need to update the product slug field to reflect this change. Over time, the search engines will drop the old page and replace it with the new URL in their indexes, at which point, you can safely remove the redirect from your database.

One last thing to note about the `redirects` framework: it's really only intended to help you move content from one URL to another. You shouldn't start adding a bunch of redirects from fake URLs in the interest of getting more people to land on each product page from a bunch of different URLs. You really don't benefit from this in any way; the URLs don't make it into Google's index, and you don't *want* to encourage people to link to pages that are just going to redirect, since you would rather have the link for inbound link value.

Google Webmasters

Google provides web developers with a couple of tools that let you gauge how well your site is faring against your own expectations. The first of these is called Google Webmasters[8], which is a free service provided to webmasters that allows them to view lots of useful data about what Google spiders are seeing in a site's content. It's also where you can submit the XML sitemap you created earlier.

To sign up for Google Webmasters, all you need is a Google account. The one that you created in Chapter 5 for using Google Checkout should work just fine for our purposes. Once you've logged in, you just need to click the "Add a site" button and add your site's hostname to the list. You should enter the same hostname that you decided upon when you set up the URL canonicalization middleware earlier in the chapter.

After submitting the site, you should be redirected to the overview page for that site. There's still one last step to do before you can start viewing data about the site: you need to *verify* that you are really the owner of the site in question. Otherwise, anyone could add the domain of any site to their Webmasters account and get data about the site from Google.

There are two methods you can use to verify that you really own the site in question: you can add a specific `meta` tag or create an HTML file with a given name at the root of your project. In our case, we must use the first option. The HTML file option won't work for our site because of the way we've set up 404 Error pages on our site. However, creating a `meta` tag is simple enough. You should see the "Meta tag" option selected on a drop-down on your site, as well as a box containing the HTML of the `meta` tag, with a name like "verify-v1." Leaving the browser window open, copy this `meta` tag out of the box and put it into your `base.html` template file, below the other description and keywords `meta` tags.

Once you've done this, go back to the Webmasters page and click the "Verify" button. (Your site needs to be up someplace public, where Google can find it, for this to work.) If you encounter any errors, go the URL of the hostname you provided and make sure that you really do see the `meta` in the source of the page, and that the content of the tag matches the tag that Google provided to you.

Once the site has successfully verified, you should be taken to the dashboard for your site, where you can now see different sections with interesting data in them, such as the queries that bring traffic into your site from Google, links to your site from other external sites, any crawl errors or missing pages, and any XML sitemaps you've submitted to Webmasters.

We haven't yet submitted a sitemap, but this sounds like a fine time to do it. In the left-hand column, you should see a collapsed section titled "Site Configuration." Expand this section and click the

---

[8] `http://www.google.com/webmasters/`

"Sitemaps" link. Here, you should be taken to a page where you can submit the path of the sitemap that you created earlier. Go ahead and add the sitemap.xml link that you created earlier (again, your site needs to be up and public for this work), and you should get a confirmation message if Google finds the file at the path you specify.

Whenever you update the content of your sitemap, you may want to let Google know about it. Google lets you submit a request to their servers telling them that you've updated your site map. Again, like most things, there's no guarantee that Google will respond to your request *immediately* and start re-indexing all of the content on your site, but every little bit helps in the SEO world.

Now that you have the sitemaps frameworks installed in your INSTALLED_APPS section, you can let Google know that you've updated your sitemap with the following command:

```
$ python manage.py ping_google
```

Besides providing information about inbound links from other sites and search queries that are driving traffic to your site, Google Webmasters also provides some excellent stats on your site's content by giving you a list of the keywords that it finds on your site, from most common to least common. This helps give you a good idea of whether or not the content you've created for your site is in line with the keyword list you generated earlier in the chapter.

Google Analytics

While Google Webmasters is quite useful, Google Analytics is a much better tool for determining how your customers use and interact with your site once they've found it. It does this by initiating a new tracking ID for each customer when they enter your site and logging every page they view until they exit your site. There is even a means of tracking purchase history, so you can figure out how much revenue your site is generating per order, tracking how those customers found your site, and tracking how customers are using your internal search pages. There are some excellent reports that Analytics provides for you by default.

As a developer, you can look at Google Analytics and say, "Hey, couldn't I do all of that myself?" Yes, you probably could. Both Python and Django have some pretty decent tools for creating reports from data. However, it's probably better that you don't, particularly if you plan to grow your site substantially over time.

THE DANGER OF "NOT INVENTED HERE"

As developers, we tend to *love* writing code, and this tends to be directly correlated with our affinity for learning. There's nothing quite like getting down and dirty writing code in order to learn how write it. You learn how things work, how to architect larger blocks of code, and learn what mistakes to avoid in the future by making a bunch of them (and then fixing them). You can read all the programming books you want, but no book is anywhere near as valuable as empiricism.

The virtues of this tend to make developers think that they should code everything for themselves from scratch, without using anyone else's code. This is referred to as the Not Invented Here (NIH) Syndrome (as in "We didn't create that, so we shouldn't use it!" The danger of this kind of thinking is that you'll spend lots of time reinventing wheels that already exist, which is time wasted. Because our business plan for this e-commerce site doesn't involve creating an Analytics Engine as a core part of our business, it's safe to outsource this particular part of the application.

As a Django and Python developer, you have a range of solutions available to you from a large community of excellent developers. I strongly encourage you to use them whenever you can.

The Data Warehouse Principle

If you plan to start tracking the activities of the customers on your site, you should seriously consider using Google Analytics to do it. The reason for this has its roots in the way you plan on treating your database once you've deployed your site into production.

Imagine that you decide you're going to create your own solution to track every page view on the site, extending the simple solution we created in Chapter 9 to track product page views so that you're tracking every page view of every customer on the site, logging repeat views more than once. Ignoring all of the extra time that you might spend developing queries for aggregating the data, templates to generate reports, and an administrative interface to access them (no small task in and of itself), you have this database table that is logging massive amounts of text containing paths to pages on your site. When your site first launches, this table will be relatively small, containing only a few hundred records, and everything will work fine. Your reports, and your site, will run just fine.

This single database table will quickly grow very large in size, and over time, performance will start to degrade very quickly. The reason is that you're using your production database in a way that it was never intended to be used. You're running all kinds of queries against it, aggregating page view data with all kinds of GROUP BY clauses and subselect SQL statements to find patterns in your customers' shopping behaviors.

When you first installed the database server in Chapter 1, remember that during the installation of MySQL, we chose the OLTP instead of OLAP. OLTP, or Online Transaction Processing, is how we configuring the database server to run for our site because our site is largely a transaction-based application. OLTP databases are optimized for retrieving, adding, deleting, and updating single records, which is the kind of activity you'd expect to see on a large e-commerce site, where customers are requesting product pages that load single records from the product table, are submitting product reviews, and executing lots of other requests that are designed to work with a few records from each table instead of all of them.

Databases that are set up for Online Analytical Processing, or OLAP, are much more suited for the type of analytical processing and business intelligence needs that arise when you start generating reports for information about your customers as a whole. In order to figure out what products your customers are viewing, or what category pages their looking at, you're going to start running queries that load all of the data from the page view table, and do a bunch of joins with the other tables in your database. Running these kinds of large, intensive queries that are designed to return a bunch of data to be used for reports is a bad idea.

Traditionally, the best means of handling this incompatibility of database uses is to migrate the data from your production database to a separate database, known as a *data warehouse*, on a regular basis. Then, you run these intensive, analytical queries against that database instead of your production one. Often times, to optimize the performance of these queries, you even restructure the database in the data warehouse, doing some de-normalization of your data to reduce the number of joins required and changing the schema to optimize how well these aggregation queries will run. While the exact principles of creating a data warehouse are *far* outside the scope of this book, the definitive text on the topic is *The Data Warehouse Toolkit: The Complete Guide to Dimensional Modeling (Second Edition)* by Ralph Kimball and Margy Ross (Wiley, 2002), if you're interested in learning more.

Great, you're thinking, so now I need to set up a separate database someplace else, figure out how to de-normalize it so that I can run reporting queries against it efficiently, and so forth. I can see I'm starting lose some of you already.

This is why Google Analytics is so good. Not only is it *extremely* easy to hook into your site, but it solves many of the problems that you would have to grapple with outlined here. Of course, there are some privacy issues associated with using Google Analytics. While you can opt to have Google store your page views for you and you can configure your Analytics account to now share the data with Google, you're still storing your data somewhere else, beyond your complete and total control. Given the nature of your business requirements, this might not be what you want.

However, did I also mention that it's free?

Signing Up for Google Analytics

Whether or not your site is up live for Google to see yet, you can do the steps in the following section now. However, even if you do install the tracking code and configure your Analytics account, your reports will be empty and not contain any tracking data. Just as with Webmasters, you'll need to use your Google account to log in and start using Analytics.

Once you've managed to get past this simple step, you just need to create a new Account for your site. This is fairly straightforward; you just put in the hostname of your site and give the account a name. Next, you provide your name, phone number, and country. After agreeing to the Google Analytics terms of use (which you should read and, of course, comply with), you'll get a snippet of JavaScript code to place at the bottom of every page of your site that should look something like the following:

```
<script type="text/javascript">
var gaJsHost = (("https:" == document.location.protocol) ? "https://ssl." : "http://www.");
document.write(unescape("%3Cscript src='" + gaJsHost + "google-analytics.com/ga.js'
type='text/javascript'%3E%3C/script%3E"));
</script>
<script type="text/javascript">
try {
var pageTracker = _gat._getTracker("UA-xxxxxxx-x");
pageTracker._trackPageview();
} catch(err) {}</script>
```

Of course, the tracking ID should be different for you, and specific to identify your site. We're going to put this code on our site now. Copy this code from the box and then go back to your project. In your `templates` directory, create a new folder called `marketing` and add a new file called `google_analytics.html`. Put this code inside that file.

Next, open up your `base.html` file and enter this code just below the jQuery script tags, but before the closing `</body>` tag at the bottom of your site:

```
{% include "marketing/google_analytics.html" %}
```

Now this tracking code will be part of every page on the site that uses the `base.html` template (which is pretty much all of them).

One of the more frustrating aspects of using Google Analytics is that when you make any changes to your tracking code, you need to wait about a day or so before you can be sure that you've done it correctly and that pages are, in fact, being tracked. This shouldn't be a big deal when you first copy that code block over, but later, when you start changing and adding Analytics code for more day-to-day marketing needs, you'll find this limitation a bit annoying. It's still a small price to pay for the functionality, if you ask me.

If your site is up live and the tracking code is in place, go ahead and click around on a few pages, just so you can check later that the tracking code is picking them up correctly. Wait a day or two, and then come back to see if there is any tracking data available for your site.

E-Commerce and Search Tracking

Now that you've got Google Analytics tracking code on your site, there are a couple of additional things you can do that will help you track the activity on your site. For one, Analytics has special reports available for e-commerce sites that allow you track conversions and other order details. There is also a report that allows you to store every internal search that users make on your site, so you can see what your customers are search for. While we're doing this in-house for the purposes of cross-selling, the report from Analytics offers enough insight to be worth the trouble it takes to configure it.

These are disabled by default, but they're very simple to enable. From the Analytics Overview page that lists all of your accounts, of which there's probably only one at this point (the one we just created), click on that account to get the overview page for that account, which lists the web sites we've submitted for tracking. From this page, click the "Edit" link in the far right "Actions" column. You should be taken to a page with one section titled "Main Website Profile Information." Click the "Edit" link at the top right of that box.

In the form you get for this page, you can change the site domain or the site profile name, the time zone, and other configuration settings. We're interested in two of the items below this: in the "E-Commerce Website" section, change the selection from "No" to "Yes" to enable the reports specifically for e-commerce. Just below this, there should another section entitled "Site Search." Select "Do Track Site Search" from the radio-button list. In the box labeled "Query Parameter," enter the letter "q," which is the parameter in the URL that will contain our search text on internal site searches. Save the changes you made and return to your profile settings page.

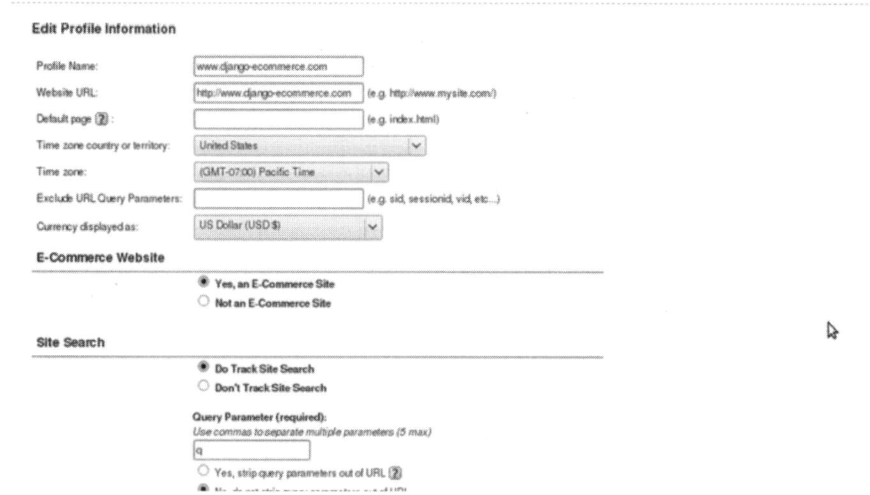

Edit Profile Information

Profile Name:	www.django-ecommerce.com
Website URL:	http://www.django-ecommerce.com (e.g. http://www.mysite.com/)
Default page ②:	(e.g. index.html)
Time zone country or territory:	United States
Time zone:	(GMT-07:00) Pacific Time
Exclude URL Query Parameters:	(e.g. sid, sessionid, vid, etc...)
Currency displayed as:	US Dollar (USD $)

E-Commerce Website

⦿ Yes, an E-Commerce Site
○ Not an E-Commerce Site

Site Search

⦿ Do Track Site Search
○ Don't Track Site Search

Query Parameter (required):
Use commas to separate multiple parameters (5 max)
`q`

○ Yes, strip query parameters out of URL ②

Figure 11-1. The Edit Profile page for your Google Analytics account.

On this page, notice that there is a section titled "Users with Access to Profile" where you can add other users with Google accounts. If you have other staff members that you would like to give access, either to view or administrate your Analytics site profile, you can do this here, without having to give them your own Google account login.

If you click back to the account overview and enter the dashboard of the site profile you just configured, you should now see a new section in the left-hand column on this page entitled "E-Commerce," as well as a new report showing your conversions. In order to get these reports to give you information about orders placed on your site, there's a small bit of tracking code that you need to add to the receipt page on your site.

Inside your project's base.html template file, add the following block to the bottom of the page, below the google_analytics.html {% include %} tag, but above the closing </body> tag:

```
{% block receipt_analytics %}{% endblock %}
```

Now, add the following to the bottom of your `receipt.html` template file:

```
{% block receipt_analytics %}

{% if order %}

<script type="text/javascript">
    // IMPORTANT: put your own tracking ID in below
    var pageTracker = _gat._getTracker('UA-xxxxxxx-1');
    pageTracker._initData();
    pageTracker._trackPageview();
    pageTracker._addTrans(
        '{{ order.id }}',              // order ID (required)
        '',                           // store name
        '{{ order.total }}',          // order total (required)
        '',                               // order tax
        '',                           // order shipping
        '{{ order.shipping_city }}',  // city
        '{{ order.shipping_state }}', // state or province
        '{{ order.shipping_country }}'// country
    );

// Loop through items in the order
{% for item in order_items %}
    pageTracker._addItem(
        '{{ order.id }}',             // order ID (required)
        '{{ item.sku }}',             // product SKU
        '{{ item.name }}',                // product name
        '',                                   // category
        '{{ item.price }}',           // product price (required)
        '{{ item.quantity }}'         // quantity (required)
    );
{% endfor %}
    pageTracker._trackTrans();
</script>

{% endif %}
{% endblock %}
```

Analytics will now track the basic information about your customer orders based on the information you've submitted to them via the tracking code. The dashboard for your site will contain some reports with information about order amounts and the best-selling products on your site. While the e-commerce order tracking functionality is much too slim to use for you entire order fulfillment process, it's still an extremely handy overview that lets you easily get a sense of how your site is progressing over time.

Even though all areas of analytics are very handy, I've found one of the most useful areas of the Analytics interface to be the "Content Overview." If you click into this section, you'll see that there is data about how customers entered the site, how they they're using your navigation, and stats about keywords that people used to find your site. One of the coolest features is the Site Overlay, which lets you navigate through your site, with information on each page about which links your customers have clicked. Each link on the page is assigned a percentage based on how frequently it was clicked when compared with all of the other links on the page. This is helpful because it gives you some insight into each page of your site from a customer's perspective.

Google Base Product Feed

Of all the things you can search for on the Internet using Google, products is the one we're interested in focusing on. Google doesn't just crawl the web for product pages on e-commerce sites and then list them in its Google Product Search results pages, RDFa or not. In order to get our product pages included for searches in the Product Search, we should create a data feed with information about the products on our site and submit it to Google.

Fortunately, there is a free Google service, called Google Base,[9] which allows you submit feeds containing all different kinds of information, including products. While it's possible to submit information about your products one at a time, the much easier and scalable solution is to create a single data feed with information about all of our products. This is as easy as creating a simple Really Simple Syndication (RSS) or Atom feed, putting it up on our site, and submitting it to Google Base, scheduling a regular interval at which they should re-download your product feed to keep your product information up-to-date in their system.

Django actually has a very good feed framework that enables you to create RSS and Atom feeds very easily, making them as easy to generate as the XML sitemap we created earlier. However, the requirements for a Google Base product feed are complex enough that we're going to take a different approach and just create the XML for the feed in a template file. We'll load up our active products, iterate through all of them in a simple {% for %} loop, and build our feed that way. It's a little clunky but a whole lot simpler than trying to hack the Django Feed framework to get the XML looking the way we want.

Create a template in your project called google_base.xml inside your marketing templates directory and add the following template code:

```
<?xml version="1.0" encoding="UTF-8" ?>
<rss version ="2.0" xmlns:g="http://base.google.com/ns/1.0">
<channel>
    <title>Modern Musician Product Feed</title>
    <description>Modern Musician Product Feed</description>
    <link>http://www.django-ecommerce.com/</link>
{% for p in products %}
<item>
<title>{{ p.name }}</title>
<g:brand>{{ p.brand }}</g:brand>
<g:condition>new</g:condition>
<description>{{ p.description }}</description>
<guid>{{ p.sku }}</guid>
<g:image_link>{{ p.image.url }}</g:image_link>
<link>{{ p.get_absolute_url }}</link>
<g:mpn>ABC123</g:mpn>
<g:price>{{ p.price }}</g:price>
<g:product_type>{{ p.categories.all|join:", " }}</g:product_type>
<g:quantity>{{ p.quantity }}</g:quantity>
<g:shipping>
    <g:country>US</g:country>
    <g:service>Ground</g:service>
    <g:price>9.99</g:price>
</g:shipping>
<g:tax>
```

---

[9] http://base.google.com/base/

```
    <g:country>US</g:country>
    <g:region>CA</g:region>
    <g:rate>8.75</g:rate>
    <g:tax_ship>y</g:tax_ship>
</g:tax>
</item>
{% endfor %}
</channel>
</rss>
```

Now, inside your views.py file in the marketing app, add the view function for this file below the view function for the robots.txt file:

```
from django.template.loader import get_template
from django.template import Context
from ecomstore.catalog.models import Product

def google_base(request):
    products = Product.active.all()
    template = get_template("marketing/google_base.xml")
    xml = template.render(Context(locals()))
    return HttpResponse(xml, mimetype="text/xml")
```

Finally, create the URL entry in the urls.py file inside your marketing app:

```
(r'^google_base\.xml$', 'google_base'),
```

Like everything else that Google offers, you'll need a Google account to create a feed. In order to submit your new Product Feed, go to the Google Base homepage. At the right of the page, there should be a "Data Feed" link. Click on this and you'll be taken to a summary page listing all of your Google Base feeds (right now, there shouldn't be any).

Click the "New Data Feed" button and you'll be taken to a page with a series of forms for you to fill out with some very basic information about yourself, your web site, and basic contact information. Make sure that you choose "Products" as the feed type. Once your feed is created, you have the option of either uploading a feed file or scheduling a regular time for Google to access your feed at a URL of your choice.

■ **Note** Creating an RSS feed by writing out the XML from scratch is potentially very error-prone, and I've done so here only in the interest of keeping this complex example simple. Some RSS feed readers, for example, will not consume the rendered Google Base template file we created previously. If you're going to create a simple RSS feed, I'd strongly urge you to look at Django's feed framework.

Clearly, because we're "lazy" (an attribute that is a programming virtue), we want to go with the latter automated option. Create a scheduled upload time, date, and frequency that are appropriate for your own organization. A weekly feed at some time very early in the morning is probably sufficient for keeping your information up-to-date, although if you're making several changes every day, you might want to schedule yours as a daily feed.

■ **Note** While I was careful to test all of the code in this book, submitting a fictional product data feed is against the Terms of Service for Google Base. That, and I didn't want lots of people finding the site and trying to buy fictional products from me.

---

500 Server Errors

In Chapter 4 of this book, we created a custom 404 Page Not Found error template file that would be returned whenever a user requests a path to a page on our site that doesn't exist. There is also the distinct possibility that our site will, in the course of running all that Python code in production, eventually return a 500 Internal Server Error, either due to some unhandled exception or untested code being deployed by a developer. If Google encounters a server error while crawling your site, it may penalize your pages or remove them from its index.

What we can do is make sure that, in the event of a server error, we return a template with an HTTP status code of 500. This lets Google know that the problem is only temporary. This also has a benefit to your human users as well, since you can put a nice message on it letting people know that your site is just experiencing difficulty, so that they know that your pages should work again the future.

Django has a default view function defined that will be called whenever your server encounters an error and your site is not configured for debug mode. All you need to do is create a template file named 500.html inside your project's templates directory with a brief message letting the user know about the error.

```
{% extends "base.html" %}

{% block title %}Internal Server Error - 500{% endblock %}

{% block site_wrapper %}We're sorry, but the site you are trying to access is currently
experiencing problems.
<br /><br />
We apologize for any inconvenience. Please try back again later.
{% endblock %}
```

By default, the view function called in the event of a server error doesn't return any context processors. This is a safe setting, since your server is already having problems in the event of an Internal Server Error. You can override this setting by specifying your own view function and hooking it into a variable called handler500 inside your project's root urls.py file, in the same way we specified the handler404 view function earlier in the book.

Summary

Now our site is optimized for search engines. We've taken steps to make sure that we've got high-quality and relevant content for each page in our title and meta tags, as well as using keywords in the body of each page. We're using hyperlinks in our site navigation, so that all pages are accessible to users by simply clicking links. We created an XML sitemap, robots.txt file, and a Google Base product feed to help Google navigate to every page on our site.

The algorithms that search engines use, especially Google, are designed to find pages that are helpful for users based on the search text that they've entered. If you put up an e-commerce site that people enjoy shopping on, there's a very good chance that they will link to your product pages and the rankings in the SERPs will come. Of course, without *any* SEO at all, you won't have users. Optimizing your site for the user experience and for search engine rankings are two different things, but they are very much interrelated, and each one will feed off of the success of the other.

As a final word of caution: there is a lot of misinformation floating around out there about SEO, as well as a lot of companies that promise to help you with your site's SEO (for outrageous fees) when in truth, they can do little more than submit your site to Google and wait, just like we did earlier in the chapter. It's not a complex process; it just requires careful planning and patience.

Now that your site is out on the Internet for everyone to find, that means that there's a small handful of people that you *don't* want finding your site: those people looking to crack into it. In the next chapter, we're going to talk about security and how you can minimize the risks associated with deploying a public-facing web application.

CHAPTER 12

■ ■ ■

Web Security Overview

B.C. Forbes once said that it's better to be occasionally cheated than perpetually suspicious. This was certainly intended to be tongue-in-cheek, and it's obvious that he said it long before the invention of the Internet. While things might go fine for a long while, a single "occasional" breach of security on your site is a terrible thing. Even a single successful attack can bring your site down to its knees and destroy everything that you've worked for. It's a sad truth, but as web developers, "perpetual suspicion" is the state of mind that we must re-affirm as part of our critical thought process when designing the architecture of an application.

While there's no such thing as a 100% secure web application (and don't let anyone tell you otherwise, no matter what they're trying to sell you), there are certainly measures you can take to greatly minimize the level of risk to you, your we bsite, and your business. In this chapter, we're going to examine some of the more common security concerns on the web, what the issues are, and the steps you can take to lower the risks associated with putting a Django web application up live on the Internet.

Securing the Site From Within

In an ideal world, your business would be run by one person: you. In theory, this is the best structure for a company because the person with a stake in the business's success, and the person running the show, are one and the same. When this is the case, that one person (you) is going to make sure that all the work they do for the business will be of the highest quality, that they use all of their resources efficiently without wasting them, and that you provide excellent customer service. Everything will be done in the best interest of the business, because as a sole proprietor, you know that how much you stand to profit from the business is directly correlated with how good of a job you choose to do.

Back in the real world, this is a tricky thing to pull off as a real business. Sure, there are sole proprietorships that manage to earn their owners a comfortable living, but those are the exception and not the rule. Most businesses require more than one person to be at the helm running things. Another problem is that they don't scale very well. As a company grows, you need to start leveraging the advantages of *division of labor* by dividing up tasks between employees.

It may seem counterintuitive, but we're going to start by looking at how we can secure the site from our own staff. Sooner or later, your site is going to grow and you're going to need to bring in outside people to help you. When this happens, you want to make sure you have mechanisms in place so that if any of these employees ever becomes an ex-employee or, due to circumstances, you end up losing trust in them, the amount of damage that they can do is minimized.

I'm not saying that you hire people who are untrustworthy…not at all. What I'm saying is that the security of your web application, when it comes to the human element, is largely beyond your control. You might hire your own nephew to help you fulfill the orders, so you've got to give him access to the

255

backend that has the order information in it. Naturally, you *trust* him, since it was only a short 20 years ago that you were helping his mother change his diapers. He's family, so there's nothing to fear.

Except that when you give him a login to your backend, let's say that he writes the username and password down on a sticky note that he puts on the monitor of the workstation you've assigned him to. And later, when you're not there, he brings in a friend to show them this little e-commerce business that *he* started, and that *he's* been running, and as he's showing his friend how things are running, the friend notices the username and password. All of the sudden, some outsider to your business has a login. And if, for some distant reason, they decide that they don't like your nephew anymore because they have some grand falling out, they might take it upon themselves to log in to that admin interface and *delete every order in there.*

Don't take too much stock in my little story, because it's just a contrived example. However, the message is very important. Once you're little e-commerce application grows, and your organization grows with it, sooner or later, things are going to grow beyond you. Right now, with a small, single site to maintain, you can easily grasp the scope of the project in your head, all at once, and foresee most of the problems that might arise. When that changes, you need to be ready. Security needs to be done up front, because when the site does start to grow, you're going to need to be worrying about other things, like whether to partner up with FedEx or UPS as your main "logistics solutions provider" or whether you should incorporate your business in Nevada or Delaware. There probably won't be time later. You need to think about it *now*, and plan for it.

When you design the security architecture of your application, you might do so with certain base assumptions in mind. Like, for example, that you'll *always hire people you can trust no matter what*. This is, of course, almost impossible to do in reality. Good security architecture takes into account that people are not perfect, that the code that people write is never perfect, and that you should expect the unexpected. No matter how you intend people to use your web application, they're going to find other ways of using it that you never even *thought* of. While not all of them will be strictly malicious, some of them are bound to be attacks designed to compromise your data.

In this section, we're going to look at Django permissions that you can apply to users in order to restrict what your administrative users can do with your data.

Django Permissions

Up until this point in the book, you've probably been using the single user login that we created when you first ran `manage.py syncdb`, when the application prompted you to create a superuser account login. This has worked great so far, since you're probably a single developer doing everything. However, giving everyone a superuser account that has access to everything is far from ideal for a real site.

Django comes equipped with the ability to assign users different permissions levels. By default, user accounts have three Boolean fields that allow you to control their access permissions to your site:

> `is_superuser`: The user will have access to everything on the site and the admin interface, with all permissions, regardless of other settings.
>
> `is_staff`: The user is allowed to log in and access the admin interface (as well as the public site), but you can manually adjust their permissions.
>
> `is_active`: If this is set to False, the user cannot access any part of the site. This is useful for removing a user while still preserving their login name and password if there's a chance you'll ever want to re-enable access.

You can set each of these on a per-user basis using the Django admin interface.

Applying Permissions to Users

So once you get your first employee and you need to set them up with an account that will let them access the admin interface of your site, the first thing you need to do is add the user account to the system. You can do this directly in the admin interface; under the "Auth" section, just click the "Users" link and then the "Add User" button, just like you've been doing with every other model so far. This will take you to a simple form, where you can have the employee enter their desired username and password. If you'd like, you can just assign them a password, give it to them, and encourage them to change it after they've first logged in.

Once you have their user account created, you just need to determine what kinds of access permissions that user needs to have. What do they need to be able to see, edit, or create in the admin interface? As one example, if they're order fulfillment, then they'll certainly need to be able to edit orders.

In order to give a user staff status, you must edit their user account in the admin interface. On the "Edit User" page, there should be three checkboxes corresponding to the three Boolean fields discussed earlier. You just need to check "Staff Status" in order to give them access.

Below this, there should be two select boxes labeled "User Permissions," where you can assign the user permissions. As you can see, each model has three permissions: add, edit, and delete. What each of these actions does is fairly self-explanatory. You just need to figure out what level of access you need to give them to your data.

Applying Permissions to Groups

Of course, after you apply permissions to a few users, you might find that you're repeating yourself quite a bit, setting up the same permissions for different employees. To make this process easier, Django allows you to create *groups* to which you can assign permissions, and then you can assign users to these groups. Any permission that you've applied to a group will be applied to all users that belong to that group. For organizations that are larger than three people and a dog, and for *any* organization that plans on growing over time, this is probably the easiest way of distributing permissions to users.

In the ASP.NET web framework, a very similar security mechanism exists, but instead of groups, they are referred to as *roles*. This is actually a much better term when trying to grasp the concept of what you're trying to set up. Think about the role that each individual plays in your organization, and what they are required to be able to do. You can give your groups names that make sense given the different departments in your organization.

For Modern Musician, I defined six different groups and gave them all different permissions based on what the employees in that group are required to do, as shown in Figure 12-1.

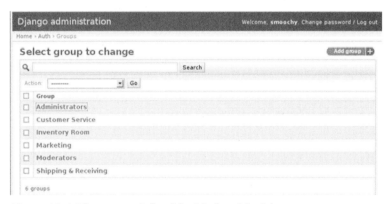

Figure 12-1. *The groups defined for Modern Musician.*

Protecting Against External Attacks

When designing your web application for security, the overall message you should pound into your brain with some kind of sledgehammer is this: never trust any input from your users. This is *especially* true when your application is a public-facing Internet web site. You need to thoroughly examine each form on your site, and make sure that you don't blindly trust anything. Your customers are trying to give you their money by shopping on your site, yes, but that doesn't mean that they're angels.

Along the same lines, retail stores use security cameras, Electronic Article Surveillance, and other means of making sure that you don't walk off with their precious inventory. Some of them have even employed people to stand at the exit doors, armed with highlighters to check customer receipts before they leave, and *God help you* if one of those Bic-wielding clerks catches you trying to walk out with something in your cart that isn't listed on the receipt.

While the effectiveness of the methods they use to prevent people from stealing things might be debatable, the reason that they do it is crystal clear. Retail establishments, if they are smart, don't trust their customers. Even though 99% of them will shop honestly and leave without any funny business, a small portion of customers will try to get away with petty theft. I don't know much about shoplifters, but most of them are probably stealing just for the thrill of getting away with something.

However, the profiles of the kinds of people that will attack your site are much different. They are technologically adept, they will try to steal more than just a few small pieces of merchandise, and the motivation driving them probably stems from more than a mere act of rebellion. More often than not, the person attacking your site is trying to extract valuable information from your site. Credit cards fetch a fair per-card price in black markets on the Internet. You need to be extremely vigilant in the design of your site, and make sure that you don't leave any gaping security holes that invite these kinds of attacks.

The Evils of Debug Mode

This might go without saying for most, but it does bear repeating because it's very important: when your site has been deployed into production, make sure that DEBUG is set to False in your settings.py file. If you don't, then any error your web application trips up on will display a traceback with source code to the end user, as well as several configuration variables about your web server, what database you're using, or payment gateway login credentials. Even just revealing that your web site is powered by the Django web framework might be enough information to get potential attackers to start formulating ideas about how to crack your site.

Often times, it's much easier to base the True or False value of DEBUG on some aspect of the development environment. For example, if you're developing on a local machine, you can set a PATH variable with a unique name and a value of True that will only ever exist on your development machine (or the machines of your fellow developers.) Then, inside settings.py, you can automate the setting of the DEBUG value like so:

```
import os
DEBUG = True if os.environ.get('LOCAL_DEBUG','') else False
```

That way, the only time DEBUG will resolve to True is when you're running the site on your local machine, and the LOCAL_DEBUG variable is found. Then, you don't have to concern yourself with switching it manually every time you update your site and want to test. Also notice the order we're assuming here: we default to production settings (e.g., DEBUG = False) unless our environment explicitly states otherwise. For security, the default assumption should be for a production environment, since it's much better to accidentally run DEBUG = False on a development machine instead of the other way around. Secure is the rule, with insecure being the exception on which we place the burden of proof.

Configuring Local Settings

Chances are good that the larger your site is, the greater number of differences there are between your development environment and your production environment. As your site grows, so will the gap between these two. In order to facilitate the greatest ease of migrating your project between the two, you need a way to set configuration variables with a little more ease than just checking for a single environment variable every time you want to conditionalize each setting.

One excellent technique is to create a separate file that contains configuration variables that are intended only for use in local development. To try this out, add the following four lines of code to the very bottom of your `settings.py` file:

```
try:
    from settings_local import *
except ImportError:
    pass
```

Now, create a new file in the root of your project called `settings_local.py`. Any configuration variables you define in this file will be imported into your project via the code we just added to `settings.py`. Even better, anything that you add to the `settings_local.py` file will override the variables you've defined in `settings.py`, which means that you can optionally add variable settings that are specific to your development environment in `settings_local.py`. If you exclude the `settings_local.py` file from your version control and don't deploy it into production, then you can use these local settings in development and the main `settings.py` file will be used when after you deploy your code.

A good example of when you might consider using this is the setting where you specify the network location of your cache backend server. (We'll look at setting up a cache server later in this chapter.) As your site grows, your cache server will likely reside on its own machine available to the production machine running your Django project over the network. However, on development machines, you won't want to refer to this cache server, as the cache server is unlikely to be available to development machines and, even if it is, you don't want to fill the cache server with development data.

However, if you specify your production cache server in a `local_settings.py` on your production application server, and your local development cache in `settings_local.py` on your development machine, you can safely run your code in both environments without clobbering the data in the production cache.

Even better, however, are the cases where you want to store passwords that you don't want to end up leaking out. If you have sensitive data stored inside `settings.py`, such as payment gateway passwords, and you suspect that you might one day release your source into the wild for others to use (and as an open source developer, I heartily encourage that), putting these sensitive variables into a local settings file that isn't part of your base source code is a good measure to ensure that the values aren't inadvertently distributed along with your released code.

Customer Registration Revisited

Back in Chapter 6, we hooked into the built-in Django authentication app to handle registration and login functionality. While this will work for you without any technical problems, there is an issue with the customer registration regarding the restrictions on passwords. Namely, there *are* no restrictions. There is no minimum password length required, meaning that a user could register with a password that is no more than a single letter "a" and successfully create an account. In addition to this, there are no constraints on password strength in the registration form. Some applications force users to create "stronger" passwords, in that they are required to contain one or more of: a combination of both uppercase and lowercase letters, at least one number, or at least one non-alphanumeric character.

In Django, this lack of enforcement is by design. The developers of the framework decided that it would be better not to have these restrictions in place by default and to let those who required them add

259

them, instead of including them by default and forcing people to disable the ones they didn't require. I don't entirely agree with this decision, because that means that over time, more and more Django applications are going to be deployed by companies that don't take security into consideration, and then users will start registering new accounts in these applications. Without any restrictions in place, these customers could be using very weak passwords to authenticate themselves, which is a concern.

The reason for this is simple: you don't want people to be able to easily determine a customer's password and get access to their account information. Attempts to hack web sites can succeed merely by selecting a username known by the attacker to be valid, and then attempting to log in to that account using every single word in a dictionary as a password, in the hopes that the successful password will be discovered by chance and will authenticate the attacker.

This is known as a *dictionary attack*. The large micro-blogging site Twitter was compromised in January of 2009 by an attacker who executed a dictionary attack using the known username "Crystal," eventually managing to authenticate himself when the password "happiness" was used. As it turned out, the user "Crystal" was actually a Twitter administrator, so the attacker found himself in a position to access every single Twitter account, including the account of Barack Obama. Twitter was very lucky that the attacker didn't cause a lot more damage than he did.

There's a very simple change you can make to minimize the risk of this: let's make a couple of quick tweaks to the registration form. First, we can give the two password fields a minimum required length. Exactly what length you decide upon for your own site depends on how secure you want your site to be. I'm going to set our password requirements to at least six characters in length, and require that passwords contain at least one character that isn't a letter or a number. We can do this by simply subclassing the Django's default UserCreationForm and overriding the fields that we want to customize. As long as we're doing this, let's take this opportunity to add an e-mail field to the registration form as well, so that as soon as the customer has signed up for an account, we'll have a valid e-mail address that we can use later, if we ever decide do any e-mail marketing.

Inside your projects accounts app, add the following to forms.py:

```
from django.contrib.auth.forms import UserCreationForm

class RegistrationForm(UserCreationForm):
    password1 = forms.RegexField(label="Password", regex=r'^(?=.*\W+).*$',
                                 help_text='Password must be six characters long ↵
                                 and contain at least one non-alphanumeric character.',
                                 widget=forms.PasswordInput, min_length=6,
                                 render_value=False)
    password2 = forms.RegexField(label="Password confirmation", regex=r'^(?=.*\W+).*$',
                                 widget=forms.PasswordInput, min_length=6,
                                 render_value=False)
    email = forms.EmailField(max_length="50")
```

Here we're taking advantage of the RegexField that you can use on Django form classes in order to ensure that the password entered contains at least one character that isn't a letter or a number. We're also putting a minimum length constraint on both the password fields so that they must be at least six characters long. In order to help facilitate a minimum of erroneous registration submissions, we've added some help text to the first password field to let the user know about our requirements.

Of course, enforcing a minimum password length and requiring that the user add at least one non-alphanumeric character might turn some of your customers away, even if you do use the help text argument to let them know in advance. Chances are good a lot of them won't read the help text you provide, and may become frustrated that they need to come up with a password that isn't merely a word in the dictionary.

One common alternative to forcing password strength is to have a bit of JavaScript on the registration page, tied to the onkeyup event of the first password textbox. As the user types, the JavaScript will analyze the strength of the password based on the type and number of characters it contains. After each keyup event, it will update an element on the page that lets the user know how strong their password is. Passwords could be rated one of three ways: "Weak." "Moderate," and "Strong." Using colors when displaying these values to the user is also immensely helpful; use red, yellow, and green for the aforementioned ratings, respectively. In this way, you encourage your customers to create a stronger password by making a "game" of it. Visually, present them with information that makes them really want to create a strong password. Make them want that "Strong" message to appear in green, and the "Weak" message in red vanish.

Like most things, good security when it comes to your customers involves carefully balancing tradeoffs between conflicting issues. On the one hand, you would like it if everyone entered a password that was 15 characters in length, and was very strong, full of ampersands and percentage signs. However, most people will choose some silly, easy-to-guess word as their password, because it's convenient for them to remember. Exactly how strong you choose to enforce the passwords in your system is a decision that will depend on you and your own specific business requirements.

One other addition to the form is the render_value argument we're passing into both of the password fields. If set to False, then the form field is not repopulated with the data from the last POST that was made to the page. So, if the user enters two passwords that don't match and the form redisplays with the error message, we don't enter the two non-matching passwords back into the inputs. Instead, we'll just force the user to completely re-enter their password and confirmation password again. It's a little extra step, but it's less error-prone and convenient for the user this way.

Next, update your view function for the registration page so that it uses this subclassed form instead of the Django default:

```
from ecomstore.accounts.forms import UserProfileForm, RegistrationForm

def register(request, template_name="registration/register.html"):
    if request.method == 'POST':
        postdata = request.POST.copy()
        form = RegistrationForm(postdata)
        if form.is_valid():
            user = form.save(commit=False)
            user.email = postdata.get('email','')
            user.save()
            un = postdata.get('username','')
            pw = postdata.get('password1','')
            from django.contrib.auth import login, authenticate
            new_user = authenticate(username=un, password=pw)
            if new_user and new_user.is_active:
                login(request, new_user)
                url = urlresolvers.reverse('my_account')
                return HttpResponseRedirect(url)
    else:
        form = RegistrationForm()
    page_title = 'User Registration'
    return render_to_response(template_name, locals(),
context_instance=RequestContext(request))
```

The only real addition here is the import and use of the new registration form class, and the fact that we're storing the e-mail address provided along with the user account.

Cross-Site Scripting Attacks

Cross-site scripting attacks (or XSS attacks) are different from most of the attacks a web application needs to worry about, in that the attacker is not necessarily attacking your site and your servers, but is instead trying to attack the other customers on your site. It involves the use of JavaScript `<script></script>` tags that can contain potentially malicious JavaScript.

The attack is carried out by finding places in a web application where input from a user is potentially rendered back as part of a page. On our site, we accept user input and render it back to the user (or other users) in the search functionality, product reviews, and product tags. That means that each of these areas is a potential security hole where the site might be vulnerable to this kind of attack.

The reason that these attacks are possible is because web browsers are literal. They receive a page full of HTML from the server and render this output to the user who requested it. If a user submits some malicious HTML to our site, we store it in the database, and later include this HTML in a page on our site, the browser cannot distinguish between this HTML from the user and the legitimate HTML that we, the site developers, put into our template files. So, not knowing any better, the browser simply renders all HTML and any JavaScript that's included in this output, regardless of its source, is executed blindly.

Testing for this problem is very simple: try submitting some JavaScript to a form on your site. For simplicity, let's start with the search functionality. After a user has entered search text and clicks the button, they are taken to a results page that reads "Search Results for [search text]". Whatever the user has entered is displayed right there at the top of the page. Enter the following bit of JavaScript into the search box:

```
<script>alert('Hello XSS!');</script>
```

If this page were vulnerable, then this JavaScript would be executed when the page was loaded and an alert box containing "Hello XSS!" would pop up as the page was loading. However, instead, you should have seen the text you typed, angled brackets and all, merely displayed on the page, without any alert box. By default, Django escapes any HTML tags that it finds in template variables before it displays them on the page.

■ **Caution** If you're using a version of Django earlier than 1.0, the auto-escaping behavior is not included. You need to explicitly use the escape template filter anywhere on your site where you display user input in a template variable.

Generally, developers are not terribly concerned when you show them that you can coerce a web site into popping up an alert box just by submitting some JavaScript as part of a form. Who really cares about some stupid little alert box? The problem is not with the alert box; the issue is that it's an indication that the site permits the user to inject JavaScript into the page, which will then be executed. JavaScript is generally used for harmless client-side functionality, such as form validation or rollover effects. However, it can also be used to steal users' cookies and craft phishing exploits to steal sensitive user information.

Maybe there's a place on your site where you *want* to render HTML that your users can input. You might be wondering if you could just strip `<script>` and `</script>` text blocks from your template variables before you display them to the user and that this would solve the problem. The problem with trying to take matters into your own hands is that attackers will be testing your site to see if there is a way around the safeguards you have in place. You might be able to do a simple search and replace on the string `<script>`, but what if an attacker submits a value containing `<scr<script>ipt>`? The middle of that text will be stripped out, but the parser will miss the outer four characters on either side, resulting in an opening `<script>` tag sneaking onto the page. Also, while today the vulnerability involves the use of script tags, tomorrow it may be another tag used to attack your site. In most cases involving security, you'll want to stick to the tried and true methods that the framework provides.

What's in a QueryString?

Often times, in a dynamic web site, you will use the URL and its contents to handle the fetching of records from the database. The perfect example is the product page: the product slug field is used to generate hyperlinks on your site to the product page, and when the page is requested, your application retrieves the product record that has the corresponding slug field. As long as each slug field contains a string of descriptive and unique text, you're unlikely to run into a security problem.

The issue arises in instances where you are looking up records based on the primary key field of a database table. More often than not, the primary key field will be an auto-incrementing integer value that's assigned to new records automatically. We use this field to look up order information in the "Order Details" page under the "My Account" section of the site, where customers can view details and products included in their past orders.

We're looking up each order by the use of its primary key, which we've been referring to as the Order Number. So, in order for a user to get the details about Order #445, they would just navigate to the following URL:

```
http://www.yoursite.com/order_details/445/
```

The problem is that any astute user will notice that the Order Number field is in the URL, and the curious ones might try changing the order number to see if they could load pages for other customer orders. The solution to this problem is simple enough: since this page requires that a customer is logged in and user information is stored along with each order, you can just add the user field to the filter() method call on the Order model manager. If you look back at the code we wrote in Chapter 6 for these pages, you'll notice that the view includes this:

```
order = get_object_or_404(Order, id=order_id, user=request.user)
```

That way, any request for an order that isn't associated with the current user will return a 404 response, instead of the page with details about that order. In this case, it might not be that big of an issue because we're not displaying any sensitive information on the Order Details page. However, in the future, this may not be the case. Later on, we might choose to include some basic credit card information, in which case you'll be much better off restricting to whom you choose to display this information. It's good to get in the habit of restricting database lookups for user information to ensure that they only ever return records that belong to that particular customer by adding the extra user field to the filter.

Cross-Site Request Forgery

Back in the days before cell phones, before everyone had caller ID right in the palm of their hand, teenagers were much more inclined to make prank calls to random phone numbers. You could pick up the phone, call someone with some kind of crazy story, and try to hook them into what you were saying. Or you ask a simple question that sounds legitimate and, when you get the answer you expect, drop some terribly witty punch line on them and hang up. Here is a classic gem that most people have heard:

Prank Caller: Hello, this is the electric company. Is your refrigerator running?

Victim: Hang on. [pause to check] Yes, it's running.

Prank Caller: Well, you better go catch it! [cue for laughter]

If you were ever the victim of such a prank, you might have found yourself angry when the facade was revealed and the comedy bombshell was dropped. The caller exploited your trust in the people who call you on the phone, and you got roped into the conversation because you believed that the person on the other end was who they claimed to be, when in fact it was a stranger spoofing their own identity. A Cross-Site Request Forgery (CSRF) attack is much like this. A CSRF attack takes advantage of the fact that a web server, without enough information, doesn't have the ability to distinguish between a legitimate request and a bogus one coming from somewhere else.

For example, imagine that the process of adding products to the shopping cart is handled via GET requests to a specific URL. The cart form, when we want to add an item to the shopping cart, makes a request to the following URL: /cart/add/?product=some-product. This in turn calls the view function, which passes the request on down the chain, and ends up creating a new record in the database in the CartItem table. The problem arises when someone places some HTML on a web page that looks like this:

```
<img src="http://www.yoursite.com/cart/add/?product=some-product" />
```

Remember, when the browser sends a request for a page to the server, the first reply we get is the HTML for that page. Then, once the browser has the HTML, it goes through the document and makes a subsequent HTTP request for each script, style sheet, or image tag that it finds. When the browser encounters the image tag here, it will initiate a new request to the URL. The user that loaded the web page with this HTML would inadvertently have the product with the "some-product" slug value added to their shopping cart. In this case, much like with XSS attacks, it's a computer that doesn't know any better. The server is "dumb." It has no way of differentiating HTTP requests that came in from form submissions and those that were made because they were embedded in HTML tags. While this example is harmless, it does illustrate the nature of the vulnerability, and how more serious attacks could be carried out, such as placing orders.

This problem is solved on our site, because we're encoding our HTML so that users cannot post HTML that might execute a CSRF Attack. However, other sites on the Internet may not be as secure. If a customer were logged in to our site, and then clicked away to a forum page on another site, where a user had posted a reply to a thread that contains the HTML image tag shown earlier, the request would be made to our site and the item would be added to the cart. The easiest solution to this problem is to ensure that no GET requests to our site manipulate any data. So, such actions as adding products to the shopping cart, placing orders, updating user profile information, or anything else that changes data in the database should only occur via POST requests. That way, arbitrary links elsewhere on the Internet cannot alter our data in any way.

Of course, while this is good practice and eliminates most of the "tire-kicking" that attackers will do against your site, that doesn't make it impossible to carry out these kinds of attacks with POST requests. It's still possible to post HTML on a web page that contains a form with the POST values that will trigger the action on our site. Right now, it would be all-too-easy for an attacker to "clone" the HTML of the form on any given product page on our site and include some JavaScript that automatically submits the form when that web page is loaded. So there's still no guarantee that the request came from our site, even given the correct POST values.

The best solution is to "sign" each form with a hidden input field that contains a unique value. When the form is submitted, you can check the value of this hidden field to verify that the form POST came from a page on our site. This might sound like a lot of work, and it probably would be some effort if we had to create a solution from scratch. Fortunately, Django includes a solution: a middleware package that you can use to generate a form validation input for all forms on your site, and this *couldn't* be any easier to use. All you need to do is put the following line into your project's MIDDLEWARE_CLASSES section:

```
'django.contrib.auth.middleware.AuthenticationMiddleware',
'django.contrib.csrf.middleware.CsrfMiddleware',
'django.contrib.flatpages.middleware.FlatpageFallbackMiddleware',
```

This middleware does two things: first, it adds a hidden input field with a validation token value to any form that makes a POST request on your site. The validation token is a hash function calculated from the user's session and the SECRET_KEY value in your project's settings.py file. Second, whenever a POST request is submitted from a form on your site, the middleware checks to make sure that the values in the post contain the hidden input field with a valid hash value. If the POST request is made without that hidden input, or without a valid hash value, we can assume that the request did not come from our site and is bogus. The CSRF middleware responds to such bogus requests with a HTTP 403 Forbidden error page.

In the course of opening the file in every chapter of this book, you may have noticed the SECRET_KEY value in your settings.py file. This value is used by your Django project for secret key hashing algorithms, for security purposes throughout the site. It was generated for you by Django when you first started the project, but you're free to change it to any random string of characters. You can generate the value using either of the methods we used to generate Cart IDs or Tracking IDs elsewhere in the book, using the random or urandom modules. According to the Django documentation, the longer the better. Naturally, too much might be overkill. If your SECRET_KEY is dozens of lines long, that will significantly slow things down unnecessarily, but a value between 50 and 100 characters cannot hurt you. Of course, if you find that the value is an empty string, you should certainly put something in there!

SQL Injection

For any database-driven web site, the real value of your site lies in the data. Consequently, this is what many attackers will attempt to do right from the start: try to steal, manipulate, or delete large quantities of your data. Of course, attackers won't have direct access to your database, since they won't have the database credentials required to connect directly to your MySQL server. Instead, this is done with an attack known as a *SQL injection* attack, which is an attempt by a user to pass their own SQL into your database server through the interface of your application, to manipulate your database contents in some way.

On the surface, this might seem like a difficult thing to do, but web sites with poor security measures in place fall victim to this kind of attack all the time. The problem lies in SQL queries that are constructed ad-hoc inside a web application based on user-submitted data. If user-supplied parameters that are passed to the database in WHERE clauses that are not properly escaped, an attacker can trick the database behind a web application into executing SQL that they've submitted as part of a form.

For illustrative purposes, take a hypothetical web application (not our own) that makes the following SQL call for the search page:

```
SELECT * FROM products WHERE name LIKE '%guitar%';
```

In this example, the user entered the word "guitar" and this was the SQL that was constructed and sent to the database. Imagine that the user entered this as the search term: a%'; DROP TABLE products;. In a situation where the site was vulnerable, this would produce the following SQL being sent to the database:

```
SELECT * FROM products WHERE name LIKE '%a'; DROP TABLE products;%
```

In this case, the SQL sent to the database retrieves all products containing the letter "a." This certainly massive result set of this query is the swan song of our product data, as the next statement deletes the product table altogether. If this were to be executed against a production database successfully, the site would almost entirely go down and return nothing but 500 Server Errors for almost every page, as the application would suddenly be trying to query from a database that no longer exists. In this case, you just have to hope that you're doing regular backups of your database, and that you can restore your data before too long.

The example here is dependent on a few assumptions. First, the attacker needed to know that our product database table was named products in order to attempt this query. In addition, the attacker would have to determine that we were using MySQL in order to know the syntax for some database commands, but DROP TABLE and the semi-colon as a delimiter between statements is actually common to a lot of the more popular RDBMS options out there.

As it happens, this problem is unlikely to come up in the course of building a Django site because most of the queries that you're going to make are done using the Django ORM. Queries made through the ORM use *bind variables*, which have their parameters automatically escaped, so that any attempts to end the SQL statement early by using a single quote don't get passed through. If someone performed this search on our site, Django would send the following:

```
SELECT * FROM products WHERE name LIKE '%a\'; DROP TABLE products';%
```

This just performs a search for products whose name contains that weird string of text that our would-be attacker entered. Thanks to Django, no harm done.

Django does allow you to write raw SQL queries and pass them to the database, both with a cursor or using the ORM extra() method. In order to eliminate any SQL injection vulnerabilities, you should use the following syntax when generating the SQL:

```
from django.db import connection

def raw_sql_query(product_name):
    sql = "SELECT description FROM products WHERE name = %s;"
    cr = connection.cursor()
    cr.execute(sql, [product_name])
```

In the normal course of things, you shouldn't ever have to do this. However, you should be mindful of the potential security hole and use the correct technique if you ever need to.

Moving the Admin Interface

By default, the Django admin interface is located at the path /admin/ in your application. However, since this is the default for all Django applications, it's very easy for the average developer to figure this out and try accessing your admin login at this path on your site. To avoid inviting any mischief to your admin login page, you might consider moving it to another path, like /sitename-admin/ or something that cannot be guessed as easily.

Naturally, just making this simple change doesn't actually do anything to secure your site. It's a form of what is known in the security community as "security through obscurity," whereby you make it a little more difficult for attackers to gather information about your site by eliminating the most obvious weak points. It's useful to apply in some cases, such as the location of the admin interface, but you want to shoot for a different principle in securing your application: "security by design." Using the latter approach, your web application is designed with security in mind from the ground up. When applied correctly, security by design is much more effective.

Storing Secrets

So far, we have several layers of security protecting the information contained in our database. By the time you have deployed your site, there should be network security in place to prevent crackers from compromising your machines, and passwords restricting access to the database server. Even though this is the case, you still shouldn't be storing sensitive information just as human-readable plain text.

In the course of running an e-commerce application, you'll no doubt encounter a situation where you need to store some kind of sensitive data that you don't want to leave sitting in the database in plain text. Passwords are an excellent example of this. There's no reason for you to leave customer passwords sitting in the database as plain text, because if your database were ever compromised, the attacker would have all of your customer's passwords and would have absolutely no trouble logging in to the site as one of your many customers. Even worse, a lot of people re-use the same username and password combinations across multiple sites, so if your site is ever compromised, it's entirely possible that an attacker might be able to use their credentials to log in to *other* sites as well.

For this reason, you'll want to use some kind of cryptographic algorithm to encrypt sensitive data. Unfortunately, there's no way that I can do the subject of cryptography any justice in this short chapter. However, in this section, I'm going to talk about some extremely basic concepts, look at how Django uses encryption to store passwords, and then take a look at how to securely encrypt and store customer credit card data using the Python Cryptographic Toolkit and the Google Keyczar library.

Storing Customer Passwords

Storing customer passwords is something that just about every web application is required to do in this day and age, since most applications require that users authenticate themselves before adding or manipulating any data on the site. Naturally, because information stored with customer accounts is intended to be confidential and only accessible to that user, we should take care to store the password in a secure fashion, so that each customer's password can't be easily obtained and used by anyone else. For this reason, when storing passwords, you shouldn't store them as plain text, but instead should encrypt the characters of the password for each customer so that the values are difficult to obtain for anybody who isn't that particular customer.

Passwords are a somewhat unique case, because once we encrypt them, we don't actually need to ever decrypt them. If you have a consistent means of encrypting passwords—that is, if you can use an encryption function that will produce identical encrypted values for the identical password values—then you never need to reverse the encryption. When a customer first registers for their new account and enters their password, you compute and store the encrypted text in the database along with their username. Later, when they come back and log in a second time, you can take the password they enter at login, apply the same encryption function as you did when they initially registered, and compare the resulting text with what you have stored in the database.

If the two encrypted strings match, then the user has entered the same password stored in the database, so we can safely assume they are who they claim to be. If they don't match, then the user has entered the wrong password, either because of a typo or because the person attempting to log in isn't really the customer who registered that account.

Because customer account passwords only need to be encrypted without decryption, we can use a very strong encryption means known as a one-way hash function. Hash functions take a string of character values, such as a password, and generate a unique hash value based on the characters. Hash functions are *deterministic*, in that the hash value computed for any given string of text will be the same, no matter how many times the value is computed.

In order to store passwords, Django uses a cryptographic hash function known as SHA-1 (SHA stands for Secure Hash Algorithm) to compute hash values for passwords. We can see this in action by dropping into a Python shell and seeing this for ourselves. The following bit of code computes the SHA-1 hash value of "password":

```
>>> import hashlib
>>> hashlib.sha1('password').hexdigest()
'5baa61e4c9b93f3f0682250b6cf8331b7ee68fd8'
```

Because SHA-1 is a one-way hash function, and isn't intended to need decryption, the actual encryption is extremely strong. That is, it would be immensely difficult for anyone to determine that the original value of the large hash value here is "password."

The results that you see are consistent when done multiple times:

```
>>> my_password = 'password'
>>> hash1 = hashlib.sha1(my_password).hexdigest()
>>> hash2 = hashlib.sha1(my_password).hexdigest()
```

```
>>> hash1 == hash2
True
```

A well-design hash algorithm ensures that the output is unique for any given string of text, so that two different passwords will never have the same hash value. Therefore, an incorrect password should never match the stored hash value. The hashed text is also case-sensitive, so "Password" would generate a different result than "password."

THE MD5 HASH ALGORITHM

Older versions of Django (prior to 1.0) used a different hash algorithm called MD5, in order to compute password hashes. This has been deprecated, although newer versions of Django still retain the functionality in the source code for backward compatibility. The algorithm used is stored with the hash value, and if your Django app finds an old MD5-computed hash in the database, it will replace it with the SHA-1 hash value the next time the user successfully authenticates.

Django actually goes one step further than this and uses a *hash salt* when computing the hash value. This is a small, randomly generated string of characters that is tacked on to the beginning of the password before the hash value is computed. The salt values are stored along with the hash value of the password when the user first registers on your site. Then, when they return to log in to your site a second time, the authentication process follows these steps:

1. Retrieve from the database the salt, the password hash value, and the algorithm that was used to compute the hash text.

2. Append the salt onto the front of the password the user has just provided at login.

3. Compute the hash value of the salt/password combination using the same algorithm as before.

4. Compare the computed hash value with the stored value. If the two values match, the passwords match, and the user is authenticated.

Django stores these three values together in a single field on the User model, delimited by a dollar sign ($) character. For example, here is the password stored for a username with the password "blah":

```
sha1$d4e4a$a725b60c877ee448c9a66515ea5672be118f2f0a
```

The first value before the first dollar sign is the algorithm used, followed by the salt used to compute the password hash value. This means that the following code will produce the same output as what you see stored after the last dollar sign in the preceding code:

```
>>> hashlib.sha1('d4e4ablah').hexdigest()
'a725b60c877ee448c9a66515ea5672be118f2f0a'
```

Using a salt to compute hash values has the added bonus of making it so that any attacker that gains access to all of your customer passwords cannot identify two different users that happen to have the same password. For example, two different customers might both use the same password of "jamesbond." If a salt isn't used, it's very easy to scan a list of password hashes and find those that are the same. If the password of one account is known, then the attacker knows that other accounts with identical hash values share that same password. Applying a salt makes trying to crack the stored hash values much more computationally expensive, and therefore much more infeasible to anyone trying to crack them.

One disadvantage of this approach is that you cannot retrieve a user password if the customer forgets it. Many sites offer to send users their password by e-mail if they've forgotten it. Since a hash is one-way, you cannot do this for your customers. The only recourse you have if a customer forgets their password is to set up a mechanism to *reset* their password to some arbitrary bunch of text, and e-mail that new password to the customer instead. For most sites, the added security of using hashes to store passwords far outweighs the convenience of password recovery.

Storing Credit Card Data

Cryptography is one of those areas of computer programming that keeps me humble. As a web developer, it's all too easy to develop an ego and start thinking that you're capable of anything. I remember the first time I created an HTML page and opened it up in a browser. The results were astonishing... wow, did I do that? Then I added in some CSS to make the colors and fonts all pretty. And it worked! Then I set up a basic database and managed to hook my web pages into them, displaying dynamic data like magic. Hallelujah, it's working! *I must be brilliant.*

Of course, real programming problems are never that simple to solve. I'm just lucky that most really tough low-level problems have already been solved by people that have come before me. The mechanisms behind cryptographic algorithms are the archetype example of a computer programming problem that is beyond most of us, and reserved strictly for those few gifted souls who are mathematically inclined. Most of us simply cannot grasp how these kinds of algorithms work, let alone implement our own custom solution.

For this reason, if you're going to store data and you have to encrypt it, then you must go with a tried and true solution that has been adopted by those in the security community. Period. While there are quite a few "hand-rolled" solutions floating around out there that claim to be more secure because they're "new" and based on some company's proprietary secret code doesn't make them secure. In fact, usually the opposite is true. Bear in mind that just because the mathematical mechanism behind all major algorithms is public and available to anyone, what makes them secure is not the specific details behind their protocols, but how hard they are to crack once they are in use.

In short, if it's good enough for the U.S. government, then it's definitely good enough for us. The last thing we want to do is start thinking we can do any better on our own.

That being said, the decision to store credit card data for your customers, anywhere on your system, is not necessarily a good idea no matter what security measures you put into place. We skipped over storing credit card information earlier, in the chapter on checkout, simply because for most small- to medium-sized e-commerce sites, storing financial information is more than likely an unnecessary risk. You may feel the urge to store it simply as a convenience to your customers, so they don't need to key in their information each and every time they come back to your site to place another order.

I disagree with this last point. If anything, making a conscious decision not to store credit card data can be touted as a *feature* of your site, not a weakness. Tell your customers right on your site that you're not going to store their information because you're thinking of them and their own personal security. For a smaller site where most of your customers are placing one-time e-commerce transactions (as opposed to a site that requires recurring monthly billing), most of them will probably not have any problem with this. Some of them will probably be relieved that you're not storing this information.

For smaller sites, this is also a good decision because the future is uncertain. Sure, today you may have a development server and a single production server, both of which run out of your company's office. Today, you have physical control over the hardware that's running your site. However, in a world where virtualization is increasing, you can't be sure where your business is going to be a year after you launch. In the Amazon's Elastic Cloud Compute, the physical hardware is an abstraction; you just deploy machine instances into the cloud and you lack the same physical control over the hardware that you did when your servers were in-house. It's a tricky prospect to consider, particularly very early on in the development process.

If you do decide to store credit card data, I'd strongly recommend that you read and comply with the PCI Security Standard in your web application. Make sure the systems on which you store the credit card information are secured by a firewall, and that *any* data you store is strongly encrypted and not merely stored as plaintext. Don't store the card verification value (CVV) anywhere. If you decide to ask customers for their CVV when they place orders, make sure that it doesn't end up in the session or log files, and definitely don't store it along with the rest of the credit card information. If you can, store the encrypted credit card information in a database that's separate from the database containing the rest of your application data, so that if a cracker compromises your credit card data, it will be devoid of any personally identifiable information, such as customer name or address.

Symmetric Cryptography

On your site, some customer information may need to be stored securely, but you won't be able to use a one-way hash function to encrypt it because you'll later need to decrypt it. If you were to hash credit card data, for example, then the best you could do is ask the customer to enter it again the next time they come back and verify that it matches the credit card data you have stored. And if you're going to make them re-enter it, you might as well just avoid any liability and not store it in the first place.

Symmetric cryptography is the kind of cryptography with which most people are intuitively familiar. There are two parties involved: one that's composing a message intended to be sent and read by the other. While in transport, the person sending the message would like it to be encrypted so that no one besides the intended recipient will be able to read its contents.

The original text of the message, which is human-readable, is known as the *plaintext*. The plaintext is converted into *ciphertext* using a cryptographic algorithm (also known as a *cipher*) and a key, which is an encrypted representation of the data that obscures the original message and renders it unreadable. The ciphertext is transmitted to the recipient, who uses the same cryptographic algorithm and the key to decrypt the ciphertext, converting it back into the original plaintext of the message. Both parties use a single key both in the encryption and decryption, which must be agreed upon by each party and not transmitted with the ciphertext message, as this would remove any security.

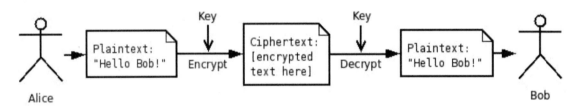

Figure 12-2. Process of encryption and decryption using symmetric cryptography.

The best library available for handling cryptography inside Python is the Python Cryptographic Toolkit. It's not part of the standard library, and it's not even written in Python. The actual parts of the library that perform low-level cryptographic functions are written in C, mostly for performance reasons. Cryptography requires some very heavy computation, and this is much faster if it's handled by a compiled language like C instead of an interpreted language like Python. The library itself provides a nice interface that lets you perform the functions inside Python.

While I'm not going to cover the mechanisms behind cryptography in this book, you might have a keen interest in learning more for yourself. The authoritative introduction to the field of cryptography is *Applied Cryptography: Protocols, Algorithms, and Source Code in C, Second Edition* by Bruce Schneier (Wiley, 1996). While it's somewhat dated at this point, and it doesn't cover the specific cryptographic algorithm we're going to implement in the next section, it's an excellent book on the subject.

Google Keyczar

As it turns out, you don't even need to understand exactly how to implement an encryption scheme using the Python Cryptographic Toolkit.[1] Google has provided a library of its own algorithm implementations, using this Toolkit, to help developers take full advantage of the encryption algorithms it offers. The mission statement behind Google Keyczar[2] is very insightful, and describes the reason that Google decided to create it for developers. From the Keyczar web site:

"Cryptography is easy to get wrong. Developers can often choose the wrong cipher mode, use obsolete algorithms, compose primitives in an unsafe manner, or fail to anticipate the need for key rotation. Keyczar abstracts some of these details by choosing safe defaults, automatically tagging outputs with key version information, and providing a simple interface."

Let's say that you've decided that you want to store some sensitive information, such as credit card data, and you decide that you need to use symmetric cryptography so that you can encrypt the data, and then decrypt it later, using a single key. You might poke around and come across information about the Data Encryption Standard (or DES). Eventually, after you dig a little deeper, you'll find that DES was replaced by the Advanced Encryption Standard (or AES), which was certified as an encryption standard in 2002 and adopted for use by the United States Government. So, since it's good enough for the NSA, you decide to use it yourself, but when you start looking into the specifics of how to implement AES for encrypting your data, you'll encounter more questions than answers. What block size should you use? What block cipher mode is most secure for your purposes? How do you generate a random and secure key, and where do you put it? You could spend hours looking for answers to all of these questions but, again, the math behind these processes is beyond most of us lowly developers, so you'll likely get exhausted while trying to find the correct answer.

Or, you could use Google Keyczar for your cryptography needs, and defer to the choices they've made in implementing AES for you.

Now, I don't intend to make Google Keyczar sound like a silver bullet that completely eliminates any work that you might need to do. There are still some very important decisions you need to make regarding the security of your system. For instance, where will the key used for encryption and decryption reside on your system? It needs to be accessible to your project, but you don't want just anyone to be able to get at it.

Google Keyczar is not an encryption library by itself. Rather, it strives to use existing libraries and just provides developers a simple interface for performing encryption that abstracts away all of the lower-level details. There is a version of Google Keyczar that is written to work with the Python Cryptographic Toolkit.

Keyczar also has a couple of dependencies you'll need to install before it will work. Because it relies on the Python Cryptographic Toolkit, you'll need to download and install that before trying to use Keyczar. A Debian installation is available via apt-get install python-crypto.

If you're using a version of Python earlier than 2.6, you will also need to download and install the simplejson module.[3] Django comes with a version of this module built-in, but Keyczar requires that you have the Python module installed. You'll also need to get your hands on a copy of the Python Abstraction Notation One library.[4]

---

[1] http://www.amk.ca/python/code/crypto.html

[2] http://code.google.com/p/keyczar/

[3] http://pypi.python.org/pypi/simplejson

[4] http://pyasn1.sourceforge.net/

Make sure that you download the Python version of the library. After extracting the .tar file, find the src/keyczar subdirectory inside the download. The keyczar directory is the one you want. Place a copy of, or create a symbolic link to, this folder somewhere on your system's PYTHONPATH, such as in your site-packages directory. To test that you've installed the library correctly, drop into a python shell and try the following import:

```
>>> import keyczar
```

If you don't get any errors, then you've successfully put Google Keyczar onto your PYTHONPATH and can now use it in your project. The utility that we're going to use inside of this directory is the keyczart.py module, which we'll use for creating our keys. Optionally, you can put this module on your PYTHONPATH as well.

Once you have it configured, you first need to generate a key that you can use for the encryption process. This is simple enough. For simplicity, we're going to generate and store the keys for encryption directly inside our project, but keep in mind that this is less than ideal. For security reasons, you probably want to store the keys in some other directory on your system that doesn't reside within your project. However, for our simple example, this is secure enough.

From inside your system's shell, in the root of your project directory, create a new subdirectory to hold your encryption keys:

```
$ mkdir keys
$ python /path/to/keyczar/keyczart.py create --location='keys' ↵
    --purpose=crypt --name='ecomstore'
$ python keyczart.py addkey --location='keys' --status=primary
$ cd keys
$ pwd
'/path/to/project/keys/'
```

Here, we create a new directory to hold our key information. Then, we use the keyczart module to create a new keyset, which means that our directory can contain more than one key for cryptographic functions. However, notice that when we create the first (and only) key for our keyset that we set its status as *primary*. At any given time, only one key in our keyset can be primary. Others can be created with their status set to active or inactive. Later, you can "promote" one of these other keys to primary if you want to rotate out the old key and replace it with a new one. For now, it's enough to create a single key with a primary status that we'll use for encryption.

Make note of the present working directory that we echoed in the last line, because we're going to use it in just a second. Now, we're going to take the new code for a quick trial run inside our project's Python shell. Drop into it using the manage.py shell command and enter the following commands. Remember to replace the path in the Read() function with your own path.

```
>>> import keyczar
>>> crypter = keyczar.Crypter.Read('/path/to/project/keys/')
>>> encrypted = crypter.Encrypt('some secret info goes here')
>>> decrypted = crypter.Decrypt(encrypted)
```

Go ahead and look at the contents of the encrypted and decrypted variables. The encrypted should be a bunch of incomprehensible junk that is our ciphertext, and the decrypted variable should contain the same text that you passed into the Encrypt() function.

■ **Note** If you've installed Google Keyczar using the `easy_install` utility, you may need to amend the first import statement in the preceding code to read `from keyczar import keyczar`, in order to ensure that your code is referencing the correct module that contains the `Crypter` module.

Even though we cannot use hash algorithms such as SHA-1 to encrypt our data, since hash functions are only one-way, it's possible to use them to "sign" encrypted data. That is, after encrypting some plaintext, generate an SHA-1 hash value from the plaintext and store this with the encrypted ciphertext. Later, when we decrypt the stored ciphertext, we compute the SHA-1 hash value from the newly retrieved plaintext and compare this value with the stored hash value. If the two hash values do not match, this means that the encrypted data we had stored was tampered with between the time it was originally encrypted and the time we decrypted it.

One of the nice things about the way Keyczar implements the AES encryption algorithm is that underneath the hood, our generated ciphertext contains an SHA-1 hash that is verified upon decrypting the data. Therefore, if anyone tampers with the encrypted data in the database, the `Decrypt()` function will raise an `InvalidSignatureError` exception. You can test this by manipulating a few of the characters toward the end of the encrypted text and trying to decrypt it:

```
>>> corrupted = encrypted.replace('mL','hh')
>>> crypter.Decrypt(corrupted)
InvalidSignatureError: Invalid ciphertext signature
```

There are a few exceptions that the Keyczar library might raise if the `Decrypt()` function receives invalid ciphertext, which we'll catch in our code.

Remember that the security of your encrypted data is based entirely on the security of your key. If the key ever gets out or is leaked, then none of your data is really secure. That is the crux of symmetric key cryptography. So remember that you should never transmit the key across an open public network (such as the Internet) without doing so securely. We've put the keys we're using in this example right into our project, so if you're using source control, make sure that you explicitly exclude any keys you intended to use in production. Also, make sure that wherever you put it after you deploy your site into production is only accessible by a few people in your organization, and that the machine you have it on is secured as well.

A Credit Card Model and Form

Let's put this new encryption functionality to work for us and take it for a test drive. In this section, we're going to create a simple model to store credit card information and a simple form class for capturing the data from customers. The following code for this demonstration can go anywhere you'd like in your project. I'm going to create a new app to house this code, called `billing`. Create this new app in your shell and add it to your project's INSTALLED_APPS section.

Inside the new app, add the following model definition to the `models.py` file:

```
from django.db import models
from django.contrib.auth.models import User

class Card(models.Model):
    data = models.CharField(max_length=500)
    user = models.ForeignKey(User)
    num = models.CharField(max_length=4)
```

```
    @property
    def display_number(self):
        return u'xxxx-xxxx-xxxx-' + unicode(self.num)

    def __unicode__(self):
        return unicode(self.user.username) + ' - ' + self.display_number
```

As you can see, we've defined a very slim model that will hold all of the encrypted credit card data in a single field. We've also created a very small string field that will hold the last four digits of the credit card number for use in display on the interface. For example, on the order details page in order history, we might show that the credit card "xxxx-xxxx-xxxx-1234" was used, instead of having to display the whole number. We've also defined a model method to return this value as a property of each model instance.

Next, we need to create a form that will actually capture all fields of a credit card as inputs from the user. Create a file named forms.py in your new billing app and add the following form class definition to it:

```
from ecomstore.billing.models import Card
from django import forms
from datetime import datetime

month_choice = [ ]
# month_choice.append(('','- Month -'))
for i in range(1,13):
    if len(str(i)) == 1:
        numeric = '0' + str(i)
    else:
        numeric = str(i)
    month_choice.append((numeric, datetime(2009, i, 1).strftime('%B')))
MONTHS = tuple(month_choice)


calendar_years = [ ]
# calendar_years.append(('','- Year -'))
for i in range(datetime.now().year, datetime.now().year+10):
    calendar_years.append((i,i))
YEARS = tuple(calendar_years)

class CardForm(forms.ModelForm):
    CARD_TYPES = (('Visa', 'Visa'),
                  ('Amex', 'Amex'),
                  ('Discover', 'Discover'),
                  ('Mastercard', 'Mastercard'),)
    class Meta:
        model = Card
        exclude = ('data','num', 'user')

    cardholder_name = forms.CharField(max_length=100)
    card_number = forms.CharField(max_length=20)
    card_type = forms.ChoiceField(choices=CARD_TYPES)
    card_expire_month = forms.ChoiceField(choices=MONTHS)
    card_expire_year = forms.ChoiceField(choices=YEARS)
```

A lot of the logic you see in this form should look much like the code we wrote for the checkout form in Chapter 5. If need be, this stand-alone form can be integrated into the checkout form, in accordance with your own needs.

Next, we're going to create a module inside this new app to actually interface with the Keyczar library and perform the actual calls to the encryption and decryption methods. Create a new file called passkey.py and add the follow little bit of code:

```
from ecomstore.settings import CURRENT_PATH
from keyczar import keyczar
import os

KEY_PATH = os.path.join(CURRENT_PATH, 'keys')

def encrypt(plaintext):
    crypter = _get_crypter()
    return crypter.Encrypt(plaintext)

def decrypt(ciphertext):
    crypter = _get_crypter()
    return crypter.Decrypt(ciphertext)

def _get_crypter():
    return keyczar.Crypter.Read(KEY_PATH)
```

Make sure that your own KEY_PATH variable contains the actual path to the keyset you created in the last section.

Now, we just need a view function and a template file we can use to take this new code for a test drive. Inside views.py, create this single view function:

```
from django.shortcuts import render_to_response
from django.core import serializers
from django.utils import simplejson
from django.template import RequestContext
from django.contrib.auth.decorators import login_required

from ecomstore.billing.forms import CardForm
from ecomstore.billing import passkey

@login_required
def add_card(request):
    if request.method == 'POST':
        post_data = request.POST.copy()
        # convert the POST variables into JSON format
        post_data.__delitem__('csrfmiddlewaretoken')
        json_data = simplejson.dumps(post_data)
        # encrypt the JSON
        encrypted_json = passkey.encrypt(json_data)
        # retrieve the encrypted JSON
        decrypted_json = passkey.decrypt(encrypted_json)
        # convert the decrypted JSON into a dictionary
        decrypted_data = simplejson.loads(decrypted_json)

        # store the newly encrypted data as a Card instance
        form = CardForm(post_data)
```

```
        card = form.save(commit=False)
        card.user = request.user
        card.num = post_data.get('card_number')[-4:]
        card.data = encrypted_json
        card.save()
    else:
        form = CardForm()
    return render_to_response("billing/add_card.html", locals(),
context_instance=RequestContext(request))
```

Lastly, inside your project's templates directory, create a new subdirectory called billing and add a template file called add_card.html. Add this template code, which contains the form and variables to check the progress each step of the way:

```
{% extends "catalog.html" %}

{% block content %}
    <h1>Add Card</h1>
    <form method="post" action="{{ request.path }}">
    <table>
    {{ form.as_table }}
    </table>
    <input type="submit" value="Submit" />
    </form>
    <br /><br />
    Original Post Data: {{ post_data }}
    <br /><br />
    Data as JSON: {{ json_data }}
    <br /><br />
    Encrypted JSON: {{ encrypted_json }}
    <br /><br />
    Decrypted JSON: {{ decrypted_json }}
    <br /><br />
    Decrypted Python Dictionary: {{ decrypted_data }}
{% endblock %}
```

In order to do this test, you'll need to create a URL entry for this view function somewhere in your project. Once you've gotten that set up, navigate to that URL on your site and you should see the credit card form as it appears in Figure 12-3.

Figure 12-3. The credit card form.

The view function itself just takes the data directly from the POST request made to the page and converts it into JSON format. Then, we pass this JSON object into the encrypt() function we created in the passkey.py file, getting back the encrypted JSON that we'll later store. Then, to ensure that everything goes smoothly with retrieval, we perform decryption on the encrypted data and convert the JSON data back into a Python dictionary.

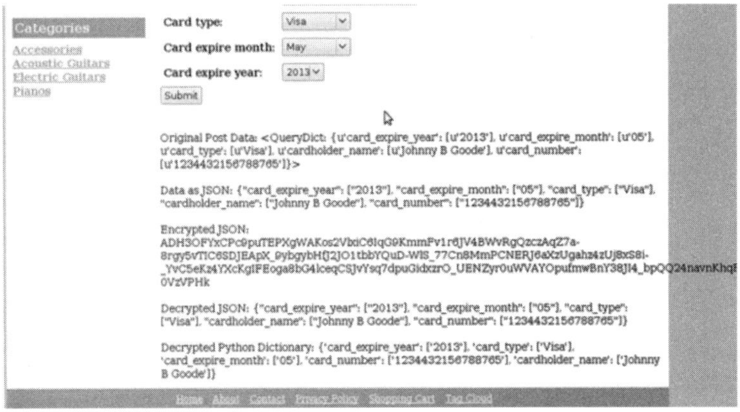

Figure 12-4. The output of processing the credit card form

You might wonder why we convert the data to JSON format, instead of just storing the QuerySet itself. One very good reason to make the extra effort and convert the POST data to JSON before storing it is portability; later, if the application is ever ported over to Ruby on Rails, or some other up-and-coming web framework, you don't want a bunch of arbitrary Django QuerySet data in your database, requiring you to decrypt everything and then convert it to some other programming language. Most major web frameworks have a means of dealing with JSON-formatted data, so you'll have an easy time dealing with the information once it's decrypted, no matter what platform you're on. Optionally, you could have chosen to store all of the data in XML format instead of JSON, using the XML document creation techniques we discussed in Chapter 5.

I also opted not to hook this particular credit card model into the admin interface. None of our employees really need access to the encrypted blobs of text data stored in our database. The only thing you might consider doing is adding the card's display number to the Order model admin page as an inline model.

How to integrate this new form and model that we've just created into the checkout process or My Account customer pages is an exercise left up to the reader.

Summary

The security battles between people who are trying to attack web sites and the developers responsible for securing those sites is an ever-escalating arms race. Keeping a site secure is not only a tricky thing to do for any site, but it's also not just one step you need to take while developing the site; it's an ongoing process. The types of attacks that crackers will use to try and compromise your site are sure to change, and you need to keep current and remain vigilant as long as your site is deployed, to ensure that your site doesn't succumb to any of these new attacks.

Security is a very diverse and extremely important topic. In this chapter, we covered a few of the basic security measures you can take when getting ready to deploy a Django site into production. We did not cover network security or how to harden the web server hosting your site, and this is certainly something you'll want to look into before actually deploying a site. If you're interested in learning more about the topics covered in this chapter, as well as other important programming security concepts, I'd recommend you take a look at *Foundations of Security: What Every Developer Needs To Know* by Neil Daswani, Christoph Kern, and Anita Kesevan (Apress, 2007).

Now that we've got that under our belt, we're going to turn our attention to another critical aspect of any highly trafficked web site: performance. In the next chapter, we're going to talk about caching and indexes, and how we can greatly reduce the query load on our database server.

CHAPTER 13

■ ■ ■

Improving Performance

A lot of web developers are fueled by delusions of grandeur. Sure, I'd like to think that, as a person, I have enough humility to make me a well-rounded and tolerable person in the presence of others. I'd like to think that my ego never gets in the way. But that's probably not entirely true. While I genuinely enjoy web programming as an intellectual challenge, some part of me is probably in this whole career field for the thrill of victory. For that moment when a project I've been hard at work on catches on in the collective minds of the world, and suddenly we're popping the bubbly and celebrating like kings of the world.

The first massive web project I ever worked on was started when I was very wet behind the ears. I believed, quite incorrectly, that if you created a database-driven web application, threw it up on a web server someplace, and threw some ads on the pages, that eventually, with some patience, the success would just *come to me*. I could just sit back, head of this new empire, and work on adding new features to the application as the demand for our product grew by leaps and bounds worldwide.

As we drew nearer to launch, I started doing research about how to make sure that the application could handle the load of several hundred visitors. Naturally, I started to grow concerned, and it quickly dawned on me that launching a site and meeting with any kind of success—that is, one visited by more than a several dozen people an hour—would just be the *start* of all the hard work. It was a critical piece of the development that I had, unfortunately for me, left until later in the development process, when I should have been doing it right from the start. Web development is comparatively easy. Developing a web application that is capable of scaling for large amounts of traffic is much more challenging. Not that this is a bad thing; I've often heard it said that performance problems are good problems to have, not least of all because it means that you've attained some respectable level of success with whatever it is you're doing.

This is not to say that you won't achieve success in running your e-commerce store, but only that scalability is important to consider early on. If you begin to get lots of traffic, the site might begin to suffer performance-wise. The more people visit your site, the harder your application, database server, and the hardware they're running on must work. In this chapter, we're going to talk about things you can do to make your site perform well under pressure. Most of this involves using a cache back end to reduce the number of times that your Django application needs to hit the database. We're also going to talk very briefly about how browsers load web pages, and how you can tweak the content of your site so that pages download faster.

A good portion of the performance tweaking you'll have to do to ensure that your application can handle your web traffic will depend largely on you, your application, and exactly what volume of traffic your site is getting. However, the techniques I'm going to talk about in this chapter should help the performance of just about any site.

The Database

In most web applications, the first bottleneck that will rear its ugly head will most likely be the database. Most highly-trafficked web sites have at least one database administrator responsible for tweaking queries, indexes, and other performance factors right at the database level. If you're not an expert database administrator, you might not be familiar with how things are working at a low level or what you can do in your Django application in order to help keep database load to a minimum.

As your site starts to get more and more web traffic, the database will probably start to feel the squeeze. It will start to get hit with queries for products, categories, products in a given category, product reviews, flat page data, and so on. If the sheer number of these queries gets too high, it's very possible that the customers using your site will start to notice that things are not running nearly as fast as they were before. The server will drag in the amount of time it takes to render and send pages to the browser.

The database in a Django web application is abstracted away below the Django ORM and the models in your project. This layer acts as a very simple interface to your data, allowing the developer to retrieve records from database tables almost as simply as if you were instantiating new objects in your Python code. Below this layer, however, there is still a database pumping away, doing the difficult task of serving up records at your web application's beck and call. It's important that you're cognizant of what the database is doing, and places where you can help lessen the load on its shoulders.

Searching your Models

When you retrieve data using model managers to get Django ORM objects, you are actually retrieving every single column from that corresponding database table. As one simple example, take the following query:

```
Product.objects.get(slug="grandmas-boy-dvd")
```

This translates roughly to the following SQL query being executed in your database:

```
SELECT * FROM products WHERE slug = "grandmas-boy-dvd";
```

This SQL statement isn't exactly what Django sends to the database. Instead of the wildcard character (*), the Django ORM actually lists every column in the table explicitly. It takes all of the data that it retrieves and creates a Django ORM model instance for each record it receives in response from the database.

Depending on what information you need to retrieve, this auto-generated query may be larger and more intensive than you really want. For example, imagine that you need to retrieve the e-mail address that is stored in the Django User model, and to do this, you retrieve the User instance via the get() method:

```
u = User.objects.get(username="joeyjoejoe")
email = u.email
```

The problem with this is that you are still sending a query to the database that is retrieving, constructing, and returning a large result set that is comprised of every column in the User table, just to get at the data in a single field. In order to just get at one or a few fields, you can list them explicitly using the values() method on the model manager:

```
u = User.objects.values("email").get(username="joeyjoejoe")
email = u["email"]
```

There is a slight drawback to using this method, however: it returns a dictionary for each model instance containing entries for each of the columns you specified in the values() method, instead of a full Django ORM object. This means that you can get at the data you need with a smaller query, but you can't call methods on your model instances. Take the pages on the site where we list product thumbnails. In these cases, we don't need every last field on the Product model for each instance; we only need a few fields to construct the thumbnail:

```
Product.active.values("name", "thumbnail").filter(...etc...)
```

Unfortunately, this won't do for a couple of reasons. First, we cannot retrieve the URL of the thumbnail image if we just get the thumbnail column in this fashion. Second, our thumbnail pages rely heavily on the use of the `get_absolute_url()` method on each model instance, in order to generate the link to the product page. In most cases, the Django ORM object will be what you want to use in your project, but there will be times when all you need is the data from one or two fields on a model, and in this case, using the dictionary provided by the `values()` method will save you a lot of database overhead.

Additionally, while it can be useful to use the `contains` and `icontains` matchers when making queries to retrieve certain records, this should not be done in every case. For example, the following query will return any products that contain "java" anywhere in the product description:

```
Product.active.filter(description__icontains="java")
```

This translates to the following:

```
SELECT * FROM products WHERE description LIKE '%java%';
```

This uses the percentage (%) wildcard character at the beginning and the end of the search string, so that it matches the string "java" if it's anywhere in the product description. However, if you don't need to scan the entire field in the database when looking for a match, you should use one of the other available ORM matchers, such as `startswith`, `endswith`, or `exact`. Don't just use `contains` because it matches everything. The use of the wildcard incurs a performance overhead, and so should be avoided in cases where it's not strictly needed.

Avoiding Expensive Joins

Very often in your web application, you will construct queries that return data from more than one table, or that need to evaluate data in more than one table in order to generate the result set. This type of query is done using a *join* between the two tables

The Django ORM makes it very easy to do joins in your queries, almost without thinking about it. Take the following query:

```
>>> Product.objects.filter(orderitem__order__user__username='smoochy')
```

This line of code is really simple, self-explanatory, and intuitive. If you understand the basic relationships we've created between the model classes throughout the rest of the book, then you should have no trouble grasping what this statement is doing. It will also give you what you want; namely, it will get all the products that the user with the username "smoochy" has ever ordered on the site. As easy and useful as this is, however, it also produces a fairly expensive SQL query that joins together four different database tables in order to get the data it needs. This query generates the following SQL query:

```
'SELECT 'products'.'id', 'products'.'name', 'products'.'slug', 'products'.'brand',
'products'.'sku', 'products'.'price', 'products'.'old_price', 'products'.'is_active',
'products'.'is_bestseller', 'products'.'is_featured', 'products'.'quantity',
'products'.'description', 'products'.'meta_keywords', 'products'.'meta_description',
'products'.'created_at', 'products'.'updated_at', 'products'.'image',
```

```
'products'.'thumbnail', 'products'.'image_caption' FROM 'products' INNER JOIN
'checkout_orderitem' ON ('products'.'id' = 'checkout_orderitem'.'product_id') INNER JOIN
'checkout_order' ON ('checkout_orderitem'.'order_id' = 'checkout_order'.'id') INNER JOIN
'auth_user' ON ('checkout_order'.'user_id' = 'auth_user'.'id') WHERE 'auth_user'.'username'
= smoochy  ORDER BY 'products'.'created_at' DESC LIMIT 21'
```

So how can you avoid making such expensive queries? You can structure the interface of your application to break up any of these expensive queries. For example, when the customer first logs in and is redirected to their "My Account" page, you can just display their list of orders to them, instead of the list of products that they've ordered. The query to get the list of orders is much smaller and only involves the use of two database tables instead of four. Then, if the customer is interested in seeing the products associated with any given order, they can click on that page and then load the products for that order. This is better because for each product page, you're only loading the products associated with that order. You're still querying data from three database tables, but the number of rows that you need to retrieve will end up being smaller for a single order than for a customer's entire order history.

However, maybe this is something that you just cannot avoid. Your boss tells you that you need to have a page for the customer that lists a summary of all the products that customer has ever ordered. In some cases, it might help you to break up the query into separate pieces, so that you only retrieve small chunks of results from the database at a time. This isn't terribly difficult to do, but it does take a few extra steps. For example, take the following two lines of code that make an earnest effort to retrieve the same results as the previous code, but with two separate database queries:

```
>>> order_ids = Order.objects.values('id').filter(user__username='smoochy')
>>> Product.objects.filter(orderitem__order__id__in=order_ids)
```

At a glance, this looks like it does what you want. However, remember that Django QuerySets are "lazy." Your database is only hit with the queries you construct when you actually evaluate the result set. Because of this, these two lines, which appear to be two separate queries, actually construct a very similar SQL statement that was generated by the single-line ORM query we made earlier. If you really want to break up a query to the database, you just need to force your code to evaluate the results you get after each query. You can do this with a simple for loop that uses the data to construct a new list. So, to break up our query:

```
>>> order_ids = [ ]
>>> for o in Order.objects.values('id').filter(user__username='smoochy'):
...     order_ids.append(o['id'])
...
>>> order_item_ids = [ ]
>>> for oi in OrderItem.objects.values('id').filter(order__id__in=order_ids):
...     order_item_ids.append(oi['id'])
...
>>> products = Product.objects.filter(orderitem__id__in=order_item_ids)
```

This results in three separate queries to the database: one to get the order IDs for the customer, one to get the IDs for the items in those orders, and a last one to retrieve the product instances associated with the IDs of those items. You haven't eliminated all of the joins, but you've reduced the number of them from three to one in your queries.

In this specific example, using three separate queries instead of a single one is probably not getting us any performance boost. In most cases, using the single, Django-generated query to get your data will be the approach you want. This is especially true in a situation where calls to the database server must be made by your application over a network. After each query, the database server has to transmit the results it generates over a network back to the server that's hosting your application. In this case, you definitely want to use the single-query approach because you want to reduce the additional network overhead that would result from three separate database queries.

However, you might encounter really huge queries that span multiple database tables that seem to be making your application drag its feet. In these cases, you might consider experimenting with several smaller queries instead of one huge one, to see if there is any gain in performance.

Creating Database Indexes

An index is an attribute on a database table that allows the database server to retrieve rows matching a given query more quickly. You create an index on a particular column. The index acts as a reference to its corresponding record, and the indexes are sorted by the contents of that column. You can think of an index as a means of "pre-sorting" data in a table by the contents of a particular column, without actually changing the order in which the records are stored in the database. When your database performs a lookup operation on that column to find matching rows, it can use the index to find those matching rows faster.

As one example, take the database table that contains the shopping cart items. Whenever a customer loads up their cart page, our application creates a query to retrieve the items where the cart_id field matches the cart ID that we retrieve from the customer's session. These items can be stored in any order, as several customers with different cart IDs might be adding items to their shopping carts on top of one another. Consequently, whenever you want to query out the items for a particular customer, the database has to scan the entire CartItem database table to find all records matching that customer's cart ID.

If we put an index on the cart_id column, the situation is drastically improved. Instead of having to scan every record in the table, the database uses the index on the cart_id column to retrieve the records. It will still have to scan the table until it finds the records that have the corresponding cart_id, but because of the index, it can stop the scan as soon as it encounters a record that doesn't match the cart ID it's looking for, since the cart IDs in the index are sorted already.

This "pre-sorting" is not the only mechanism that MySQL uses to make indexes fast. Internally, MySQL uses other algorithms that enable the lookup to use a B-tree, which is a good deal more efficient for searches than a top-to-bottom scan. If you're not familiar with B-trees, don't worry; all you really need to know is that when it comes to performance in database lookups, they are an unequivocal ally.

You might be wondering why we don't just sort the entire table by the cart_id column and store the records that way. There are a couple of reasons for this. First, it would slow down INSERT operations, as any new records created would have to be placed at a specific point in the table, relative to other records, based on an insertion sort algorithm. Second, and more importantly, you might want to have an index on more than one column in any given table. Since it's not possible to store the rows of a database table sorted by more than one column at a time, indexes afford you the ability to quickly look up data based on the contents of one or more columns.

So where should you use indexes? WHERE, indeed? There are no hard and fast rules about where to apply indexes, but as a general rule of thumb, you should apply and test indexes to columns that are used in the constraint part of your query, namely, inside of the WHERE clause. These are the columns that your database server will be scanning through in order to determine which rows in a table to return, which is the very operation that we're interested in speeding up. For example, take the following query made through the ORM to retrieve the cart items for a given cart ID:

```
CartItem.objects.filter(cart_id="abcdefghij")
```

This translates to:

```
SELECT * FROM cart_items WHERE cart_id = "abcdefghij";
```

In this case, the `cart_id` column is included in the WHERE clause of the generated SQL, meaning that we should consider creating an index on it. In order to create an index on a field, you can add a simple `db_index` argument to the model definition:

```
cart_id = models.CharField(max_length=50, db_index=True)
```

Now, when you run `manage.py syncdb`, an index will be created on the `cart_id` field. If you already have the table created, you'll need to go into your database and do this yourself.

```
mysql> CREATE INDEX 'cart_items_cart_id' ON 'cart_items' ('cart_id');
Query OK, 23 rows affected (0.02 sec)
Records: 23  Duplicates: 0  Warnings: 0
```

If you need to figure out the syntax, you can always just run the `manage.py sqlall` for your `cart` app and copy the line of output SQL that Django will use to create the index. One other very obvious place that we're lacking an index where it will likely affect performance is in our stats app, where we're logging product views for each customer with a given tracking ID, similar to the cart ID. Add an index to the `PageView` abstract base class, on the `tracking_id` field.

Another place where you can add indexes and get a potential performance boost is columns used in JOINs. If you've been following along in this book so far, most of the fields that are used in JOINs are already indexed for us. By default, Django creates an index on every default primary key ID field for each model, and any foreign key fields that reference those IDs.

So, which queries in your application could be improved with the use of indexes? Unfortunately, there is no automatic way of discerning exactly where you should be using indexes. There are some general guidelines you can follow, but you should add indexes one at a time, testing performance both before and afterward, instead of just indexing every column that you find used in a JOIN or WHERE clause and hoping that it will help matters.

Lastly, it is very important to note that while the use of database indexes does help performance, using too many indexes all over the place can definitely hurt you much more than it will help. Indexes can potentially consume a lot of disk space. Also, while indexing columns in the appropriate places does speed up data retrieval, it does slow down any write operations on the table, as the indexes have to be created or updated along with their corresponding records.

Deleting Old Data

While the use of indexes will greatly help queries on larger data tables, it can also be helpful to keep the data that you're storing to a minimum. Take the shopping cart: right now, items in the shopping cart are being deleted after a customer goes through the checkout process. However, there is nothing being done to remove the shopping carts that have been abandoned by customers who showed up, added things to their cart, and left the site without checking out. Your data table for shopping cart items might grow very large over time. Furthermore, because user sessions expire after 90 days of inactivity, we know it isn't likely that shopping carts that haven't been modified in 90 days will ever be retrieved by our web application.

Because of this, you want to give yourself a way to remove old shopping carts that have expired and will not be needed by customers any longer. In concept, this seems simple, but there's one catch: we cannot simply delete items that are greater than 90 days old. This ignores the possibility that someone keeps coming back to our site once a month and adds a new item each time. If they add five items over five months, and then we delete all the items over 90 days old, that person will return to find that two of the items have disappeared from their shopping cart!

While unlikely, this is something that we need to take into consideration. The workaround for this problem is to group the shopping cart items by their cart ID value, and use the `date_added` field of the most recently added or modified shopping cart item when doing our calculation. The code for doing this is simple enough. Add the following method to your `cart.py` file:

```python
from django.conf import settings
from django.db.models import Max
from ecomstore.settings import SESSION_AGE_DAYS
from datetime import datetime, timedelta

def remove_old_cart_items():
    print "Removing old carts"
    # calculate date of SESSION_AGE_DAYS days ago
    remove_before = datetime.now() + timedelta(days=-settings.SESSION_AGE_DAYS)
    cart_ids = [ ]
    old_items =
CartItem.objects.values('cart_id').annotate(last_change=Max('date_added'))
        .filter(last_change__lt=remove_before).order_by()
    # create a list of cart IDs that haven't been modified
    for item in old_items:
        cart_ids.append(item['cart_id'])
    to_remove = CartItem.objects.filter(cart_id__in=cart_ids)
    # delete those CartItem instances
    to_remove.delete()
    print str(len(cart_ids)) + " carts were removed"
```

First, we calculate the `datetime` value of 90 days ago, by using the Python `datetime timedelta` object and the number of days that sessions persist from our `settings.py` file. Then, we query out the cart ID of the shopping cart items grouped by the cart ID, and use the built-in `annotate()` ORM method to create an entry in our results dictionary called `last_changed`, which tells us when the customer with that shopping cart ID last modified or added an item to their cart. We further filter the results by taking only those cart IDs that haven't been modified in the last 90 days. Then, we create a list of those cart IDs, retrieve the cart items associated with those cart IDs, and then delete them.

Before this will work, we need to revisit the session expiration value in our `settings.py` file. This value, `COOKIE_SESSION_AGE`, takes a number of seconds as a value. In Chapter 4, when we specified that the length of our sessions would be 90 days, we multiplied out the number of seconds in a minute, by the number of minutes in an hour, and so forth, in order to calculate the number of seconds in 90 days. We just need to break out the day portion of this equation and give it its own constant:

```python
SESSION_AGE_DAYS = 90
SESSION_COOKIE_AGE = 60 * 60 * 24 * SESSION_AGE_DAYS
```

Now that we've created the function, the real question then becomes: how do we call this function? We can test it right now by dropping into a Python shell, importing the `cart` module, and then calling the function. However, this isn't really something that we'd want to do on a regular basis. For our application, we're going to hook up this new function so that you can delete the old shopping carts by making a simple call to the `manage.py` module that you've been using for other system administration tasks throughout the book. That way, you can make the following call from your shell to remove the carts:

```
$ python manage.py delete_old_carts
```

This actually isn't as difficult as it might sound, since Django makes it very simple to add your own functions to manage.py. First, you just need to create a subdirectory inside your cart app called management. Inside this new subdirectory, create a commands subdirectory. Add to both of these the obligatory __init__.py file to mark them both as Python modules. Inside the commands app, just create a Python file with the name of the function that you want to call from manage.py. In this case, create a file called delete_old_carts.py.

Before we start adding code to the file, here is how the directory structure should look in your cart app:

```
--cart/
  --management/
    --__init__.py
  --commands/
    --__init__.py
    --delete_old_carts.py
```

Inside the delete_old_carts.py file, you just need to create a class that inherits from one of the BaseCommand classes. There are two that you might want to use when creating your own manage.py commands: NoArgsCommand and AppCommand. AppCommands take the name of one of the apps in your project, like when you run manage.py sqlall [app_name] in order to see the SQL that will be used to create database tables. Since what we're doing doesn't require an app for an argument, this is not what we need here. Instead, we're going to create a subclass of NoArgsCommand:

```python
from django.core.management.base import NoArgsCommand
from ecomstore.cart import cart

class Command(NoArgsCommand):
    help = "Delete shopping cart items more than SESSION_AGE_DAYS days old"
    def handle_noargs(self, **options):
        cart.remove_old_cart_items()
```

For larger applications, adding common commands to manage.py is a good way of organizing the more common commands that developers need to use. One added benefit of this approach is that if we ever choose to distribute our cart app, the delete_old_carts command will go with it. However, it's probably debatable whether or not the delete_old_carts functionality really belongs as a part of the manage.py module. After all, it's more a site administrator task and isn't directly related to the development of the site. For this reason, you probably *should* be conservative about what functions you choose to hook into manage.py. Otherwise, you may end up with a large number of commands that have little to do with the site's configuration and more to do with the application you're developing. The deletion of old shopping carts has no business being alongside the dumpdata or syncdb commands, simply because it's specific to this particular project. For this one example and for simplicity, I choose to add this function to manage.py, instead of some other approach. Optionally, you could create a form to run the function somewhere in the admin interface templates.

If you need to maintain access to abandoned shopping cart information, say, for marketing purposes, you could take a different approach. Instead of just deleting the old carts, you could copy them to another model designed to hold old shopping cart data.

Caching with Memcached

Memcached[1] is an object-caching server that allows you to drastically reduce the number of times your Django web application needs to hit your database server in order to serve up content. Conceptually, you can think of Memcached as one big Python dictionary, in which you can store objects or lists of objects, identified by a unique key name you use to look the information up in the Memcached server. This is designed to take load off of the database server. When we need data, we can avoid a potential database hit by checking the cache for the data we want. If the object in question is found in the cache, we just use that. If the item isn't found in the cache, or if the item has expired in the cache, we then got to the database, get the data we need, and update the cache with a copy of the data for the next time.

The first thing you'll need to do before starting to use Memcached is to install the software required on your machine. Once you have the server itself installed on your system, you'll need to install bindings for Memcached that allow Python to be able to communicate with Memcached.

There are a couple of options; the first is the `cmemcache` module.[2] This option is the fastest, but if you're just starting out programming, I would recommend that you start with the slightly slower, but much easier to install, `python-memcached` module.[3]

Once you have the software installed, you just need to tell your project about it. Inside `settings.py`, add the following line to hook up our Memcached server:

```
CACHE_BACKEND = "memcached://127.0.0.1:11211/"
```

This tells our project that we have Memcached running on localhost, and can be accessed on port 11211. Of course, if you installed Memcached somewhere other than your local machine, you'll need to edit the configuration to match your own. In order to test that this is working properly, try running `manage.py runserver` from your shell. If the `CACHE_BACKEND` value is invalid, Django will tell you about it.

Memcached should be running after you install it, and requires a fixed amount of RAM allocated to it. By default, it will be running with 64 MB. You might want to tweak this setting based on the resources available to your system and how well the cache is performing on your site.

In this section, we're going to examine how you can make use of Memcached in your Django application. First, we'll look at the simple way of using caching in templates using the `{% cache %}` tag. Then we'll look at the more flexible means of using Memcached right in your Django view functions using Django's cache API.

The Virtue of Stale Data

As developers, we tend to over-estimate just how important it is to have the most up-to-date information display on our site. While we're developing, we're often troubleshooting issues with fetching data and using it in pages, and we develop a kind of affinity with changing information in the database and then seeing it change instantly on the site, the next time we reload the page. This situation is all well and good for development, but unfortunately, for a moderately trafficked web site in production, having the most recent data available to users of your site immediately is generally a luxury you cannot afford.

In a completely imaginary scenario I just cooked up in my head, pretend that your company web site has a category page with information that you plan to change with a ludicrous frequency of once a

---

[1] http://www.danga.com/memcached/

[2] http://gijsbert.org/cmemcache/

[3] ftp://ftp.tummy.com/pub/python-memcached/

day. (It's interesting that you have so much time on your hands...don't you have a company to run?) Let's imagine further that this page gets hit, on average, twice a minute. So 120 times each hour, someone loads the page. Without any caching functionality in place, the database server gets hit with the request for the category details, its products, and any other data on that page. This single page might be composed of more than one database query, so the number of actual database hits might be more than 120 per hour.

On the other hand, if you were to cache the items on that page and set it so that the cache was updated once every hour, then the number of requests for that page to the database drops from 120 to 1. Of course, there is still the risk that you might end up with some users who are viewing stale data. Imagine that you set the timeout in the cache to be one hour. If you change that category information right after the cache is updated, this means that potentially 120 users might see expired category data over the course of the next hour, until the cache is re-populated with the new information.

I would, of course, argue that the chances are very good that the people viewing these 120 stale requests won't really know or care that they're viewing old data. You're much better off with the caching in place so that your database server is free to do more important things that require real-time database interface, like, say, the checkout process. And later, in the section "Signals for Cache Invalidation," we're going to see that this isn't going to be a problem for us, since we can automatically update the cache if we modify a Category model instance.

Template Caching

Django comes equipped with a built-in cache template tag, which allows you to cache HTML fragments in your templates. Take the list of categories at the left side of each page, which is contained in `tags/category_list.html`. When each page is loaded, the template must hit the database in order to render the list of active categories. If you want to cache the HTML output of this tag, just add the following bit of template code to that file:

```
{% load cache %}

{% cache 3600 category_list %}
    {# template content here #}
{% endcache %}
```

This will cache the HTML output of the category links for one hour. To see this in action, go ahead and pull up a browser with the site running. If you start clicking on category pages, something should stand out. When we set up the category link list, we added styles so that if the customer was on the page for any given category, that category would not be rendered as a hyperlink in the sidebar. This isn't happening anymore. The reason for this is that the category links are no longer dynamic. They are as they appeared the first time you loaded the page with the cache tags in place, and will be for another hour.

Naturally, this solution is not going to work for us in this particular case. However, this solution can be applied to the list of `FlatPage` links in the footer. They're dynamic, but the actual HTML of the links doesn't change from page to page. This is the perfect place to actually use template caching. Open the `footer_links.html` template and add the caching tags, just as you see them in this section. Just give them a different name, such as `footer_links` instead of `category_list`. With this in place, you've saved a database hit for the flat page links on every page and saved the template rendering system some unnecessary work.

Template caching is useful at times, but for the most part, I believe the merits of putting your caching functionality right in the templates are few. Django templates are very slim files that are intended only to contain formatting for presentation with variables interspersed, and very little logic outside of a few {% if %} and {% for %} block statements. In most cases, handling caching in this fashion doesn't really separate logic from presentation, and won't really give you the kind of control that you need.

The Low-Level Cache API

Django provides a low-level means of interacting with your Memcached cache back end right in your Python code. The Django cache API allows you to perform the same Create, Read, Update, and Delete (CRUD) commands that you're allowed to perform on your database server. Django provides a very simple set of commands that allow you to manage information stored in your project's cache.

You can test the syntax from inside a Python shell in your project. In order to set a new item in the cache, you use the `set()` function, providing the cache key name and the value of the object you want to store:

```
>>> from django.core.cache import cache
>>> cache.set('cache_key', 'Value to store')
```

The `set()` function also takes a third parameter, an int value in seconds, which allows you to explicitly set how long the item in the cache will last before it expires. If you try to access the entry in the cache *after* the timeout window has passed, a value of `None` is returned instead.

Then, you can access this value using the `get()` function on the cache and passing in the cache key name:

```
>>> cache.get('cache_key')
'Value to store'
```

When you attempt to retrieve a value from the cache and find an entry corresponding to the key name that you entered, this is referred to as a *cache hit*. It's also possible that you might attempt to look up a key that doesn't exist in the cache, or a value with an expired timeout value (known as a *cache miss*), in which case you'll get a null value returned to you:

```
>>> cache.get('does_not_exist')
```

The `get()` function also takes a second argument, which is a default value that will be returned in the event of a cache miss:

```
>>> cache.get('does_not_exist', 'Value not found')
'Value not found'
```

In these latter few examples, the value that we stored was just a simple string. However, you're not limited to storing just string values. You can store entire model instances, too:

```
>>> product = Product.active.get(slug="ruby-axe-guitar")
>>> cache.set(product.slug, product)
>>> cache.get(product.slug)
<Product: Ruby Axe Guitar>
```

Then, to explicitly purge an item from the cache, just use the `delete()` function:

```
>>> cache.delete(product.slug)
```

The only thing you need to determine is how you will name the keys in your cache. You are free to use any value you like, but you must make sure that the name you choose will be unique for each item you plan to store in the cache. Otherwise, you might override another object in the cache if you try to set an item in the cache and there is a collision between different key names. Even worse, if you override a `Product` instance with a `Category` instance because they have the same cache key value, your code will run into some serious errors if it starts treating a `Category` instance as if it were a `Product` one.

The value you choose for key name should also be available in the context where you plan to query the cache. It doesn't help performance very much if the cache key value you choose to use for each model instance requires a database hit in order to fetch the cache key. For example, in the product page view, you can't use the ID field of the `Product` instance because you would have to query the ID from the database, and then query the cache. The goal is reduce the number of database hits, so this approach defeats the purpose of using the cache.

At a glance, it might seem like the slug field for each model is a good candidate, as they are guaranteed to be unique for each model instance and available in the view function. However, there is no guarantee that a `Product` instance and a `Category` instance will not share the same slug value. Furthermore, as you create more and more model classes with slug fields, the chances that there will be a naming conflict will increase with the mere use of the slug value.

A much better alternative is to use the slug field, along with something that identifies the model class. The easiest way to do this is to use the `get_absolute_url()` method you created on your model classes. This has the added benefit of being available in the context of the view functions without requiring a hit the database. As long as we've structured our URL entries to be unique for the model pages, they're also guaranteed to be unique for each model instance.

■ **Caution** According to the FAQ on the Memcache wiki,[4] the maximum key length is 250 characters. If your site contains unusually large URLs, you may need to modify your approach, as truncated URLs increase the likelihood that there will be a collision between two keys.

First, let's decide upon and set a timeout value for items in the cache. Inside your project's `settings.py` file, add the following line and set it to the number of seconds you would like to persist items in the cache. Here, I'm setting it so that items are kept in the cache for one hour:

```
# seconds to keep items in the cache
CACHE_TIMEOUT = 60 * 60
```

Open your `views.py` file for the `catalog` app and add the following code to the product view function to use Memcached to load products before falling back on the database:

```
from django.core.cache import cache
from ecomstore.settings import CACHE_TIMEOUT


def show_product(request, product_slug, template_name="catalog/product.html"):
    product_cache_key = request.path
    # get product from cache
    p = cache.get(product_cache_key)
```

---

[4] http://code.google.com/p/memcached/wiki/Start?tm=6

```
    # if a cache miss, fall back on database query
    if not p:
        p = get_object_or_404(Product.active, slug=product_slug)
        # store in cache for next time
        cache.set(product_cache_key, p, CACHE_TIMEOUT)
    categories = p.categories.filter(is_active=True)
```

You can replicate this logic for the show_category() view function just as easily:

```
def show_category(request, category_slug, template_name="catalog/category.html"):
    category_cache_key = request.path
    c = cache.get(category_cache_key)
    if not c:
        c = get_object_or_404(Category.active, slug=category_slug)
        cache.set(category_cache_key, c, CACHE_TIMEOUT)
    products = c.product_set.filter(is_active=True)
```

Now, let's revisit the category list on the side of the page. We decided that we couldn't cache the results right in the templates, but there's nothing to say that we cannot cache the results of the list of categories fetched from the database right in the inclusion tag function itself. Inside the catalog_tags.py file, modify the category_list() inclusion tag function so that it uses the cache first:

```
from django.core.cache import cache
from ecomstore.settings import CACHE_TIMEOUT

def category_list(request_path):
    list_cache_key = 'active_category_link_list'
    active_categories = cache.get(list_cache_key)
    if not active_categories:
        active_categories = Category.active.all()
        cache.set(list_cache_key, active_categories, CACHE_TIMEOUT)
```

Django Signals for Cache Invalidation

Of course, all of these solutions work well in the views, but they still leave us with the concern of stale data. If you update or delete a product, the page for that product won't vanish right away, but instead stick around until the entry for that product expires in the cache. It would be much nicer if, after an update or delete operation is performed on a model instance, the cache would be updated automatically.

Django actually does provide a very easy mechanism to handle this case, using *signals*. Django models come with a few built-in signals that we can use in our application: pre_save, post_save, pre_delete, and post_delete. These four signals on models are sent out pretty much when you would expect them to, given their names. In order to make use of them, we just need to register *receiver functions* for these signals. In the case of our Memcached server, we can set up receiver functions to update the cache when a product model instance is altered or removed.

For example, in our case, we want to make sure that the cache is updated whenever a product is updated. The two signals we can use for these two cases is post_save. Any receiver function that we register with post_save will only fire after a successful save operation. We don't want to use pre_save in this case, because we don't want to update the cache until we're sure that the save operation has completed.

Create an app called `caching` inside your project. Inside this new app, create a new file called `caching.py` and create the following two function definitions:

```
from django.core.cache import cache
from ecomstore.settings import CACHE_TIMEOUT

def cache_update(sender, **kwargs):
    item = kwargs.get('instance')
    cache.set(item.cache_key, item, CACHE_TIMEOUT)

def cache_evict(sender, **kwargs):
    item = kwargs.get('instance')
    cache.delete(item.cache_key)
```

Now, in order to make sure that these receiver functions get called after save and delete operations, we just need to register them with our models. Open your `catalog/models.py` file and add the following imports to the top of the file, and the signal connections to the bottom of the file after all of the model definitions:

```
from django.db.models.signals import post_save, post_delete
from ecomstore.caching.caching import cache_update, cache_evict

# model definitions here.

post_save.connect(cache_update, sender=Product)
post_delete.connect(cache_evict, sender=Product)
post_save.connect(cache_update, sender=Category)
post_delete.connect(cache_evict, sender=Category)
```

There's one last thing we need to do before this is complete: the caching functions are expecting each model instance to have a property named `cache_key`, which our models don't currently define. We can set this as a property on the model by adding the following function definition to both your `Category` *and* your `Product` model classes:

```
@property
def cache_key(self):
    return self.get_absolute_url()
```

Now, whenever we create, update, or delete a `Product` or `Category` instance, the cache will be updated with the new object. You can hook up this caching scheme to as many models as you would like. All you need to do is register the caching functions you just created with every model you want to use make sure that each model for which you would like to cache has a property named `cache_key` that is unique for each instance.

You can test that this is working by firing up a Python shell in your project:

```
>>> from ecomstore.catalog.models import Product
>>> from django.core.cache import cache
>>> product = Product.active.get(name="Ruby Axe Guitar")
>>> cache.get(product.cache_key)  # cache is empty
>>> product.save()
```

```
>>> cache.get(product.cache_key)  # product now in cache
<Product: Ruby Axe Guitar>
```

Notice, of course, that this will only work if you perform the update through the admin interface or a Python shell. If you make updates to your product data in a way that doesn't call the `save()` or `delete()` method on an instance, the cache won't be updated. For example, if you edit your data in bulk using Django's `update()` command, or from inside your MySQL shell or other database admin tool, those methods won't get called and the data in your cache will remain stale until it expires.

A Quick Word about Django Signals

Signals are an extremely useful tool for many things in a Django project, cache invalidation being just one of them. There are many places in your application that you might consider using one of the built-in signals. As one small example, refer back to Chapter 6 when we created our `UserProfile` class to store additional order information for each user. We created a `retrieve()` function, which first checks to see if an instance of `UserProfile` exists for the given user, creates it if does not, and then returns the instance to our view. Instead of doing the check-if-exists-and-create-if-it-doesn't logic every time the checkout view function loads, you can use Django signals to hook up a function to create a `UserProfile` instance each time a `User` model instance is created, which ensures that each user always has a profile.

Signals allow you to keep separate parts of your application decoupled. Take the `UserProfile`, for instance: it doesn't matter how many registration forms we have for creating `User` instances. If we hook up a `post_save` signal, the corresponding profile will always be created, saving you from having to duplicate the auto-creation of the profile each time you create a registration form.

Consult the Django documentation[5] for other signals that are built-in and how you can use them to keep your application flexible.

Front-End Engineering

Despite what people with always-on, high-speed Internet connections might tell you, bandwidth is still a limited resource for a lot of people. For this reason, page load time is still something you should consider when designing your pages. The focus here is on improving the experience that the customer has when they first come to your site. You don't want to spend lots of money on marketing just to have would-be customers come to your site and have to wait at least 30 seconds (which is a really long time) for your home page to load. The exact numbers vary by the speed of the Internet connection, but on average, after around eight seconds[6] of waiting for a web page to load, people start getting impatient and just assuming that the slow response is an indicator that something is wrong with the site, and they decide to go elsewhere.

There is one key concept that you need to be aware of to appreciate the problems we're going to address in this section: most HTML pages are not single documents that are downloaded all at once. When a user requests a product page on your site, for example, your Django application server will call the view function, load the necessary data from the database for that product, and render it all as part of the template. This rendered HTML template page is then returned to the customer and displayed in the browser window.

---

[5] http://docs.djangoproject.com/en/dev/topics/signals/

[6] Andrew B. King, *Website Optimization* (Sebastopol, CA: O'Reilly, 2008), p. 147.

However, this is far from the last step of the process. Once the customer has the rendered HTML page downloaded, the browser then goes through the HTML tags on the page looking for additional static media components, such as graphics, CSS style sheets, and JavaScript files. It then makes a subsequent HTTP request for each of these additional page components at the path specified in the HTML.

To help illustrate this concept, consider the following example. Generally, the extra components included in your HTML pages are fetched by the browser from your own server, under your own domain. However, this isn't required to make these requests work. If you included the URL of an image file on someone else's site in the `src` attribute of an image tag on your site, then the browser would request the image from that URL when the page was loaded. For example, if you include the following image tag on your site, the page will load and display the logo from the Google homepage:

```
<img src="http://www.google.com/intl/en_ALL/images/logo.gif" alt="Google logo" />
```

While this is entirely possible, it's definitely a bad idea. Loading images from someone else's site for use in your own pages is known as "bandwidth stealing," and is certainly bad practice. For one thing, you lose control of what is being displayed on the page. What if Google changes the location of their logo and removes the old one? Your own site will be left with an empty "Missing Image" error. Even worse, when you use someone else's images, you are at the mercy of the person controlling the content you're stealing. Some webmasters will, upon discovering that someone is stealing their content, replace the images on their own site with new files and change the old ones to contain obscene words or images. More importantly, you also open yourself up for being sued for infringing on someone else's copyright.

The point here is not that you can save on bandwidth by using someone else's images; the point is that graphics on your page are not part of the HTML page that the user downloads. In the Google example, we don't embed Google's logo in our page. You didn't download a copy of it and put it on your server. It's just being requested from Google's servers by the browser each and every time the page is loaded.

And here's the kicker: the majority of the load time for a web page lies in the downloading of these external components, and *not* in the HTML page itself.

This behavior shouldn't come as a surprise to anyone who was using a dial-up Internet connection back in the 1990s. Back then, web surfing was fraught with excessive wait times. You would navigate to a page, the text on the page would load, and then you'd sit back and wait for the images to load and fill in the content of the page. These subsequent HTTP requests for additional page components are also the mechanism that allows attackers to carry out Cross-Site Request Forgery attacks, which we discussed in Chapter 12.

Now, all of those components might not be downloaded with each and every page requested by a single customer. Browsers are capable of caching static media files on the client side. Imagine the first time that a brand new customer finds their way onto your site. They will load the homepage, and the browser will then download the CSS, scripts, and graphics needed to render that page. A lot of these items will be stored in the browser's cache for future requests. That way, when the user clicks on each product page, the browser will first check its cache for each additional component. If it finds the needed style sheet or graphic in the cache, it will use that one. If the object isn't present in the cache, then the browser will make an HTTP request to the server.

For the most part, the HTML, CSS, JavaScript, and graphics files for your site are what they are. While it may seem that there is little you can do in order to make things run faster for the user, there actually are steps you can take to improve the user experience without changing much of your actual code. The factors that you should consider when architecting the pages on your site fall into three categories:

- Move CSS and JavaScript into separate files.

- Reduce the number of external components.

- Optimize the external components.

In this section, we're going to look at these factors and how they affect the HTML, CSS, and JavaScript files of your site. Our foray into front-end engineering will not be comprehensive, but if you're interested in learning more about how to speed up your site, I'd refer to the Yahoo! performance guidelines[7] on which this section is based.

Move CSS and JavaScript Into Separate Files

CSS and JavaScript code can be placed right inside your HTML page, in `style` and `script` tags within the `head` element. For very small sites, it might be perfectly fine to include a few little bits of code embedded right in each page. But as the site grows, you'll find that you're repeating yourself across multiple pages. The same basic CSS styles are required to make the navigation look the way you want, and this CSS is inside every single page. Aside from the fact that if you ever need to edit the CSS you'll have to do it in more than one place, these extra bytes of CSS style text are making every page much heavier than it needs to be. Why should we worry about how "heavy" each page is? Simply put, the more bytes that you have crammed into an HTML page, the longer it will take for a person to download it. It will increase the wait time for each person trying to load the pages of your site.

Of course, if we move all of the CSS and JavaScript from your HTML page and put them into separate files, this doesn't actually reduce the number of bytes that the user needs to download in order to view your page. However, it does help the *progressive rendering* of the page. The actual HTML page will be downloaded first, and then each of the additional style sheets and JavaScript files included in the page will be downloaded. It doesn't reduce the overall size of things but it does help give the user some visual feedback much quicker.

Keeping all of your CSS and JavaScript out of your HTML pages also has some serious SEO benefits. The Google spiders don't view your page the same way that human users do. When they load a page from your site, they are looking for the content on that page to get a sense of what the page contains. You want to make sure that the actual content of your page is as close to the top of the page as possible. If you have loads of CSS and JavaScript in the `head` element of each page, then Google has to crawl through all of that extra junk at the top of the HTML document in order to get to the body element.

This is the approach that we have taken in this book so far. We have broken out our CSS and JavaScript files into separate files that are included in the HTML pages of our site.

Reduce the Number of External Components

Of course, now that we know splitting our CSS and JavaScript out into separate files is a good thing to do, we have to consider the flip side of the same coin: can you ever have too many external files? Naturally, just as you can cram too much into your HTML pages themselves, you shouldn't have an excessive number of external page components, either. Remember, bandwidth is a bottleneck, and each of those additional components requires an HTTP request and response that must be transmitted over the network. There is a lot of overhead associated with each request and response, so it's very important that you keep the total number of requests to a minimum.

When we look at reducing the number of external components, we should consider how many there are on a *per-view* or a *per-template* basis. Think about your product page: there might be tons of JavaScript functions in your `base.js` file making the elements on your product page sing and dance for your customers. Most of the JavaScript that we have in that file right now is for the Ajax functionality we created for the product page in Chapter 10. However, the `base.js` file is downloaded when each new customer visits the home page for the first time.

---

[7] http://developer.yahoo.com/performance/rules.html

There is an obvious tradeoff in this situation. When the user ends up clicking through the home page to a product, the product page will load faster because the JavaScript functions required for the product page were already loaded when the user visited the home page. This added speed comes at the expense of making the initial load time of the home page slower. There's also a mistaken assumption here: that the customers will always enter your site through the home page. In an e-commerce site, you will likely use your product pages as *landing pages* for marketing purposes. In truth, you really have *no* idea exactly where any given customer is going to enter your site.

For much larger projects, instead of lumping all of your JavaScript functions into a single massive file, consider breaking them up into separate files and making them available to the pages of your site on a per-template basis, as they are needed. Django makes this extremely simple; just create a template block section at the bottom of your base template file where you can include script tags referencing external JavaScript files:

```
<script src="/static/scripts/base.js" type="text/javascript"></script>
{% block other_scripts %}{% endblock %}
```

Then, move all of the JavaScript that is specific to your product page out of your `base.js` file and put it into another JavaScript file called `product.js`. Inside your `product.html` template file, add the follow below the `content` block:

```
{% block other_scripts %}
    <script src="/static/scripts/product.js" type="text/javascript"></script>
{% endblock %}
```

There will be JavaScript functions that are required by every page. For example, there is the function to validate the contents of the search box when the form is submitted. This JavaScript should be included in every page. We'll put these types of JavaScript functions into our `base.js` file. In this way, for any given template, there should be no more than two external JavaScript file downloads required for any given page.

You can also apply the same solution to the CSS file. While we have one relatively small file at the moment, you might consider breaking out the styles into separate style sheets and including them in your templates on an "as needed" basis in the same way.

Optimize External Components

After the browser has downloaded an HTML page, it goes through the contents of the page in order, from top to bottom, looking for external components that it needs to download to finish rendering the current page. One very important thing you should do in order to optimize this process for the user experience is to move all of your CSS link includes to the top of the page, at the very top of the head tag, and put all JavaScript script includes at the bottom of the page, just before the closing body tag.

Let's look at both of these one at a time. First, you want the CSS to be loaded before the rest of the page because you want the styles available to the page before the content starts loading. Have you ever visited a web site and had a brief view of bare, un-styled HTML load before you, and then a few seconds later the entire layout, styles, and appearance of the page suddenly change in a flash? This is because the content of the page was loaded before the style sheet. The gap in time between the two might not be noticeable over a fast Internet connection, but for slower connections, it's very apparent to the end user.

For this reason, make sure that the link elements that are hooking in your style sheet files are close to the top of your head tag, only below the Content-Type meta tag in your head element.

JavaScript files are exactly the opposite. They can be large files that take an awfully long time to download. Having these files at the top of your web pages can drastically increase the amount of time that it takes for the entire page to load, as the content is downloaded only after *all* of the components above it have finished downloading. In almost all cases, excluding those times when you need a script to be present before the content of the page, you'll want to keep all your JavaScript files as the very last thing on each page.

Summary

In this chapter, we touched upon the practices that Django developers can use in order to speed up the performance of their site. In most cases, the database will be the item that causes most of your grief when the site climbs in the search pages and you start getting steady amounts of traffic to your pages. However, this is not the only potential bottleneck. If the database tweaks don't yield any improvements, you might try profiling other aspects of your application, such as the Python code itself, to make sure that there aren't any blocks of code that are performing poorly. For the most part, however, as long as you cache all the database query results that you can, and set the timeouts to be as long as you can manage, the performance of your site should be fairly smooth; that is, until Slashdot writes an article about your site, prompting you to get so many hits an hour that your web server literally catches fire. (That's a bridge you can cross when you come to it.)

In the next chapter, I'll talk about an absolutely critical stage of the development of any application: testing. We're going to look at how the Django testing client can help you automate testing the functionality of your application.

CHAPTER 14

∎∎∎

Django Testing

In order to facilitate the production of higher-quality code (and maintain the sanity of developers), Django comes equipped with an automated testing suite. Writing perfect code is next to impossible. It can be done, but there's a very good reason that computer keyboards have a "Backspace" key on them: people make mistakes. While a few developers probably like to think that they embody super-human qualities such as never writing faulty code, the simple truth is that we all make mistakes without realizing it at first.

In this chapter, we are going to take a look at the Django test suite and how you can use it to ensure that the code you've written for your web site is behaving the way you expected. We're going to write two kinds of tests: unit tests and functional tests. There are several other kinds of tests that might be done on a much larger web application, such as browser, regression, usability, integration, acceptance, performance, and stress tests. However, for simplicity in this introductory chapter, we're just going to stick with unit and functional tests. For small- to medium-sized web sites, these two kinds of tests are likely to catch most of the bugs that might get introduced in your code.

Django also comes equipped with another type of test that you can write: *doctests*. Doctests are little snippets of code that resemble the interaction you might see inside your Python shell. You put these tests inside the docstring on your models and, when the test runner executes, it will attempt to execute the bits of code you have in the docstring and check to make sure that the results it gets when it executes those lines are the same as the results you have written in your docstring.

Doctests can be very useful in some cases, but I'm not going to cover them in this chapter. This is largely because I haven't ever encountered a type of test I wanted to do but couldn't do with the Django testing framework instead of a doctest. Furthermore, at the risk of starting a Python flame war, I believe that doctests are clutter inside your application's docstrings, which are really intended to serve as comments that describe what your code is supposed to do. On the whole, I felt that focusing our efforts on the regular Django testing framework in depth instead of trying to include doctests basics would yield you a higher return on your invested time.

While writing tests for a Django web application is not terribly difficult, learning how to manage the state of them can be a difficult task. We're going to write functional tests to make sure that the interface is behaving the way you would expect, and write unit tests to ensure that the behavior of your models is the way you would expect. Lastly, we'll write some basic security tests to make sure that the measures we took in Chapter 12 are in place and working as we would expect them to be.

Why We Test

Even if you are some superstar developer who is able to produce hundreds of lines of bug-free code a day, there is still the problem with the interrelated parts of your web application. That is, the dependencies in one app rely on the code that runs in another app someplace else. Sure, you can take great pains to architect your code so that all the separate parts are loosely coupled, but that won't completely eliminate the problem. Testing makes the maintenance of a large application much easier. When you edit one app, you can potentially break the code in other places on your site, and because it's just not feasible to manage all of these dependencies inside your head, you need to test your code.

This might not sound like a very big problem in theory, but as your application grows in complexity, so too does the need for testing. Imagine that customers can add products to their shopping cart from the product page, from product thumbnails, and from their wish list pages. You make a small change to how products get added to the shopping cart, and you update the product page and product thumbnail template...but you forget about the wish list page. One month later (in this story, not many people are using your wish list pages), a customer complains that they're having trouble adding products to the cart from their wish list, leaving you with the task of figuring out what's wrong.

There's a problem with this. I don't know about you, but I have trouble remembering details about the code that I wrote an *hour* ago. I can drudge up the memory and the logic behind what I did pretty easily, but I still need to drag the waters. One *whole month later*, and there's no recovering the logic behind what I did from my own head. At that point, I have to approach the code I wrote as though it were someone else's code. I just need to read through it and dissect what's it's doing, which tends to be much more difficult than fixing code when it's fresh in your mind.

The moral is that new bugs are much easier to deal with if you catch them earlier rather than much later. Preferably, all the automated tests are run every time you make a change,before you check your code into your version control repository, to ensure that your changes haven't broken any existing functionality. Lots of coding methodologies, like agile development practices, have the writing of tests baked right into the procedure. I don't really think it matters what coding method your organization uses; writing tests is immensely helpful to the production of quality code, regardless of the rest of your process.

Adding automated testing to your code is probably just one more step in a testing process you already do without realizing it. Whenever you write the code for a new web page, the first thing you do is fire the page up in a browser to make sure that everything is formatted correctly and appears the way you intended it to. Writing Python code to test the state of your application for you is this kind of manual testing on steroids. It's faster, more thorough, and it's easy. And when you take the trouble to make a process easy for yourself, you're much more likely to do it.

However, I don't want to spend lots of time in this chapter trying to convince you of *why* you should be writing tests. If I haven't piqued your curiosity by this point, then chances are I won't be able to.

Ideally, we would have been writing tests for our code right from the start, adding them in conjunction with each piece of our application to ensure that we had test coverage for every part. I opted not to do this, simply because the flow of the book would have been hampered had I included tests in every chapter. However, in a real-world application (and a much more perfect book, perhaps), I would have been writing my tests right alongside my models, views, and templates, every step of the way. Getting started now, in any case, is better than not doing it at all.

How to Test Code

One of the tenets of the Test-Driven Development methodology is that the developer should write the test code first, run it with the expectation that they will fail (because the actual code doesn't exist yet), write the actual code, and then re-run the tests with the expectation that they will succeed. I've never really been able to get my brain around coding in this fashion... although in the agile development world, writing tests first makes sense, particularly if you're coding without any written specification. Writing tests before writing code forces you to *design* what you're going to write. In spite of this, I still don't think writing tests first really replaces the need for a spec up front... but to each their own. Personally, I don't start coding until I have a specification and I write my tests after I write the code, but that doesn't make it the right approach 100% of the time. Use whatever techniques you find help you test your code effectively.

Writing tests is all about gauging expectations. When the code you've written runs, what do you *expect* to happen? At the most basic, here is how you can approach writing tests:

1. Determine the state of things before any action is taken, list the characteristics, and test them.

2. Write code to execute the action in question.

3. Determine which characteristics the action in #2 should have altered, and test that they've changed.

That three-step process is a little esoteric. Let's consider a very simple case to test a customer coming to our site and logging in. We first expect that the user will not be authenticated, so we check their session and make sure that it doesn't contain any authentication data. Then, we emulate the event of the customer logging into the site. Finally, we check that the customer's session now has valid authentication data in it.

While tests can get much more complicated than this, and you'll find yourself testing multiple things in the "before" and "after" stages of each action, the basic strategy remains the same: to determine that your application is responding to inputs the way you expect.

Creation of the Test Database

The Django test runner should not run tests on your development or production database. Often, you'll want to run tests that perform creation, manipulation, or deletion of large amounts of data in your database, and you don't want all of these changes to persist after your test suite has run. For this reason, Django creates a separate database on which to run your project's tests. This database is given the same name as your development database, prefaced with test_.

When the Django test runner tries to access to the test database, it will use the same credentials stored for your production database. Right now, the MySQL user in our settings.py file doesn't have permission to create a new database named test_ecomstore, let alone the permissions to create tables and start mucking around with the data. For this to work, we need to first make sure that the MySQL login our project uses has permission to create and manipulate the test database. Inside of MySQL, run the following two commands:

```
mysql> CREATE DATABASE test_ecomstore;
mysql> GRANT ALL ON test_ecomstore.* TO 'ecomstore'@'localhost';
```

Now the test database is created, and our project will be allowed to access it when tests are run.

Python & Django Test Methods

To aid in testing, Python and Django offer default test methods that allow you to check the conditions of your application while the tests are running. These allow you to assert that certain things are true at any given point, or to cause the test to fail if the condition you're testing for is not met.

Some of the more common and useful test methods available on the basic Python unittest.TestCase instance are listed in Table 14-1.

301

Table 14-1. The Python unittest.TestCase testing methods

Method Name
assertEqual(actual, expected)
assertFalse(expression)
assertNotEqual(actual, expected)
assertRaises(ExceptionClass, method)
assertTrue(expression)
failIf(expression)
failIfEqual(actual, expected)
failUnless(expression)
failUnlessEqual(actual, expected)

Some of these are functionally equivalent. For instance, using `failUnless()` and `assertTrue()` are both testing that the argument you've passed in evaluates to `True`. Any Python value that evaluates to `False` will cause the test to fail. When there is more than one option available to you, use the one that's most logical for the given situation. As one simple guideline, try to avoid double negatives. For example, instead of this:

```
self.failUnless(not logged_in)
```

just reverse the logic of the process. If you really expect the `logged_in` variable to have a value of `False`:

```
self.assertFalse(logged_in)
```

This will greatly enhance the readability of your testing code. All of these methods take an optional string parameter after the required arguments, which is a message that will be displayed when the expression fails. For example:

```
self.assertFalse(logged_in, 'User is logged in!')
```

There are also available test methods on the enhanced Django `TestCase` class, which inherits from the Python `unittest.TestCase` class. These extra methods are designed to help you use the Python `unittest` base class in order to write tests that check conditions specific to the web environment, such as the flow between pages, form errors given invalid input, and templates used to render view responses:

Table 14-2. *The Django TestCase testing methods*

Method Name
assertRedirects(response, url)
assertFormError(response, form, field, [error1, error2…])
assertTemplateUsed(response, template_name)
assertTemplateNotUsed(response, template_name)
assertContains(response, value)
assertNotContains(response, value)

The good news is that if you're a Python developer and you've been using the unittest base class for writing unit tests, starting to use the Django TestCase subclass for web testing will be a very easy transition for you. If the Django TestCase methods still don't make much sense to you at this point, keep on reading. We're going to use all of them in the tests we're going to write in this chapter.

Anatomy of a Test Class

So when you create your test classes, where should you put them? If you're using at least Django 1.1, the easiest thing to do is simply to put them in the tests.py file that Django creates inside every app in your project. If you're using an earlier version of Django, you can easily create tests.py files for your apps manually. When you run the test runner, it will look in each of your INSTALLED_APP directories and load any test classes that it finds inside your tests.py files.

Inside these files, you define test classes that inherit from the Django TestCase class, and create methods inside each test class. When you run the test runner, each class is instantiated and each of the test methods inside the class runs. Here is how an example test class you define might look:

```
class MyTestClass(TestCase):
    def test_something(self):
        pass

    def test_something_else(self):
        pass
```

Test methods are prefaced with test_. Test classes can contain other helper methods that don't start with test_ that can be called by test methods, but these are not called by the test runner directly. In the context of test methods, the pass placeholder keyword for empty Python blocks takes on a logical, more literal meaning.

When you write your tests, it helps immensely if you give them descriptive names that describe exactly what part of your application their testing, as well as the nature of the response that you're expecting. That way, when you run your tests and one of the test methods encounters a failure, you'll have some context about the problem that was encountered just by reading the name of the test method that failed.

Testing the Product Catalog

So let's start by writing a few small sample tests for our application, to see how the test methods and Django test classes are designed to be used. These first tests that we're going to write are not really unit tests in the strictest sense of the word. They are more *functional tests*, because we're testing that our application is working as expected when a user is browsing the product catalog. We'll get to some basic unit tests for our models a little later.

In this section, after writing some rudimentary tests for a new customer accessing the home page, we'll look at how to run Django tests. We'll also look at how overriding the setUp() and tearDown() methods on test classes can reduce the repetition in your tests, by giving you a simple means of defining code that runs before and after each method.

Writing Functional Tests

First, let's consider the simplest of all cases: a new user comes to the site, not logged in, and loads the catalog home page. What kinds of things can we expect to happen in this case? Well, we expect that the home page will load without any errors, so we can check the status code of the response and make sure that it's the 200 that's indicative of a success. Open the tests.py file in your catalog app. If there is any placeholder code in there already that Django added when it created the app, you can remove all of it and replace it with the following:

```
from django.test import TestCase, Client
from django.core import urlresolvers

import httplib

class NewUserTestCase(TestCase):
    def test_view_homepage(self):
        client = Client()
        home_url = urlresolvers.reverse('catalog_home')
        response = client.get(home_url)
        # check that we did get a response
        self.failUnless(response)
        # check that status code of response was success
        # (httplib.OK = 200)
        self.assertEqual(response.status_code, httplib.OK)
```

Inside this new test class, we create a new instance of the Django client test class, Client, which is designed to help simulate the actions of a user. We make our new Client instance request our home page, using the get() method on our test client instance. There are two methods you can call on the test client instance in order to make requests to pages in your test methods: get() and post(). Each makes the request using its corresponding HTTP verb, and both take the URL path of a page on your site. Mostly, we're going to use get() to emulate catalog browsing, but later we'll use post() to test form submissions.

We check to see that a response was returned, and that the status code indicates a success. Notice that we're using the urlresolvers module in order to get the URL path of the homepage before we navigate to it. This is very useful and, just like in our actual web application, makes our code much less prone to 404 Page Not Found errors due to simple typos. Also, if we ever choose to update our URL entries to be something different, the tests won't break because of it.

Also notice that instead of hard-coding the value of 200 to check for the status code, we're falling back on the `httplib` module to provide the numerical HTTP status codes for us, looking them up by their enumerated names. Table 14-3 shows the names of the status codes that you'll be using most frequently in testing your application.

Table 14-3. httplib HTTP Common Status Codes

Status	HTTP Status Code
httplib.OK	200
httplib.MOVED_PERMANENTLY	301
httplib.FOUND	302
httplib.FORBIDDEN	403
httplib.NOT_FOUND	404

In order to run these tests and ensure that users can, in fact, load our home page, let's take the test runner for a spin right now. To run the tests for a single app in your project, you can use the syntax `manage.py test [app name]`. Run the following in your shell:

```
$ python manage.py test catalog
```

You should see a lot of code output that's creating all of the tables and indexes for the test database, and then some output about how your tests succeeded. If there were any errors in the syntax of your code, the test runner will fail to start up. You cannot test a project that won't run under normal circumstances.

Note When you run your tests for the first time, you may get an error about the test database already existing, and a prompt for a "yes/no" about whether it should try and create it. This is because we created the database `test_ecomstore` earlier in the chapter manually. Remember, the test database is created at the start of each run and then dropped at the end. If you ever interrupt the test runner before it has a chance to get to the last step (say, by using Ctrl-C), then it will get confused the next time it starts because it wasn't expecting the database to exist already. As a courtesy, it prompts you before overwriting this existing database. In most cases, and in this one as well, you'll be all right typing "yes".

You can run tests for your entire project by merely omitting the name of the app from this call in your shell. If you run this, however, it may take a little while, as all the tests bundled with Django will be run in addition to your own tests:

```
$ python manage.py test
```

Before we go much further, I should point out one very important test method that the Python and Django test cases provide: the `setUp()` method. When you run your tests, the Django test runner will call the setUp() method on each test class instance before it runs any of the test methods. This is useful in cases where you want to create variables that will be used across multiple test methods.

Take our test Client class: as we start adding test methods, we'll find ourselves creating an instance of this class in every method. Instead of all this repetition, we can simply instantiate the Client class once, in the setUp() method of the class, assign the instance as a *variable* on the test class, and use that client instance on the class in our test methods. So, to refactor the work we just did:

```
class NewUserTestCase(TestCase):
    def setUp(self):
        self.client = Client()

    def test_view_homepage(self):
        home_url = urlresolvers.reverse('catalog_home')
        response = self.client.get(home_url)
        # check that we did get a response
        self.failUnless(response)
        # check that status code of response was success
        self.assertEqual(response.status_code, httplib.OK)
```

The setUp() method can contain assertions and tests for failures itself. As a practical means of demonstrating this point, let's add code that tests to ensure that the user is not authenticated. We can check this by looking at their session data. Authenticated users will have an entry named _auth_user_id in their session dictionary, while anonymous users won't have this yet. We can retrieve this from the Django auth module, by grabbing the SESSION_KEY constant:

```
from django.contrib.auth import SESSION_KEY

class NewUserTestCase(TestCase):
    def setUp(self):
        self.client = Client()
        logged_in = self.client.session.has_key(SESSION_KEY)
        self.assertFalse(logged_in)
```

The setUp() method is run before each test method in the class. As an illustration of this, the following test class will run successfully without any failures:

```
class ExampleTestCase(TestCase):
    def setUp(self):
        self.my_value = 1

    def test_setup_method(self):
        self.my_value = 0

    def test_setup_method_2(self):
        self.assertEqual(self.my_value, 1)
        self.failIfEqual(self.my_value, 0)
```

If, in the course of running the setUp() method, the test runner encounters any failure or exceptions in the code, the test will return an error response and it will be assumed that the test has failed. There is also a corresponding tearDown() method, which runs after all of the test methods, and is useful for performing any cleanup operations on data that you don't need.

Go ahead and re-run the tests for the catalog app a second time, to make sure that these few additions correctly assert themselves without any unexpected problems.

Managing Test State with Fixtures

Now let's test some of the other pages, which are bound to be a bit more complex than the home page. Let's add a single test method for navigating to an active category page. Add this method inside your tests.py file:

```
from ecomstore.catalog.models import Category

class NewUserTestCase(TestCase):
    ... code omitted here ...

    def test_view_category(self):
        category = Category.active.all()[0]
        category_url = category.get_absolute_url()
        # test loading of category page
        response = self.client.get(category_url)
        # test that we got a response
        self.failUnless(response)
        # test that the HTTP status code was "OK"
        self.assertEqual(response.status_code, httplib.OK)
```

Now if you go back and run the tests for the catalog app, you should get some interesting results. While the test database is still created and the tests run, you should see a message about a failure we encountered when the test suite was trying to load one of the categories. This is because our test database is empty by default. While the categories table does exist, it doesn't contain any category data. Because we're trying to get the zero-index on an empty result set, an IndexError is raised trying to get the category.

Testing a data-driven dynamic web site without any data won't be sufficient for our purposes. In order to populate your test database schema with some actual data you can reference in your test methods, you *could* create new objects from scratch right in your setUp() method, using the standard Django ORM methods. However, this is a lot of extra typing you need to do, and clutters up your test classes with all kinds of code that does little more than create some basic classes.

A much superior approach to loading initial data is to use *fixtures*. Fixtures are test files that reside in your project's apps folders, containing JSON or YAML-formatted data that conforms to the schema of your database tables.

Django provides a means for you to create fixtures from your test database, by simply dumping the data from the database you've been using for development all along. If, at this point, your product database already contains thousands of products, you might not want to run this, since it might take a while to run. If that's the case, simply choose another app that has a small amount of data in it, and run this command:

```
$ python manage.py dumpdata catalog --indent=2
```

This produces some nicely formatted JSON text that we can use as fixtures in our test cases. The dumpdata command dumps JSON data by default, but you can also choose YAML as the outputted format if you'd prefer. Inside your catalog app, create a new subdirectory called fixtures. Then, go back and run this command to dump the data into that directory, into a file named initial_data.json:

```
$ python manage.py dumpdata catalog --indent=2 > catalog/fixtures/initial_data.json
```

This will create a fixtures file that contains all of the categories, products, and product reviews currently in our development database. The file name initial_data (followed by any extension for a data format that Django supports for fixtures, such as .json or .yaml) means that the test runner will load this data into the test database after it creates the test database and before it runs any test methods.

You're free to edit this file by hand. As a matter of fact, in order to test that our ActiveProductManager is working, we should make sure that at least one of the products in our fixtures file has its is_active field set to False. Open the new initial_data.json file, choose one of the catalog.product model records, and make sure that at least one has is_active set to 0, which is False in JSON. (At this point, I'm assuming you have more than one product in your database.) When you run Django tests, any fixtures found in your apps is loaded into the database. Fixtures are loaded before each test is run, so you are free to wipe out all existing data in one of your test methods, even though other subsequent test methods might depend on this data. For example, given an initial_data.json file that contains fixtures with Product model data in them, the following two tests succeed:

```python
from ecomstore.catalog.models import Product

class MyTestCase(TestCase):
    def test_delete_all(self):
        for p in Product.objects.all():
            p.delete()
        # check that the data
        self.assertEqual(Product.objects.all().count(),0)

    def test_products_exist(self):
        self.assertTrue(Product.objects.all().count() > 0)
```

Fixtures can also be specified in each test class, by passing in a list of fixture file names to a property of the test class called, aptly enough, fixtures. The following will scan the project's fixtures directories for any fixture files with these names:

```python
class MyTestCase(TestCase):
    fixtures = ['products', 'categories']

    def test_something(self):
        # test stuff here
```

Including the extension of the fixture file is optional. In this case, the test runner will look for any files that have valid fixture extensions, such as .json or .yaml, and load them into the test database before running any test methods for that class.

Category Testing

So, now that we have some fixtures in place, let's get back to the category testing that we were trying to do before. Inside `tests.py` in your catalog app, add the following lines to the test class we created in the last section:

```
class NewUserTestCase(TestCase):
    ... code omitted here ...

    def test_view_category(self):
        category = Category.active.all()[0]
        category_url = category.get_absolute_url()
        # test loading of category page
        response = self.client.get(category_url)
        # test that we got a response
        self.failUnless(response)
        # test that the HTTP status code was "OK"
        self.assertEqual(response.status_code, httplib.OK)
        # test that we used the category.html template in response
        self.assertTemplateUsed(response, "catalog/category.html")
```

Let's have a quick look at template testing. One of the test methods we've been using is `assertTemplateUsed()`, which takes a response and the path to a template file in our templates directory as an argument. The method checks that the template file specified was used by the view function in generating a response. So far, we've just been putting the name of the template file into the function to check it.

While this works, it's less than ideal because if we ever change the name of the template that the URL is using, it will break the test, even if we correctly update the URL entry and the view function with the view template name. A much better solution is to look up the name of the template being used to render the response by retrieving the value of the `template_name` keyword argument using the `resolve()` method on the URL. You can test this inside a Python shell in your project:

```
>>> from django.core import urlresolvers
>>> urlresolvers.resolve('/product/something/')
(<function show_product at 0x11e0488>, (),
    {'template_name': 'catalog/product.html', 'product_slug': 'some-product'})
>>> urlresolvers.resolve('/product/something/')[2]['template_name']
'catalog/product.html'
```

So, we can refactor our existing test method to look up the `template_name` variable on the URL entry and use that value in the line that checks the template used:

```
from django.core import urlresolvers

class NewUserTestCase(TestCase):
    # other test methods here

    def test_view_category(self):
        category = Category.active.all()[0]
        category_url = category.get_absolute_url()
```

```
# get the template_name arg from URL entry
url_entry = urlresolvers.resolve(category_url)
template_name = url_entry[2]['template_name']
# test loading of category page
response = self.client.get(category_url)
# test that we got a response
self.failUnless(response)
# test that the HTTP status code was "OK"
self.assertEqual(response.status_code, httplib.OK)
# test that we used the category.html template in response
self.assertTemplateUsed(response, template_name)
```

This test method is pretty good, but at the moment, it's really only testing that Django is successfully generating and returning the response with the correct template file. There's nothing here to test that the content on the page is what we expect it to be. This is what the assertContains() method is used for. This method takes two required arguments: a response object and a string that you expect to occur in the document body of the response. If the test method finds the string in the content of the response, the test succeeds. We can put this to good use by testing that the category page contains the category name and the category description:

```
def test_view_category(self):
        category = Category.active.all()[0]
        category_url = category.get_absolute_url()
        # get the template_name arg from URL entry
        url_entry = urlresolvers.resolve(category_url)
        template_name = url_entry[2]['template_name']
        # test loading of category page
        response = self.client.get(category_url)
        # test that we got a response
        self.failUnless(response)
        # test that the HTTP status code was "OK"
        self.assertEqual(response.status_code, httplib.OK)
        # test that we used the category.html template in response
        self.assertTemplateUsed(response, template_name)
        # test that category page contains category information
        self.assertContains(response, category.name)
        self.assertContains(response, category.description)
```

Now that we've got all the basic methods used in test methods covered, let's use all of them to write a brief test method to ensure that our product view is working correctly. Put the following method inside your test class:

```
    def test_view_product(self):
        """ test product view loads """
        product = Product.active.all()[0]
        product_url = product.get_absolute_url()
        url_entry = urlresolvers.resolve(product_url)
        template_name = url_entry[2]['template_name']
        response = self.client.get(product_url)
```

```
    self.failUnless(response)
    self.assertEqual(response.status_code, httplib.OK)
    self.assertTemplateUsed(response, template_name)
    self.assertContains(response, product.name)
    self.assertContains(response, product.description)
```

Don't forget to add the `Product` model to the import statement or else this won't work!

■ **Note** Your product names or descriptions might contain characters that will be escaped by Django when they're rendered in your templates. We'll see how to get around this in your tests when we write the code for the search later in this chapter.

One other issue that you'll encounter is an error with the logging of the product page view. The `ProductView` model we created in Chapter 9 for tracking the pages that customers are viewing requires a valid IP Address... something that the Django test runner does not simulate on the `Client` instance. So, in order to make our tests succeed, we need to add a little bit of additional logic to the `log_product_view()` function in our `stats.py` file:

```
v.ip_address = request.META.get('REMOTE_ADDR')
if not request.META.get('REMOTE_ADDR'):
    v.ip_address = '127.0.0.1'
v.user = None
```

Test classes can also contain other methods that exist only to act as helper methods for your test methods. Take a look at the lines of code that are getting the name of the template file given the URL; the code to do this might be repeated across several of your test methods. You can create such a method by simply defining a method that doesn't start with `test_`, and called from your test methods using the `self` keyword:

```
def get_template_name_for_url(self, url):
    """ get template_name kwarg for URL """
    url_entry = urlresolvers.resolve(url)
    return url_entry[2]['template_name']
```

Helper methods on test classes can also contain assertions, and they will cause the test to fail if the assertion fails. However, they won't be called by the test runner by default. You must call them explicitly from within either `setUp()` or one of your test methods for them to run. For this reason, it's generally best practice to leave your assertions in your test methods and only use helper methods to reduce repetition of common tasks.

The response object also comes equipped with a `context` property. This is useful for testing the existence of variables that you expect to appear in the returned response. For example, our product view function should be returning a variable called `form` with each product page response. We can test that this variable is included in the response by asserting that it exists in the response context, and checking that it is an instance of the correct form class:

```
from ecomstore.catalog.forms import ProductAddToCartForm

# check for cart form in product page response
cart_form = response.context[0]['form']
self.failUnless(cart_form)
# check that the cart form is instance of correct form class
self.failUnless(isinstance(cart_form, ProductAddToCartForm))
```

There are other variables returned in the product page view that we could also test for in the response context. For example, each product page is supposed to return a variable called product_reviews. Testing for this variable is a little trickier. For instance, the following code will not work:

```
product_reviews = response.context[0]['product_reviews']
self.failUnless(product_reviews)
```

This will work if we are certain that the product we've selected for our test has at least one product review. However, if the product has no reviews, then the variable product_reviews will be an empty list, which will cause the failUnless() method to fail in the preceding case. On top of this, if the variable product_reviews is missing from the dictionary, then the first line of the preceding code will raise a KeyError exception.

A much better approach for testing the existence of variables in response contexts is to check that they exist by using the get() function available on Python dictionaries, and returning the Python null value None if the object doesn't exist. Then, check that the return value is not None:

```
product_reviews = response.context[0].get('product_reviews',None)
self.failIfEqual(product_reviews, None)
```

Testing the ActiveProductManager

One of the assumptions we've made about our code is that inactive categories and products will not be returned to the user interface. We can test this simply by trying to load an inactive product and checking that Django returns a 404 Page Not Found error.

Add the following class to the test file and re-run your tests. Remember to make sure that at least one product in the initial_data.json fixtures file you created earlier is set to inactive:

```
class ActiveProductManagerTestCase(TestCase):
    def setUp(self):
        self.client = Client()

    def test_inactive_product_returns_404(self):
        """ test that inactive product returns a 404 error """
        inactive_product = Product.objects.filter(is_active=False)[0]
        inactive_product_url = inactive_product.get_absolute_url()
        # load the template file used to render the product page
        url_entry = urlresolvers.resolve(inactive_product_url)
        template_name = url_entry[2]['template_name']
        # load the name of the default django 404 template file
        django_404_template = page_not_found.func_defaults[0]
        response = self.client.get(inactive_product_url)
```

```
    self.assertTemplateUsed(response, django_404_template)
    self.assertTemplateNotUsed(response, template_name)
```

One thing to notice here is that we cannot test the HTTP status code of the 404 page, because when Django serves up the custom Page Not Found page we created, it actually uses an HTTP status code of 200 and not 404. So, in order to test that the inactive product is not being loaded, we're using the template assertion methods to check the behavior.

Product Catalog Model Tests

Now that we've tested some of the basic parts of the interface, let's jump back down to the model level and write some tests to check the configuration of our model classes. TestCase classes are pretty simple to create for your models, so your test code should have a TestCase class for each model you've defined in your projects.

Writing unit tests to check the models in a web project often entails writing tests to check the create, update, and delete operations of any given model. These can be very simple to define. For example, when writing a test class to test the Product model, you could just check the total count of products in the database before and after a create and delete operation, making sure that the count incremented or decremented by one in each case, respectively. Or you could run an update on a model instance by calling the save() method, and then check to make sure that those changes were actually stored.

Writing these simple tests to check the CRUD operations of a model class is very simple. You just write test methods that exercise the Django ORM techniques you've been using through the rest of the book. In my opinion, testing for these kinds of things is testing to ensure that Django is doing what it's supposed to do and not testing the specific code that you've written for your project. As such, I won't be including any of them in this book.

There are more interesting things that we can test for that check the code we have written. For example, on the Product model, we have defined a model method called sale_price(), which will return the price if an old price is specified on the model and is greater than the price field. This is exactly the kind of logic we should be testing when we write our test classes.

Inside your catalog/tests.py file, add the following test class for the Product model:

```
from decimal import Decimal

class ProductTestCase(TestCase):
    def setUp(self):
        self.product = Product.active.all()[0]
        self.product.price = Decimal('199.99')
        self.product.save()
        self.client = Client()

    def test_sale_price(self):
        self.product.old_price = Decimal('220.00')
        self.product.save()
        self.failIfEqual(self.product.sale_price, None)
        self.assertEqual(self.product.sale_price, self.product.price)

    def test_no_sale_price(self):
        self.product.old_price = Decimal('0.00')
        self.product.save()
        self.failUnlessEqual(self.product.sale_price, None)
```

This defines a setup() method that retrieves an active product for us to use in all of our test methods, and sets a default price. In this case, it really doesn't matter what the actual price of the product was; we can just set it to some value that helps us write our tests. The test methods check that the sale_price() method returns a value of None when the old price is less than the price field, and that the sale price returned matches the price field when there is an old price greater than price.

There are other methods on the Product model class that we can check. There is also a __unicode__() method that should return the name of the product, as well as the get_absolute_url() method, which, for active products, should return a valid product page. Add the following two test methods to the ProductTestCase class:

```
def test_permalink(self):
    url = self.product.get_absolute_url()
    response = self.client.get(url)
    self.failUnless(response)
    self.assertEqual(response.status_code, httplib.OK)

def test_unicode(self):
    self.assertEqual(self.product.__unicode__(), self.product.name)
```

The latter two cases are fairly self-explanatory. Writing a test class for the Category model class is similar, and quite a bit simpler:

```
class CategoryTestCase(TestCase):
    def setUp(self):
        self.category = Category.active.all()[0]
        self.client = Client()

    def test_permalink(self):
        url = self.category.get_absolute_url()
        response = self.client.get(url)
        self.failUnless(response)
        self.failUnlessEqual(response.status_code, httplib.OK)

    def test_unicode(self):
        self.assertEqual(self.category.__unicode__(), self.category.name)
```

One other thing we can check for at the model level is any validation we expect to be present. Django doesn't provide validation at the model level at the time of this writing, but there are still a couple of very basic things we can test for at the model level in our application. For example, looking at the product model, we know that we cannot save a ProductReview instance without a valid product or user set in the foreign key field. An attempt to save an orphaned product review without a corresponding product will raise an IntegrityError. To test for this, we can assert that the error is raised after any attempt to call the save() method an invalid instance:

```
from ecomstore.catalog.models import ProductReview, Product
from django.db import IntegrityError

class ProductReviewTestCase(TestCase):
    def test_orphaned_product_review(self):
        pr = ProductReview()
        self.assertRaises(IntegrityError, pr.save)
```

There are a couple of fields that have default values set in the `ProductReview` model definition: is_approved and rating. As long as we provide a product review with both a product and a user, the save should occur successfully, and those two fields should contain the default values defined in the fields on the model. To make sure that this is true, we can create a new product review, iterate through all the fields on the model, and check that fields with a default value fall back on the provided default:

```
from django.contrib.auth.models import User

class ProductReviewTestCase(TestCase):
    # other code here

    def test_product_review_defaults(self):
        user = User.objects.all()[0]
        product = Product.active.all()[0]
        pr = ProductReview(user=user, product=product)
        pr.save()
        for field in pr._meta.fields:
            if field.has_default():
                self.assertEqual(pr.__dict__[field.name], field.default)
```

Note that in order for this to run without errors, you need to make sure that you create some fixture data for the users of your site. We can dump the data from the Django auth app into one of our own apps fixtures subdirectory so that at least one User instance will be present in the database for the test runner. Even though we're testing the catalog app only at the moment, the fixture data from all apps is loaded before the test runner starts running the tests. So, to dump the auth data and user logins into the accounts directory in our project, use the following commands:

```
$ mkdir accounts/fixtures
$ python manage.py dumpdata auth --indent=2 > accounts/fixtures/initial_data.json
```

You should create a `TestCase` subclass for each of your models and test the logic of it that is specific to your application. What you want to focus on are the parts of your models that get exposed via the user interface. Once you have a Django `ModelForm` that's created from the model class, then you want to start testing that the form instance enforces all of those rules. If there are relations between your models, or if any fields are required, test for `IntegrityError` exceptions when calling the save() on an instance.

Testing Forms & Shopping Cart

Now that we know a user can make it to the product pages without technical difficulties, let's test that the customer can add a product to their shopping cart. There is actually a lot going on in this simple operation. The user is submitting a form containing very basic data with a POST request to the product page that we need to validate. If the data is valid, then we need to create the new cart item and redirect the user to the cart page.

Let's have a look at emulating a successful add-to-cart operation, as well as testing the before and after expectations we have about the process. Inside your cart app, add the following test code to tests.py:

```
from ecomstore.catalog.models import Product
from ecomstore.cart.models import CartItem
from ecomstore.cart import cart
```

315

```
from django.test import TestCase, Client
from django.core import urlresolvers
from django.db import IntegrityError
from django.contrib import csrf
from django.conf import settings

import httplib

class CartTestCase(TestCase):
    def setUp(self):
        self.client = Client()
        self.product = Product.active.all()[0]

    def test_cart_id(self):
        home_url = urlresolvers.reverse('catalog_home')
        self.client.get(home_url)
        # check that there is a cart_id set in session
        # after a page with cart box has been requested
        self.failUnless(self.client.session.get(cart.CART_ID_SESSION_KEY,''))

    def test_add_product(self):
        QUANTITY = 2
        product_url = self.product.get_absolute_url()
        response = self.client.get(product_url)
        self.assertEqual(response.status_code, httplib.OK )

        # store count in cart_count variable
        cart_item_count = self.get_cart_item_count()
        # assert that the cart item count is zero
        self.failUnlessEqual(cart_item_count, 0)

        # perform the post of adding to the cart
        cookie = self.client.cookies[settings.SESSION_COOKIE_NAME]
        csrf_token = csrf.middleware._make_token(cookie.value)
        postdata = {'product_slug': self.product.slug,
                    'quantity': QUANTITY,
                    'csrfmiddlewaretoken': csrf_token }
        response = self.client.post(product_url, postdata )

        # assert redirected to cart page - 302 then 200
        cart_url = urlresolvers.reverse('show_cart')
        self.assertRedirects(response, cart_url, status_code=httplib.FOUND,
target_status_code=httplib.OK)

        # assert cart item count is incremented by one
        self.assertEqual(self.get_cart_item_count(), cart_item_count + 1)
```

```
        cart_id = self.get_cart_id()
        last_item = CartItem.objects.filter(cart_id=cart_id).latest('date_added')
        # assert the latest cart item has a quantity of two
        self.failUnlessEqual(last_item.quantity, QUANTITY)
        # assert the latest cart item is the correct product
        self.failUnlessEqual(last_item.product, self.product)

    def get_cart_item_count(self):
        cart_id = self.get_cart_id()
        return CartItem.objects.filter(cart_id=cart_id).count()

    def get_cart_id(self):
        return self.client.session.get(cart.CART_ID_SESSION_KEY)
```

Have a look at the test_add_product() method. You'll notice that before we actually make a POST to the product page that we expect to be successful, we have to add the hidden input to make sure that form is valid. In Chapter 12, we added a middleware class to our project to help reduce the likelihood of Cross-Site Request Forgery attacks. This ensures that every POST request we make with a form on our site is checked to make sure that the request is valid by checking that it has a valid hash value in a hidden form input named csrfmiddlewaretoken. Because we're generated the POST data by hand, we need to generate this value and add it to the dictionary by hand.

This process is simple enough. We first retrieve the cookie from the test client's session using the value from the settings module. Notice that, in this case, we're importing settings from django.conf and *not* from our own project root directory. Then, we call the _make_token() function from the CSRF middleware class, passing in the cookie value. We just add the return value from this call to the data of the POST request. If you omit this value from the form, your HTTP status code will not be the 200 OK that you're expecting, but will instead be a 403 Forbidden error.

Now that we've covered successful additions to the cart, let's look at the list of things that can go wrong when a user submits a form. The quantity might be empty, or it may contain a value that isn't a valid integer. We can easily add some test methods to our class to check these errors:

```
from ecomstore.catalog.forms import ProductAddToCartForm

class CartTestCase(TestCase):
    # other test methods here
    def test_add_product_empty_quantity(self):
        product_url = self.product.get_absolute_url()
        postdata - {'product_slug': self.product.slug, 'quantity': '' }
        response = self.client.post(product_url, postdata )
        expected_error = unicode(ProductAddToCartForm.
            base_fields['quantity'].error_messages['required'])
        self.assertFormError(response, "form", "quantity", [expected_error])

    def test_add_product_zero_quantity(self):
        product_url = self.product.get_absolute_url()
        postdata = {'product_slug': self.product.slug, 'quantity': 0 }
        response = self.client.post(product_url, postdata )

        # need to concatenate the min_value onto error_text containing %s
```

```
        error_text = unicode(ProductAddToCartForm.
            base_fields['quantity'].error_messages['min_value'])
        min_value = ProductAddToCartForm.base_fields['quantity'].min_value
        expected_error = error_text % min_value

        self.assertFormError(response, "form", "quantity", [expected_error])

    def test_add_product_invalid_quantity(self):
        product_url = self.product.get_absolute_url()
        postdata = {'product_slug': self.product.slug, 'quantity': 'bg' }
        response = self.client.post(product_url, postdata )
        expected_error = unicode(ProductAddToCartForm.
            base_fields['quantity'].error_messages['invalid'])
        self.assertFormError(response, "form", "quantity", [expected_error])
```

assertFormError() takes the response object from the POST, the name of the form as it appears in our view function, the name of the field we expect to have the error, and finally, a Python list of expected error messages. It's important to notice that, in the interest of not repeating ourselves, we're actually going to the name of the form class and pulling out the error that we expect the form to raise when we submit it. Then, we just check for the presence of that particular error in the response on that form and field.

Testing the Checkout Form

Next, we're going to write some tests for a very important aspect of our site: the checkout process. I'm not going to cover checkout in great detail, but we're going to take a quick look at how you can check for errors on form fields without listing each and every field by name. While it's all well and good to check for errors on specific fields on a small form like Add To Cart that contains only a single quantity field, we'd really like to be able to check that all of the fields are being validated without having to hard-code a check for each one. This is easy enough to do.

Before we start writing tests for the checkout, there's one last important point to keep in mind: the user needs to have at least one item in their shopping cart to successfully access the checkout page. Otherwise, the site will redirect them back the cart page. So, as a part of our basic setUp() method, we need to create a Client instance that has an item in the cart.

In your checkout directory, add the following test class to tests.py:

```
from django.test import TestCase, Client
from django.core import urlresolvers

from ecomstore.checkout.forms import CheckoutForm
from ecomstore.checkout.models import Order, OrderItem
from ecomstore.catalog.models import Category, Product
from ecomstore.cart import cart
from ecomstore.cart.models import CartItem

import httplib

class CheckoutTestCase(TestCase):
    def setUp(self):
```

```
        self.client = Client()
        home_url = urlresolvers.reverse('catalog_home')
        self.checkout_url = urlresolvers.reverse('checkout')
        self.client.get(home_url)
        # need to create customer with a shopping cart first
        self.item = CartItem()
        product = Product.active.all()[0]
        self.item.product = product
        self.item.cart_id = self.client.session[cart.CART_ID_SESSION_KEY]
        self.item.quantity = 1
        self.item.save()

    def test_checkout_page_empty_cart(self):
        """ empty cart should be redirected to cart page """
        client = Client()
        cart_url = urlresolvers.reverse('show_cart')
        response = client.get(self.checkout_url)
        self.assertRedirects(response, cart_url)

    def test_submit_empty_form(self):
        """ empty form should raise error on required fields """
        form = CheckoutForm()
        response = self.client.post(self.checkout_url, form.initial)
        for name, field in form.fields.iteritems():
            value = form.fields[name]
            if not value and form.fields[name].required:
                error_msg = form.fields[name].error_messages['required']
                self.assertFormError(response, "form", name, [error_msg])
```

Take a look at the last test method: one of the great things about Django forms is that you have access to all of the fields on an instance of that form. First, we post a completely empty instance of the form to the checkout page. Then, we're iterating through all of the fields in the checkout form and, if they don't have a value but are required by the form definition, assert that the "required" error message was raised by posting the form.

Security Testing

Security is a very important aspect of any web application and, like any other important part of our site, we should test it. There are a couple of very simple tests we can add to our test classes to make sure that our site is performing basic security measures.

First of all, any time that user input is displayed back on a page, we expect that Django will escape any HTML found in the template variable tags to eliminate any possibility of Cross-Site Scripting attacks. We can test for this by adding a simple test class that performs a basic search and ensures that the search text appears, HTML-encoded, on the results page. Inside your search app, add the following code to the tests.py file:

```
from django.test import TestCase, Client
from django.core import urlresolvers
from django.utils import html

import httplib

class SearchTestCase(TestCase):
    def setUp(self):
        self.client = Client()
        home_url = urlresolvers.reverse('catalog_home')
        response = self.client.get(home_url)
        self.failUnless(response.status_code, httplib.OK)

    def test_html_escaped(self):
        search_term = '<script>alert(xss)</script>'
        search_url = urlresolvers.reverse('search_results')
        search_request = search_url + '?q=' + search_term
        response = self.client.get(search_request)
        self.failUnlessEqual(response.status_code, httplib.OK)
        escaped_term = html.escape(search_term)
        self.assertContains(response, escaped_term)
```

Here, we perform a search for a search term that contains the dreaded <script></script> tags. In our test method, we encode the search text using the escape() function in the django.utils.html module and then check that the results template contains the escaped text, instead of rendering the potentially harmful tags.

We can also check that a POST request with form data that isn't signed by our CSRF middleware fails. Earlier in this chapter, when we wrote test methods for adding products to the shopping cart, we needed to add a special entry to the POST data we were submitting in order to pass the validation check by the CSRF middleware. For security purposes, we can test that a POST request to add an item to the shopping cart fails the security check if this special input is missing.

Inside your CartTestCase class, add the following method to check that a POST missing the validation input field fails, and returns an HTTP 403 Forbidden error status code:

```
def CartTestCase(TestCase):
    # other test methods here

    def test_add_to_cart_fails_csrf(self):
        quantity = 2
        product_url = self.product.get_absolute_url()
        response = self.client.get(product_url)
        self.assertEqual(response.status_code, httplib.OK )

        # perform the post of adding to the cart
        postdata = {'product_slug': self.product.slug,
                    'quantity': quantity }
        response = self.client.post(product_url, postdata )

        # assert forbidden error due to missing CSRF input
        self.assertEqual(response.status_code, httplib.FORBIDDEN )
```

Lastly, we can also test to make sure that the encryption and decryption methods we created for our credit card data in Chapter 12 are working as we'd expect them to. Inside `billing/tests.py`, add the following single test class:

```
from django.test import TestCase, Client
from ecomstore.billing.passkey import encrypt, decrypt

class EncryptionTestCase(TestCase):
    def test_encrypt_decrypt(self):
        to_encrypt = 'Some text here'
        self.failUnlessEqual(to_encrypt, decrypt(encrypt(to_encrypt)))
        self.failIfEqual(to_encrypt, encrypt(to_encrypt))
```

This test class doesn't actually do anything to test how *secure* the actual cipher we're using is. It merely tests that the encryption and decryption functions are working the way we expect them to, and that the ciphertext is not equal to the plaintext.

While there are certainly other security tests you could perform on your site, and there are definitely other places you could apply these two test cases, for brevity's sake, these are all of the security tests that I'm going to include in this book. However, security testing is a very important (and oft-overlooked) aspect of writing tests for web applications.

Summary

It's extremely important to keep in mind that just because you've written tests for your application, and just because you can run all of them without a single failure, that doesn't mean that your application is perfect. If you've forgotten to test some part of your application, then you won't detect any failures if that area of your web site breaks for some reason. And, of course, these kinds of tests only check for errors in the way that your application is supposed to *function*. If the interface of your web site is a terrible garble of HTML that no customer could possibly stand to look at, the tests you've written in this chapter certainly won't catch that problem. (That's what *usability* testing is for.)

As you start writing tests for your Django project, and having nightmares every night wondering whether or not you've got sufficient code coverage in your tests to check for every possible failure in your application (I'm only kidding about that... sort of), you'll find yourself starting to look much deeper into what Django has to offer. If you take testing into consideration from the outset, I strongly believe that you'll end up with a better application that will cause you much less grief maintenance.

Personally, I've found writing tests to be a very useful form of code review for myself. We often make silly little mistakes in the logic of our application, and having to write tests forces me to re-examine the thought processes and assumptions behind my initial work. They're also immensely helpful when you're creating parts of your application that can't easily be tested by manual means.

Now that the tests have been written and they run without fail, we're ready to show off the work we've done throughout the rest of this book to the world. Let's get this bad boy deployed onto the web so we can start selling products.

CHAPTER 15

■ ■ ■

Deployment

As web developers, we tend to squirm at the thought of having to actually deploy the code that we've just written into production. We are usually excited at the prospect of getting our site up, in the hopes that other people find it, write about it in magazines, and make us an overnight success story. But the devil's in the details. As you start to switch over from development to deployment, you start taking on a role that more closely resembles that of a system administrator than a web developer. You stop writing and debugging code, and start worrying about server configuration settings, network security, and the cost of bandwidth. It's a very different hat to wear, and for a lot of developers, it's territory filled with problems that we'd just rather let someone else solve.

Since a lot of developers regard the deployment stage of a web project as the final step and as a necessary evil required to expose the wonderful fruits of their development labors to the rest of the Internet community, they leave it until the very end. In most cases, for more substantial projects, this is not the most efficient approach. Much like testing, in a best-case scenario, you would have deployed your site to a production environment right from the start. That is, in Chapter 2, right after you first configured the base templates for our project, you would have gone the extra step and deployed those small template files to a production environment.

The reason for this is that deployment, just like development, is fraught with the unexpected and the unanticipated. I'm not even referring to the fact that your site might not be able to handle the loads of traffic that it receives in a production environment. Even without considering the gobs of people that (hopefully) will descend upon the pages of your site and put strain on the web server, there are difficulties you will encounter just from copying the files from your development machine to your production environment. If you spend months developing a large application and then expect to deploy the whole thing to a production environment within a week, you're in for a big surprise (or, more accurately, a lot of little ones).

Unfortunately, deployment is a highly subjective area of development no matter what web framework you might be using. There are any number of operating systems and hardware arrangements to which you might be deploying. In this chapter, I'm not going to talk about system administration or the many ugly details of server configuration. Since this is a development book, we're just going to look at those few extra steps that you'll need to take in order to make your e-commerce site ready for the wild. This includes making sure that the web server can serve your Django pages, that static media is not being served by your Django application, and that SSL is properly configured for your environment.

In the Django community, there are some tools that help developers through deployment. Among them are Capistrano[1], which helps automate the deployment process, and virtualenv[2] and buildout[3],

---

[1] http://www.capify.org/

[2] http://pypi.python.org/pypi/virtualenv

[3] http://www.buildout.org/

which help sandbox a runtime environment for a particular Django project. I won't be covering these tools in this chapter, since my experience with them is severely limited and I wouldn't be able to do them justice. I'd encourage you to poke around online and learn more about these tools before you jump into deploying a site for yourself.

Lastly, at the outset, I'd like to mention that I'm not a spokesperson for any particular vendor that provides web hosting, Git repositories, or any other software that's discussed in this chapter. It's difficult to talk about the how-to's of deployment without some concrete examples, which you can use and tweak based on your own needs. Talking in a lot of funky abstractions in an effort to make this chapter all things to all people just wouldn't be very useful to anyone. So, in an effort to help the widest possible range of people, I've opted to discuss a very simple deployment case using some of the more common software packages.

The Django Philosophy

At the moment, all of the different functions being done by your Django application are probably being done by a single machine. Your development computer is running a database server, a Memcached backend server, and a Django web application, which is in turn handling both dynamic web pages and the static media. Your machine is handling not only every request that you're making, but all of the responses as well. Everything should be running very quickly for you each time you fire up the site in a browser, because there's no network latency (everything's happening on just your local computer) and because there is only a single person making requests (you). For smaller sites, running all of these things on a single machine in production isn't necessarily a bad idea; if your site is small enough and you can get away with it, then by all means, I encourage you to do so.

When you get to the point where you need to scale your application, there are a couple of choices. The first is to scale *vertically*. Using this approach, you seek to scale an application by throwing it onto one massive computer that's loaded up with tons of RAM and a multi-core processor. There are several drawbacks to this approach, the most notable being the high cost. Even though the cost of memory and hardware is falling all the time, the incremental financial cost for adding power to a single machine increases faster than the capabilities you're purchasing.

A much better option is scale *horizontally*. Using this approach, you structure your application so that it can operate across several commodity machines. This is the guiding principle behind Google's own proprietary database storage engine, named BigTable[4]. BigTable was designed by Google engineers to manage large quantities of data across thousands of commodity machines. As a matter of fact, most large web applications use horizontal integration as a means of keeping their architectures scalable. Among the more notable examples of companies that integrate their web architectures horizontally are Facebook, Ebay, and Amazon.

The Django philosophy is squarely on the horizontal integration side of the debate. Basically, the creators of Django believe that when you deploy your project, you should employ a logical division of labor between the different parts of your application by their basic functionality. This requires a little bit more planning at the start of development, but is not terribly difficult to implement. Django lends itself very well to being deployed across lots of commodity hardware.

As a matter of fact, despite that all of the work we've done so far has been done on a single machine, the functionality of the application is fairly decoupled. If tomorrow, you absolutely needed to break your application up across several small server machines, you could do so pretty easily. All you'd need to do is change the configurations in settings.py and the pieces would all be able to talk to one another, between different machines. This is the great thing about the Django philosophy of "shared nothing." If you modularize the functions of your application, then it will scale with much less effort, and won't necessarily require the aid of server machines so expensive that only organizations like NASA can afford them.

---

[4] http://labs.google.com/papers/bigtable.html

Ideally, at a minimum, you'd be able to use four different machines: a database server; a Memcached server; a static media server for CSS, JavaScript, and graphic files; and an application server for Django dynamic pages. After you've got this set up, you just need to change configuration settings in your `settings.py` file and configure your web server to route requests to their respective machines on a network. We're not going to take this approach in this chapter: rather, we're just going to deploy all of our code to a single machine. However, we are going to invoke the "Horizontal Integration" model explicitly, so that you can easily move the different parts around as your application requires.

We're going to tackle the content of this chapter in three phases. In phase one, we're going to set up an Apache web server to handle all of the network traffic to our site, using mod_wsgi to enable Apache to interface with our Django project. In phase two, we're going to set up NginX web server, which will serve as the front-end web server serving requests for static media, such as style sheets and JavaScript files, and forwarding requests for dynamic Django pages to the Apache server. In the last phase, we're going to enable SSL for both of them so that any pages with URLs that have been marked with the ENABLE_SSL flag will be served securely, using HTTPS instead of HTTP.

The examples in this chapter are going to be done on a machine with the Ubuntu Linux Server 8.10 operating system installed. I chose to use Ubuntu not only because it's an excellent operating system to use as a web server, but it's also readily available. If you choose to deploy your Django application onto a hosting plan that provides you with your own VPS (see the next section "Finding a Hosting Plan"), or onto machine instances in Amazon's Elastic Cloud Compute,[5] you will find that several versions of Ubuntu are available for a fresh install. In addition, its integration with Django is extremely simple.

Of course, Ubuntu Server operating systems tend not to be run and configured using a Graphical User Interface. It's possible to do so, but you are discouraged from doing so for security and performance reasons. Because of this, I'm going to be configuring the hosting environment in this chapter from the command line. If you're very GUI-dependent and don't much like the command line, the topics in this chapter might be a little difficult to read if you're unfamiliar with the basic `ls` and `cd` commands so common to Unix systems.

Coverage of Windows-specific requirements for deploying Django will be very limited. I'll point you to solutions and software that are comparable to those we'll use in this chapter, but be warned: in my experience, integrating Django with IIS is a somewhat tricky endeavor.

Finding a Hosting Plan

Before you get started with deployment, you do have quite a few decisions to make. What web server software package will you use? On what hardware will your Django application reside? When you're shopping around for a hosting provider for your Django application, I do have one piece of advice: try to get root shell access. Throughout the course of this book, most of the development process has required us to execute commands inside our system's shell.

There are lots of hosting providers out there that offer "Python" support, but what this really means is that they provide hardware that will execute Python code. They come with a very low price tag, but considering the amount of time and effort that you'll spend trying to jump through hoops to get them to give you what you want far outweighs the savings. In the long run, you'll be much happier if you go with a provider that gives you root access to the shell, and the ability to configure your own machine and install any software that you would like.

Fortunately, in the era of virtualization, this isn't as hard to come by. There are several hosting plans offered by companies that come with a Virtual Private Server (VPS). You don't actually get your own dedicated physical server, but you do get your own virtual machine that behaves just like your own machine. You can install your own operating system, and any other applications that are required by your Django site. While hosting plans that include a VPS tend to cost a little bit more than those shared

---

[5] `http://aws.amazon.com/ec2/`

hosting providers that have "Python support" on a bunch of commodity Linux boxes, what you'll save in time trying to get everything working with a shared hosting plan will more than make up for it.

Personally, I haven't investigated every VPS option out there, but in the Django community, people tend to have very fond things to say about Webfaction[6] and Slicehost[7] for hosting Django applications. The companion site for this book (http://www.django-ecommerce.com/) is hosted using Slicehost, and my whole experience using their interface to manage my server has been very good. Make sure you find a hosting plan that is affordable, and meets your other business and technical requirements.

Phase One: Apache and mod_wsgi

Up until this point in the book, you've more than likely been using Django's built-in development server to run and preview your site, available via the manage.py runserver command. While this works fine for development, the built-in server was never intended to handle the volume of traffic that your site is going to see once it's been deployed. For this kind of load, you need to use a much stronger web server that's suitable for production use.

You have several options in this regard, as there are many open source web servers available that allow you integrate Django and start serving pages. In this section, we're going to start by using Apache 2.2[8] as the web server. All of the requests to the site will be handled by Apache, whether they are for static media or for dynamic Django-driven pages. The architecture that we're going to create in phase one will look something like Figure 15-1.

Figure 15-1. *All requests from the client are served by Apache and Django.*

Apache is a very widely used web server on the Internet, and it currently hosts the overwhelming majority of web sites built using open source technologies.[9] If you'd like to learn more about Apache, read the online documentation, or to find an install method different from the one we're going to use in the following section, visit the Apache web site.

Installing the Apache Web Server

The first thing you'll need to do is install Apache 2.2. In this chapter, since I'm using an Ubuntu Linux server for our demonstration, I'm going to install the Apache web server and other software using a Debian package manager known as Advanced Packaging Tool (APT). This tool allows you to install software directly from the command line. So, in order to install Apache 2.2 on an Ubuntu Server machine, you would type the following from the command line:

---

[6] http://www.webfaction.com/

[7] http://www.slicehost.com/

[8] http://www.apache.org/

[9] http://news.netcraft.com/archives/web_server_survey.html

```
$ apt-get install apache2 apache2.2-common apache2-mpm-prefork apache2-utils apache2-
threaded-dev
```

This command installs five packages, listed one at a time after "install," in order to make sure that all the packages required for your server are available on your machine.

SIDEBAR: NOTES ON UBUNTU SERVER

For security reasons, Ubuntu allows you to configure user accounts that have different levels of permission. If you are working on an Ubuntu server and you get a message when trying to install packages such as "Permission Denied," then you don't have a sufficient permission to install software on your system. You need to either log in using a root account, or you need to add your current user account to the "sudoers" file on your machine. This allows you to install software by prefacing your commands with sudo, which will prompt you for your user account password before executing the command:

```
$ sudo apt-get install apache2 ...etc...
```

In the rest of the examples in this chapter, I'm going to preface the commands with sudo in the hopes that your system is configured to require this. However, if you're operating as the root user, you don't need to include the sudo in order to run the commands.

For more information about how to configure user accounts in an Ubuntu server environment, as well as other important security topics, I'd recommend reading *Beginning Ubuntu Server Administration* by Sunder van Vugt (Apress, 2007), which I found to be a very useful reference in configuring my Ubuntu server.

Additionally, package managers on Linux systems can be extremely useful, but there's one caveat: when you run the install command, it scans the list of available packages and selects the available package of the same name. In some cases, you can explicitly choose which version of the software you would like to install by picking the right name. In other cases, you might not be so lucky. For example, you can install Django via apt-get install django, but if you do this, then you can't be sure what version you're installing until you check the installation afterwards.

Once you have Apache installed, you just need to start up your server and test that the default Apache page is working. To do this, just run the following command:

```
$ sudo /etc/init.d/apache2 start
```

In order to stop Apache, you just use stop instead:

```
$ sudo /etc/init.d/apache2 stop
```

And to perform both a start and stop all in one go, you just use the restart command:

```
$ sudo /etc/init.d/apache2 restart
```

Once you have your Apache server up and running, try loading the default page by visiting http://[IP Address]/ in your browser, putting the IP address of the machine on which your server is running. If you're running a Debian version of Linux, you should get a very simple page with only the text "It works!" in large header letters. Other distributions may have a default Apache page; if you have any doubts, refer to the Apache documentation for your own system to make sure you've done everything correctly.

Next, you need to configure your environment so that Apache can talk to Django, which is not possible by default. There are a couple of options for hooking Apache into Django, the most popular among them being mod_python and mod_wsgi. For our project, we're going to use mod_wsgi. mod_wsgi is an Apache module that allows your Apache server to communicate with Python applications, including your Django project. Fortunately, Django includes support for exposing your project as a WSGI application, so the process of hooking this up is very simple.

First, you need to install the mod_wsgi module on your system. Run the following at the command-line:

```
$ sudo apt-get install libapache2-mod-wsgi
```

Now that we've got this going for us, we need to copy our project onto this machine before we start configuring Apache to start serving our pages. How you do this depends largely on how you've been managing the source code for your project. Back in Chapter 1, I mentioned that I'm assuming (optimistically, and for your own sake) that you're using some version-control software, such as Git or Mercurial, in order to maintain your source code in some remote repository. The simplest way to get your source code onto your deployment machine is just to clone the remote repository into a directory on your local machine. On my server, I just clone my projects into my user's home directory, which is located at the path /home/[username]/ on Ubuntu.

■ **Note** If you're working with Windows Server 2003 and IIS 6.0, you'll be interested in looking at the isapi-wsgi module, which was created to help integrate IIS with Python WSGI applications. You can obtain the source code and learn more about this at: http://code.google.com/p/isapi-wsgi/.

Before getting too much further, remember that you also need Django, MySQL, and any other software or Python modules required by your project to be installed on this machine as well. You also need to create the database for the project on your server machine. Refer back to Chapter 2 for the process by which you create the database and the MySQL user account. Of course, if you've got a dedicated database server that doesn't reside on your local machine, then you don't need to do this.

Once you have your database created and a database user account set up with credentials that match those in settings.py, you just need to run the manage.py syncdb utility in order to create all of your database tables and their indexes on the new machine.

Creating the mod_wsgi File and Apache Virtual Host

First, we need to create a wsgi script inside our project that will integrate Apache with our project. This script can reside in the root of your project, but for cleanliness, we're going to put it into a subdirectory. Create a new directory in your project called apache, and create a new file inside it named django.wsgi. Open this file and add the following code:

```
import os, sys

# path to directory of the .wsgi file ('apache/')
wsgi_dir = os.path.abspath(os.path.dirname(__file__))
# path to project root directory (parent of 'apache/')
project_dir = os.path.dirname(wsgi_dir)
# add project directory to system's PATH
sys.path.append(project_dir)
# add the settings.py file to your system's PATH
```

```
project_settings = os.path.join(project_dir,'settings')

# explicitly define the DJANGO_SETTINGS_MODULE
os.environ['DJANGO_SETTINGS_MODULE'] = 'ecomstore.settings'

import django.core.handlers.wsgi
application = django.core.handlers.wsgi.WSGIHandler()
```

Of course, make sure you change ecomstore in this example if your project has a different name than mine.

Now, we just need to configure Apache to start routing requests to our server to this script. To do this, we're going to create an Apache virtual host on our Ubuntu server. Virtual hosts are the easiest way to maintain more than one site on a single machine. Later, if you want to host another Django or other web site on the same server, you can simply create a separate virtual host to handle the traffic for that site.

■ **Note** One thing you need to do is make sure that the domain name for your project is pointed at the IP address of your server by creating a DNS record. How you do this depends largely on where you are hosting your project, and the domain registrar from whom you purchased the domain name.

Navigate to the ServerRoot of your Apache 2.2 server, which, on Ubuntu, is located at the path /etc/apache2. In this directory, you will see two directories named sites-available and sites-enabled. In order to create a virtual host for your project, create a new file inside sites-available, and name it something that uniquely identifies your project, such as the domain name of your site. Inside this new file, add the new virtual host:

```
NameVirtualHost *:80

<VirtualHost *:80>
    ServerAdmin admin@your-domain.com

    # ServerName is required for a virtual host
    ServerName www.your-domain.com
    ServerAlias your-domain.com

    Alias /static /path/to/your/project/static

    # DocumentRoot is required for a virtual host
    DocumentRoot /path/to/your/project
    WSGIScriptAlias / /path/to/your/project/apache/django.wsgi

    ErrorLog /var/log/apache2/error.log

    # Possible values include: debug, info, notice, warn, error, crit,
    # alert, emerg.
    LogLevel warn

    CustomLog /var/log/apache2/access.log combined
</VirtualHost>
```

The use of a name-based virtual host requires a `NameVirtualHost` directive, with an argument that matches that of your virtual host. Notice that we've specified a `ServerName` and a `ServerAlias`, so that requests to both the www and non-www URL of our site will be routed to our project, and corrected by the `URLCanonicalizationMiddleware` class we created back in Chapter 11. Of course, you'll need to edit these settings so that they apply to your site, replacing your-domain with the actual domain name of your site and /path/to/your/project with the actual path to the project, wherever it resides on your system. And, of course, you might wish to change the e-mail address of the administrator.

In addition, we've used the `Alias` directive in order to point Apache at the directory containing our static media files. Any requests that come in to site with a URL path of /static will be served by Apache out of this directory in our project, without involving Django in any way. Below this are the directives that connect Apache and Django together. `DocumentRoot` points the virtual host at the directory containing our Django project, and `WSGIScriptAlias` points at the django.wsgi file we created previously.

■ **Note** If you're interested in learning lots more about how to configure virtual hosts or the Apache web server as a whole, I'd recommend checking out *Pro Apache: Third Edition* by Peter Wainwright (Apress, 2004), which is an invaluable introduction and overview of everything Apache has to offer.

In order to enable our new virtual host, you need to create a symbolic link from inside the sites-enabled directory, which points at the virtual host configuration file in your sites-available directory. On Debian installations, there is a utility you can use in order to do this. Run the following in order to create this link. If your virtual host file is named something other than ecomstore, be sure to use that name instead.

```
$ sudo a2ensite ecomstore
```

After you've done this, navigate to Apache's sites-enabled directory on your system and have a look at the contents of the folder. You should see another default symbolic link inside the folder that points to the "It works!" page that we saw earlier. For good measure, go ahead and delete this symbolic link now. You can also run the following to disable this default site:

```
$ sudo a2dissite default
```

To make sure that Apache is listening for income requests on the server, you need to make sure that the ports.conf file in the ServerRoot directory contains the following line, instructing the server to listening for incoming network requests on port 80 of the web server:

```
Listen: 80
```

Now, the ultimate test in order to see whether or not you've implemented this correctly is to remove the URL entry that is currently serving static media via Django. In the urls.py file in the root of your project, comment out or completely remove the following lines:

```
#(r'^static/(?P<path>.*)$', 'django.views.static.serve',
#    { 'document_root' : os.path.join(settings.CURRENT_PATH, 'static') }),
```

If you've conditionalized these lines to only be present when DEBUG is set to True, then you don't need to worry about removing these lines now.

After this has been done, you just need to restart your Apache web server in order for the virtual host to take effect:

```
$ sudo /etc/init.d/apache2 restart
```

Provided that there are no other configuration errors in your project, you should be able to navigate to the domain name of your site in your browser, and the requests for your project will all be routed to the project directory.

Phase Two: Nginx for Static Media

Right now, Apache is handling all of the requests for static media. Ideally, you'd be able to create a static media server on a separate machine from your Django application, so that requests for graphics and CSS style sheet files would be routed to and served by this machine. That way, your application server is free to spend its processing power on more important tasks, such as serving up Django pages.

NginX[10] (pronounced "Engine-X") is a fully functional web server that can be better suited for serving static media than Apache. In this section, we're going to configure NginX to act as our public-facing web server, accepting all incoming requests for our project. It will then divide up these requests between those for dynamic Django-driven pages and those for static media files, forwarding the requests for dynamic pages to the Apache virtual host we set up in the last section, and handling any requests for static media without involving our Django project at all. The architecture will look much like Figure 15-2.

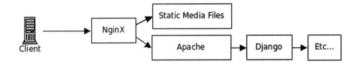

Figure 15-2. NginX to divide up requests between static media files and Apache / Django.

Unfortunately for my Windows readers, a full discussion of how to integrate an NginX with IIS is well outside the scope of this book. If you plan to use IIS and serve static media using NginX, I'd recommend using two separate servers instead of trying to use NginX to forward requests to IIS running on the same machine.

Installing and Configuring NginX

Naturally, before you start using NginX, you need to install it. Fortunately, there is a Debian package available using the apt-get syntax:

```
$ sudo apt-get install nginx
```

The configuration of NginX mirrors many of the aspects of Apache configuration. For example, in order to configure our single web site, we're going to create an NginX virtual host file. To do this, navigate to the ServerRoot of NginX, which, much like Apache, is located at /etc/nginx on your Ubuntu path. You'll

---

[10] http://www.nginx.org/

see the same two directories in this folder: `sites-available` and `sites-enabled`. These two directories serve the same function in NginX as they did in Apache: you put your site virtual host configuration files in the first and create symbolic links in the second for each site you would like to enable.

Create a new file for the virtual host inside `sites-available`, and again give it a name that uniquely identifies your site. The domain name of your site or some other self-describing string will do perfectly. Add the following to this file to create the virtual host:

```
server {
    listen 80;
    server_name www.your-domain.com your-domain.com;

    location / {
      access_log /var/log/nginx/localhost.access.log;
      proxy_pass http://127.0.0.1:8080;
    }

    location /static {
        root /path/to/your/project;
    }
}
```

The architecture that we're invoking here is very straightforward. Our NginX virtual host, once enabled, will listen for incoming requests on port 80 of our web server. Any request that comes in to the web server with a URL path that starts with /static will be served by our NginX web server. We've set the root of this location to the root of our project. So, if a request comes in for http://www.your-domain.com/static/some-image.gif, NginX will look in /path/to/your/project/static/some-image.gif for a file that it should be serving as a response.

However, any request with a URL path that doesn't begin with /static is a request for a Django dynamic page, and we forward this request to the Apache virtual host that we created in the last section. It won't work quite yet, because our Apache virtual host is still listening on port 80 for incoming requests, and the origin of those requests is not confined to requests from 127.0.0.1 (aka localhost), but we're going to fix that in a just a moment.

There is one slight drawback with this simple approach. As it stands right now, all of the requests that get forwarded by NginX to Apache will appear to have come from the IP Address 127.0.0.1, which is localhost. Technically, this is accurate, but you don't want the IP addresses in your log files or application to get swallowed by this proxying of requests from NginX to Apache. In order to fix this, we need to install the reverse proxy add forward module for Apache, known in shorthand as mod_rpaf. Fortunately, there is an APT installation available in order to make this available on your server.

```
$ sudo apt-get install libapache2-mod-rpaf
```

Now, we need to configure NginX to forward the IP address from each incoming request along with each request that it makes through the proxy to Apache. Add the following three lines to the first location setting in your NginX virtual host file for your site:

```
location / {
      access_log /var/log/nginx/localhost.access.log;
      proxy_pass http://127.0.0.1:8080;
      proxy_set_header X-Real-IP $remote_addr;
      proxy_set_header Host $host;
      proxy_set_header X-Forwarded-For $proxy_add_x_forwarded_for;
    }
```

After this is done, you just need to enable the site by going into /etc/nginx/sites-enabled and creating a symbolic link to the virtual host file inside your sites-available directory. Run the following from inside /etc/nginx in order to create the link:

```
$ sudo ln -s sites-available/ecomstore sites-enabled/ecomstore
```

Updating the Apache Virtual Host

Now that we've got the NginX virtual host set up, we need to make a couple of edits to our Apache virtual host in order to handle the changes we've made to our NginX. Open the Apache virtual host file for your site and change the opening element of your virtual host from this:

```
<VirtualHost *:80>
```

to this:

```
<VirtualHost 127.0.0.1:8080>
```

Above the virtual host configuration at the top of the file, update the NameVirtualHost directive as well:

```
NameVirtualHost 127.0.0.1:8080
```

Our virtual host will now be listening for requests originating from IP address 127.0.0.1, which is all requests that are coming from NginX on our local machine, on port 8080. The use of port 8080 is an arbitrary number. You can specify a different number if you're already using this port for another application. However, just make sure that you use a number above 1024, as most port numbers below this value are reserved by operating systems and applications for other uses.

While you're inside the Apache virtual host, add the following three lines inside the bottom of virtual host so that the mod_rpaf module can handle the forwarding of external IP addresses from NginX proxied requests:

```
CustomLog /var/log/apache2/access.log combined

RPAFenable On
RPAFsethostname On
RPAFproxy_ips 127.0.0.1
</VirtualHost>
```

And, as one final change, we need to make sure that Apache itself is listening for incoming requests on the port number we specified in our virtual host (in our example, port 8080). Open the ports.conf file you edited in the last section and change the line so that Apache will now listen on port 8080:

```
Listen 8080
```

If everything is set up correctly, your web site should still be serving media under the path /static, but just not with Apache.

After you've done all of this, you just need to make sure that your Apache and NginX servers are both running and, if they are, restart them for the changes we've just made to take effect. You can start, stop, and restart NginX in the same way as Apache, using the same commands. In order to restart both of your servers, run the following on the command line:

```
$ sudo /etc/init.d/nginx restart
$ sudo /etc/init.d/apache2 restart
```

Once you've done this, you should have your static media being served by NginX, with dynamic requests being forwarded to Apache and Django.

Phase Three: Configuring SSL

For all of its complexity, our web application is still missing one very critical feature: SSL. Right now, all of our pages are being served over HTTP, which is an insecure protocol. That means that if you were to accept credit card information from a customer who submits an order form on your site, there is no encryption or security of any kind protecting the information in transit. Anyone with a little technical prowess would be able to sniff the packets of information as they were transmitted over the Internet and could, without any difficulty, steal the credit card information of your customer.

Secure transmission of information over the Internet is done using the Secure Sockets Layer (hence, SSL) and a protocol called HTTPS, which is different from ordinary HTTP responsible for transmitting most pages. HTTPS communication, by default, happens on a different port than HTTP; while HTTP uses a default port of 80, HTTPS communicates over 443. More importantly, HTTPS encrypts all information sent back and forth between your server and the client using *asymmetric cryptography*.

Asymmetric cryptography differs from the symmetric cryptographic protocols that were discussed briefly in Chapter 12 in that there are two different keys being used for encryption and decryption functions. The problem with traditional cryptography that uses a single key in Internet communications is that your web server might be communicating with hundreds of browsers with which it has had no past correspondence, and there is no way for both the server and client to use a single key for encrypting information. This is because there is no way for the server to securely transmit the key to the client. And if your web server needs to send the encryption key to each client "in the clear" in order to create a secure connection with each client, then the key can be intercepted and used by anyone. In this case, you haven't secured your network traffic at all. In order for symmetric cryptography to work, the key must be secret.

Asymmetric cryptography makes use of *public-key cryptography*. Using this form of cryptography, there are two keys: one public and one private. A public key is distributed freely to each of the clients, while the private key is stored securely on the server and never shared with anyone. The two keys are mathematically related, and this allows some very interesting behavior. First, before being transmitted, messages are encrypted by the server using the private key. After they have been received, they are decrypted by the client using the corresponding public key. Then, any correspondence sent from the client to the server is encrypted using the public key and decrypted with the private key on the server. This not only means that information is securely encrypted in transmission, but also that the ciphertext of the message acts also as a means of verifying that the person sending the message is who they claim to be. If the client or the server cannot decrypt the information received from the other end, then it's presumed that the incorrect key was used for encryption and the sender is not who they claim to be. In this way, the encryption keys act as digital signatures that allow the client and the server to verify where the message came from.

There is a little bit more to SSL and secure communication than this, but this description will suffice for our purposes. There is a third piece to this puzzle: certificate authorities. You see, it's possible for anyone to simply generate a certificate and private key for their web server and start serving pages. However, there is no way for the average web user, surfing around the Internet on random sites, to determine whether or not each web site is legitimate. In order to combat this problem, a third-party arbitrator, called a certificate authority, digitally signs the server's certificate. When the secure pages of a site are loaded, the browser checks that the certificate of a site has been verified by a reputable certificate authority. If the certificate hasn't been verified, the browser displays an error message about the server's certificate being invalid.

In principle, this works because malicious sites are much less likely to go through the hassle of getting their certificates verified by a certificate authority. In reality, however, it has its limitations because it assumes that Internet consumers are paying attention to the errors that their browser is spitting at them.

Also, just because a site's certificate has been signed, that does not mean that the site in question is secure. It's merely a measure designed to help savvy consumers distinguish between legitimate and potentially fraudulent web sites, and to reduce the amount of overall mischief on the Internet.

The most well-known certificate authority is probably Verisign;[11] however, they are not the only option for getting your certificates verified. The process of getting your certificate verified by a company such as Verisign is fairly painless. In order to get your certificate digitally signed by a reputable certificate authority, you first need to generate a Certificate Signing Request (CSR) that contains basic information about you and your site (we're going to do this in a moment). You then submit the CSR to a certificate authority of your choosing, and the certificate authority will return a certificate to you, which you can then install on your NginX server to handle secure communications. Once you have done this, browsers should cease their warning messages about your site's legitimacy.

For development and testing purposes, it's perfectly possible for us to generate our own private key, as well as the corresponding signed certificate request. This will allow you to test your pages using SSL. Our own self-signed certificates, however, are not suitable for production use. Have you ever tried to access a web page over HTTPS and gotten a cryptic message about how the authenticity of the current site couldn't be verified? This is the scary error that users will see if you don't get your certificates signed by a reputable certificate authority.

For the generation of the key and certificate, we're going to use the OpenSSL[12] library that comes installed on most Linux distributions, including our very own Ubuntu server. First, somewhere on your Ubuntu server, create a directory where you can play around and generate the files required to set up SSL. In my case, I created a directory named sandbox inside the home directory on my server. The first thing you need to do is generate the private key that the server will use in communication.

```
$ openssl genrsa -des3 -out ecomstore.key 1024
```

Executing this command will asked you for a passphrase; enter a simple password to make the key generation process happy. This will create the private key inside of a file named ecomstore.key inside of the directory.

The next step is to create the certificate signing request. Enter the following command, which uses the private key file you just created to generate a file named ecomstore.csr, which contains the details about the certificate:

```
$ openssl req -new -key ecomstore.key -out ecomstore.csr
```

After you run this, you will be prompted with a series of questions about your site, such as the locality in which you conduct business, company name, and e-mail address. There is one very critical misnomer here, of which you must be aware and answer correctly. It will ask you for your "Common Name," with the unhelpful text in parentheses, "(eg YOUR name)." This is not asking you for your own name, which was bestowed upon you by your parents the day you were born. Here, you need to enter the domain name under which you intend to operate your site. This *must* match the domain you plan to use in your URLs. You must be explicit and distinguish between www versus non-www domain names. If you intend to operate under www.your-domain.com, you must enter this and not your-domain.com. If the domain and what you enter doesn't match exactly, your customers will get funny browser warnings when they try to access the secure pages of your site.

At this point, you now have a Certificate Signed Request file, which is what you would submit to a certificate authority in order to obtain a signed certificate for your server. However, for our example, we're going to go ahead and do this process ourselves.

---

[11] http://www.verisign.com/

[12] http://www.openssl.org/

Next, we need to remove the passphrase that we entered for the key file. To do this, rename the key file inside the same directory:

```
$ mv ecomstore.key ecomstore.key.backup
```

Then, use the new key file to generate another key file that doesn't require a passphrase. You will need to enter the passphrase you entered before in order to make the following command run:

```
$ openssl rsa -in ecomstore.key.backup -out ecomstore.key
```

The passphrase on the key file does afford us a little extra security, but there is another very good reason that we chose to remove it: If you leave the passphrase, then you will be prompted for the password every time you restart your NginX server. This also includes any times when your server machine reboots for any reason, such as after a power failure or other server application error. The NginX server will hang, unable to restart completely until you return to the terminal and enter your passphrase. During that time, customers will be unable to access your site. Because of this, I've opted to remove the passphrase completely.

Now, we just need to create the actual certificate file using the private key file and the certificate signed request:

```
$ openssl x509 -req -days 365 -in ecomstore.csr -signkey ecomstore.key -out ecomstore.crt
```

This will create the ecomstore.crt certificate file, which will expire in one year. In order to make these available to our server, we just need to copy them into the relevant directories on our server. They can reside wherever you would like, but on Ubuntu server, private key files and certificates are kept in the /etc/ssl/private and /etc/ssl/certs directories, respectively. So, to complete the whole operation, you just need to copy the two files into their directories:

```
$ sudo cp ecomstore.key /etc/ssl/private/
$ sudo cp ecomstore.crt /etc/ssl/certs/
```

At this point, you don't need to keep the files that you created just a moment ago. You can keep them around until you've confirmed that they work, but make sure that you at least remove the private key ecomstore.key file from the directory you just used. You want to keep this key a secret, and don't want to leave it lying around in insecure places.

SIDEBAR: CERTIFICATES ON WINDOWS SERVER

In order to generate a certificate for a site running under IIS 6.0, you might want to follow a slightly different set of steps that don't require installing OpenSSL. In order to generate a certificate, open the IIS Manager, and expand the Web Sites list. Right-click on the site for which you'd like to create a certificate and choose Properties from the menu.

You should see a tab labeled "Directory Security." Under this tab, there is a button reading "Server Certificate." Click this button and you will be taken a wizard. Follow the steps to create a new certificate, and save it to a text file. Later, you can submit this certificate to a certificate authority.

Now, we just need to make sure that NginX is listening for requests coming in for HTTPS. Remember that our server is currently listening on port 80 for regular, insecure web traffic, but right now, it won't serve requests for traffic on 443, which we require. For this, we need to add another server entry to our NginX virtual host file.

Open the file and add the following, below the first server entry:

```
server {
    listen 443;
    ssl    on;
    ssl_certificate        /etc/ssl/certs/ecomstore.crt;
    ssl_certificate_key    /etc/ssl/private/ecomstore.key;
    server_name www.your-domain.com your-domain.com;

    location / {
      access_log /var/log/nginx/localhost.access.log;
      proxy_pass http://127.0.0.1:8080;
      proxy_set_header X-Real-IP $remote_addr;
      proxy_set_header Host $host;
      proxy_set_header X-Forwarded-For $proxy_add_x_forwarded_for;
      proxy_set_header X-Forwarded-Ssl on;
    }

    location /static {
        root /path/to/your/project;
    }
}
```

There are a few key differences between this and the other server entry in the file. The first is the port number on which we're listening for incoming requests. Right after that, there are three new entries that enable SSL on our site. These three lines configure the ssl setting to on, and then point the virtual host to the locations of the certificate and private key files on our machine.

The final key difference of which you should be aware if the additional proxy_set_header entry we've added to our code. This is because of a small bug that arises in the SSLRedirect class due to our server configuration. Right now, our Django application has its pages served by Apache, which is currently ignorant of any of the SSL settings we've set up in NginX. A secure request that comes into the site at an HTTPS URL will be forwarded from NginX to Apache, which will send the request to our Django project. The SSLMiddleware will catch the request and check if it is secure by using the request.is_secure() method. However, because the request coming into Apache from NginX is *not* secure, the SSLRedirect will assume that the request should be insecure and attempt to redirect our request to an insecure URL. However, when this happens, the SSLRedirect will catch the redirect, find that the SSL parameter in the URL entry is set to True, and attempt to redirect to a secure page.

What we have here is an infinite loop that will redirect back and forth between secure and insecure until your web server or browser gets fed up and stops trying to serve the request. This is fixed by adding the header to all requests from NginX to Apache. If you open the SSLMiddleware.py file and scroll down to the _is_secure() method, you should see the following two lines:

```
if 'HTTP_X_FORWARDED_SSL' in request.META:
    return request.META['HTTP_X_FORWARDED_SSL'] == 'on'
```

This checks each request for an HTTP header called HTTP_X_FORWARDED_SSL. As long as we add this header to each request that is proxied from NginX to Apache, the _is_secure() method will return True, our pages will be served securely, and the infinite loop can be safely avoided.

Now that you have this configured in your virtual host files, go into settings.py and set the ENABLE_SSL configuration variable to True. After restarting both Apache and NginX, you should now be able to see your secure pages served over HTTPS in the browser instead of HTTP. Of course, if you signed your own certificate instead of using a certificate authority, you will initially see a pretty unfriendly error message in the browser when you first try to load the page. Remember to get your certificate signed before you actually deploy your site!

Transferring Data with Django

There's a pretty good chance that you've spent copious amounts of time in the rest of this book adding data to the database that resides on your local development machine, and now, you need to transfer all of that information over to the production machine. However, you cannot simply "copy" a database from one server to another. You need to take additional steps to transfer data between machines.

Fortunately, this isn't too difficult using a couple of the built-in Django commands. In Chapter 14, we created JSON fixture files using the manage.py dumpdata command. There is another command that allows you to take JSON file data and load it into your database: manage.py loaddata. Therefore, it's possible to use dumpdata on your development machine to create a JSON file containing all of your product catalog information, transfer that file to your production server, and then use loaddata in order to load the data into your production database.

So, to create a file holding all of the data from your catalog app, you would do the following:

```
$ python manage.py dumpdata catalog > catalog_data.json
```

This creates a JSON file named catalog_data.json in the root of your project. If you're using version-control software to copy your files over, you just need to add this file to the repository. Then, pull this file down from the remote repository onto your production machine and execute the loaddata command:

```
$ python manage.py loaddata catalog_data.json
```

This will install the records from your development database into your production one.

■ **Note** If you've been maintaining different sets of data on both your development machine and your production machine, you might encounter difficulty in trying to merge the two. This example assumes you want to copy data from database tables in your development machine to an empty table in your production database.

Database engines such as MySQL and PostgreSQL also come with utilities that allow you to dump data from a database server into a file and extract the contents of that file into another database server. For MySQL users, you want to use the mysqldump[13] utility, which lets you dump a schema, one or more tables of data, or even an entire database into a file with some very simple commands. PostgreSQL users can do this using the equivalent pg_dump[14] command.

The Admin Interface Styles

One piece that is still missing from our site in deployment is the CSS styles that are required to beautify the Django admin interface. After your site has been deployed, the link tags referencing the style sheets

---

[13] http://dev.mysql.com/doc/refman/5.1/en/mysqldump.html

[14] http://www.postgresql.org/docs/8.1/interactive/app-pgdump.html

338

for the admin interface are no longer pointing in the correct direction. Fortunately, this is a very simple thing to remedy; we just need to create a link to the directory where the Django style sheets reside, and then set a simple configuration variable.

The media files for the Django admin interface reside in your Django source code, under `django/contrib/admin/media`. Find where this directory resides on your system, and create a symbolic link to this folder inside your project's static directory. Give the link a descriptive name, such as `admin_media`:

```
$ ln -s /path/to/django/contrib/admin/media admin_media
```

Now, we just need to tell our admin interface templates to look at this location for the media files. Open your `settings.py` file, find the `ADMIN_MEDIA_PREFIX` line, and change it to read:

```
ADMIN_MEDIA_PREFIX = '/static/admin_media/'
```

This should make your admin interface templates appear nice and pretty.

Summary

In this chapter, we took a quick look at how to configure two of the most popular open-source web servers, Apache and NginX, in order to serve your Django pages and your static media files by configuring virtual hosts. With the architectures we constructed in this chapter, the different parts of your application are now decoupled enough that you could feasibly spread your application across a few different server machines, if and when you need to scale it. We also took a brief look at how to create your own private key and self-signed certificate for your server so that your Django application can now serve their pages securely using SSL.

In the next chapter, we're going to have a look at what it takes to get a Django web application up and running on Google App Engine, which is Google's cloud infrastructure for hosting Python applications. We're going to build a very simple shopping cart application, using the techniques we've learned in the rest of the book.

## CHAPTER 16

Django on Google App Engine

In mid-2008, Google finally opened up Google App Engine for use by the public. Google App Engine is a cloud infrastructure onto which developers can deploy Java- or Python-based web applications. This is an exciting prospect; Google has finally created a cloud into which we can deploy web sites. Much like Amazon's own Elastic Cloud Compute service, it's an option that abstracts away the hardware from developers and system administrators into a series of web service calls over the Internet. The hardware architecture of the App Engine cloud is maintained by Google's engineers, so all you need to do is concern yourself with deploying your Django project and managing the data properly.

It's important to point out, very early on, that the Google App Engine and Django are *not* the same thing. Google App Engine is a cloud infrastructure for web hosting that's *capable* of hosting Django-based applications. The App Engine is actually able to host a site created using any framework that uses Python and supports the Web Server Gateway Interface (WSGI) standard interface. App Engine actually has its own framework that developers are allowed to use, known as the webapp framework. I'm not going to cover webapp in this book, but a good deal of its syntax and structure is borrowed from Django. In webapp, variables in templates are enclosed by double curly braces, for example.

This chapter will not be a comprehensive introduction to Google App Engine. Instead, we're going to look at what it takes to get a basic shopping cart application up and running using the Django web framework deployed onto the Google App Engine. We're going to be duplicating the work that we've done in the rest of this book in a lot of ways. Some of you might have skipped right to this chapter in the book, in the hopes that I would shed some light on exactly how you deploy a Django application onto the Google App Engine. I will make an effort to touch upon the basic concepts. Unfortunately, I won't be able to touch upon all the subjects covered in the rest of this book, go into topics with as much depth, or create an application of comparable complexity in just a single short chapter. For the rest of you that have already read the other chapters in this book, try to think of this chapter as a brief review of Django examples from the other chapters in this book, using App Engine–specific data storage techniques.

■ **Note** In Django terms, an "app" refers to a subset of your overall project; projects are comprised of several apps that break up parts of the project's functionality. In the Google App Engine documentation and in this chapter, entire projects that you will deploy onto the App Engine are referred to as "apps." If I mention "deploying your app," then I'm referring to the whole of your Django *project*, which might be several Django "apps."

The Inconvenient Truth

So the Google App Engine sounds pretty excellent as far as a hosting option goes, and it even supports Django. Does that mean that we simply dump our project files into their cloud infrastructure and start running the site from there?

Not exactly. While the App Engine does support Django, there are enough differences that deploying the project we've created in this book onto the App Engine would be far from simple. First of all, the Django model classes that we have created are different than the ones you will need to create to use App Engine's datastore. The classes are required to subclass from a different App Engine data class, and the declaration of each field requires a different set of data types. Secondly, the queries that are required to select or manipulate the data in the App Engine datastore is also very different than the Django ORM syntax we've been using.

Because of the number of these incompatibilities and the sheer depth to which they are embedded in our project, I'm going to start from scratch and create a new shopping cart application in this chapter. We'll be able to replicate some of the logic from the rest of this book. Of course, if you're really interested in a challenge, you could just upload the Django project that we've create in this book into the App Engine and work through all of the errors that you encounter one at a time. This would be painful, but it might have some value as a learning experience. If you have a masochistic personality and would like to do this, I'd encourage you to read this chapter before you attempt to do so.

Signing Up For An Account

In keeping consistent with the steps required for the rest of the Google tools that we've used throughout the rest of this book, the first thing we need to do before creating our applications is to sign up for the App Engine using a Google account. Unlike the rest of the Google goodies we've used, however, signing for the App Engine requires an extra step: you'll need to have a mobile phone capable of receiving SMS text messages handy in order to complete registration. You can start the registration process at: http://appengine.google.com/, as shown in Figure 16-1.

Figure 16-1. Signing up for a developer account with Google App Engine.

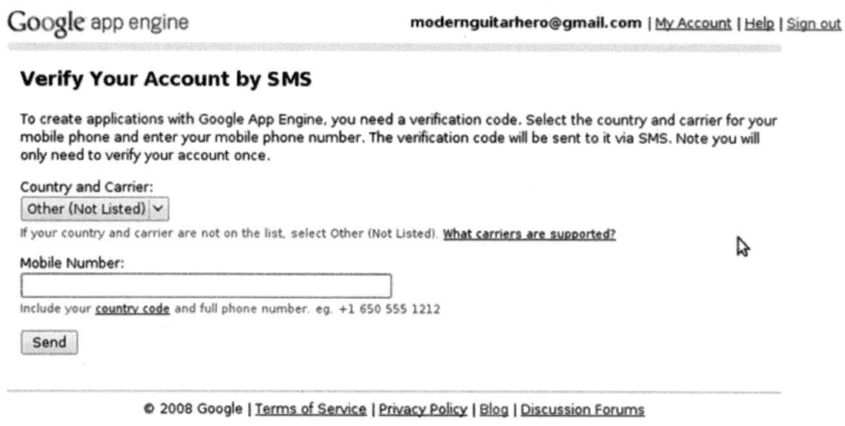

Figure 16-2. *Verifying yourApp Engine account via SMS. Keep a cell phone handy.*

The verification process using your mobile number is shown in Figure 16-2. Once you've successfully registered, you just need to do two more things: create an application and download the SDK. When choosing a name for your app, keep in mind that it will be used in the URL of your application. If you decide to name your app mybluedjango, for example, then your app will be available at: http://mybluedjango.appspot.com/.

Next, you need to download the App Engine SDK for the Python environment. You can download the appropriate copy of this from: http://code.google.com/appengine/downloads.html. You can put the actual google_appengine directory anywhere on your system that you'd like, but you need to add this folder to your system's PATH before you'll be able to run any App Engine projects locally, using the manage.py runserver command.

The Django App Engine Patch

In the olden days (e.g., mid-2008), it was fairly difficult to get a Django project running on the App Engine. There were a lot of extra configuration steps you needed to take just to get a basic site running, and even when you did go through all of that trouble, there were still lots of things that were missing. Support for the admin interface, for example, didn't exist. The Django authentication system wasn't compatible with the datastore. Just about all of the slick features that come with Django out of the box weren't available for use on the App Engine.

Now for the really great news: there is a project out in the wild, ripe for the taking, which is known as the Google App Engine Patch.[1] The App Engine Patch project was started and done mostly by Waldemar Kornewald in order to bridge the gap between regular Django development and the Google App Engine environment. Because of his efforts, there is support for sessions, the admin interface, and many of the default Django apps that we've been using throughout the rest of the book. It also supports the Django testing framework so that you can run all of your project tests. The project also includes a utility for integrating with Amazon's Simple Queue Service (SQS) from within your Python code, which is an immensely useful offering when you need to do intensive computing tasks but don't want your app to be bogged down.

---

[1] http://code.google.com/p/app-engine-patch/

The Django App Engine Patch actually adds a lot of other interesting capabilities as well. For example, when you go to deploy your project from your local development machine into the cloud, you would normally use a Python file provided in the App Engine SDK distribution named appcfg.py. When you're ready to deploy your project, you would run the following command:

```
$ python ./appcfg.py update [your_project_dir]/
```

The Patch project actually includes this command as part of manage.py, so that when you want to deploy your code, you just run the following from inside your project's root directory:

```
$ python manage.py update
```

As a Django developer, this should make you feel right at home. Don't worry about actually uploading your code yet. We'll get to that step in a second. First, you just need to download a copy of the App Engine Patch project. Once you've gotten the project, create a copy of the project and name the copy something similar to the name of your App Engine app that you just created after signing up. We're going to work on the copy of the project, so that if you want to start other apps on the App Engine, you can use the untouched copy of the Patch project as a starting point.

Next, we need to edit the YAML configuration file. Open the app.yaml file inside the project and have a look at its contents. First, there should be a listing of configuration variables for your project. You need to change the "application" value to match the name of the app you created after registering. So, if you named your project mybluedjango, you would enter that.

Below these, there is a section titled "handlers." This contains a list of URLs that can be mapped to files on your site, and allows you set permissions levels for directories or files, if necessary. There are three things we need to make sure are present in the handlers section. First, an entry to hook up the Remote API script included with the SDK, which will allow us to remotely add data the App Engine datastore for our project from within a local Python shell. Second, an entry to specify which directory in our project will serve static media. Lastly, we need a catchall entry to map all incoming requests that aren't handled by any other handler to the main.py file in the common/appenginepath subdirectory.

After all is said and done, here is what your app.yaml file should contain:

```
application: [your app name]
version: 1
runtime: python
api_version: 1

default_expiration: '3650d'

handlers:
- url: /remote_api
  script: $PYTHON_LIB/google/appengine/ext/remote_api/handler.py
  secure: optional
  login: admin

- url: /media
  static_dir: _generated_media
  secure: optional

- url: /.*
  script: common/appenginepatch/main.py
  secure: optional
```

The order of the items you list in the handlers section matters. You should configure them to be more restrictive and more specific, to less restrictive and more general. The first item, which hooks up the `remote_api` script we'll be using later, is restricted. Only an administrator of the app is allowed to access it. The next entry is telling the project to look for a directory named _generated_media at a URL path of /media for our static files. And the last entry is designed to handle any request coming into the site that doesn't match any of the other URLs. The `main.py` file is doing the heavy lifting for your project. It's similar to the `django.wsgi` file we created in the last chapter in order to interface our project with Apache and mod_wsgi.

There are a couple of other extra goodies that the App Engine Patch gives you by default, of which you should be aware before you start actively developing your site. First, there is the static media generator; if you remember back to Chapter 13, we talked about keeping your CSS and JavaScript files small and few in number, so that there is a minimum of network bandwidth required in order to view your site for the first time. The App Engine Patch comes equipped with a utility that does some very handy things. Whenever you run the `manage.py` update command, it automatically combines all of your JavaScript files and CSS style sheets into a single combined file. Then, it compresses the two files using the YUI Compressor, which is a Java-based tool created by Yahoo! that removes all the extraneous whitespace and comments from your static media files. It writes the output of this compression process into the _generated_media subdirectory, where your project will look for your files. The whole process makes the static media that you deploy onto the App Engine much smaller than it would have been otherwise, and will dramatically improve the overall speed of your site from a user standpoint.

If you want to make use of this utility (and I strongly suggest that you do), there are a couple of extra steps you'll need to take in order to make sure that this works the way you expect it to. First, you'll need to have Java installed and available on the PATH of your development machine so that the YUI Compressor tool can run. If you've been using Eclipse as your IDE up until this point in the book, chances are good that you've already got it on your system. Second, you need to list all of your CSS and JavaScript files in your `settings.py` file. Open `settings.py` and you'll see a section titled `COMBINE_MEDIA`. This is where you tell the media generator utility about each of your code files.

For sites deployed into production, you need to change the version number of the `MEDIA_VERSION` each time you make a change to any media files. This will change the URL path of the static media files, so that cached versions of the generated media will be replaced with updated versions. If you forget to do this, users out in the wild will still be experiencing old CSS and JavaScript until it expires in their browser's cache; this is probably not what you want!

While the compression of your static media will happen automatically whenever you run `manage.py` update, there is also another utility you can use to generate the media by hand. Just run the following inside your project to create the newest version of your files in _generated_media:

```
$ python manage.py generatemedia
```

App Engine Patch also comes with some basic CSS inside the `blueprintcss` directory that contains base styles for your HTML that's designed to cut down on your development time. While I found many of the defaults to be particularly helpful, you are free to remove it by removing the `blueprintcss` app from the INSTALLED_APPS of your project. Even if you don't plan to use it, keep in mind that it's present in your project. When you start creating templates for your site, you might start seeing your HTML pages behave in a strange way, with margins, padding, or other styles that you didn't create in your own CSS. If this happens, it's likely coming from this app, and you'll need to override the styles in order to change them.

Finally, if you start developing your site locally, there's one very important point to keep in mind about data: by default, if you're running the site on a development machine, the App Engine SDK writes data to a flat file in your operating system's temporary directory. Files inside this directory tend not to stick around very long; generally, they're deleted each time you restart your machine. This means that any product data, session information, or user accounts that you create on your local development machine are fleeting. Be very careful about entering new data for your site, and make sure that it's ending up in the App Engine datastore. In this chapter, when we get around to adding data, we're going to make sure that we do so on the deployed version of our app, so that important data is not wiped out.

Getting the Test Page Running

So let's take this new project for a test drive. In order to deploy your project, you just need to execute the `manage.py update` command that we saw in the last section. During the upload process, you should be prompted for your Google Account e-mail and password. This is just to make sure that you are an administrator of the named app and are authorized to change things; go ahead and enter them. You won't need to do this every time. After the first upload, the `appcfg.py` script will save a cookie on your computer so that you don't need to authenticate yourself every time after that. During the initial upload, you might also be prompted about creating a superuser account for your app. If you plan on using the admin interface to add data (which you will), then you should definitely create a superuser account now.

Provided that everything runs smoothly and the app ends up deployed without any errors, you can now view your app at the `appspot.com` URL. It should look something like Figure 16-3:

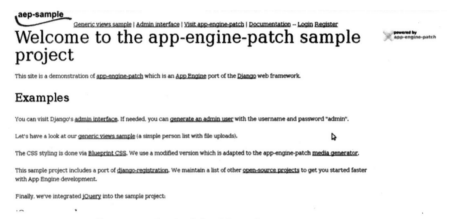

Figure 16-3. *Hello App Engine Path for Django!*

Our Google App Engine Store

Since we're starting over, I'm going to scrap the Modern Musician site and create a new e-commerce store that specializes in selling coffee, tea, and other accessories that help office workers get through their often mind-numbing days.

The first thing we need to do is edit the base template files so that the look and feel of the site becomes our own. This is fairly straightforward; App Engine Patch comes equipped with a `templates` directory, so the first thing we need to do is create the base template files. Open the `base.html` template file inside this directory and have a look at its contents. There are only a couple of edits that we're going to make. We're going to replace the rest of the contents of the body section of the template with our own content block, named `site_wrapper`. Then, for performance reasons, we're going to move the block that contains the JavaScript includes to the bottom of the page, just before the closing body tag. Also, update the title tag to reflect the name of your own site. Here is what `base.html` should look like after you've finished these edits:

```
<!DOCTYPE html
    PUBLIC "-//W3C//DTD XHTML 1.0 Transitional//EN"
    "http://www.w3.org/TR/xhtml1/DTD/xhtml1-transitional.dtd">

<html xmlns="http://www.w3.org/1999/xhtml"
```

```
        dir="{% if LANGUAGE_BIDI %}rtl{% else %}ltr{% endif %}"
        xml:lang="{% firstof LANGUAGE_CODE 'en' %}"
        lang="{% firstof LANGUAGE_CODE 'en' %}">
    <head>
      <title>{% block title %}{% endblock %} - Bleeker Street Coffee</title>
      <!-- other stylesheet includes omitted here -->

      {% block extra-head %}{% endblock %}
    </head>
    <body>
      {% block site_wrapper %}{% endblock %}

      {% block js %}
        <script type="text/javascript" src="{{ MEDIA_URL }}combined-{{ LANGUAGE_CODE
}}.js"></script>
      {% endblock %}
</body>
</html>
```

Next, we need to create a template that will house the layout of the site, which inherits from
base.html. Create a catalog.html template file and put the following template code into it:

```
{% extends "base.html" %}

{% load store_tags %}

{% block title %}{{ page_title }}{% endblock %}

{% block site_wrapper %}
<div id="main">
    <div id="middle">
        <div id="banner">
          <h1>
            <a href="/">
              Bleeker Street Coffee
            </a>
          </h1>
          <div id="navigation">
              <a href="/">Home</a> |
              <a href="/cart/">Cart</a>
          </div>
        </div>
        <div id="sidebar">
          {% category_list %}
          <br /><br />
          <a href="http://code.google.com/p/app-engine-patch/">
          <img src="{{ MEDIA_URL }}global/powered-by-app-engine-patch.png"
              alt="powered by app-engine-patch" />
          </a>

        </div>
        <div id="content">
          <div id="padderIEcontent">
```

347

```
        {% block content %}{% endblock %}
      </div>
    </div>
  </div>
</div>
{% endblock %}
```

You should notice a couple of things here. To start with, this example is loading a custom template tag named category_list. Obviously, because we haven't created this tag, this won't run quite yet. We're going to get to that in the next section, when we create the app to house our product catalog data. Secondly, notice that I've included a hyperlinked App Engine Patch logo as a means of tipping my hat to the developers of the App Engine Patch. If you're allowed to do this in your own project, I'd encourage you to do the same.

Before we start creating apps, have a look at the root of the App Engine Patch project. There is a simple demo Django app provided for you, named myapp. If you are having any trouble figuring out how to start adding model classes to your code, you can work off of the examples provided for you in the models.py inside this app.

Let's create the app for our catalog data. Create an app named store inside your project. The first thing we need to do is create some models that will hold catalog information in the datastore. Open the newly generated models.py inside this new app, and add the following code to it:

```python
# -*- coding: utf-8 -*-
from django.db.models import permalink, signals
from google.appengine.ext import db
from ragendja.dbutils import cleanup_relations

class Category(db.Model):
    name = db.StringProperty()
    description = db.TextProperty()
    created_at = db.DateTimeProperty(auto_now_add=True)
    updated_at = db.DateTimeProperty(auto_now=True)
    is_active = db.BooleanProperty(default=True)

    class Meta:
        verbose_name_plural = 'Categories'

    def __unicode__(self):
        return self.name

    @permalink
    def get_absolute_url(self):
        return ('store_category', (), { 'category_key': self.key()})

    @property
    def products(self):
        return Product.gql('WHERE category = :1', self.key())

class Product(db.Model):
    name = db.StringProperty()
    description = db.TextProperty()
    created_at = db.DateTimeProperty(auto_now_add=True)
    updated_at = db.DateTimeProperty(auto_now=True)
    is_active = db.BooleanProperty(default=True)
```

```
is_featured = db.BooleanProperty(default=False)
price = db.FloatProperty()

category = db.ReferenceProperty(Category)

def __unicode__(self):
    return self.name

@permalink
def get_absolute_url(self):
    return ('store_product', (), { 'product_key': self.key()})
```

If you've worked with Django models before, this should look fairly similar. There are only a couple of differences. First, notice that our model classes are subclasses of db.Model, which is the App Engine datastore base class. Also, the type of fields that we're declaring on the models is different, and specific to the App Engine. For example, for smaller string values, you should use db.StringProperty, much like models.CharField on Django models. Similarly, for large amounts of text that might be very long, you should use db.TextProperty, which is similar to models.TextField.

There isn't a corresponding field type in the App Engine for each of the Django model field types, but the basic ones are there and should suffice for the majority of your needs. One small adjustment we had to make is that product price is now a float field on the model instead of the Django decimal field.

More importantly, though, is the means by which we are specifying a relationship between the Category and Product models. Unfortunately, the App Engine Patch doesn't yet support many-to-many relationships between Django models using the admin interface (I'm hopeful that there will be someday soon). For now, to keep things simple, I've created a basic one-to-many relationship between categories and products; that is to say, a category can have multiple products, but each product only belongs to a single category.

Let's have a look at how this is done using the App Engine syntax. In order to understand how this works, a little bit of background on the App Engine db.Model class is in order. After each model instance is saved in App Engine's datastore, a unique key is generated for each model instance. This key is actually an instance of the google.appengine.db.Key class. Each key contains ID field of the model instance, the combined name of the app (e.g., store) and model class, and the name of your Django app (e.g., mybluedjango). Therefore, this key guaranteed to be unique across all model instances not only for your own App Engine app, but all other apps as well.

You can get the key instance of a model instance by calling the key() method on the instance. We're doing this in order to build our URLs for the pages. When used in the context of URLs and in templates, the key instance is converted into a unicode string. You might be wondering why we don't just use a slug field that has keyword-rich URLs for search engine spiders; the reason is that there is no way to apply a unique constraint on a db.Model field. Creating a StringProperty field to act as a slug field is a bad idea, as it would be possible to end up with multiple model instances with the same key.

In order to create the relationship, we create a ReferenceProperty on the Product model, which references the Category model class. On each Product instance, this will act as a foreign key field that references the key value of the associated category instance. Then, on the Category model, we create a custom method named products, which retrieves all of the products that have been assigned to that category. Note the property decorator on this function, so this method is not actually callable.

Because we want to make use of these models using the Django admin interface, we need to register these models with the admin site. To do this, create a file named admin.py inside your store app and enter the following code into it:

```
from django.contrib import admin
from store.models import Product, Category

class CategoryAdmin(admin.ModelAdmin):
```

```
    list_display = ('name', 'description', 'created_at', 'updated_at')
    exclude = ('created_at', 'updated_at')

admin.site.register(Category, CategoryAdmin)

class ProductAdmin(admin.ModelAdmin):
    list_display = ('name', 'description', 'created_at', 'updated_at')
    exclude = ('created_at', 'updated_at')

admin.site.register(Product, ProductAdmin)
```

Before moving on, let's create the category list for the left-hand column on the site. Create a directory inside of store named templatetags, and inside of it, add two files: the standard __init__.py and a store_tags.py file. Inside the latter, add the following:

```
from django import template
from google.appengine.ext import db
from store.models import Category

register = template.Library()

@register.inclusion_tag("store_category_list.html")
def category_list():
    query = db.Query(Category)
    query.filter('is_active = ', True)
    query.order('name')
    categories = query.fetch(20)
    return {'categories': categories }
```

This references a template file that doesn't yet exist. Next to templatetags, there should be another directory named templates. This is where we're going to put all of the template files for the store app. In it, create a file named store_category_list.html, and add in the following code for the links:

```
<h3>Categories</h3>
<ul id="category_list">
{% for category in categories %}
    <li>
    <a href="{{ category.get_absolute_url }}">
        {{ category.name }}
    </a>
    </li>
{% endfor %}
</ul>
```

There's really nothing new here. For those of you who noticed that the templates directory we just created isn't part of the TEMPLATE_DIRS tuple for our project: that's a good observation. However, don't worry about this issue. I'll discuss this further when we get to the next section, where we create the template files for each app in our project.

For a moment, let's go back to the actual code of the category_list() function. db.Query(Category) generates an instance of google.appengine.db.Query, which represents all Category instances from which we can actually query Category instances. Similar to Django syntax, you can also use a method named filter() in order to trim down the Query object result set based on some criteria you specify. The filter method we used previously creates a Query object that will only return categories where is_active is True.

You can also specify how a Query object will order its results by using the order() method and passing in a field name. Just like Django, you could reverse the order by prefacing the field name with a dash (-):

```
>>> query.order('-name')
```

Once you have a Query object, you need to call one of the methods that will actually execute the query you've just constructed. Calling the get() method on this Query object, for example, will return one result: the first result that it finds. Because there is more than one category, this clearly won't do.

The fetch() method is the one you should use when you're interested in a list of results. The fetch() method requires that you pass in an integer value for the number of results that you would like returned to you. At the time I'm writing this, the maximum number of results you can query for using the fetch() method is 1,000. You cannot simply make a query for every single model instance in the datastore.

Using the fetch() method properly in your projects requires using the second optional argument you can pass in, which represents an offset. Using this, you can paginate your results across multiple pages, like we did in Chapter 8 when we built the search results pages. The offset of the first result is always zero. Therefore, to get the first 20 results, you could make the following query:

```
>>> query.fetch(20, 0)
```

The offset is zero by default, so this is the same as calling query.fetch(20). Now, if you want to get at the next 20 results, you'd use the following:

```
>>> query.fetch(20, 20)
```

This retrieves the 20 instances, starting with the 21st result. To get the third page, starting with the 41st result, you would use an offset of 40:

```
>>> query.fetch(20, 40)
```

And so forth. You can automate this with some very simple math based on the page number of records you're interested in retrieving. The offset is calculated using the following formula:

```
OFFSET = RESULTS_PER_PAGE * (PAGE_NUMBER - 1)
```

For the simple examples in this chapter, I'm going to limit my queries to the first 20 results, and I'm going to hard-code the value of 20 inside my fetch() methods. For a project of any substantial size, however, you should take the extra effort and implement a pagination system, so that the number of results isn't peppered throughout fetch() method calls all over your site.

To complete the base template files, we need to add in the CSS that will style up the base templates that we just created. Inside your project, there should be a directory named media. Open the look.css file inside there, empty the contents, and replace it with this CSS:

```
*{padding:0;margin:0;}
body{font-family:Verdana;font-size:0.9em;}
.bn{border:none;border:0;}
.fl{float:left;}.fr{float:right;}
.cb{clear:both;}

div#main{
    width:100%; }

div#middle{
    width:900px;
    margin: 0 auto; }
```

351

```
div#banner{
    height:100px;
    background-color:green;
    position:relative; }

div#banner h1{
    padding-top:25px;
    padding-left:10px; }

div#banner h1 a{
    color:White;
    text-decoration:none;
    font-size:2em; }

div#navigation{
    position:absolute;
    bottom:0;
    right:0;
    padding:5px; }

div#navigation a{
    color:yellow;
    font-weight:bold; }

div#sidebar{
    float:left;
    width:200px;
    padding-top:10px;
    text-align:left; }

h3{
    background-color:Maroon;
    color:White;
    font-size:1.0em;
    padding:3px;
    font-weight:bold; }

div#content{
    float:left;
    width:700px; }

div#padderIEcontent{
    padding:10px;
    padding-left:30px; }

h1, summary{
    font-size:1.3em;
    font-weight:bold; }

ul#category_list{
    list-style:None;
    padding:0;
    margin:0;
```

```
        padding-left:5px; }

ul#category_list li a{
        color: Maroon;
        text-decoration:None;
        font-weight:bold; }

ul#category_list li a:hover{
        text-decoration:underline; }
```

The Brubeck Shopping Cart App

We're almost at the end of a book that's about creating web sites with Django using the Python programming language and so far, there's yet to be any reference to old-time jazz musicians or John Cleese quotes. I apologize for this. As an act of contrition, I'm going to name the shopping cart app that we'll use to manage shopping cart information on the App Engine after one of my favorite jazz musicians: Dave Brubeck.

Create an app named brubeck inside your project. You certainly know the drill by now; we're going to starting by creating some model classes in models.py:

```
# -*- coding: utf-8 -*-
from django.db.models import permalink, signals
from google.appengine.ext import db
from ragendja.dbutils import cleanup_relations

from store.models import Product

class CartItem(db.Model):
    quantity = db.IntegerProperty()
    date_added = db.DateTimeProperty(auto_now_add=True)
    cart_id = db.StringProperty()
    product = db.ReferenceProperty(Product,
                                    collection_name='products')

    @property
    def total(self):
        return self.quantity * self.product.price

    @property
    def name(self):
        return self.product.name

    @property
    def price(self):
        return self.product.price

    def get_absolute_url(self):
        return self.product.get_absolute_url()
```

This is a fairly simple model class; there are really no new concepts here. We have a ReferenceProperty acting as a reference to a Product instance. There is also a field for storing cart IDs.

This begs the question: how will we generate cart IDs? Create a file named cart.py inside the brubeck app and add the following code:

```python
from google.appengine.ext import db
from brubeck.models import CartItem
from store.models import Product
from decimal import Decimal

import base64
import os

CART_ID_SESSION_KEY = 'cart_id'

def get_cart_id(request):
    cart_id = request.session.get(CART_ID_SESSION_KEY, '')
    if not cart_id:
        cart_id = _generate_cart_id()
        request.session[CART_ID_SESSION_KEY] = cart_id
    return cart_id

def _generate_cart_id():
    return base64.b64encode(os.urandom(36))

def add(request, product_key):
    postdata = request.POST.copy()
    quantity = int(postdata.get('quantity', 1))
    product = Product.get(product_key)
    item = CartItem.all().filter('product = ', product)
        .filter('cart_id = ', get_cart_id(request)).get()
    if not item:
        item = CartItem()
        item.product = product
        item.quantity = quantity
        item.cart_id = get_cart_id(request)
        item.put()
    else:
        item.quantity = item.quantity + quantity
        item.put()

class Cart(object):
    def __init__(self, request):
        cart_id = get_cart_id(request)
        query = CartItem.all().filter('cart_id = ', cart_id)
        self.items = query.fetch(20)
        self.subtotal = Decimal('0.00')
        for item in self.items:
            self.subtotal += Decimal(str(item.total))

def get(request):
    return Cart(request)

def update_item(item_key, quantity):
    key = db.Key(item_key)
```

```
    item = CartItem.get(key)
    if item:
        if quantity <= 0:
            item.delete()
        else:
            item.quantity = int(quantity)
            item.put()

def remove_item(item_key):
    key = db.Key(item_key)
    item = CartItem.get(key)
    if item:
        item.delete()
```

This is all very familiar. In order to track items in customers' shopping carts, we need a way of uniquely identifying each customer. We do this by generating a random string of characters for the cart ID, which we write to a cookie on the customer's browser. We store this unique value along with each item that the customer has added to their cart. When we need to get all of the items in any given customer's shopping cart, we just load the ones that have the cart ID matching that of the value stored in the cookie.

Notice that when we go to save newly generated cart items, or update existing ones, we call put() on the instance and not save().

The only major difference between this and the cart.py module we created in Chapter 4 is that we've created a custom Cart class to hold a subtotal Decimal object and a list of CartItem objects, which is a slightly more object-oriented approach to passing cart data around between the model and the view.

Now, create a file named forms.py and add this to it:

```
from django import forms
from brubeck.models import CartItem


class ProductAddToCartForm(forms.ModelForm):
    class Meta:
        model = CartItem
        fields = ('quantity',)

    quantity = forms.IntegerField(widget=forms.TextInput(attrs={'size':'2',
                                                    'value':'1',
                                                    'class':'quantity'}),
                            error_messages={'invalid':'Please enter a valid
quantity.'},
                            min_value=1)
```

This is the form class that we will use on the product page template.

Now, in order for us to test that things are working the way that they're supposed to, we need to add some data to our project. This is done simply by using the Django admin interface provided for us. After your app has been deployed onto the app engine, just go to http://your-app-name.appspot.com/admin/, log in using the superuser account you created earlier, and add some categories, as well as products to go with them.

Views and Templates

Now that we have the back end set up, we need to focus our attention on the interface. Let's start with the view functions and the URL entries that we need to create for the store app. Open the store/views.py file and add the following:

```
from django.shortcuts import render_to_response
from django.template import RequestContext
from google.appengine.ext import db
from django.core import urlresolvers
from django.http import HttpResponseRedirect

from store.models import Category, Product
from brubeck.forms import ProductAddToCartForm
from brubeck import cart

def index(request,
          template_name='store_index.html'):
    page_title = 'Welcome'
    query = db.Query(Product)
    query.filter("is_featured =", True)
    query.filter("is_active =", True)
    featured_products = query.fetch(20)
    return render_to_response(template_name, locals(),
        context_instance=RequestContext(request))

def show_category(request, category_key,
                  template_name="store_category.html"):
    key = db.Key(category_key)
    query = Category.gql('WHERE __key__ = :1 AND is_active = True', key)
    category = query.get()
    if not category:
        raise Http404('Category not found!')
    products = category.products
    page_title = category.name
    return render_to_response(template_name, locals(),
        context_instance=RequestContext(request))

def show_product(request, product_key,
                 template_name="store_product.html",
                 form_class=ProductAddToCartForm):
    key = db.Key(product_key)
    query = Product.gql('WHERE __key__ = :1 AND is_active = True', key)
    product = query.get()
    if not product:
        raise Http404('Product not found!')     page_title = product.name
    if request.method == 'POST':
        postdata = request.POST.copy()
        form = form_class(postdata)
        if form.is_valid():
            cart.add(request, product_key)
            redirect_url = urlresolvers.reverse('show_cart')
            return HttpResponseRedirect(redirect_url)
```

```
    else:
        form = form_class()
    return render_to_response(template_name, locals(),
        context_instance=RequestContext(request))
```

Now, create a `urls.py` file inside `store`, and add the URL entries:

```
from django.conf.urls.defaults import *
#from django.core.urlresolvers import reverse

from brubeck.forms import ProductAddToCartForm

urlpatterns = patterns('store.views',
    (r'^$', 'index', {'template_name':'store_index.html'},'store_home'),
    (r'^category/(?P<category_key>.+)/$', 'show_category',
        {'template_name': 'store_category.html'}, 'store_category'),
    (r'^product/(?P<product_key>.+)/$', 'show_product',
        {'template_name': 'store_product.html',
         'form_class': ProductAddToCartForm},
            'store_product'),
)
```

The one thing you might notice here is that we've specified the name of the form class as a keyword argument for the `show_product()` view function. This way, if anyone using this app ever wants to use a different form class, they can just change the form class in the URL, and the view will automatically use the new form instead.

Switch gears for a second and go back to the brubeck shopping cart app. Inside `views.py`, add this single view function for the cart page:

```
from django.shortcuts import render_to_response
from django.template import RequestContext
from django.core import urlresolvers
from django.http import HttpResponseRedirect

from brubeck.models import CartItem
from brubeck.forms import ProductAddToCartForm
from brubeck import cart

def show_cart(request, template_name='brubeck_cart.html'):
    if request.method == 'POST':
        postdata = request.POST.copy()
        submit = postdata.get('submit','')
        item_key = postdata.get('cart_item_id')
        if postdata.get('submit','') == 'Update':
            quantity = postdata.get('quantity', 1)
            cart.update_item(item_key, quantity)
        if postdata.get('submit','') == 'Remove':
            cart.remove_item(item_key)
    shopping_cart = cart.get(request)
    page_title = u'Shopping Cart'
```

```
    return render_to_response(template_name, locals(),
context_instance=RequestContext(request))
```

Then, create a urls.py file and add the one URL entry:

```
from django.conf.urls.defaults import *

urlpatterns = patterns('brubeck.views',
    (r'^$', 'show_cart', {'template_name':'brubeck_cart.html'}, 'show_cart'),
)
```

Now, we need to create our template files for each app. In the rest of the book, we created a single directory for our templates, and divided up the template files into subdirectories named after the apps the templates for which they were created. In this chapter, we're going to take a slightly different approach. Django allows you to create a subdirectory named templates inside each individual project app. When you reference the name of a template file, it will check the template directories you specified in TEMPLATE_DIRS in settings.py. If it doesn't find it there, it will then turn to the templates subdirectories that it finds inside each of your INSTALLED_APPS. This is particularly handy if you plan on distributing your apps; that way, you can include default template files with your app.

This is what we're going to do for this project. Of course, going this route, we have to be careful to avoid any naming collisions between templates. It would be all too easy for a group of people to decide that they should create an index.html to act as the home page for their given app. In this case, Django will load the first template file that it finds whenever it needs to load this template file with this name. That means that the first app with a templates/index.html will always be used when index.html is referenced, and the index.html in the apps that follow will be effectively hidden. Also, if a developer ever creates a single index.html file inside one of the listed TEMPLATE_DIRS, this one will override any other index.html provided at the app level.

To avoid this, I'd recommend giving your template files names that are prefaced by the name of the app in which they are contained. Earlier, when we created the template file for the category list of links for the left column, we called it store_category_list.html. As long as we follow the convention of prefacing the template name with the app name, the likelihood of a naming problem should be greatly reduced.

The store app requires three new template files: one for the homepage, one for the category page, and one for the product page. First, create one for the homepage called store_index.html and inside, enter this:

```
{% extends "catalog.html" %}

{% block content %}
    <h1>Welcome</h1>
    <br />
    {% for p in featured_products %}
        {% if forloop.first %}
            <h3>Featured Products</h3>
        {% endif %}
        <a href="{{ p.get_absolute_url }}">
            {{ p.name }}
        </a>
        <br />
    {% endfor %}
{% endblock %}
```

Next, create the one for category page. Create a file called store_category.html and add:

```
{% extends "catalog.html" %}

{% block content %}
    <h1>{{ category.name }}</h1>
    <br />
    {% for p in products %}
        <a href="{{ p.get_absolute_url }}">
            {{ p.name }}
        </a>
        <br />
    {% endfor %}
{% endblock %}
```

Now, to top the store app off, add a store_product.html template file and put this in it:

```
{% extends "catalog.html" %}

{% block content %}
    <h1>{{ product.name }}</h1>
    <br />
    Price: ${{ product.price }}
    <br />
    Description: {{ product.description }}
    <br /><br />
    <form action="." method="post">
        {{ form }}
        <br />
        <input type="submit" value="Add To Cart" />
    </form>
<br />
{% endblock %}
```

We're almost through with all of this mind-numbingly repetitively template code. We just need to create a template file for the cart page. Inside the brubeck app, create a templates directory and then, inside of that, create a file named brubeck_cart.html. Enter the following code into it for the cart page:

```
{% extends "catalog.html" %}

{% block content %}
    <table width="100%" id="shopping_cart">
        <summary>Shopping Cart</summary>
        <thead>
        <tr>
            <th>Product</th>
            <th>Quantity</th>
            <th></th>
            <th></th>
            <th>Price</th>
            <th>Total</th>
        </tr>
        </thead>
        <tfoot>
```

```
            <tr>
                <td colspan="6" style="text-align:right;">
                        Cart Subtotal: ${{ shopping_cart.subtotal }}
                    <br /><br />
                    <input type="submit" value="Checkout" />
                </td>
            </tr>
            </tfoot>
    {% if shopping_cart.items %}
        {% for item in shopping_cart.items %}
        <tr>
            <td width="300px">
            <a href="{{ item.get_absolute_url }}">
                {{ item.name }}
            </a>
            </td>
            <td>
                <form action="." method="post">
                <input type="text" name="quantity" value="{{ item.quantity }}" size="2" />
                <input type="hidden" name="cart_item_id" value="{{ item.id }}" />
            </td>
            <td>
                <input type="submit" name="submit" value="Update" />
                </form>
            </td>
            <td>
                <form action="." method="post">
                    <input type="hidden" name="cart_item_id" value="{{ item.id }}" />
                    <input type="submit" name="submit" value="Remove" />
                </form>
            </td>
            <td>${{ item.price }}</td>
            <td>${{ item.total }}</td>
        </tr>
        {% endfor %}
    {% else %}
        <tr>
            <td colspan="6">
                Your cart is empty.
            </td>
        </tr>
    {% endif %}
    </table>
{% endblock %}
```

For the purposes of styling up the table on the cart page, and in the interest of demonstrating how to use the media generator utility that comes with the App Engine Patch, find the subdirectory inside the brubeck app called media, and add a file named brubeck.css to it. Add the following CSS bits:

```
table#shopping_cart th{
    background-color:Maroon;
    color:White;
}
```

```
table#shopping_cart td{
    height:30px;
}
```

Now, you just need to make sure that this code is included when the generatemedia.py script is run. Inside settings.py, find the COMBINE_MEDIA section and add the brubeck.css file to the CSS section. Note that you don't need to include the media directory in the path of the file you specify here, as the utility will scan these directories automatically.

```
'combined-%(LANGUAGE_DIR)s.css': (
        'global/look.css',
        'brubeck/brubeck.css',
    ),
```

And that's it! Make sure these two new apps are in INSTALLED_APPS, and that the URLs modules you created for each app are included in the urlpatterns in urls.py in the root of your project. After this, your app should be ready to deploy on the App Engine. Run the manage.py update utility, enter your password if need be, and your app should be available at the appspot.com URL, preceded by your app name.

Managing Database Indexes

When working with models for the Google datastore, you need to be aware of *indexes*, how they are used, and, most importantly, how they are created. When you make queries to the datastore, there needs to be an index defined for each particular query that your application will make while running in production. These queries need to be managed through the use of a file named index.yaml in the root of your project.

The index.yaml file contains a single entry, named indexes, that lists the indexes required by the queries your application will make to the datastore. The App Engine Patch comes with this YAML file, which contains a couple of indexes that have been defined for your application by default:

```
indexes:
- kind: django_admin_log
  properties:
  - name: content_type
  - name: object_id
  - name: action_time

- kind: django_admin_log
  properties:
  - name: user
  - name: action_time
    direction: desc
```

The model to which the index belongs is specified using the kind attribute, and the fields to which the index pertains are listed using the properties attribute, with a name attribute for each field you want to index.

The good news is that for most simple queries, these indexes are generated automatically for you when you run the development server on your local machine. The development server checks for any indexes that are missing on models or fields that are being used in each query and automatically adds them to this file. You also have the option of managing these indexes manually. Take a look in the index.yaml file again; below the index definitions you should see a line reading:

```
# AUTOGENERATED
```

Any indexes that are added by the development server automatically when your queries execute will be added below this line, and updated as needed by your application queries or model field changes. Any indexes that you want to add or manage manually should go above this line. You have the option of moving any auto-generated indexes from below this line to the manual area above.

The tricky part is in making sure that the indexes are up to date for your application before you deploy it into production. While this happens automatically for you, it will only happen if each datastore query in your code is executed on the development server. You can do this by firing up the development server and walking through your web application in its entirety every time you make a change, but as your project gets larger, this approach quickly becomes too large a task to handle yourself.

The lesson here is that you must always have good tests, with sufficient code coverage, if you want your code to run on the App Engine. For example, let's say that you have a block of code in your application that looks like this:

```
if condition1:
    # some query here.
elif condition2:
    # some other query here.
else:
    # yet another query here.
```

For this code, you need to create three separate test cases that handle each of these three possible conditions so that the indexes required by these three queries get updated. As mentioned in Chapter 14, you should be writing automated test cases to make sure that your application is working as expected. On the App Engine, this polite suggestion becomes almost mandatory for maintaining indexes on larger applications.

Before going too much further in developing your project, you should read the App Engine documentation[2] to learn more about indexes and how they are related to your project's queries.

■ **Note** If you notice that the # AUTOGENERATED is there, but the indexes still aren't being added, you may be dealing with an issue[3] where the indexes won't be generated if the line endings of your file are '\r\n'. This tends to happen when you're using an editor that appends odd line ending characters when you edit this file, such as on Windows machines. If this is happening to you, you should be able to get the indexes to generate by either deleting the file or fixing the line endings.

Error Logs, Remote Data API, and Network Programming

In the course of developing your Django project, you'll likely run into some server errors. Fortunately, the App Engine console keeps a log of these errors that you can use to see what exactly went wrong in your code. Go back to http://appengine.google.com/, and log in using your Google Account. You should be presented with a list of your App Engine apps. Click the one that you're working on, and you'll be taken to the dashboard for that project.

---

[2] http://code.google.com/appengine/docs/python/datastore/queriesandindexes.html

[3] http://code.google.com/p/googleappengine/issues/detail?id=1548

In the navigation column at the far right, you'll see one link a couple below the dashboard one titled "Logs," Click this link and you'll be taken to a page summarizing the list of most recent server errors. This provides valuable traceback information when your application hits an error.

Figure 16-4. *The Logs page containing server error info for our app.*

If you're a seasoned Python developer, and you've grown accustomed to being able to manipulate large quantities of model data inside a Python shell using simple commands, you might be a little disappointed that this isn't available to you. As a matter of fact, it's as simple as using the `--remote` argument after the `manage.py shell` command:

```
python manage.py shell --remote
```

This command allows you to query for and edit model instances in the remote datastore just as if they were on your local machine.

Also, if you're interested in doing any network programming, the App Engine provides its own API for that via the `urlfetch` module. You would use this API if you're interested in integration with a third-party payment processor, like the examples we created for Authorize.Net or Google Checkout back in Chapter 5. Wherever you use the `urllib2` or `httplib` modules to create connections and get responses, you would just replace it with the following `urlfetch` syntax:

```
from google.appengine.api import urlfetch

url = 'http://www.authorize.net/path/'
postdata = {'name1': 'value1', 'name2': 'value2'}
response = urlfetch.fetch(url, payload=postdata)
content = response.content
# do something with your content here.
```

Note that the bandwidth you consume in making network calls from within your app is billable per the terms of service agreement, once you've surpassed the free amount provided.

Summary

If this chapter was your first introduction to using Django on the Google App Engine, consider yourself very lucky. Those of us who were working with Django when the App Engine was first released back in 2008 were extremely excited at the thought of being able to host our Django projects on the App Engine. That excitement quickly degenerated into disappointment, as we realized that while the App Engine infrastructure supported Django *in theory*, there were enough incompatibilities to dash our hopes. Between the missing admin interface, the lack of Django sessions support, and the fact that all of the data model classes needed to be changed, it seemed that it just wasn't possible without rewriting all of our existing code almost entirely from scratch.

Django developers owe Waldemar Kornewald and the other developers of the App Engine Patch project a debt of gratitude. Thanks to them, most of the comforts of Django that we all love are very real possibilities on the App Engine. The App Engine is constantly changing, and I suspect that it will continue to do so in coming years. I invite you to read the documentation, both for the App Engine and the Django App Engine Patch project, to learn more in-depth about their capabilities. Go forth, create your own apps, and try to have as much fun as you can in the process.

Index

■T

■XYZ

You Need the Companion eBook

Your purchase of this book entitles you to buy the companion PDF-version eBook for only $10. Take the weightless companion with you anywhere.

We believe this Apress title will prove so indispensable that you'll want to carry it with you everywhere, which is why we are offering the companion eBook (in PDF format) for $10 to customers who purchase this book now. Convenient and fully searchable, the PDF version of any content-rich, page-heavy Apress book makes a valuable addition to your programming library. You can easily find and copy code—or perform examples by quickly toggling between instructions and the application. Even simultaneously tackling a donut, diet soda, and complex code becomes simplified with hands-free eBooks!

Once you purchase your book, getting the $10 companion eBook is simple:

❶ Visit **www.apress.com/promo/tendollars/**.

❷ Complete a basic registration form to receive a randomly generated question about this title.

❸ Answer the question correctly in 60 seconds, and you will receive a promotional code to redeem for the $10.00 eBook.

233 Spring Street, New York, NY 10013

Offer valid through 4/10.